Jesus Christ Through History

Jesus Christ Through History

Dennis C. Duling

Canisius College

Under the General Editorship of
Robert Ferm
Middlebury College

HARCOURT BRACE JOVANOVICH, PUBLISHERS
San Diego   New York   Chicago   Atlanta   Washington, D.C.
London   Sydney   Toronto

To the Memory of Norman and to Gretchen

Library of Congress Catalog Card Number: 78-70506

ISBN: 0-15-547370-0

Printed in the United States of America

Cover photo by Sheldon Machlin, courtesy of
Ford Foundation

Preface

In the summer of 1970, I introduced a new course entitled "The Problem of Jesus—History and Myth." The course was not meant to be a history of the Christian church, or of Christian thought, or even of Christology in the purely doctrinal sense, though it drew on these fields as necessary. Rather, in discussion with students, it was decided to pursue something more general and oriented to what I, a "New Testament person," might find especially important in the history of Western thought about Jesus Christ. For one of my particular background, this meant sketching a contemporary view of the historical Jesus, some New Testament images of Jesus Christ, the outlines of early Christological creedal development, an impression about medieval faith in Jesus, the views of such important Protestant reformers as Luther and Calvin and of a Catholic reformer (Ignatius Loyola), and then picking up with the type of material represented in part by Albert Schweitzer's *Quest of the Historical Jesus,* but including the Roman Catholic Modernist Alfred Loisy, a representative *Religionsgeschichtler* (Wilhelm Bousset), and some major themes of Rudolf Bultmann and the post-Bultmannians. With a bit of naïve enthusiasm, we set off on our quest for some of the best thinking about Jesus Christ in Western civilization. It is perhaps no surprise that somewhere in the middle of the course, a student wryly commented (in reference to the course title) that she had not known that Jesus had had such a complex problem!

In a summer term at Boston University, I changed the name of the course to "Jesus Christ—History and Myth" and tried to give it some flavor by including audiovisual aids, attempting to characterize such phenomena as the Renaissance, the Reformation, the Enlightenment, and the Weimar Republic in Germany. I also added a section on a Methodist thinker, John Wesley, and one on a Protestant Evangelical, J. G. Machen, and included lengthier biographical comments about the thinkers, elaborating as much of their *Zeitgeist* as necessary for minimal understanding.

When the possibility emerged that the course might provide the basis for a book, suggestions by a number of scholars led to a rearrangement of the material into the general outline it now has. I also added more specific material from the medieval period—St. Thomas Aquinas and St. Francis—and, after some gentle complaining by my spouse that no women were represented, I settled on a section about St. Teresa of Ávila. It is perhaps unfortunate that I have not included as a major subdivision a Jewish representative; scholars, however, will note that the discussions about the historical Jesus in Chapter 1 are indebted in places to a very important Jewish contribution to this subject: *Jesus the Jew,* by Geza Vermes. I have also included a brief discussion of the views of the late S. G. F. Brandon, who was much indebted to Jewish scholarship.

I hope that this book will fill a void in literature on the study of Jesus Christ. There are excellent books on specific periods of the study of Jesus, such as Schweitzer's classic; there are more technical books, such as the standard works on New Testament Christology or the history of some phase of Christian thought; and there are a number of books on the lives and thought of particular scholars. But I am unaware of any *general* book that attempts to combine historical and biographical sketches of key scholars and their periods with careful summaries of their thought about Jesus Christ in just this fashion. If it is a strength to make accessible a general book, it is also clear that experts in particular historical fields may find some of my descriptions limited in perception. But I hope the generalities will be enough on target to make the book a useful teaching tool and, if nothing else, drive students more deeply into the primary sources. It will become clear that I am highly indebted to many scholars in many areas. To facilitate further reading, I have attempted to mention works of a general nature in the notes at the ends of chapters. What is written here is, nevertheless, my responsibility.

There are a number of persons and institutions that I should like to mention because they have been important in the course of writing. In the early stages, Professors Carter Lindberg and Kent Brown of Boston University made helpful suggestions on the Reformation and Wesley sections, and Howard Kee of Boston University and Vernon Robbins of the University of Illinois made a number of helpful criticisms. Dr. Stephen Bruce of Ohio Northern University did an excellent job of proofreading my initial draft. Professors Robert Grant of The University of Chicago and Dr. Michael Fahey, S.J., of Concordia University, Montreal, read through the final draft and made many suggestions and corrections. Charleen Krofft, formerly of the Department of Philosophy and Religion at Ohio Northern University, accomplished the difficult task of typing the first draft, and her successor, Janet Martin, helped with some revisions. Pamela Thimmes, O.S.F., a graduate student at Canisius College, and Patricia Irr, O.S.F., dedicated many hours to preparing the Indexes. I am thankful to Professor Ronald Benson of Ohio Northern University for the use of his philosophical library, and to Professor Harold Hinderliter of Ohio Northern University, Dr. David Kreider of Auburndale, Massachusetts, the Reverend Leon Oliver and the Reverend Helen Oliver of Martha's Vineyard, Massachusetts, and Mrs. W. C. Littlefield of Ogunquit, Maine, for providing space and facilities for writing. The staffs of the libraries at Boston University, Ohio Northern University, Harvard Divinity School, The University of Chicago Divinity School, Ohio State University, The University of New Hampshire at Durham, and Andover Newton School of Theology also deserve mention.

Finally, there are several people who really made this book possible. It was William A. Pullin, at Harcourt Brace Jovanovich, who first became interested in its possibilities as a textbook and who asked me to submit a sample; he then initiated the project and controlled its development. Professor Robert Ferm of Middlebury College, Vermont, supported the project from the beginning, read both drafts, and gave invaluable suggestions about its organization and content; I am especially indebted to him. For the very fine job of meticulous editing of the final draft, I give my special note of sincere thanks to John Holland and Judy Burke. Most of all, I owe my greatest debt to my mentor, the late Professor Norman Perrin of the University of Chicago. My acquaintance with Professor Perrin goes back to his very first years at Chicago, when he taught his students with the personal attention every graduate student should have; it was he who encouraged this book and gave it his wholehearted support. His service to American New Testament scholarship is well recognized, and he will be missed. To my wife, Gretchen, I owe the indispensable quality of understanding someone who seems at times to become more absorbed in a project than in a family and who waits patiently for the times when we communicate and play with Teddie Anne and Stephen. To Norman Perrin and Gretchen Duling I have dedicated the book.

Dennis C. Duling

Contents

III   JESUS CHRIST IN THE GREAT CHURCH   63

IV   JESUS CHRIST IN THE PROTESTANT AND
CATHOLIC REFORMATIONS   100

V   JESUS CHRIST IN RATIONALISM, PIETISM, AND
ROMANTICISM   133

I

The Historical Jesus

A description of the historical Jesus presupposes the solution to a great many problems in the study of Jesus Christ. Because the historical approach to this study is a distinctively modern one, this chapter could as well have been placed at the end of the book. It is placed at the beginning because our theme, which is the place of Jesus Christ in thought and belief throughout history, centers on a historical person. Yet it should not be forgotten that the picture we give of him is, like the other approaches in succeeding chapters, an interpretation. To account for some of the factors in this interpretation, it will be helpful to sketch briefly the recent "quest of the historical Jesus" and some of the reasons that led to this approach.

THE NEW TESTAMENT GOSPELS AND THE QUEST OF THE HISTORICAL JESUS

By the latter half of the second century c.e. (the Common Era of both Jews and Christians), the move to reduce the number of authoritative gospels in the early church to four was well under way. About 170 c.e.

Tatian, a native of Syria, produced out of (at least) four gospels a single "gospel harmony" called the *Diatessaron* (Greek: "through the four"), which attempted (with minor exceptions) to omit no episode that was distinctive in a particular gospel. This probable limitation to four gospels was given a rationale about 185 C.E. by the early church theologian Irenaeus of Lyons (in Gaul, modern France). Irenaeus, who was aware of the attitudes toward the gospels in the churches of Asia Minor, Rome, and Gaul, wrote,

> And it is impossible that the Gospels can be either more in number or, on the other hand, less than they are. For since there are four zones of the world in which we are, and also four principal winds, and since the Church is scattered throughout the whole world, and since the pillar and support of the Church is the Gospel and the Spirit of life, it is natural that she should have four pillars breathing out immortality all over and rekindling man.[1]

Irenaeus's argument from the fourfold nature of the world was presumably less important than the facts that key churches in Asia Minor, Rome, and Gaul were using these gospels, that such gospels supported an emerging attitude about correct belief, and that they were thought to have been written by disciples of Jesus (Matthew and John) or followers of Paul (Mark and Luke). The same four gospels were also defended in North Africa and Egypt in the same period. The evidence from early church writers on the number of gospels is supported by the papyrus texts P[45] and P[75], which are the earliest New Testament papyrus fragments to contain more than one gospel, both from the late second or early third century. The fourfold gospel is also confirmed by the first known official list of books in the New Testament canon (Greek: *kanōn*, "[measuring] reed"), the Muratorian Canon from Rome, about 200 C.E. Finally, the same four gospels—Matthew, Mark, Luke, and John, in that order—were made authoritative for the larger part of the Church in the Festal Letter of Athanasius in 367 C.E., which listed the twenty-seven books now in the New Testament.

Meanwhile, the opponents of Christianity were arguing that because the four gospels did not agree in every detail, they were inaccurate. Augustine of Hippo (in modern Algeria), who had accepted Athanasius's limitations on the canon, responded to such criticisms by saying that each of the successive gospels knew and used the earlier one(s), that they were in general agreement, and that they should be seen together as a "harmony" (*On the Harmony of the Evangelists*), though Augustine did not, like Tatian, literally produce such a harmony. This harmonizing tendency was fostered by the churches and is still evident, for example, in Christmas pageants that bring together stories of the wise men in Matthew's gospel with the shepherds in Luke's. In various periods actual harmonies were again produced. The "lives" of Jesus based on them were written to encourage people to live by the example of Jesus.[2] In addition, by the fourth and fifth centuries great thinkers of the Church were attempting to define with philosophical precision the sense in which Jesus was both a god and a man (see Ch. 3). Neither the piously oriented "lives" nor the doctrinal creeds were based on a historical interest in the modern sense.

Within the last two hundred years or so, the question of the differences among the four gospels has arisen again.[3] If they are not exactly alike, can they all be correct? What is the relationship between or among them? By about the middle of the nineteenth century, German scholars who were taking the lead in the quest of the historical Jesus were separating the Gospel of John from the first three gospels, primarily because of its style of expression, the order it gave for the events of Jesus' life, and the distinctive types of miracles and discourses it included. Whatever its (long-acknowledged) "spiritual" value, the Gospel of John was judged to be relatively unimportant as a *historical* source for the life and teachings of Jesus.

What, then, of the first three gospels, Matthew, Mark, and Luke? The practice had emerged of putting them in parallel columns in order to look at them together. Hence they were named the *synoptic* gospels (Greek: *optic,* from "to see"; *syn,* "together"), and the problem of their proper relationship became known as the *synoptic problem.* The orthodox view of the Church was that Matthew had been a disciple of Jesus, that his gospel had been written first and was the most important (it had been placed first in the New Testament), and that each of his successors (including John) had used the others in turn. The new "solution" to the synoptic problem was that instead of Matthew, Mark was the earliest (the hypothesis of "Markan priority") and that Matthew and Luke had used Mark plus a "sayings source" (now lost, but referred to by scholars as the Q document), which accounted for the identical or similar non-Markan passages in their gospels (the "two-source hypothesis").

Thus, it was thought, the source problem was solved. On the basis of the Markan priority, all sorts of logical and linguistic arguments were put forward to prove that Mark presented a basically trustworthy life of Jesus. In other words, the new historical approach sought to go behind the Christ of the Creeds to the real *historical* Jesus, and to do so it abandoned the "gospel harmony" for the "Markan hypothesis." Usually, this historical Jesus was perceived as an ethical teacher whose teaching was timeless.[4]

Yet by the early twentieth century a number of scholars, again in Germany, had come to doubt that the Markan hypothesis could provide the basis for a historically accurate life of Jesus. In this period it became increasingly important to discover the process that led to the formation of the Gospel of Mark, that is, to understand the various stages of *oral* tradition *about* Jesus. Yet, at some point decisions had to be made about which were the earliest layers of the "Jesus tradition" embedded in the sources. (The method that sought to trace the development of the stories about Jesus and his teachings which underlay Mark and the other gospels was called *form criticism*.[5]) Moreover, when a glimpse of Jesus' shadow appeared, he was not the simple ethical teacher of the earlier quest, but a more remote, strange figure whose ·teaching centered in the reign of God at the end of the world. This perspective became important in the "new quest" of the historical Jesus in the period after World War II.[6]

Since the 1950s, except for those who never accepted this approach to the historical problems, the discussion about Jesus has tended to take the "new quest" orientation. (Some scholars have either temporarily or permanently abandoned such a quest to work on other matters—for example, the thought of a particular evangelist—or have launched out on new problems of method.) What follows, then, will be based in large measure on the results of the "new quest."[7]

NONBIBLICAL SOURCES ABOUT JESUS

Apart from the Christian gospels there are several literary sources from the ancient world that mention Jesus of Nazareth. They can be divided into three types: Roman authors, Jewish authors, and nonbiblical Christian sources.

Roman Sources [8]

About 110 C.E. Pliny the Younger, a Roman governor of Bithynia in Asia Minor, consulted the emperor Trajan (reigned 98–117 C.E.) about the "depraved and extravagant superstition" that was rapidly spreading in his district. Pliny also mentioned in passing that the Christians met early in the morning, sang antiphonal hymns "to Christ, as to a god," and swore oaths of morality. Interesting as Pliny's account is about early Christianity, Pliny said that it came from informers against the Christians and the Christians themselves; therefore it is not independent of the Christian movement. Since the historian seeks independent evidence, Pliny's account adds no new information about Jesus himself.

Another fragment comes from a Roman writer, Julius Africanus, from the early third century C.E. He wrote that "Thallus, in the third book of his history, calls this darkness an eclipse of the sun, but in my opinion he is wrong!" If this allusion is to Thallus the Samaritan, who died in Rome about 60 C.E. (Josephus, *Wars* 18.6.4), then Thallus's writing would be an early reference to the darkness at the crucifixion. Nonetheless, this would indicate little more than that the passion story was known in Rome by the middle of the century and that the enemies of Christianity were attempting to explain a Christian miracle by natural means.

Close to the time of Jesus, the Roman historian Suetonius (75–160 C.E.) mentioned that the emperor Claudius (reigned 41–54 C.E.) expelled the Jews from Rome (about 51 C.E.) because of a riot instigated by a certain "Chrestos" (*Life of Claudius* 25.4). However, because this occurred about a generation after Jesus' death, either the reference is to another Chrestos, or Suetonius was speaking about Jewish–Christian conflicts at Rome and the report is misinformed or confused about Chrestos.

Tacitus (60–120 C.E.), another Roman historian, reported that the Christians were blamed for the burning of Rome during the reign of the emperor Nero in 64 C.E. and, in passing, stated that the name of this "pernicious superstition" came from "Christus" (*Annals* 15.44). This reference is the most solid piece of information from a Roman writer, but it, too, gives no more information than what Tacitus might have learned from Christians or non-Christians at Rome.

In short, the Roman sources offer some interesting information about the growing Christian movement and presuppose the actual existence of Jesus, but they offer no new or independent facts about him.

Jewish Sources [9]

The first non-Christian, Jewish literary sources about Jesus are found in the writings of Flavius Josephus (37–100? C.E.), who became the official Jewish historian for the Romans. In one passage (*Antiquities of the Jews* 20.200) Josephus reported the execution of Jesus' brother, James, and referred to him as "the brother of Jesus, who was called Christ—James was his name." The passage may be authentic, but it offers no new information about Jesus.

The second passage (*Antiquities* 18.63–64), sometimes called the "Testimonium Flavianum," is worth quoting:

> About this time there lived Jesus, a wise man, [if indeed one ought to call him a man.] For he was one who wrought surprising feats and was a teacher of such people as accept the truth gladly. He won over many Jews and many of the Greeks. [He was the Messiah.] When Pilate, upon hearing him accused by men of the highest standing among us, had condemned him to be crucified, those who had in the first place come to love him did not give up their affection for him. [On the third day he appeared to them restored to life, for the prophets of God had prophesied these and countless other marvellous things about him.] And the tribe of the Christians, so called after him, has still to this day not disappeared. [10]

Certain phrases in this passage (bracketed here) can scarcely have come from a Jewish author, for they express specifically Christian beliefs about Jesus. Either they were inserted by Christians who copied the texts of Josephus through the centuries, or (since the passage is like the little Christian sermons about Jesus in the writings of Luke) the passage *as a whole* was a Christian insertion. In either case, the information is meager and confirms what is already known, though its stress on a "wise man" is interesting and provides some historical reinforcement. In short, there *may* be an authentic notice in Josephus about Jesus as a "wise man" and miracle worker who gathered followers and was crucified under Pontius Pilate, information that agrees with, but does not add to, New Testament materials.

The second major source for Jewish references to Jesus is the Jewish Talmud, the heart of which is a deposit of legal–ritual applications of the Jewish Law to concrete situations of daily life.[11] This deposit includes (originally oral) discussions of important rabbis, called Tannaim, who flourished during the first two centuries of the Common Era. In them are references to Jesus as Jesus Ben Pandîrā, that is, son of Pandîrā (a variation is Panthera), as well as various polemical comments about Jesus and Mary. These rabbis made numerous attempts to identify Pandîrā. Usually, later traditions thought of him as Mary's lover (that is, Mary was an adulteress or a harlot). A funeral urn of a Roman archer by the name of Tiberius Julius Abdes Pantera, once stationed in Palestine and transferred to Germany in 9 c.e., has been discovered; however, modern scholars have been unwilling to make the connection with Pandîrā and have viewed the Talmudic legends as attempts to refute the Christian stories of Jesus' origins. Perhaps a better explanation is that the name Pandîrā was originally a Hebrew corruption of the Greek *parthenos,* meaning "virgin."

What is sometimes taken more seriously is the Talmud's view that Jesus was executed because he was a miracle-working magician who led the people astray. Joseph Klausner, a Jewish scholar, summarized the most important Talmudic traditions about Jesus:

> There are reliable statements to the effect that his name was Yeshu'a [Jesus] of Nazareth; that he "practiced sorcery" (i.e., performed miracles, as was usual in those days) and beguiled and led Israel astray; that he mocked at the words of the Wise [the official scribes who interpreted the Law]; that he expounded scripture in the same manner as the Pharisees; that he had five disciples; that he said he was not come to take aught away from the Law or to add to it; that he was hanged (crucified) as a false teacher and beguiler on the eve of Passover which happened on a sabbath; and that his disciples healed the sick in his name.[12]

The only thing here that differs essentially from the gospel traditions is that Jesus had five disciples, who in some traditions are given names of somewhat dubious origin.

Thus the Talmudic accounts, like the Roman ones, are interesting additions from the ancients; yet, partly because of their polemical nature, they give little certain information that is not already available from the gospels. A comparison of Josephus's comments and the Talmud makes it clear that in Jewish tradition, Jesus was considered primarily a miracle worker who gathered followers and led them away from the truth.

Christian Agrapha and Apocrypha

In addition to the Roman and Jewish non-Christian sources, there are a number of isolated sayings attributed to Jesus in Christian sources but not found in the four gospels of the New Testament.[13] These *Agrapha* include "words of the Lord" in the nongospel sections of the New Testament (e.g., Acts 20:35: "To give is more blessed than to receive."); additions to the manuscripts of the gospels by early Christian copyists (e.g., Luke 6:4, Manuscript D: "When on the same day he saw a man doing work on the Sabbath, he said to him: 'Man! if thou knowest what thou doest, blessed art thou! But if thou knowest not, thou art cursed and a transgressor of the law.'"); sayings found in early Christian writings from the early second century to the Middle Ages (e.g., from the mid-second century, Justin Martyr, *Dialogues* xxxv, 3: "There will be dissensions and squabbles."); isolated bits and pieces of papyri (e.g., from about 300 c.e., Oxyrhynchus Papyrus 1224: "[He who today] stands far-off will tomorrow be [near][to you]"); many sayings in apocryphal gospels (e.g., from the second-century Coptic Gospel of Thomas, saying 42: "Jesus said: become passers-by."); sayings attributed to Jesus in the Talmud (e.g., Jerusalem Taanith 65[b]: "Rabbi Abahu said: 'If a man say to thee "I am God," he is a liar; if [he says, "I am] the son of man," in the end people will laugh at him; if [he says] "I will go up to heaven," he saith, but shall not perform it.'"); and numerous Islamic sayings in the Koran and even one saying known from the eighth century, now inscribed on the south main portal of the mosque in Fathpur-Sikri, India, in 1601 ("Jesus, on whom be peace, has said: the world is a bridge. Go over it, but do not install yourselves upon it."). These particular examples, except for the Talmudic and Islamic sayings, are valued by some scholars as highly as the New Testament gospel sayings.

In addition to the Agrapha, there are well over fifty Christian gospels and gospel fragments which, in the process of the growth of orthodox Christianity during the first four centuries, were excluded from the authoritative texts by the major orthodox churches and thus ultimately omitted from the New Testament itself. These are in the New Testament Apocrypha (Greek: *apocrypha,* "hidden," meaning originally "holy," then "spurious").[14] They may be divided into three categories: those of the New Testament type, those of "Gnostic" type (related to Gnostic Christianity, an early form of Christianity that was eventually considered heretical by the orthodox churches), and those which sought to supplement or elaborate the New Testament stories about Jesus. This literature is too voluminous to illustrate in any detail, but we will mention several examples.

Among the New-Testament-type materials is Oxyrhynchus Papyrus 840, a little parchment from the fourth or fifth century written on both sides in miniature. This was probably an amulet, that is, a little charm worn on the person to protect against evil. The first few lines are a conclusion of a speech by Jesus in Jerusalem; then comes a visit to the Temple where Levi, a Pharisaic chief priest, castigates Jesus and the disciples for neglecting the purification rites of bathing and changing one's clothes. Jesus responds,

> Woe unto you blind that see not! Thou hast bathed thyself in water that is poured out, in which dogs and swine lie at night and day, and thou hast washed thyself and hast chafed thine outer skin, which prostitutes also and flutegirls anoint, bathe, chafe, and rouge, in order to arouse desire in men, but within they are full of scorpions and of [bad]ness [of every kind]. But I and [my disciples], of whom thou sayest that we have not im[mersed] our-selves, [have been im]mersed in the liv[ing . . .] water which comes down from [. . . B]ut woe unto them that . . .[15]

One scholar, Joachim Jeremias, believes that in substance this papyrus "ranks as high as the Synoptic account."[16] Besides such gospellike fragments, it is known that several Jewish–Christian gospels existed, for example, the Gospel of the Nazaraeans, the Gospel of the Ebionites, and the Gospel of the Hebrews.

The second type of Apocryphal "gospels" comes from the Gnostic Christian groups. These are mostly in the form of dialogues in which the risen Jesus appears and imparts knowledge (Greek: *gnōsis,* "knowledge," in this case religious knowledge for salvation, knowledge about the universe and man) to his disciples. Gnostic "revelation discourses" of this type are well illustrated by the Coptic language Gospel of Thomas, a collection of 114 sayings attributed to Jesus and recorded by one Didymos Judas Thomas, which was discovered in 1945 near Nag Hammadi in southern Egypt. The "gospel" in its present form is from the fourth or fifth century, but it is thought to go back to a Greek original of the early second century. An example of a saying is its version of the parable of the Lost Sheep (cp. Luke 15:3–7; Mt 18:10–14):

> Jesus said: The Kingdom is like a shepherd who had a hundred sheep. One of them went astray, which was the largest. He left behind ninety-nine, he sought for the one until he found it. Having tired himself out, he said to the sheep: I love thee more than the ninety-nine.[17]

This parable (and ten others), various sayings, and the *form* of the document as a collection of sayings raise the intriguing question of the document's relationship to the New Testament tradition of Jesus' sayings. Scholars have various answers to this question, but some think that the forms of certain sayings are earlier than the canonical gospel forms.[18]

The third major division of the New Testament Apocrypha consists of materials which, by definition, are not independent of the New Testament but are attempts to supplement or elaborate New Testament stories about Jesus' infancy, relatives, work, and sufferings. A particularly interesting example is the *Infancy Story of Thomas* (not to be confused with the Coptic Gospel of Thomas), which was written by a gentile Christian sometime after 200 c.e. The following is the beginning section of the document:

1. I, Thomas the Israelite, tell and make known to you all, brethren from among the Gentiles, all the works of the childhood of our Lord Jesus Christ and his mighty deeds, which he did when he was born in our land. The beginning is as follows.

2. 1) When this boy Jesus was five years old he was playing at the ford of a brook, and he gathered together into pools the water that flowed by, and made it at once clean, and commanded it by his word alone. 2) He made soft clay and fashioned from it twelve sparrows. And it was the sabbath when he did this. And there were also many other children playing with him. 3) Now when a certain Jew saw what Jesus was doing in his play on the sabbath, he at once went and told his father Joseph: "See, your child is at the brook, and he has taken clay and fashioned twelve birds and has profaned the sabbath." 4) And when Joseph came to the place and saw (it), he cried out to him, saying: "Why do you do on the sabbath what ought not to be done?" But Jesus clapped his hands and cried to the sparrows: "Off with you!" And the sparrows took flight and went away chirping. 5) The Jews were amazed when they saw this, and went away and told their elders what they had seen Jesus do.

3. 1) But the son of Annas the scribe was standing there with Joseph; and he took a branch of willow and (with it) dispersed the water which Jesus had gathered together. 2) When Jesus saw what he had done he was enraged and said to him: "You insolent, godless dunderhead, what harm did the pools and the water do to you? See, now you also shall wither like a tree and shall bear neither leaves nor root nor fruit." 3) And immediately that lad withered up completely; and Jesus departed and went into Joseph's house. But the parents of him that was withered took him away, bewailing the youth, and brought him to Joseph and reproached him: "What a child you have, who does such things."

4. 1) After this again he went through the village, and a lad ran and knocked against his shoulder. Jesus was exasperated and said to him: "You shall not go further on your way," and the child immediately fell down and died. But some, who saw what took place, said: "From where does this child spring, since his every word is an accomplished deed?" 2) And the parents of the dead child came to Joseph and blamed him and said: "Since you have such a child, you cannot dwell with us in the village; or else teach him to bless and not to curse. For he is slaying our children."

5. 1) And Joseph called the child aside and admonished him saying: "Why do you do such things that these people (must) suffer and hate us and persecute us?" But Jesus replied: "I know that these words are not yours; nevertheless for your sake I will be silent. But they shall bear their punishment." And immediately those who had accused him became

blind.   2) And those who saw it were greatly afraid and perplexed, and said
concerning him: "Every word he speaks, whether good or evil, was a deed
and became a marvel." And when Joseph saw that Jesus had so done, he
arose and took him by the ear and pulled it hard.   3) And the child was
angry and said to him: "It is sufficient for you to seek and not to find, and
most unwisely have you acted. Do you not know that I am yours? Do not
vex me."[19]

Other stories tell of the boy Jesus raising one of his playmates from the
dead, of his healing activity, and of his stretching boards so that they
would be the right length for his father in the carpenter shop!

In conclusion, it is possible to say that no new knowledge about
Jesus is found in sources outside the New Testament beyond some possible variations on some of his teachings. A hypothesis that has sometimes been put forward in the modern period is that Jesus never really
lived;[20] though these sources offer very little information about the historical Jesus, they are nonetheless strong evidence that the ancients
never had such doubts.

ASPECTS OF THE LIFE OF JESUS

Today one almost never sees a book titled *The Life of Jesus*. Novels,
plays, films, and rock operas about Jesus' life are written and/or performed, but they are recognized as imaginative portrayals by creative
artists. Scholarly works on the life of Jesus in the biographical sense are
no longer written. Yet something, however sketchy, can be said about
the life of Jesus, and more can be said about his teaching. The following
sketch, as mentioned earlier, is indebted to the "new quest" of the historical Jesus.[21]

Date of Birth

It is not known precisely when Jesus was born. The Gospels of Matthew
(ca. 85–90 C.E.) and Luke (ca. 85–90 C.E.) both state that Jesus was
born in the days of Herod, the king of Judea (Mt 2:1; Luke 1:5), that is,
Herod the Great, who is known to have died in 4 B.C.E. There has been
an attempt to identify the star of the Magi in Matthew's account (Mt 2:2,
7ff.) with the conjunction of the planets Jupiter and Saturn in 7 B.C.E.,
but the legendary motif of a great person born under the sign of a star
was very widespread in the ancient world.[22] Luke 2:1ff. further associ-
ates Jesus' birth with the census under Caesar Augustus (reigned 27
B.C.E. to 14 C.E.) in 6 C.E., that is, ten years *after* the death of Herod (if

Acts 5:37 compared with various Josephus accounts on the census is correct). If, then, Matthew and Luke were approximately correct, how could Jesus have been born at least four years "before Christ"? The reason is that about 525 C.E., a Scythian monk and abbot of a Roman monastery, Dionysius Exiguus, who began to date time from Jesus' birth, miscalculated the date by at least four years!

If the exact year is uncertain, the day is totally unknown. The traditional date, December 25, was a later adaptation of the Christian Church to the commonly accepted date of the birthday of the sun in the Roman Empire, that is, the "return" of the sun after the winter solstice (about December 21).

Place of Birth

The place of Jesus' birth is debated. The Bethlehem location is related to the belief that Jesus was descended from the lineage of David, probably itself an inference from the belief that he was the Messiah of the lineage of David. When Luke places the family in Bethlehem of Judea for the birth, he takes them there for the census (Luke 2:1ff.); but, as noted, that poses a historical problem. Matthew puts the family at Bethlehem in the very beginning (Mt 2:1ff.), and this is followed by the flight into Egypt and resettlement in Nazareth. John 7:40–42 reflects a controversy about Jesus' geographical origins and may imply a similar controversy about his descent:

> When they heard these words, some of the people said, "This is really the prophet." Others said, "This is the Messiah." But some said, "Is the Messiah to come from Galilee? Has not the scripture said that the Messiah is descended from David, and comes from Bethlehem, the village where David was?

From this tradition, it appears that Jesus came from Galilee. Many scholars accept this view and note that Mark, usually considered the earliest gospel, thinks Jesus came from Nazareth (Mark 1:9) and frequently calls him a "Nazarene" (Mark 1:24; 10:47; 14:67; 16:6). In Matthew 21:11 he is called "the prophet from Nazareth of Galilee." If Jesus was *born* in Nazareth, the Bethlehem tradition presumably arose in connection with the belief in his Davidic Messiahship.

Parents and Lineage

The tradition that the mother of Jesus was named Mary is widespread (Mark 6:3; Mt 1–2; Luke 1–2; John 2:1ff.; 19:25–27; Acts 1:14). Paul says only that Jesus was "born of a woman" (Gal 4:4); he, Mark, and

John seem to have no interest in a virgin birth.[23] Both Matthew and Luke find support for belief in the virginity of Mary in Isaiah 7:14, a passage which in Hebrew contains the general term *'almāh,* which means "young woman" and may or may not imply virginity. Yet its equivalent in the Greek Old Testament, *parthenos,* which is more frequently used for a virgin, is the term found for Mary's virginity in Matthew and Luke. Paradoxically, Matthew and Luke also trace Jesus' Davidic lineage through the line of Joseph (Mt 1:1ff.; Luke 3:23ff.). Luke seems to express the contradiction when he says that Jesus was born of Joseph "as was supposed" (Luke 2:23), and Matthew apparently attempted to handle the difficulty by tracing the line down to Joseph, but at that very point concluding with the statement that Jesus was born of Mary, the wife of Joseph, as though Joseph had nothing to do with it (Mt 1:16, though there are textual variants)! One recent and intriguing view is that the Hebrew term *bethulah* in rabbinic tradition could refer to a "virgin mother," that is, one who has married and conceived after her first ovulation but prior to the onset of her first menstruation (marriageable age was normally at the beginning of puberty), though this strains some of the texts as they stand. Since a Messiah born from David's line in Judaism was not connected with a virgin, and since Mary's virginity is absent from Paul and Mark, a frequent explanation is that the virgin birth motif came into early Christianity late in the first century C.E. as a belief about the divine origins of Jesus through the Spirit, and that this motif had to be maintained alongside the contradictory acceptance of Jesus' Davidic descent through Joseph. The rabbis then countered the Christian stories about Mary's virginity with their own stories about her immorality.

Related to this issue is the Christian tradition of Mary's perpetual virginity.[24] Jesus, according to Mark 6:3 (cp. Mt 13:55), had brothers whose names are given. Sisters are also mentioned. Early Christian explanations were that these children were Joseph's by a previous marriage, or that a sister of Mary bore the children, or that the term "brother" in Greek (*adelphos*) went back to a Semitic term meaning "kinsman." Mark, writing in Greek, undoubtedly meant "brother"; indeed, another Greek term exists for the notion of "kinsman" (Col 4:10). Neither did Matthew mean the perpetual virginity of Mary when he wrote "Joseph . . . knew her not until she had borne a son" (Mt 1:25). Historically, of course, the whole question is moot!

The earliest views of Jesus' descent from David are found in little creeds and confessions (Rom 1:3–4; 2 Tim 2:8), which are elaborated in the Matthaean and Lukan genealogies (Mt 1:1ff.; Luke 3:23ff.). These genealogies are built up out of Old Testament materials and do not agree with each other. Thus they are probably confessions about Jesus' identity as a descendant from David, from Abraham (so Matthew and Luke), and indeed from Adam (so Luke). Jesus was, by descent, confessed as Son of David, Son of Abraham, and Son of God. The title "Son of David" addressed to Jesus by those in need of healing (especially Mark 10:46ff.) is not focused on descent and, in any case, may have been added to the stories. The debate about Jesus as Son of David (Mark 12:35–37) involves a complicated argument about "the Messiah" in general and may have been transmitted as an example of Jesus worsting his opponents. The early Church tradition that Christian leaders of Davidic descent related to Jesus were rounded up and interrogated by the Romans in the late first century (Eusebius, *Ecclesiastical History* 3.19–20) may also be a Christian claim about Jesus' Davidic descent. In short, though quite early, belief in Jesus' Davidic descent shows signs of being a confession related to the belief that he was the Messiah.

Chronology of Ministry

As we stated, the date of Jesus' birth is uncertain, though most scholars think that sometime just prior to 4 B.C.E. is likely. There is a similar problem with respect to the precise dates of Jesus' ministry and death. The Gospel of Luke reports that John the Baptist appeared in the fifteenth year of the reign of the emperor Tiberius (14–37 C.E.), that is, about 28 C.E. and Luke seems to fix the beginning of Jesus' ministry at this point (Luke 3:1ff.), whereas the Gospel of Mark puts it after John the Baptist was imprisoned (Mark 1:14) and the Gospel of John represents their ministries as overlapping (John 3:25ff.). Since all the evangelists have interpretive reasons for their chronologies, the precise beginning of Jesus' ministry is unrecoverable.

The length of his ministry and the date of its end are also only approximate. The Gospels of Mark, Matthew, and Luke picture a public life of one year; John's account, since he mentions three Passovers (John 2:13, 23; 5:1; 6:4; 11:55), allows for the possibility of more than two years. A highly debated issue in this connection is whether Jesus ate a Passover meal with his disciples. The synoptics say that he did and that he was crucified the following day (which, since Jewish calendars began the day at sunset, was the same calendar date, Nisan 15). The Gospel of John says that the meal and crucifixion were on the previous day, Nisan 14. These *calendar* dates in connection with the Passover cannot be reconciled, and both are highly interpretive. Where they agree is that the *day* of the week, whether the beginning of Passover or not, was Friday (cp. Mark 15:42; 16:1; Mt 27:62; 28:1; Luke 23:54; 24:1). Some estimate of the year in which either Nisan 14 or 15 fell on a Friday would be about 30 C.E., though this is further complicated by uncertainty about the lunar calendar. John's gospel would agree with this

Rembrandt, *Portrait of Christ* THE METROPOLITAN MUSEUM OF ART,
NEW YORK

if, as he says, Jesus' early ministry was during the forty-sixth year of the
rebuilding of the Temple, that is, about 27 or 28 c.e. (John 2:20). Luke,
who has in view a shorter ministry, claimed that Jesus was about thirty
when he began his ministry (Luke 3:23). If he was born in 4 b.c.e., and
if his ministry was about one year (Luke follows Mark), the year of the
crucifixion would be about 27 c.e., but we must recall that Luke's chronologies in connection with the census are suspect. In summary, Jesus
was crucified sometime late in the third decade c.e. or about 30 c.e., a
date that is certain enough for historical purposes.

Galilee and the Zealots [25]

It is generally accepted that Jesus grew up, was educated, and began his ministry in Galilee, a judgment that has important implications for his language and thought-world. Modern scholarship accepts the view that Jesus' mother tongue was Aramaic, the spoken language of Palestinian Jews in this period. This language, known from a few ancient sources (especially the Jewish Talmud), was a sister language of biblical Hebrew that persisted as a holy language. Though Galilee was surrounded by cities where Greek was spoken, the Galilean countryside remained strongly Aramaic. The claim that Jesus' language was Aramaic is reinforced by Aramaic terms found in the gospels (Mark 5:41; 7:34; 14:36; Mt 6:24); however, it should be remembered that the early Christians immediately after the time of Jesus were Aramaic speaking, as well.

Among the Jews and Romans, Galilee was considered a hotbed of political revolution. The Jews had a long history of political revolt against foreign oppression and, under the Romans, the core of leadership came from Galilee. Despite the sharp criticisms of Galilean revolutionaries by the Jewish historian Josephus, it is probable that these *Zealots* (Greek: *zealos*, "zeal" [for the Jewish law]) were considered national heroic leaders by the common people. Since the most secure historical fact about Jesus' life is that he was crucified by the Romans for sedition against the Roman state, the question arises: Was Jesus a Galilean revolutionary, that is, either a Zealot or associated with the Zealots?

This question has occasionally been answered yes by scholars, especially since the 1920s. Some of the arguments for Jesus' Zealot links are these: As a youth Jesus was influenced by Zealot revolutionaries in Galilee; one of Jesus' disciples was Simon the Zealot (Luke 6:15; Acts 1:13); Judas Iscariot's name may be related to the Latin *Sicarii*, those noted by Josephus as fomenting assassinations (with the *Sica*, a dagger?); Jesus asks whether they came out after him in the garden as though he were a "brigand" (Luke 22:52); Jesus was crucified between two "brigands" (Mark 15:27); Luke says that Jesus' followers had swords in the garden (Luke 22:35–39); Jesus said, "I have not come to bring peace, but a sword" (Mt 10:34); some of Jesus' sayings, such as "Render to Caesar the things that are Caesar's, and to God the things that are God's" (Mark 12:17), should be seen as calls for revolution; Jesus' teaching about the kingdom of heaven was anti-Roman; Jesus' cleansing of the temple was really more like a guerrilla attack against it; and, most important, the gospels were written after the Romans decimated the Jews in 66–70 C.E. and tend to portray Jesus as a pacifist at a time when the Christians wanted to distinguish themselves from the Jews and get along with the Roman state. Thus, goes the argument, it was not an accident that Jesus was crucified for sedition. Was he in sympathy with the Zealot movement?

Though these arguments give the impression of being realistic and certainly indicate that Jesus was not simply a mild-mannered quietist who never became involved in contemporary issues,[26] they have this effect only when they are so interpreted and when they are viewed in the context of the Zealot movement. Usually, the above passages are interpreted differently. For example, the claim that the Galilean rebels influenced the young Jesus is an argument from silence, for nothing so specific is known of his youth. The focus of the Zealot hypothesis is on the final days in Jerusalem, and though Jesus was crucified for sedition, it is normally held that this was a misinterpretation by the authorities. Most important, this argument, though recognizing quite correctly that Jesus has been reinterpreted in the gospels, tends to avoid what is crucial for every historical reconstruction: a thorough evaluation of Jesus' teachings as a whole. In the last analysis, most historians think that the "Zealot hypothesis" goes *around* the major teaching texts in its view of reinterpretation and that this is what permits one to see Jesus in the historical context of the Zealot movement; though slippery, the dominant method is to sift *through* the texts as they stand.

Jesus' Disciples[27]

While in Galilee, Jesus attracted followers. Though the Talmud mentions only five disciples (the Gospel of John mentions only five by name), all four gospels state that Jesus had twelve disciples, and the synoptics and the Book of Acts present them in the form of lists (John 6:67ff.; 20:24; Mark 3:16–19; Mt 10:2–4; Luke 6:14–16; Acts 1:13). Since Paul refers to "the Twelve" in a tradition believed to be very early (1 Cor 15:5)—he does not otherwise refer to "the Twelve"—the number twelve should probably be accepted as accurate. Nonetheless, it is often concluded that Jesus did not attempt to set up a "new Israel" of twelve tribes in the sense of an institutional church (in the past Roman Catholics and Protestants have differed on this issue; see the discussion of the views of Loisy in Ch. 9) and that he did not train pupils to preserve his oral teaching in the rabbinic sense (a view which has also been defended by some scholars); rather, if the number did not arise very early in the churches, which some believe, it probably symbolized the "new Israel" in an "otherworldly" sense related to Jesus' teaching about the end of the world.

Jesus and John the Baptist[28]

Jesus' relation to John the Baptist is strongly rooted in the gospel tradition and the Book of Acts (Acts 1:22; 10:36–37; 11:16; 13:24) and is without doubt historical. The gospels claim that John was from a family of priests (Luke 1:5ff.), that he was ritually pure as regards the dietary laws (Mark 1:6; cp. Lev 11:22), and that he baptized the many people who went out to be purified in the Jordan River (Mark 1:5). These connections with priesthood, baptism, and the Jordan are especially intriguing because, since the discovery of the Dead Sea Scrolls in 1947, much is known about the Essenes, a priestly sect that initiated proselytes by baptism and was located just south of where the Jordan empties into the Dead Sea. There were also other baptizing sects along the Jordan. One such sect, the Mandaeans, which has a Gnostic orientation and claims connections with John the Baptist, still exists in modern Iran and Iraq. Intriguing theories about John's possible relation to these groups are numerous but highly debated.

The heart of John's preaching was the prophetic call to all people to repent and be baptized, for God's reign would come very soon. John spoke of "one who is coming," a figure who would be the judge not only of Israel, but of the whole world (Mt 3:12). Thus his baptism of repentance was the last preparation before the End. Josephus states, with some plausibility, that Herod Antipas, the son of Herod the Great and ruler of Galilee, executed John because he feared that John's great influence over the people might lead to a revolt (*Antiquities* 18:116–19; see also Mark 6:14–19).

As noted above, Jesus was baptized by John, but the exact connection between them remains uncertain. It appears that the statements in which John was not sure of Jesus' identity and in which Jesus expresses a somewhat qualified admiration for John reflect accurate historical conditions during Jesus' life (Mt 11:2–19). This goes against the Christian tradition, which tries to play John down (Acts 19:1ff.; John 1:15; 3:30). Yet, even though the synoptic gospels preserve a high estimate of John, they nonetheless interpret him in a subordinate way, namely, as the prophet Elijah come again, the expected forerunner of the Messiah (Mal 2:23 [English 4:5]; Ecclesiasticus 48:10 [also known as Jesus ben Sirach; canonical for Roman Catholics, but apocryphal for Protestants]; the Mishna; cp. Mt 11:14), and so they describe him with the colorful descriptions of Elijah (2 Kings 1:8; cp. Zech 13:4; Mark 1:6; contrast John 1:21).

In summary, the historical core appears to be that Jesus was baptized by John, that he was in some way connected with the baptist movement (Jesus' teaching reflects John's in part), that he paid John high tribute, and that the Christian and baptist movements eventually came into conflict. Yet it is probable that Jesus himself did not baptize (John 4:2 contradicts John 3:22 and 4:1). Moreover, several other features of Jesus' ministry contrast with John's, namely, his miracle-working activity, the fact that he went directly to the people, and most important, his teachings about ritual purity and the kingdom of heaven.

Jesus as Exorcist and Healer [29]

The gospels are full of the miracle-working activity of Jesus. There is some background for this type of activity in Palestinian Judaism. In Palestine, unlike much of the ancient Near East, professional healers had not always been respectable. By about 200 B.C.E. they were accepted, but healing was even then believed to be a divine gift to be preceded by prayer. Because of the influence of Zoroastrian religious beliefs on the Jews during the long Persian occupation of Palestine (538–331 B.C.E.), evil demons and helping angels began to play a significant part in beliefs about disease and health (see the Book of Tobit, chs. 6 and 8 [also known as Tobias, this book is canonical for Roman Catholics but apocryphal for Protestants]). Venerable ancestors were said to have performed exorcisms of demons (for example, Abraham by praying, laying his hands on Pharaoh's head, and rebuking demons [in a Dead Sea Scrolls writing, *Genesis Apocryphon* 20:16–19]; David by playing his harp [in a noncanonical Jewish narrative called LibAntBib 60:1–3]; Noah by medicines and herbs [in a noncanonical pseudepigraph, Jubilees 10:10–14]; and especially Solomon, whose wisdom included incantations for healers and formulas for exorcism that were passed on as magico-medical lore [Josephus, *Antiquities* 8:44–45]).[30] Josephus and the rabbinic literature also have references to famous spirit-filled, or "charismatic," miracle workers in Palestine who, like Jesus, were termed "men of deed." A famous example was Hanina ben Dosa, a first-century C.E. Galilean *Hasîd* ("pious one") who was believed to have healed people at a distance by means of prayer; he lived in poverty and was renowned for his lack of interest in legal and ritual affairs.

How did Jesus fit this pattern? Though the forms of the miracle stories follow typical patterns of such stories both within and outside of Palestine, it is generally concluded that Jesus exorcized demons and healed diseases, a picture corroborated by Josephus and the rabbis (see pp. 5–7). It is interesting to note that Jesus is portrayed within Palestine as on the verge of breaking with legal–ritual traditions, either in healing by touch on the Sabbath (Mark 1:29–31) or simply in coming into frequent contact with those considered ritually unclean. Before discussing his relation to the Hebrew law in general, we must first consider the heart of Jesus' teaching and another way in which he is both like and unlike his Jewish contemporaries.

ASPECTS OF JESUS' TEACHING

The Jewish Myth of God's Future Reign

It is common in Western culture to use the term "myth" in a derogatory sense. Behind this lies a history of the criticism of myth as irrational, pagan, immoral, and untrue. Yet today's scholars of myth think that for those who believe in the myths, they have a very profound kind of truth.[31] Myths are stories about the gods or other supernatural beings and about events occurring in another place and especially "in another time" (*in illo tempore*)—usually the time of "beginnings," though occasionally a unique "historical" time such as a "golden age" may be referred to. Myths are symbolically rich narratives about the way "the world" and "human life" *really* are, and meaningful life in the present is interpreted through them. They deal with the perennial problems of human life, and they are considered sacred stories which, in a variety of symbolic ways, provide vivid and authoritative patterns of meaning and valuable models for individual morality. They also tell of the origin of the group or nation and offer lenses through which complex human experience becomes simplified.

The enactment of sacred events of myth is *ritual;* to "reparticipate" in the myth's various levels of symbolic reality (whether conscious or unconscious) is to participate in ritual, that is, to worship. In ritual, worshipers emerge from profane, chronological ("historical") time and space, where there is change, dissolution, and disorder, into sacred and wholly different time and space, where there is permanence, harmony, and order. Through ritual, chaos is overcome, and new creation occurs. Wholeness, healing ("therapy"), and real freedom result. Archetype and repetition, myth and ritual—these, along with sacred places, times, things, and persons, are the heart of the mythical consciousness.[32]

One form of myth that occurs mostly in less traditional societies is called an *eschatological myth.* (Greek: *eschaton,* "end"). In such a myth the symbolism of the Beginning is transposed to the symbolism of the End. Eschatological myths hope for the *re*-establishment of the beginnings, the *re*-creation of the original paradise. As creation myths express belief in life and its origins, so eschatology expresses the inevitability of death, destruction, and judgment—but also the possibility of new life beyond death, of a new creation. To reenact death in anticipation is to reenact the possibility of new life in anticipation: The ritual becomes a reparticipation (an act of remembering) in the Beginning and an anticipatory participation in the End.

In ancient Israel there was a myth of God's (Yahweh's) rule over his people, which eventually became an eschatological myth.[33] With a monarchy as the basic political form of government, it is not surprising that a myth about God and his kingdom (especially Pss 47; 83; 95–99) arose. In this myth, Yahweh as king was characterized especially as creator, judge, and conquering warrior: He was creator of the world and ruled over it as a king; he was a judge who judged the nations justly; he was a powerful military figure who defeated his enemies. As Yahweh was king, so he had a kingdom (Hebrew: *malkuth Yahweh,* cp. 1 Chron 28:5). By the later Old Testament, this kingdom had lost its geographic limitations and become a universal "rule" or "reign" extending to all of creation. Yahweh's reign was said to be unending (Pss 145:13; 103:19).

After the final destruction of the nation "Israel" (Judah) in 587 B.C.E., "Judaism," a new form of religion centered in the Mosaic law, emerged. Jewish thinkers began more and more to conceive's God's universal reign as a future one, that is, to see it in terms of an eschatological myth. One form of this myth stressed beliefs such as that "this age" is an evil age, that the end of "this age" is near, that "this age" will be destroyed by God, that the End will be marked by great cataclysmic signs in the universe, and that the "age to come" will be totally different—like the primeval paradise of long ago. All of this is put in the form of a seer's fantastic, colorful, and highly symbolic vision, a revelation. This type of eschatology is called *apocalyptic* (Greek: *apocalyptō,* "I uncover," "I reveal"), and it shows the tendency found in eschatological myths to calculate the period before the End by means of the symbolism of four successive (and degenerating) kingdoms. For the author of Daniel (Dan 2:44), the fifth kingdom will be final, victorious, and everlasting and will be characterized by Yahweh's miracles ("signs and wonders," cp. Dan 3:33 [English 4:3]). Then, in Daniel 7, the four kingdoms are viewed as four supernatural beasts, while Yahweh's kingdom is given to a heavenly, mythical being "like a (son of) man." Dan 7:13–14 reads,

> I saw in the night visions,
> and behold, with the clouds of heaven
> there came one like a son of man
> and he came to the Ancient of Days
> and was presented before him.
> And to him was given dominion and glory and kingdom,
> that all peoples, nations, and languages should serve him;
> his dominion is an everlasting dominion,
> which shall not pass away,
> and his kingdom one that shall not be destroyed.

Here again, the kingdom is universal and eternal. The unusual feature is that it is given to one like a "son of man," an aspect not found in other early texts. The judgment of the nations is absent here, but it is picked up in another Jewish text from about 63 B.C.E. (Psalms of Solomon 17:3):

> But we hope in God, our Savior;
> For the might of our God is forever with mercy,
> And the Kingdom of God is forever over the nations in judgment.[34]

One of the best expressions of the eschatological myth of the reign of God is found in ritual, that is, in the Kaddish prayer, recited by Jews at various points in each of the three daily synagogue services (and on certain other occasions):

> Magnified and sanctified be his great name in the world which he has created according to his will. May he establish his kingdom in your lifetime and in your days and in the lifetime of all the house of Israel even speedily and at a near time.[35]

In this frequently recited prayer, nearness and urgency are stressed.

The eschatological myth just described is, in part, hypothetical. It does not appear as an isolated myth, whole and complete in one text, and it does not seem to have been a central idea in all of pre-Christian Judaism. There were many other notions among the Jews, such as the expectation of a prophet (Elijah, or one like Moses) and both priestly and royal messiahs. A somewhat more political expectation is reflected in the Psalms of Solomon, where the Son of David is expected to accompany the new reign of God. It is also clear that at least by the middle of the first century C.E., the Zealots wished to expel the Romans on account of their hope for the reign of God. The eschatological myth thus took various forms; in the teaching of Jesus it took still another form.

Jesus' Transformation of the Myth of God's Future Reign [36]

In many respects Jesus was in continuity with his Jewish heritage. He taught an eschatological myth of God's reign and ritually celebrated with his disciples the anticipation of its coming. As Jews prayed for the coming of God's kingdom (Kaddish prayer), so Jesus taught his disciples to pray, "Thy Kingdom come" (Mt 6:10). In characteristic fashion, the heavenly reign of God was expected to come to earth in the near future, and it was associated with the Judaic ritual anticipation of the "messianic banquet," that is, a heavenly banquet with God and/or his Messiah in the future Paradise (Isa 25:6–8; 1 Enoch 62:14; Exodus Rabbah 25:8 [a Jewish commentary]; Dead Sea Scrolls IQSa 2.11–22, cp. IQS

6.4–5; Mt 8:11). Many have suggested that Jesus' fellowship meals with
his disciples and the outcasts were ritual anticipations of just such a
messianic banquet.

However, Jesus' view of God's kingdom was also a transformation
of the eschatological myth. In the first place, there was a shift in the
meaning of the *language*.[37] Jesus spoke of the kingdom the way the
rabbis spoke of the Messiah and other texts spoke of the "new age": It
"comes," and one prays for its coming. In the second place, there was a
shift in the *context* of his teaching. In Judaism the eschatological myth
was found primarily in apocalyptic literature; for Jesus that apocalyptic
element was greatly reduced, so that the cosmic symbolism was not
strong. Jesus did not *describe* the kingdom that was now dawning (Luke
17:20–21). Third, God's kingdom was preached not only as future, but
as already *present*. Being not far from the kingdom of God (Mark 12:34)
meant loving God and neighbor. It was something like the love and trust
of a child (Mt 18:3). An ethical element began to predominate, for the
poor possessed the kingdom (Luke 6:20; Mt 5:3); in fact, human rank
might be reversed in the kingdom (Mt 11:11; Luke 7:28). In addition,
though Jesus denied that miraculous signs would herald the coming of
the kingdom, the kingdom was nevertheless already present upon those
who were exorcized of demons (Luke 17:20); in a sense, the kingdom
was preached as being already present in Jesus' victorious battle with
the evil and demonic forces of the universe. The orientation toward the
present and toward ethics meant that the commitment of the disciples
had to be total (Luke 9:62), and it was especially difficult for those who
were materially rich (Mt 10:23b, 25).

Thus we see that there is a shift of language through the reduction
of the mythical symbolism of apocalyptic eschatology, a focus on the
present through the stress on a reality that is "in the midst of you," a
reversal of usual human values through the offer of hope for the poor
and lowly, a concentration on childlike love, and a need for absolute
commitment. Moreover, the kingdom is present in the exorcism of demons, which, though it presumes a mythic battle between the forces of
good and evil in the cosmos, indicates that the victory over evil is *already* in process.

These shifts are indicative of a strong move toward giving sacred
significance to what is "profane," thus modifying the traditional mythical separation between what is set aside as "holy" and the everyday
"secular." One might suggest that for Jesus the mythical reality which
speaks of another time is transformed, in thought, language, and the activity of extra-cultic, or "secular," *living,* into a reality which includes
this world and this time. The remnants of the eschatological myth of the
kingdom of heaven persist; but they are also being transformed by a
move toward making the world itself sacred.

Jesus was not an apocalyptic seer. His "reduced apocalyptic" was more characteristic of a revival of prophecy, which was thought to have died out in Israel but was awaited in connection with the End. In Judaism there was expected either a returning Elijah who would work miracles (Mal 3:23 [English 4:5]; Sir 48:10) or a prophet–teacher like Moses (the Dead Sea Scrolls; see p. 21). Whether or not Jesus implied that he was a charismatic prophet (Mark 6:4; Mt 13:33), it is apparent that his miracle working raised the question whether he was Elijah, and it was also asked whether he was John the Baptist come back to life, or some other prophet (Mark 6:15; 8:28; Luke 4:25–27; 7:16, 39; 22:64; 24:19; Mt 21:11, 46). It is also certain that the early Church identified him with the "prophet like Moses" (Acts 3:17–26). Perhaps, then, the prophet of the kingdom, or reign, of God ought to be placed alongside the exorcist and healer as an apt description of the historical Jesus.

Jesus and the Law [38]

Law in Judaism was more than simply civil law; it was God's "cosmic law," a total way of life. Rooted in the first five books of the Hebrew Scriptures (called the Torah) and expanded by an elaborate oral interpretation that sought to apply it to specific situations in everyday life, the Judaic written law and elaborate legal–ritual customs regulated every phase of daily existence, from the sacrificial cultus to personal ritual cleanliness. The Essene sect along the Dead Sea was, among other things, a scribal community dedicated to copying and interpreting the Scriptures; the Sadducees, a conservative and aristocratic party, would not accept anything they did not find in the Torah, such as the belief in angels, demons, and the resurrection of the dead; and the Pharisees, a learned group of lay scholars, considered themselves the guardians of the holy legal–ritual tradition. Though the common people of the period (the "people of the land") could not carry out all the legal prescriptions, by and large it can be said that Judaism was a "people of the book," and the interpretation of the book was a matter of great significance. Thus there arose famous teachers of the law, who are named by the Talmud as "rabbis" (Hebrew: *rabbi,* "my great one," or "teacher").

That Jesus was addressed as "Rabbi," especially by the common people and opponents (presumably in derision), is debated. If the conception of rabbi in Jesus' period was the same as that found in the later rabbinic literature (in which a rabbi is one who bases all truth on the Scriptures, teaches in the synagogues, gathers pupils around him in a school, and debates the fine points of the law with other authoritative scribes), then Jesus was not a rabbi. Jesus taught in synagogues, but he also taught in open spaces, along the seashore, during his travels, and

in the Temple precincts. Among his followers were those whom stricter
rabbis considered to be of lesser status, such as the uneducated, the
poor, women and children, the frequently hated tax collectors, and prostitutes. Most importantly, Jesus was known as an authoritative teacher
who was willing to oppose his own view to the beloved Torah. The
source of this authority was not some unusual expertise in the Torah itself, for many of the sayings *attributed* to Jesus were also said by the
rabbis; rather, Jesus spoke with directness and simplicity about daily
life, and it is very likely that his authority was buttressed by the power
of his exorcisms and cures. This authority is echoed in the frequent
formulas, "You have heard it said, . . . but I say to you," and "Truly,
truly, I say to you." In so speaking, Jesus criticized the performance of
external actions for their own sake, even if prescribed by Torah. Strict
observance of the Sabbath was modified by "The Sabbath was made for
man, not man for the Sabbath" (Mark 2:27); at times he seemed to deny
the significance of the central place of worship, the Jerusalem Temple
(Mark 13:1ff.); at other times he demanded reconciliation with one's
brother before sacrifice at the altar (Mt 5:23ff.); he encouraged fasting
without ostentatiousness (Mt 6:16ff.); and in contrast to the usual Jewish teaching, he strictly forbade divorce (Mark 10:2ff). This boldness
was especially evident in his sayings about clean and unclean food, that
is, his claim that what defiles one is not what comes from outside oneself (Mark 7:15). Similarly, Jesus' view on burial of the dead, an absolute responsibility in Judaism, was so radical that it seems scarcely
believable for a Jew: "Leave the dead to bury their own dead" (Luke
9:60a).[39] Finally, as mentioned above, Jesus gathered about him outcasts who were considered unclean and ate with them. For this reason
it was said that he, in contrast to the ascetically oriented John the Baptist, was ". . . a glutton and a drunkard, a friend of tax collectors and
sinners!" (Mt 11:19). In short, as Jesus blurred the distinction between
sacred and secular in his kingdom of God teaching, so he blurred that
distinction in his approach to the law.

Jesus' Parabolic Teaching

Related to Jesus' shift of the Jewish eschatological myth to the present
and his secularizing of Jewish legal–ritual tradition were his parables.[40]
These were figurative forms of speech drawn from daily life or nature
that opened up a new reality in such a way that his hearers were challenged to make a decision. The parables were attempts to engage
hearers by creating images to evoke strong feelings. They confronted
the listeners and challenged them to alter their perception of reality.

They had "shock value" and could be directed to opponents as well as to friends and followers.

In contrast to John the Baptist's focus on judgment, Jesus' parables expressed the tremendous surprise and joy of the reign of God.[41] It was like unexpectedly discovering buried treasure, or finding a long-sought pearl of great price—so much so that one would sell all one's possessions to obtain it (Mt 13:44–46). This joy was also felt when something lost was found again, especially persons accounted sinners and outcasts such as a prodigal son who had been in daily contact with the unclean pigs and whores (Luke 15:11–32). Similarly, Jesus said that there is great rejoicing over a lost sheep (Mt 18:12–13) or a lost coin (Luke 15:8–9). Such teaching was implicitly a defense of Jesus' own association with those considered lost, especially in his meals with the outcasts. His parable of the great banquet (Mt 22:1–14; Luke 14:16–24; Gospel of Thomas 64), though the surviving versions of it have been reworked, was an indication that those who responded were, among others, the poor. It was absolutely crucial to make a decision, and in order to bring home the point, Jesus told another parable of a roguish figure, an unjust steward (Luke 16:1–9), who was compelled by circumstances to act decisively.

The problem in accepting Jesus' challenge, of course, was that it flew in the face of many long-cherished ideas. In one parable a despised tax collector who asked mercy for his sins was accepted before the pious and self-assured Pharisee (Luke 18:9–14). Those who heard the parable of the good Samaritan (Luke 10:29–37) might have expected a pious Jew to be more helpful to a person attacked along the road than a ritually pure priest or a Levite, but certainly not, as Jesus' story said, a hated Samaritan! It was better to refuse and repent later than to accept and then disobey (Mt 21:28–32). Yet God would certainly respond to those who counted the cost (Luke 14:28–32), and, like a friend who is disturbed in the night (Luke 11:5–8) or a hardnosed judge who is incessantly bothered by a poor, complaining widow (Luke 18:1–8), he would hear their cry. One could not be absolutely sure that the usual standards of human justice would apply to God's justice, for God might be generous at the very end, as the vineyard owner was with the laborer who began to work only late in the day (Mt 20:1–16).

Jesus' parables were pervaded with the view that love of God and of one's fellow human being, the most important Jewish commandments (Mark 12:28–34), were more important than the legal–ritual externals. Such love was to go beyond society's customary status classifications; it required even turning the other cheek when one is struck, giving more than requested, going the extra mile (Mt 5:39b–41). It required merciful forgiveness, as God has forgiven (Mt 18:23–25). With such an ethic future "success" was assured (Mark 4:3–9; Gospel of Thomas 9). This was true—even radical—obedience.

Finally, Jesus' teaching did not develop a social ethic in the usual sense of a program for social reform. Certainly, his ethic of love for humanity as represented in the parables implied that the downtrodden, the poor, the outsider must be accepted; but the specific applications of that view in new situations were not spelled out in detail. Likewise, he proclaimed no political ethics in the usual sense; obedience was not the same as obedience to the state (Mark 12:13–17). Whatever the circumstances, the challenge to one's usual point of view was always present, and commitment to God was final.

Jesus' Final Days [42]

Our sketch of Jesus' life and teachings has emphasized that Jesus emerged out of the baptist movement as an authoritative miracle worker and as a prophet of a transformed myth of the reign of God. In addition, Jesus came into conflict with many traditions of his religion, especially in placing the ethic of love above obligatory rules and sacred rituals and in accepting outcasts and persons of lower status. Though the opponents of Jesus are stereotyped by the gospel writers, it is probable that many of the Pharisees were upset with Jesus' legal–ritual nonconformity and that they engaged him in occasional debate (Mark 12). In the same way, the Sadducees objected to his (Pharisaic!) belief in the final resurrection of the dead (Mark 12:18–27).

Aside from such religious opposition, it appears that the hardcore opponents of Jesus arose within the political establishment. Since he was not a Zealot revolutionary, it may well be that Jesus, like John the Baptist, was feared because he had gained a following among the masses. In any case the evangelists state that he had opponents from the very beginning of his ministry in Galilee. Luke records that King Herod Antipas of Galilee, who believed Jesus was the executed John the Baptist come back to life, plotted against him. When some Pharisees warned him, Jesus is said to have replied,

> Go and tell that fox, "Behold, I cast out demons and perform cures today and tomorrow, and the third day I finish my course. Nevertheless, I must go on my way today and tomorrow and the day following; for it cannot be that a prophet should perish away from Jerusalem." (Luke 13:32–33)

This comment may have a historical core, but it reflects the influence of early Christians in its view that Jesus knew of his death. The same problem arises with the passion narrative as a whole, for it is a powerful drama dominated by deeply felt Christian convictions. Thus, even though it is a more connected story than the rest of the gospel materials, historical reconstruction remains conjectural.

It seems probable that Jesus rode into Jerusalem in the final days on a donkey, an event that later tradition interpreted as the entry of the King Messiah foretold in Zechariah 9:9. He also wielded his authority against the religious–economic establishment by attempting to put an end to the commonly accepted practice of exchanging foreign currency in the outer precincts of the temple. Thus the chief priests who wished to maintain order sought to respond quickly, *before* the actual feast of the Passover began, "lest there be a tumult among the people" (Mark 14:2). This little statement contradicts the synoptic gospels' view that Jesus celebrated a Passover meal with his disciples and was then convicted for blasphemy in a late night trial by the Sanhedrin (the Jewish Supreme Court), after which he was crucified on the first day of the Feast (Nisan 15). Yet it is probably accurate, since there are good reasons for believing that Jesus did not celebrate the Passover and was not crucified on the first day of the Feast: Jesus' last meal was not linked to the Passover by Paul or John, and many crucial features of a Passover meal (including the Passover lamb and the unleavened bread) are missing from the accounts of the supper. Furthermore, night trials and single sessions were strictly forbidden by (admittedly later) rabbinic laws about trial procedure. According to the same laws, Jesus said nothing blasphemous (that is, nothing against the Divine Name) at the trial. Indeed, the punishment for blasphemy was stoning, and there is a good deal of evidence indicating that only the Romans could carry out capital punishment in this period.[43] Though the Passover hypothesis has its defenders, all these complications lead many scholars to think it more probable that Jesus ate a customary fellowship meal *prior* to the beginning of Passover, perhaps on the previous night as the Gospel of John suggests, and that it was later viewed as a Passover meal in connection with the notion of a new Passover for the new Israel, the church.

There is no reason to doubt that Jesus was betrayed by one of his own—the motive can only be conjectured—and that he was arrested in the Garden of Gethsemane, turned over to the Jewish authorities, tried by them, and delivered to the Roman authorities as politically dangerous. Presumably, Pilate agreed with this estimate, though later Christian tradition attempted to exonerate him and fix the guilt more directly on the Jews and their disbelief that he was the Messiah. The release of the Zealot Barabbas may also be accurate, though the custom of releasing a criminal at Passover cannot be traced. If so, the irony is that the politically revolutionary hero Barabbas was permitted to go free, while Jesus was condemned on a political charge.

The final end was that on a hill called Golgotha outside Jerusalem, the miracle worker and teacher of Nazareth, deserted by his followers and mocked by the Roman troops, was crucified for sedition against the Roman state. A little sign was probably carried about his neck—at least that was the custom—and was affixed to the cross. It read, "King of the

Jews." By intercession of the courageous Joseph of Arimathea, Jesus of Nazareth was buried in a tomb according to the Hebrew law.

SUMMARY

During the early centuries of Christianity, the majority of churches came to accept four gospels, Matthew, Mark, Luke, and John, but the strong tendency in successive centuries was to interpret them as a "gospel harmony." By the eighteenth century, differences among the four gospels were beginning to lead to theories about their interrelationship, the overwhelming consensus in the nineteenth century being in favor of the two-source theory and the Markan hypothesis. However, the quest of the historical Jesus, built on the Markan hypothesis, was countered by many twentieth-century scholars who began to see that the gospels were products of developing oral tradition in which the stories about Jesus were altered to meet new needs. The new quest of the historical Jesus in the twentieth century has attempted to sift the documents carefully to arrive at a critical estimate of the Jesus who actually lived.

There are a number of nonbiblical sources about Jesus from non-Christian Romans and Jews and from attempts to expand the biblical materials. Though such materials indicate that no one doubted the actual existence of Jesus, they offer no really new information about him beyond that found in the gospels. Indeed, the Christian Apocrypha give evidence about how the stories about Jesus grew and developed in the decades after the writing of the materials eventually accepted into the canon.

A critical estimate yields a minimal amount of material about the "life" of Jesus. He was probably born about 4 B.C.E., perhaps in Nazareth, and his mother was Mary. Sometime late in the 20s Jesus emerged out of the baptist movement, not as a Zealot but as an exorcist, healer, prophet of a transformed myth of the kingdom of God, legal–ritual revisionist, and parable teacher. All these features made him attractive to a growing number of followers, some of whom became the twelve disciples. His teaching about the presence of the kingdom, his placing the standard of love above religious conformity, and his acceptance of various outcasts backed by a certain nonconformist parable teaching brought about resistance from religious authorities. At Jerusalem he was betrayed by one of his own, tried, and handed over to the Roman authorities, who crucified him as a political criminal.

NOTES

1. Irenaeus, *Against Heresies* 3.11.8, quoted in Daniel J. Theron, *Evidence of Tradition* (London: Bowes & Bowes, 1957), p. 107.

2. On the gospel harmonies in general, see Harvey K. McArthur, *The Quest through the Centuries* (Philadelphia: Fortress Press, 1966), pp. 96–113.

3. See Ch. 7. William R. Farmer, *The Synoptic Problem* (New York: Macmillan Co., 1964), gives a history of the problem of the relation of the first three gospels, but his solution is usually contested; see Reginald H. Fuller, "The Synoptic Problem: After Ten Years," *Perkins Journal* **28** (Winter 1975), pp. 63–68.

4. See Ch. 7. See also Albert Schweitzer, *The Quest of the Historical Jesus,* trans. W. Montgomery (New York: Macmillan Co., 1968), ch. 14 (originally published in German, in 1906).

5. See Ch. 9.

6. The "new quest" is said to have been launched by Ernst Käsemann, "The Problem of the Historical Jesus," in *Essays on New Testament Themes*, Studies in Biblical Theology, no. 41, trans. W. J. Montague (London: SCM Press, 1964), pp. 15–47 (originally published in German in 1953); see also Ch. 9.

7. For a general discussion of the "new quest," a standard treatment is James M. Robinson, *A New Quest of the Historical Jesus,* Studies in Biblical Theology, no. 25 (London: SCM Press, 1959).

8. A well known treatment, with sources, appears in Maurice Goguel, *Jesus and the Origins of Christianity,* 2 vols., trans. Olive Wyon (New York: Harper & Brothers, Torchbooks, 1960), vol. 1, "Prolegomena to the Life of Jesus," pp. 91–104.

9. Ibid., pp. 70–91; Joseph Klausner, *Jesus of Nazareth: His Life, Times, and Teaching,* trans. Herbert Danby (Boston: Beacon Press, 1964), pp. 18–54 (originally published in 1925).

10. Josephus, *Antiquities of the Jews,* Loeb edition, vol. 9, trans. L. H. Feldmann (Cambridge, Mass.: Harvard University Press, 1965); further discussion is found in Howard C. Kee, *Jesus in History,* 2nd ed. (New York: Harcourt Brace Jovanovich, 1977), pp. 42–45.

11. A standard work is Hermann L. Strack, *Introduction to the Talmud and Midrash* (New York: Harper & Row, Torchbooks, 1965), especially chs. 1 and 2 (originally published in German in 1931).

12. Klausner, *Jesus of Nazareth,* p. 46.

13. J. Jeremias, "Isolated Sayings of the Lord," in *New Testament Apocrypha,* ed. Edgar Hennecke and Wilhelm Schneemelcher, trans. A. J. B. Higgins et al., English translation ed. R. McL. Wilson (Philadelphia: Westminster Press, 1963), vol. 1, pp. 85–90.

14. J. Jeremias and W. Schneemelcher, "Papyrus Fragments of Apocryphal Gospels," in Hennecke–Schneemelcher, *New Testament Apocrypha,* pp. 91–116.

15. Ibid., p. 94.

16. Ibid., p. 93.

17. *The Gospel According to Thomas,* ed. and trans. A. Guillàumont, H.-Ch. Puech, G. Quispel, W. Till, and Yassah 'Abd Al Masīḥ (New York: Harper & Row, 1959), pp. 53–54.

18. Norman Perrin, *Rediscovering the Teaching of Jesus* (New York: Harper & Row, 1967), pp. 253–54, summarizes alternative viewpoints.

19. Hennecke–Schneemelcher, *New Testament Apocrypha,* pp. 392–94.

20. Arthur Drews, *The Christ Myth* (Chicago: Open Court, 1910); William Benjamin Smith, *The Birth of the Gospel: A Study of the Origin and Purport of the Primitive Allegory of the Jews* (New York: Philosophical Library, 1957) (originally published in 1927); responses to this movement came from Johannes Weiss, *Jesus von Nazareth: Mythus oder Geschichte* (Tübingen: J. C. B. Mohr [Paul Siebeck], 1910) in German; from Maurice Goguel, *Jésus de Nazareth, mythe ou historire?* (Paris: Payot, 1925) in French, cp. Goguel, *Jesus and the Origins of Christianity,* vol. 1, pp. 65–69; and from Frederick C. Conybeare, *The Historical Christ: An Investigation of the Views of Mr. J. M. Robertson, Dr. A. Drews, and Prof. W. B. Smith* (Chicago: Open Court, 1914) in English.

21. The sketch is indebted especially to Günther Bornkamm, *Jesus of Nazareth,* trans. Irene and Fraser McLuskey with James M. Robinson (New York: Harper & Row, 1960) (originally published in German in 1956); Hans Conzelmann, *Jesus,* ed. John Reumann and trans. J. Raymond Lord (Philadelphia: Fortress Press, 1973) (originally published in German in 1959); Norman Perrin, *Rediscovering;* and Geza Vermes, *Jesus the Jew* (New York: Macmillan Co., 1973). The last is not a "new quest" scholar.

22. E. Stauffer, *Jesus and His Story,* trans. Dorothea M. Barton (London: SCM Press, 1960), pp. 36–38, defends the astronomical evidence; see the extract from Stauffer in Hugh Anderson, *Jesus,* Great Lives Observed Series (Englewood Cliffs, N.J.: Prentice-Hall, 1967), pp. 164–67.

23. For the question of the virginity of Mary that follows, see Thomas Boslooper, *The Virgin Birth* (Philadelphia: Westminster Press, 1962); Vermes, *Jesus the Jew,* pp. 213–22.

24. On the virginity of Mary, see Raymond E. Brown, *The Virginal Conception and Bodily Resurrection of Jesus* (New York: Paulist Press, 1973).

25. Vermes, *Jesus the Jew,* ch. 2; the modern scholar best known for the view that Jesus was in sympathy with the revolutionary Zealot movement was the late S. G. F. Brandon, *Jesus and the Zealots* (New York: Charles Scribner's Sons, 1967); a succinct statement of the evidence is found in Oscar Cullmann, *Jesus and the Revolutionaries* (New York: Harper & Row, 1970); see also Martin Hengel, *Victory Over Violence,* trans. David E. Green (Philadelphia: Fortress Press, 1973).

26. For a critique, see Walter Wink, "Jesus and Revolution: Reflections on S. G. F. Brandon's *Jesus and the Zealots,*" *Union Seminary Quarterly Review* **25** (1969), pp. 37–59.

27. Conzelmann, *Jesus,* pp. 33–35; R. E. Brown, "The Twelve and the Apostolate," in *The Jerome Biblical Commentary,* ed. Raymond E. Brown, Joseph A. Fitzmyer, and Roland E. Murphy (Englewood Cliffs, N.J.: Prentice-Hall, 1968), part 2, pp. 795–99.

28. For the historical questions, see Bornkamm, *Jesus of Nazareth,* pp. 44–52; Charles H. H. Scobie, *John the Baptist* (Philadelphia: Fortress Press, 1964).

29. Vermes, *Jesus the Jew,* pp. 22–26, 58–82; some background mate-

rial is given in Dennis Duling, "Solomon, Exorcism, and the Son of David," *Harvard Theological Review* **68**:¾ (1975), pp. 235–52.

30. Scholarly judgment places these materials prior to, or contemporaneous with, the time of Jesus; see Duling, "Solomon, Exorcism, and the Son of David," p. 242.

31. Kees Bolle, "Myth and Mythology," in *New Encyclopedia Britannica,* Macropaedia 12, Knowledge and Depth (Chicago: Encyclopaedia Britannica, 1974), pp. 793–804; on primitive religions, see W. Richard Comstock, *The Study of Religion and Primitive Religions* (New York: Harper & Row, 1971).

32. Mircea Eliade, *Myth and Reality,* trans. Willard R. Trask (New York: Harper & Row, Torchbooks, 1963), pp. 5–6; on eschatological myth, see Eliade, *Myth and Reality,* ch. 4, "Eschatology and Cosmogony," and Bolle, "Myth and Mythology," pp. 799–800.

33. Helmer Ringgren, *Israelite Religion,* trans. David E. Green (Philadelphia: Fortress Press, 1966), pp. 220–38; on the Davidic royal conception, see Dennis Duling, "The Promises to David and Their Entrance into Christianity—Nailing Down a Likely Hypothesis," *New Testament Studies* **20** (1973), pp. 55–77.

34. R. H. Charles, *The Apocrypha and Pseudepigrapha of the Old Testament,* 2 vols. (Oxford: Clarendon Press, 1913), vol. 2, pp. 647–48.

35. For discussion see Norman Perrin, *The Kingdom of God in the Teaching of Jesus* (Philadelphia: Westminster Press, 1963), p. 19; Perrin, *Rediscovering,* pp. 57–58.

36. Perrin, *Kingdom,* gives the history of thinking about the kingdom of heaven; Perrin, *Rediscovering,* ch. 2, discusses the texts; in his *Jesus and the Language of the Kingdom* (Philadelphia: Fortress Press, 1976), chs. 2 and 4, Perrin speaks of the kingdom as a symbol that calls forth the Israelite myth of God acting as king on behalf of his people, which can also have a future referent. I have attempted to see the myth of the kingdom of God as an "eschatological myth" in Eliade's sense (see note 32). Helmut Koester, "The Role of Myth in the New Testament," *Andover Newton Quarterly,* N.S. ⅞ (1966–1968), pp. 180–95, especially 186ff., sees the kingdom in terms of Jewish eschatological myth.

37. Perrin, *Kingdom,* pp. 58–60; more generally, Amos N. Wilder, *The Language of the Gospel: Early Christian Rhetoric* (New York: Harper & Row, 1964), chs. 1 and 7.

38. Bornkamm, *Jesus of Nazareth,* ch. 5; Conzelmann, *Jesus,* pp. 51–67; Vermes, *Jesus the Jew,* pp. 52–57, 80–82.

39. Vermes, *Jesus the Jew,* pp. 28–29.

40. On the "secularizing" language of the parables, see Wilder, *Language,* ch. 5; for further discussion of recent interpreters of parables see Perrin, *Jesus and the Language of the Kingdom,* ch. 3.

41. The following discussion is indebted to Perrin, *Rediscovering,* chs. 2, 3, and 4.

42. Conzelmann, *Jesus,* ch. 11; Bornkamm, *Jesus of Nazareth,* ch. 7; Eduard Lohse, *History of the Suffering and Death of Jesus Christ,* trans. Martin O. Dietrich (Philadelphia: Fortress Press, 1967); see also William R. Wilson, *The Execution of Jesus* (New York: Charles Scribner's Sons, 1970) and Gerard S. Sloyan, *Jesus on Trial* (Philadelphia: Fortress Press, 1973), both of which have extensive bibliographies.

43. Wilson, *Execution,* ch. 1.

II

Jesus Christ
in Early Christianity

The early Christians did not write a "life and teachings of Jesus" like that presented in Ch. 1. They wrote what they wanted to remember, as well as what they believed, confessed, experienced, sang, and prayed about the one who had lived and died. For some he was a heroic human being, or a spirit-filled miracle worker, or a suffering, righteous martyr; for others he was the Messiah resurrected to divine status, or a returning Savior and Judge, or a heavenly divine Being who had existed from eternity. The early Christians expressed their views about Jesus in the thought patterns of their own day, and what appears in the New Testament is a great variety of images, frequently mythic or quasi-mythic, often mixed or united with some of the recollections of the type isolated in Ch. 1. The purpose of this chapter is to look at the background of some of these images in the environment in which early Christianity arose and to suggest a possible explanation of why Jesus was so interpreted. As in Ch. 1, the perspective represents a particular historical attitude, and to that extent it is an interpretation that might well have been placed at the end of the book.

BELIEF IN THE RESURRECTION OF JESUS

The notion of resurrection was widespread in the ancient world.[1]
Usually it took the form of a myth about the return to earth of a god or
goddess imprisoned in the underworld, its context being the renewal of
vegetation and/or the agricultural process of sowing and reaping. Thus
resurrection and fertility went hand and hand, the return of the deity
symbolizing the return of nature's growth processes.

    In contrast to this widespread mythical view of resurrection in con-
nection with nature, Jewish views of resurrection, strongly influenced
by Zoroastrian ideas in the period of Persian domination (538–331
B.C.E.), centered in the survival of people after death followed by judgment (Dan 12:2). One Jewish belief was that the individual soul would
hover two or three days next to the destructible body and then go to the
(under-)world of departed souls, a view which was sometimes influenced by the Greek conception of the immortal soul that inhabits the
body and returns to its rightful home after death. Much more dominant
was the form that pictured the transformation of bodies at the end of the
world. Either *all* "sleeping" bodies would be awakened for judgment at
the end of the world (Testament of Benjamin 10:6–10), or—and this
view seems to have been related to the martyrdom of Jewish national
heroes in the second century B.C.E.—only the *righteous* among the
"sleeping" would be "awakened" (I Enoch 25:6), either to an existence
in some other place (heaven) or to a newly transformed earth, a paradisical "world to come" in contrast to "this (evil) world" (Testament of Levi
18:9–11 [Testament of the Twelve Patriarchs, a pseudepigraph written
just prior to or during the Christian Era]). Thus there was no single
doctrine of the resurrection of the dead in Judaism, and this diversity is
reflected in postbiblical Jewish literature, which had its origins in the
beliefs of the Pharisees. Yet it is known that the pious Pharisee prayed
daily for the coming resurrection (the Eighteen Benedictions), and the
New Testament shows that the Sadducees, in contrast, rejected the
belief because they did not believe it was in the Torah (Acts 23:6ff.;
Mark 12:18–25). Jesus and the early Christians were Pharisaic on this
point.

    If Jesus believed in the resurrection of the dead at the end of the
world (Mark 12:18–25), did he predict his own individual suffering,
death, and resurrection? The gospels say so in a group of passion predictions about the Son of Man (Mark 8:31; 9:31; 10:32–34; cp. 9:1,
10:45). While it is not unimaginable that Jesus had "precognition," or at
least premonitions of his death in dangerous situations (Martin Luther

King did), the passion predictions in their present form are too heavily confessional and precise to have come from Jesus. The point is that one cannot base belief in Jesus' resurrection on his own prophetic statements, for those statements were probably ascribed to him later.

A further difficulty is that there is no actual description of Jesus' resurrection from the dead in the New Testament. Rather, there are stories of the empty tomb and of appearances of the resurrected Jesus to his followers, some of which occur on earth, either in Galilee (Mt 28:16–20; John 21) or (near) Jerusalem (Luke 24; John 20), and others of which picture him in heaven (Acts 3:21; 7:56). Most scholars believe that the stories at the end of the gospels have been so edited that it is difficult to know precisely what happened. Moreover, it is probable that Luke, when he was writing his Gospel and the Book of Acts, had at his disposal both earthly and heavenly appearance stories and ordered them in a sequence of resurrection to earth (earthly appearances) for forty days (Acts 1:3) and then ascension to heaven (heavenly appearances). What one seeks, then, are early accounts of the resurrection traditions, and that search is carried on by isolating passages whose form and content indicate that they come from someone or some group other than the author, that is, from a time earlier than the author. "Structures" of belief can be uncovered from some of these early traditions, most of which are probably little creeds, confessions, and hymns. Moving on from Jesus's death and resurrection, one can hope to discover patterned images of the Christ figure.

One of the most important New Testament passages for an early view of Jesus' resurrection is 1 Corinthians 15:3b–5. Because it is introduced with known technical terms for passing on religious tradition and contains many un-Pauline expressions, the passage is considered to have been taken over from some early church, perhaps Antioch or Damascus, or even Jerusalem.[2] With its introduction (the technical terms are italicized), it reads,

> 3) For I *delivered* to you as of first importance what I also *received,* that Christ died for our sins in accordance with the scriptures,   4) that he was buried, that he was raised on the third day in accordance with the scriptures,   5) and that he appeared to Cephas, then to the twelve.

Since this passage must be earlier than the early 50s, the date of 1 Corinthians, it is very early. Yet Jesus is called not "the Christ" (i.e., the Messiah) but "Christ" as a personal name, so that there is some change in meaning in the word "Christ." The reference to death "for our sins in accordance with the scriptures" might be an attempt of some early Christians to root the notion of the sacrificial death of a victim as a way of atoning for sins (see pp. 52–54) in a particular scriptural text related to Jesus' life, perhaps the Suffering Servant of Isaiah 53 (cp. Mark 14:45b; 14:24; Rom 8:32; 1 Tim 2:6). If so, Jesus was being identified as the Suffering Servant, that is, as the ugly, despised, rejected, sorrowful man (king?) who bears the sorrows of others and is led like a lamb to the slaughter, but who will (as God's servant) be exalted and lifted up as one "very high" (Isa 52:13–53:12). It was said of him that "he bore the sin of many" (Isa 53:12). In any case, the formula in Paul states that he was resurrected "on the third day," which meant not simply the soul's hovering near the body for three days, but a specific belief based either on the Scriptures in general or on a specific "prophecy" such as "After two days he will revive us, on the third day he will raise us up, that in his presence we may live" (Hos 6:2), but applied individually to Jesus.[3] Whatever the precise background of these statements, one fact is certain: At a very early period, Jesus' death and resurrection were being argued by Christians as part of God's plan, and associated with them were high estimates of him.

JESUS AS THE RESURRECTED MESSIAH, SON OF GOD (AND LORD)

Stories of Jesus' resurrection have led to a quest for the reasons why early Christians believed it occurred. If the possibility that Jesus predicted it is set aside, then remains the possibility that early Christians interpreted texts which spoke of the "raising up" (which originally meant "coming forth") of important figures, especially the Davidic king, as references to the resurrection. Since such texts were set within a whole royal enthronement tradition in ancient Israel and Judaism, it will be helpful to recall some of the major ideas of the royal "ideology."

The monarchy in ancient Israel was an adaptation to the political and religious patterns of the ancient Near East.[4] In Israel it was said that Yahweh made a promise to David through the prophet Nathan about the kingship, the heart of which was 2 Samuel 7:11b–15a:

> Moreover the Lord (YAHWEH) declares to you that the Lord will make you a house. 12) When your days are fulfilled and you lie down with your fathers, I will raise up your son after you, who shall come forth from your body, and I will establish his kingdom. 13) He shall build a house for my name, and I will establish the throne of his kingdom for ever. 14) I will be his father, and he shall be my son. When he commits iniquity, I will chasten him with the rod of men, with the stripes of the sons of men; ·15) but I will not take my steadfast love from him . . .

Here there are three basic elements: (1) the promise that David's son (literally, "seed") would succeed him, implying the whole Davidic line; (2) the perpetuation of the kingdom and throne forever, even though the king might have to be chastised from time to time; (3) the close relationship between Yahweh and the king, expressed in terms of a father who will "raise up" his son.[5] Throughout Israel's history, the various items in this "promise tradition" were remembered and celebrated in the religious life of the nation in connection with the Jerusalem temple and the "house" (palace).[6]

The Davidic monarchy was destroyed by the Neo-Babylonians in 587 B.C.E.; they in turn were overcome by the Macedonian Greeks, who conquered Palestine in 331 B.C.E. In 168 B.C.E. a revolt against the Greek-descended Seleucids of Syria produced, once again, an independent kingdom, which lasted until the assumption of power by the Romans in 63 B.C.E. During the latter part of this century of independence, the non-Davidic Maccabees ruled as priest–kings. They were anointed, purified with water, involved in a cultic meal of bread and wine, and presented with a scepter—in other words, the images for enthronement were drawn from the old monarchy. Building on psalms such as Psalm 2 and Psalm 110, the Israelites pictured the king in an ascent to the heavenly regions, in which he stood ministering in God's presence as his Son, servant, and priest, declaring his mysteries to the people (T. Levi).[7]

Along with this temporary rejuvenation of the monarchy, there was an increasing tendency among the Jews (especially because of the corruption of the non-Davidic Maccabees and the return of foreign oppression with the Romans) to hope for an ideal king of the line of David. About the time of the Roman occupation in 63 B.C.E., an unknown (Pharisaic?) author wrote the Psalms of Solomon, which recalled the ancient promises again:[8]

> 17:5) Thou, O Lord, didst choose David (to be) king over Israel,
>   And swaredst to him touching his seed that never should his
>   kingdom fail before Thee. . . .
> 23) Behold, O Lord, and raise up unto them their king, the Son of David,
>   At the time in which Thou seest, O God, that he may reign over
>   Israel Thy servant.
> 24) And gird him with strength, that he may shatter unrighteous rulers,
>   And that he may purge Jerusalem from nations that trample (her)
>   down to destruction.

The Messiah ("anointed of the Lord," v. 36) would "thrust out sinners" (v. 25), "gather together a holy people" (v. 28), "judge the tribes of the people" (v. 28), "judge peoples and nations in the wisdom of his righteousness" (v. 31), "rebuke rulers and remove sinners by the might of his word" (v. 41), "be mighty in his works" (v. 44), and, as God's servant, bring Israel "good fortune" (v. 49). It appears that in some quarters of Judaism the hope was for both an ideal king and an ideal priest (Testament of Simeon 7:1–2)[9]—a view found in the Dead Sea Scrolls.[10] In many Scroll passages the Davidic king ("seed," "root," "branch") is said to be "raised up" and to be God's Son; it may be that with the idea of resurrection as a link, the heavenly themes which had sometimes accompanied the enthronement conception were developed as a heavenly enthronement.

There is no Jewish text known from the immediate pre-Christian period that claims that the Messiah would survive death or that he would be raised from the dead in anticipation of the general resurrection. Yet Christians had such beliefs about Jesus from very early days. The extent to which they were aware of the *actual* royal enthronement ideology of the ancient Near East in general or of the Israelite monarchy in particular is a matter for speculation. In any case, the Scriptures (specifically the Psalms and Isaiah 53) spoke of the king's suffering (indeed, 2 Samuel 7 and the promise tradition frequently mentioned chastising the king), and many passages tell of God's deliverance of the king from near death (Ps 118:17ff.). Some early Christians seem to have found their specific "proof text" in Psalm 16:10, "For thou dost not give me up to Sheol, or let thy godly one see the Pit." In Acts 2, "me" and "thy godly one" are interpreted not as a reference to David (who is speaking in the psalm) but as David's prophecy about the Messiah to come. Though not all is absolutely clear, the speech attributed to Peter takes the "prophecy" to mean either that the Messiah would not die (Acts 2:29) or, more likely, that God would not permit the "bonds" of death to hold him in Sheol, the gloomy underworld of departed spirits (Acts 2:24).[11] If the latter, belief in Jesus' resurrection might have grown out of the (Jewish?) notion that death would not contain the Messiah.

Whether or not this is the case, the belief that Jesus was resurrected to become the Son of God is found in a very early, pre-Pauline formula, Romans 1:3–4, which with Paul's introduction reads,

> 1) Paul, a servant of Jesus Christ, called to be an apostle, set apart for the gospel of God   2) which he promised before hand through his prophets in the holy scriptures,   3) the gospel concerning his Son, who was descended from [literally, "born of the seed of"] David according to the flesh   4) and designated Son of God in power according to the Spirit of holiness by his resurrection from the dead, Jesus Christ our Lord . . .

There may well be some Pauline additions in this text, but the basic notion of the passage is contrary to Paul's belief that Jesus Christ was God's Son sent to earth. This notion is that Jesus, being descended from David, was qualified to become the royal Son of God and that he became such on his resurrection from the dead, not before.[12] Thus the passage has points of contact with the royal ideology just traced, though the resurrection is an added factor.

The same general view of Jesus' resurrection as a heavenly enthronement is linked with the Psalm 16:10 argument about death in the speech in Acts 2:22–36. Again, the viewpoint is not that of the author, who accepted Jesus' divine sonship in connection with his life

(Luke 3:21–22, 38). After statements about Jesus' miracle· working, crucifixion, and inability to be held by death (Ps 16:10), the speech recalls the promise that one of David's descendants would be placed on his throne. But the heavenly motifs reappear when it is said that Jesus, in contrast to David, was resurrected and exalted at God's right hand, for as David prophecies in Psalm 110:1, "The Lord said to my lord [meaning, in this context, the Messiah], 'Sit at my right hand until I make your enemies your footstool.' " The speech concludes, "Let all the house of Israel therefore know assuredly that God has made him both Lord and Christ, this Jesus whom you crucified" (Acts 2:36).

A similar view is found in the speech attributed to Paul in Acts 13:17–41. Here Jesus is said to fulfill the prophecy, "I will give you the holy and sure blessings promised to David" (Isa 53:2), by not being held by death (Ps 16:10) and, being raised, by becoming the Son of God as foretold in Psalm 2:7: "Thou art my son; today I have begotten thee" (v. 33). In short, imbedded in the speeches in Acts is the claim that God "raised up" Jesus to the heavens at God's right hand; thus he became Messiah, Lord, and Son of God.[13]

JESUS AS THE COMING HEAVENLY REDEEMER (SON OF MAN)

A common conception among some Jews and Samaritans of Jesus' day was that there would be "raised up" (come forth) a new "prophet like Moses," Moses being the supreme lawgiver of ancient Israel. This expectation was based on Deuteronomy 18:15, in which Moses said, "The Lord God will raise up a prophet like me from among you." In Acts 3:21, Jesus is seen to have been that "prophet like Moses," now "raised up" (resurrected) to heaven, where he waits for the final days of "universal restoration." At that time he will *return* as Messiah. In the present he is a "Messiah designate," that is, he has not yet reached his full and complete status. The stress seems in this passage to be on who he *was* and who he *will be*, not who he *is*. Part of the speech again attributed to Peter, reads,

> ". . . 20) and that he may send the Christ appointed for you, Jesus, 21) whom heaven must receive until the time for establishing all that God spoke by the mouth of his holy prophets from of old. 22) Moses said, 'The Lord God will raise up for you a prophet from among your brethren as he raised me up. You shall listen to him in whatever he tells you. 23) And it shall be that every soul that does not listen to that prophet shall be destroyed from the people.' "

According to some scholars this "two-foci" Christology (having a past focus and a future focus) is the most primitive point of view in the early church about Jesus: He is resurrected, but not yet the Messiah in his full status.[14]

The notion that Jesus would be the Redeemer at the End was characteristic of early apocalyptic Christianity, probably among groups which not only continued to transmit the ("reduced") apocalyptic sayings of Jesus but also produced new sayings of this type through the utterances of spirit-filled prophets and seers who spoke for Jesus, just as he had spoken to them in the past. A number of scholars think that some sayings attributed to Jesus in the gospels actually came from such prophetic utterances and that their central notion was the idea of Jesus as the coming Son of Man.[15] Again, it will be helpful to review some of the background for this conviction.

Recall from Ch. 1 that in Daniel 7, an eternal kingdom was to be presented to a heavenly figure, a "Son of Man," who would be served by all peoples and nations. Linguistically, the term "Son of Man" referred primarily to one of the species mankind, something like "a certain human being." But the designation could occasionally take on a dignified meaning with reference to a human being, as when the prophet Ezekiel is addressed as "Son of Man," or a self-effacing meaning in reference to oneself, as sometimes occurs in nonbiblical Jewish literature.[16] A few gospel sayings may reflect such meanings (cp. Mt 8:20; 11:19); yet, because the New Testament stresses the Son of Man as a specific mythic figure who will fly with the clouds of heaven and come as Judge and Savior, like the one found in Daniel 7, we may limit our discussion to this mythical meaning.

At least two Jewish documents that refer back to Daniel 7 speak of the Son of Man as a specific, individual figure. In the "Similitudes of Enoch" (I Enoch 37–71), "the Son of Man" is "named" (brought into existence) before anything else in creation (the motif of his preexistence), sits on a "throne of glory" (the frequent motif of light), remains hidden to all but the elect, and is expected to come at the End to judge angels, demons, and people. "On that day" he will condemn the oppressors of the elect, destroy sinners, bring salvation to the righteous (including Gentiles), and eat with the elect, who will be resurrected forever.[17] A second document, IV Ezra, exhibits two associated conceptions. In Ch. 12 the Messiah is hidden until the "end of days," at which time he will "spring from the seed of David," judge the ungodly, and, after rebuking them, destroy them. In Ch. 13, which builds on Daniel 7:13–14, there is a dream in which one in "the form of a man" comes up from the chaotic sea, flies with the clouds of heaven, and makes everything fall away by his gaze or the sound of his voice; then, when an army of men wage war against "the Man," he carves out a mountain, flies to it, destroys his enemies, and, descending, is joined by a peaceable multitude. The interpretation in the document is that the Man is preexistent (v. 25) and is the Son of God (vs. 32, 51).[18] In short, the author clearly is developing ideas from the royal enthronement tradition and combining them with mythical materials, especially Daniel 7.[19]

Was there then a "Son of Man" *conception* prior to Jesus? This question is complicated by the dates of the Similitudes (uncertain: first century C.E.?) and of IV Ezra (late first century C.E.), for these are the only apocalyptic Son of Man sources in Judaism apart from Daniel 7. Furthermore, these sources refer back to Daniel 7 and could be built on it in a purely literary fashion; in that case there would be no widespread popular conception. The way one answers this question will influence the problem of the synoptic Son of Man sayings.[20]

One common theory is that such a conception was available for Jesus to use, for the Son of Man is mentioned sixty-eight times in the synoptic gospels, always in the third person. Perhaps, then, Jesus used the term to refer to an apocalyptic, mythical figure *other* than himself, but in relation to himself, as in Luke 12:8–9: [21]

> Everyone who acknowledges *me* before men, *the Son of Man* also will acknowledge before the angels of God; But he who denies *me* before men *will be denied* before the angels of God.

In this case the Son of Man would judge or save in accordance with one's response to Jesus. However, the gospel writer who records the saying believed that Jesus was referring to himself.

There are other "reduced apocalyptic" sayings in this category. The coming Son of Man will be ashamed of anyone who is ashamed of Jesus and his followers (Mark 8:38); his coming will be sudden, "like lightning from the east, flashing as far as the west" (Mt 24:27); people who carry on with business as usual will discover that some will be taken, but others left, as in the days of Noah (Mt 24:37–41); or they will be consumed with fire and sulphur, as in the days of Lot (Luke 17:26–30). Repentance at Jesus' preaching is a necessary prerequisite, as the men of Nineveh repented at the preaching of Jonah (Luke 11:30).

If Jesus of Nazareth did not speak these things, then it appears that early Christian prophets spoke them in his name, whether he was being distinguished from the Son of Man or being identified with him. (The increasing tendency to suggest their origin in the early Church is our reason for omitting them from Ch. 1 and placing them here.) [22] In either case, it is usually accepted that because many of them are preserved in the "sayings source" Q (reconstructed by comparing portions of Matthew and Luke that are not in Mark; see the opening section of Chapter 7), this stratum of material represented an apocalyptic Son of Man point of view. Thus there was probably an early Christian community—the "Q community"—that stressed Jesus' role as a prophet and wise man, passed on such sayings as a means of comfort and exhortation, and created new ones through the continuing tradition of prophecy. Moreover, other Son of Man sayings appeared that were even more apocalyptically colored, continuing the tradition of Daniel 7 and even verbally reflecting that tradition. Mark 13:24–27, though attributed to Jesus, is usually thought to come from an early Apocalpse after Jesus' time because of its high apocalyptic flavor: [23]

> ". . . But in those days, after that tribulation, the sun will be darkened, and the moon will not give its light,   25) and the stars will be falling from heaven, and the powers in the heavens will be shaken.   26) And then they will see the Son of Man coming in the clouds with great power and glory.   27) And then he will send out the angels, and gather his elect from the four winds, from the ends of the earth to the ends of heaven. . . ."

How did such notions arise? One possible explanation is that Jesus was identified with the Son of Man in heaven when he was pictured as being "raised up" to the right hand of God.[24] The author of Luke and Acts preserved such a primitive picture in his portrayal of Stephen's vision, though he stated that the Son of Man was standing, rather than sitting as Psalm 110:1 says (Acts 7:55–57):

> 55) But he, full of the Holy Spirit, gazed into heaven and saw the glory of God, and Jesus standing at the right hand of God;   56) and he said, "Behold, I see the heavens opened, and the Son of man [Dan 7:13] standing at the right hand of God" [Ps 110:1].

The Evangelist Mark preserved a similar picture when he dramatized what happened when Jesus stood before the High Priest in Jerusalem (Mark 14:61b–62):

> 61b) Again the high priest asked him, "Are you the Christ, the Son of the Blessed?"   62) And Jesus said, "I am; and you will see the Son of Man [Dan 7:13] sitting at the right hand of Power [Ps 110:1], and coming with the clouds of heaven [Dan 7:13].

The apostle Paul did not use the name "Son of Man" for Jesus; yet he did expect the coming of "the Lord" from heaven "with a cry of command, with the archangel's call, and with the sound of the trumpet of God," after which the dead would rise and the living would be caught up with them "in the clouds to meet the Lord in the air" (1 Thess 1:8–9; 4:15–18). In 2 Thessalonians, which comes from Paul's circle if not from Paul himself, it is mentioned that the rebellion would come first and that the "man of lawlessness," the "son of perdition," would take his seat in the temple before the End came. In 1 Corinthians 15, Paul gave the following picture of the End, noting that the heavenly Christ had to reign until the enemies were vanquished (1 Cor 15:23–28): [25]

> 23) But each in his own order: Christ the first fruits, then at his coming those who belong to Christ.   24) Then comes the end, when he delivers the kingdom to God the Father after destroying every rule and every authority and power.   25) For he must reign until he has put all his enemies under his feet [Ps 110:1].   26) The last enemy to be destroyed is death.   . . .   28) When all things are subjected to him, then the Son himself will

also be subjected to him who put all things under him, that God may be everything to every one.

For Paul such descriptions were words of encouragement and comfort to Christians. The Gospel of Matthew also gave encouragement to disciples and followers of Jesus, and it was directly linked to the Son of Man (Mt 19:28–29):

> 28) Jesus said to them, "Truly, I say to you, in the new world, when the Son of man shall sit on his glorious throne, you who have followed me will also sit on twelve thrones, judging the twelve tribes of Israel.   29) And every one who has left houses or brothers or sisters or father or mother or children or lands, for my name's sake, will receive a hundredfold, and inherit eternal life.

Such apocalyptic views of Jesus found expression in the apocalyptic book of Revelation.[26] Here the Davidic Messiah, called the "lion of the tribe of Judah, the Root of David" (Rev 5:5) and "the Root and Offspring of David, the Bright Morning Star" (Rev 22:16b), is the Lamb of God who is sacrificed (Rev 4:6ff.), who is given a place on God's throne (Rev 3:21) and receives authority over the nations. He conquers Satan and the powers of darkness, and after a 1000-year reign with the resurrected martyrs, Satan being released and finally destroyed, he participates in judging those who are now finally raised from the dead; the evil ones are flung into a lake of fire, and the good ones receive life in the new Jerusalem that descends from heaven (Rev 20–21). The author of Revelation, a certain John of Patmos, describes the figure "coming with the clouds" (Rev 1:7) in this way (Rev 1:12–19):

> 12) Then I turned to see the voice that was speaking to me, and on turning I saw seven golden lampstands,   13) and in the midst of the lampstands one like a son of man, clothed with a long robe and with a golden girdle round his breast;   14) his head and his hair were white as white wool, white as snow; his eyes were like a flame of fire,   15) his feet were like burnished bronze, refined as in a furnace, and his voice was like the sound of many waters;   16) in his right hand he held seven stars, from his mouth issued a sharp two-edged sword, and his face was like the sun shining in full strength.
> 17) When I saw him, I fell at his feet as though dead. But he laid his right hand upon me, saying, "Fear not, I am the first and the last,   18) and the living one; I died, and behold I am alive for evermore, and I have the keys of Death and Hades.   19) Now write what you see, what is and what is to take place hereafter."

Such passages show that early apocalyptic Christianity awaited the End with hope and confidence, finding encouragement and comfort in times of stress and persecution. Its focus was on the future, and to a lesser extent on the past; it was on the future Son of Man, who would come with judgment and salvation, who was also the prophet, the servant, and the teacher who had lived among them. Already in Paul, however, there emerged a stress on the present that had perhaps been implicit in the concept of the enthroned king, God's Son, as well as in the larger mythical background from which the apocalyptic Son of Man may have been derived.

JESUS CHRIST IN THE NEW TESTAMENT HYMNS

We mentioned in Ch. 1 that about 110 c.e. Pliny the Younger wrote to the emperor Trajan about the rapidly spreading Christian "superstition" in his district: By interrogation he had learned ". . . that on an appointed day they [the Christians] had been accustomed to meet before daybreak, and to recite a hymn to Christ [*carmen Christi*], as to a god, . . ."[27] Such "hymns" (or at least antiphonal litanies) about the divine Christ seem to have been a common part of early Christian worship (1 Cor 14:26); like confessional formulas, they are embedded in the New Testament texts and can be isolated by their style and content. These are called the New Testament "Christological hymns," and they picture Jesus as preexistent in heaven as a divine being who descended to earth, became human, and reascended to heaven, though not every stage of this pattern is explicit in every hymn. What is specifically different in these hymns is the theme of preexistence, and for that further religious parallels must be considered.

Belief in the full deity of the king, or the pharaoh, or even the Roman emperor (as in "emperor worship," which Greek and Roman rulers adopted from the East) affected the New Testament in various ways,[28] but it has never proved a sufficient explanation for belief in Jesus Christ as a preexistent deity. Likewise, the apocalyptic Son of Man, though sometimes pictured as preexistent in Judaism, was never considered in Jewish texts to descend to earth; moreover, the synoptic Son of Man materials are known for their avoidance of the notion of preexistence. As a result, the quest for the source of the preexistence theme has broadened into the larger religious sphere of the Greco-Roman world, and three major possible sources have been identified: These are speculation about Wisdom (Hebrew: *ḥokmâ;* Greek: *sophia*); speculation about the Word (Hebrew: *dābar;* Greek: *Logos*); and the myth associated with the origin of Man, the Anthropos (Greek: *anthrōpos,* "man[-kind]") myth, which is sometimes split into the Heavenly Man myth and the First Man myth and is thought to have reemerged in Christian times as the Gnostic Redeemer myth.

Wisdom in the ancient world was usually depicted as a woman. In ancient Mesopotamia she was a mother-goddess, and in Egypt, which influenced Israel rather directly in this area, the goddess Isis was especially characterized by wisdom.[29] In Israel there was an increasing tendency to make her (both Hebrew *ḥokmâ* and Greek *sophia* are feminine gender) into a person distinct from God, that is, to personify her, or to "hypostatize" (Greek: *hypostasis,* "substance," as in Hebrews 1:3) her. Thus in Proverbs 8:22–27 she was said to be the first thing created, and in verse 30 she was a participant in creation ("then I was beside him, like a master workman . . .").[30] Other texts carried her function further. In the Dead Sea Scrolls she was a "divine thought" (CD 11:11), and in wisdom literature influenced by Greek thinking she was "an image of His eternal light" (Wisd 7:26). The rabbis suggested that her role in creation was like that of the divine Torah, also personified.[31] Most important, 1 Enoch 42:1–2 thought of her in a descent–ascent pattern:

> 1) Wisdom found no place where she might dwell;
>   Then a dwelling-place was assigned her in the heavens.
> 2) Wisdom went forth to make her dwelling among the children of
>   men.
>   And found no dwelling-place;
>   Wisdom returned to her place,
>   And took her seat among the angels.

Thus the Wisdom of God preexisted, descended to earth, and ascended again.

Another possible link with belief in Jesus Christ's preexistence was "Word" speculation. In many ancient texts from Babylonia, Egypt, and Israel (cp. Pss. 33:6; 107:20), Wisdom became virtually identified with God's Word.[32] Perhaps Greek influences further fed the process of hypostatizing the Word. In the Greek perception the Word, or the *Logos,* was a rational principle that made the world a dependable, orderly place (Heraclitus), or it was God's mind or reason, which "emanated" (radiated) from God and penetrated everything, controlling, guiding, and directing everything (the Stoics). By the second century B.C.E., Palestinian Jewish thinkers influenced by the Greeks (Sirach 39:17b) were giving the *Logos* a virtually independent existence (IV Ezra 6:38ff.). Especially at Alexandria, Jews were influenced by Greek thinking. There the author of the Wisdom of Solomon had a conception in which both Wisdom and *Logos* participated in creation (9:1: "God . . . Who has made all things by thy Word, and by thy Wisdom has formed man"), the *Logos* being in the mind of God, but also part of the rational nature of man. In the Wisdom of Solomon, the *Logos* was also the sustainer of creation, the medium of intercourse between God and man, an angel, and the name of God.[33] Philo of Alexandria, a Jewish contemporary of Jesus who was influenced by Platonic and Stoic thought, combined a number of conceptions:[34]

> Thou didst beget Him, Thy only Son, before all the ages by Thy will, Thy power, and Thy goodness, without any agency, the only Son, God the

Logos, the living *Sophia,* the first-born of every creature, the angel of Thy great counsel, and Thy High-Priest, but was King and Lord of every intelligible and sensible nature, who was before all things, by whom are all things.

In this passage Word and Wisdom are identical and preexistent, and they are also the only Son, the "first-born," an angel, the high-priest, the king, and the lord.

There is a third major set of ideas in Philo related to preexistence, and these may be considered under the heading of the Anthropos myth, which Philo sometimes relates to Word and Wisdom. In the ancient world there was a widespread myth about the first man created on earth, the father of the human race, who was also a primeval king and hero who was slain in battle. This figure was frequently said to be "born" from the chaotic waters and was sometimes thought to be both male and female (androgynous), sometimes perceived as a shining sun deity in the heavens, and sometimes imagined as a cosmic giant. He was the Great Man, the Perfect Man.[35] The appearance of the First Man myth in Judaism (Ezek 18:12, 17; Job 15:7; rabbinic speculation about Adam [Hebrew: *'Ādām,* "Man," "Mankind"]) led in some instances to the attempt to give another explanation for the origin of evil. For some it was not Adam but Eve who was responsible (Life of Adam 12ff.; Slavonic Enoch 30:11ff.); for others the angels fell when they had lust for human women (I Enoch; cp. Gen 6). Philo's solution was that there were *two* Adams, the First–Heavenly Man (Gen 1:27: ". . . then the Lord God created man in his own image, in the image of God he created him"), and the Second–Earthly Man, who sinned (Gen 2:7; Gen 3):[36]

There are two types of man: the one a heavenly, the other an earthly. The Heavenly Man being made in the image of God is altogether without part of lot in the corruptible or terrestrial substance . . . the Heavenly Man was not moulded but stamped in the image of God. (*Allegory of the Holy Laws* 1.31ff.)

The identification of the First Man with the Heavenly Man was common in ancient religions,[37] especially among the Persian Zoroastrians, whose earlier conceptions may have influenced the Jews, and among the Mandaeans, whose descendants still exist today in Iraq and Iran and whose views may have had connections with early Christian ideas.[38] Traces of the Heavenly Man as the archetype for human beings are also found in Egypt (the Hermetic literature, *ca.* 100–200 C.E.), in Syria (the cult of Attis), in the religion of Mani from Iran (an ecclectic religion combining features of Zoroastrianism, Judaism, Christianity, and Buddhism), and in Gnosticism (Greek: *gnōsis,* "knowledge"). The latter was a highly dualistic and syncretistic religious movement which stressed that this world of darkness was created by an inferior creator deity, but that one could be redeemed out of this world by means of

secret "knowledge." Rudolf Bultmann once summarized what he
thought was its "redeemer myth":

> The Gnostic myth recounts—with manifold variations—the fate of the
> soul. It tells of its origin in the world of light, of its tragic fall and its life as
> an alien on earth, its imprisonment in the body, its deliverance and final as-
> cent and return to the world of light. The soul—or, more accurately in the
> language of Gnosticism itself, man's true, inner self, is a part, splinter, or
> spark of a *heavenly figure of light,* the original man. Before all time . . . the
> demonic powers of darkness . . . tore the figure of light into shreds and
> divided it up, and the elements of light were used by the demons as cohe-
> sive magnetic powers which were needed in order to create a world out of
> the chaos of darkness as a counterpart of the world of light, of which they
> were jealous. . . . Naturally, interest is concentrated on these sparks of
> light, which are inclosed in man and represent his innermost self. The
> demons endeavour to stupefy them and make them drunk, sending them to
> sleep and making them forget their heavenly home. Sometimes their at-
> tempt succeeds, but in other cases the consciousness of their heavenly ori-
> gin remains awake. They know they are in an alien world, and that this
> world is their prison, and hence their yearning for deliverance. The su-
> preme deity takes pity on the imprisoned sparks of light, and sends down
> the *heavenly figure of light,* his Son, to redeem them. This Son arrays him-
> self in the garment of the earthly body, lest the demons should recognize
> him. He invites his own to join him, awakens them from their sleep, re-
> minds them of their heavenly home, and teaches them about the way to re-
> turn. His chief task is to pass on the sacred passwords which are needed on
> the journey back. For the souls must pass the different spheres of the
> planets, the watch-posts of the demonic cosmic powers. The Gnostic re-
> deemer delivers discourses in which he reveals himself as God's emissary:
> "I am the shepherd," "I am the truth," and so forth. After accomplishing his
> work, he ascends and returns to heaven again to prepare a way for his own
> to follow him. This they will do when they die and the spark of light is
> severed from the prison of the body. His work is to assemble all the sparks
> of light. That is the work he has inaugurated, and it will be completed when
> all the sparks of light have been set free and have ascended to heaven to
> rejoin the one body of the figure of light who in primordial times fell, was
> imprisoned and torn to shreds. When the process is complete, this world
> will come to an end and return to its original chaos. The darkness is left to
> itself, and that is the judgement.[39]

This "gnostic redeemer myth" is a scholarly structure based on the several oriental myths; in this highly developed form it is too late to have
influenced the New Testament. Yet an earlier form of the myth *may*
have existed to influence the Christological hymns.

Having noted the possible religious associations for the theme of
preexistence, we can now look more closely at the New Testament. The
first pre-Pauline "Christological hymn" is Philippians 2:6–11:[40]

6) Who, Being in the form of God,
    Did not think it robbery to be equal with God,
7)   But emptied himself,
    Taking the form of a slave.

Becoming in the likeness of men
And being found in fashion like a man
8)   He humbled himself,
Becoming obedient unto death (the death on the cross)

9)   Wherefore God highly exalted him
And bestowed upon him the name above every name,
10)   That in the name of Jesus every knee may bow
        (in the heavens and on earth and beneath the earth,)
11)   And every tongue confess,
"Jesus Christ is Lord!"
(to the glory of God the father.)

To be "in the form of God" (v. 6a) means "to be equal with God" (v. 6b), a conception that has in view a divine being. In direct contrast is taking "the form of a slave," and thus the redeemer rejects his divine status and "empties himself," becoming "in the likeness of man . . . in fashion like a man." This view is not like that of the powerful apocalyptic Son of Man who judges at the End, and "like a man" is nowhere else in Greek a translation of the Aramaic for "Son of Man."[41] Thus the idea is probably not indebted to the apocalyptic Son of Man in Daniel or related Jewish texts. The simple "slave" notion does not so easily remove the possibility that the suffering Servant of Isaiah 52:13–53:12 is present, for although the language is different, the same term for "slave/servant" (Greek: *doulos*) does occur in another Old Testament Servant poem (Isa 49:3, 5) and in Mark 10:44, which is clearly influenced by Isaiah 52–53. "Obedience unto death" may reflect Jesus' actual death and indicate a Christian point of view. The preexistent one who is equal to God becomes a human being who suffered and died. The phrases in verses 10 and 11 are taken directly from Isaiah 45:23. In this regard it should be noted that whereas the first two stanzas make the Redeemer the actor, the third makes God the actor, and the language in the third stanza sounds very much like heavenly enthronement. It is therefore possible to suggest that the hymn indicates a merger of the preexistence–descent idea with the resurrection–enthronement idea, even though resurrection is not specifically mentioned. In any case the acclamation that "Jesus Christ is Lord" shows that the hymn is advanced enough to think of the name "Christ" as a personal name (not as meaning "the Messiah") and that it is using the concept of "Lord" (cp. Acts 2:36).

The hymn dramatically portrays the myth of the Redeemer in three distinct stages: (1) preearthly existence (2) earthly existence (in the "likeness of men"), and (3) postearthly existence ("exaltation"). Paul is fond of stressing Jesus' death on the cross (cp. especially 1 Cor 1), and because the reference to it breaks the rhythm of the passage, the phrase is usually attributed to Paul himself. The descent–ascent pattern suggests the religious possibilities just discussed: Wisdom, *Logos,* and the Anthropos myths. Because of its Jewish coloring, the hymn has most frequently been traced to a variation of Wisdom speculation, which perhaps merged with an *early* form of the Anthropos myth (since, as noted, the full conceptions cannot be documented prior to the Christian period). Only the Egyptian Hermetic literature, which is closely related to Gnosticism, comes close with regard to dating (ca. 100–200 C.E.). Yet because of certain similarities to the above myths, a more recent tendency is to think of a "developing myth," or emergent "mythical configuration," which syncretistically combined Wisdom, *Logos,* and the Anthropos myths in their earlier stages.[42] Before drawing this conclusion, however, it is important to take a brief look at the other Christological hymns.

Colossians 1:15–20 reads,[43]

15) Who is the image of the invisible God, the firstborn of all creation;
16) For in him was created everything in the heavens and on earth,
    (the visible and the invisible,
    whether thrones or lordships,
    whether rulers or authorities)
Everything was created through him and unto him.

17) And he is before everything,
    And everything is united in him,
18) And he is the head of the body (the church)

    Who is the beginning, the first-born of the dead,
    (that he himself might be pre-eminent in everything)
19) For in him all the fullness was pleased to dwell,
20) And through him to reconcile everything unto himself.

Without the portions in parentheses, this appears to be a three-stanza hymn in which the third stanza has elements that parallel the other two stanzas.[44] But it can also be seen that there is a pattern in the three: The first stanza stresses the creation of the world, the second stresses the preservation of the world, and the third the redemption of the world.

In the first stanza the Redeemer figure participates in creation, a feature which was especially characteristic of Wisdom and the *Logos.* He is called the "image" (*eikōn*) of the invisible God and the firstborn (*prōtotokos*) of all creation, both of which are specific attributes of *Logos,* Wisdom, and the Heavenly Man/First Man, especially in Philo and the Wisdom of Solomon.[45] The second stanza, which stresses preservation, calls him "the head (*kephalē*) of the body (*sōma*)"; without the Christian interpretation of "the body" as the Church, this reflects the common Hellenistic picture of the world as a cosmic giant (Philo spoke of the *Logos* as the head of the universe, and Gnostic sources envision the All as a giant human being).[46] In contrast to the Philippians hymn, the third stanza of the Colossians hymn specifically mentions the resurrection (v.18b: "the firstborn of the dead," meaning first in time and importance, like firstborn sons in patriarchal societies), and in this case the resurrection marks the new beginning of a new humanity. In him the "fullness" (*plērōma*) was pleased to dwell, "fullness" meaning either God's attributes or, from the Gnostic perspective, all the intermediary powers of the universe between the world of light and the world of darkness.[47]

The third major "hymn" (some would prefer to call it religious poetry) is found imbedded in the prologue to the Gospel of John (John 1:1–18):[48]

1) In the beginning was the Word,
   And the Word was with God,
   And the Word was God.
2) He was in the beginning with God.

3) Everything was made through him,
   And apart from him was nothing made which was made.
4) In him was life,
   And the life was the light of men.

5) And the light shines in the darkness,
   And the darkness did not overcome it. . . .

9) He was the true light,
   Which enlightens every man,
   Coming into the world.

10) He was in the world,
    And the world was made through him.
    And the world did not know him.

11) He came to his own.
    And his own did not receive him.

Some interpreters include in the hymn parts of verses 12, 14, and 16:

12) But to all who received him, . . .
    He gave power to become children of God. . . .

14) And the Word became flesh
    And dwelt [literally, "tented"] among us. . . .
    We have beheld his glory,
    Glory as of the only Son from the Father. . . .

16) And from his fullness have we all received,
    Grace upon grace.

This "hymn" centers around the *Logos*, or Word, alluding in the first verse to Genesis 1:1 ("In the beginning God created the heavens and the earth") and in general to God's creative Word in Genesis 1:3ff. ("And God said, 'Let there be light' "). The first stanza (vs. 1–2), which appears to state that the Word both is and is not God, at once calls to mind the hypostatization of Wisdom and Word in Jewish literature. Indeed, the creative activity of the Word is expressed in verses 3 and 10. The dualism of light and darkness and the theme of true life might suggest broader (Gnostic) associations, though such dualism was also known in the Dead Sea Scrolls.[49] If verses 12, 14, and 16 were part of the original "hymn," it might have arisen within Christianity prior to John. Finally, it should be noted that this "hymn," in contrast to the other two, stresses especially the "preexistence" and incarnation ("descent") of the *Logos,* not the ascent; nonetheless, if one accepts the latter verses, the *Logos* is identified with the "only Son from the Father" who is characterized by "glory" (*doxa,* associated with light, as in "throne of glory"), frequently a heavenly designation (see 1 Tim 3:16, quoted below).

There are in addition to these three longer "hymns" a number of shorter "hymns" or "hymnic confessions" that reflect the same mythic structure. 1 Timothy 3:16, in contrast to the Philippians hymn, stresses the uniqueness of the Incarnate One:[50]

Who was manifested in the flesh,	A
Was vindicated in the spirit,	B
Was seen by angels	B
Was proclaimed among the nations	A
Was believed on in the world,	A
Was taken up into glory.	B

One need only compare the "A" phrases with the "B" phrases to see that the structure of the "hymn" is "preexistence" (implied), earthly existence, and heavenly existence, that is, descent–ascent.

1 Peter 3:18–19, 22 has a similar structure, but once again (as in the Philippians hymn) it shows influence by the traditions of heavenly enthronement at the right hand of God and of the subjection of enemies:[51]

18c) Having been put to death in the flesh,
     Having been made alive in the spirit,
19) Having gone to the spirits in prison,
     He preached. . . .
22) Who is at the right hand of God,
     Having gone into heaven,
     Angels and authorities and powers have been made subject to him.

A similar combination of Wisdom–*Logos*–Heavenly/Primal Man is found in the exaltation of the priest–king at God's right hand in Hebrews 1:3:[52]

Who, being the reflection [*apaugasma*] of his glory and the stamp [*charak-
  tēr*] of his essence [from *hypostasis*]
Bearing everything by the word [*rhēma*] of his power,
Having made purification for sins,
Sat down on the right hand of the majesty on high.

Finally, one may cite a modified version of Ephesians 2:14–16: [53]

14) [For] he is our peace,

Who has made us both one,
And has broken down the dividing wall of the fence (the enmity), . . .

15b) In order to make the two into one new man in him (making peace),
16a) And to reconcile both in one body to God (through the cross). . . .

In this passage the "dividing wall of the fence" refers to the hostile wall
between God and the redeemed, a theme also found in the Mandaean
literature and picked up in early Christian literature as well.

At this point it will be helpful to summarize the structure of the
hymns again, elaborating the simple preexistence–earthly existence–
postearthly existence theme mentioned at the outset. According to Professor Jack Sanders, the fuller structure is as follows: [54]

1. *The Redeemer possesses unity or equality with God:* "being in
   the form of God" (Phil 2:6); "image of the invisible God" (Col
   1:15); "before everything" (Col 1:17); "reflection of his glory and
   stamp of his essence" (Heb 1:3); "In the beginning was the
   Word, and the Word was with God, and the Word was God. He
   was in the beginning with God" (John 1:1–2)
2. *The Redeemer is mediator or agent of creation:* "For in him
   was created everything in the heavens and on the earth" (Col
   1:16); "Everything was made through him, and apart from him
   was nothing made which was made" (John 1:3)
3. *The Redeemer is himself a part of (or the sustainer of) creation:* "first-born of all creation" (Col 1:15); "everything is
   united in him, and he is the head of the body" (Col 1:17b–18);
   "bearing everything" (Heb 1:3); "In him was life, and the life
   was the light of men" (John 1:4)
4. *The Redeemer descends from the heavenly to the earthly
   realm:* "But emptied himself, taking the form of a slave. Becoming in the likeness of men, and being found in fashion like a
   man . . ." (Phil 2:7); "And the light shines in the darkness, and
   the darkness did not overcome it" (John 1:5); "He was the true
   light, which enlightens every man, coming into the world" (John
   1:9)
5. *He dies:* "He humbled himself, becoming obedient unto death"
   (Phil 2:8); "the first-born of the dead" (Col 1:18); "manifested in
   the flesh" (1 Tim 3:16); "Put to death in the flesh" (1 Pet 3:18)

6. *He is made alive again:*   "first-born of the dead" (Col 1:18); "vindicated in the spirit" (1 Tim 3:16); "made alive in the spirit" (1 Pet 3:18)

7. *He effects a reconciliation:*   "Who is the beginning" (Col 1:18); "For in him all the fullness was pleased to dwell" (Col 1:19)"; "For he is our peace, who has made us both one, and has broken down the dividing wall of the fence . . . in order to make the two into one new man in him . . . And to reconcile both into one body to God . . ." (Eph 2:14–6); "proclaimed among the nations, believed on in the world" (1 Tim 3:16); "in which he went and preached to the spirits in prison" (1 Pet 3:19); "having made purification" (Heb 1:3)

8. *He is exalted and enthroned, and the cosmic powers become subject to him:*   "Wherefore God highly exalted him, and bestowed upon him the name above every name, that in the name of Jesus every knee may bow . . . and every tongue confess, 'Jesus Christ is Lord!' . . ." (Phil 2:9–11); "seen by angels, taken up in glory" (1 Tim 3:16); "Who is at the right hand of God, having gone into heaven, angels and authorities and powers have been made subject to him" (1 Pet 3:22); "Sat down on the right hand of the majesty on high" (Heb 1:3)

This structure, representing an emerging mythical configuration, bears enough resemblance to the religious myths traced out above to suggest the following conclusion: The Christological hymns have as their background the hypostatization of Wisdom and Word that had merged with an early form of the Anthropos myth in its movement toward what later became a more elaborate (Gnostic) Redeemer myth. This would account for the preexistence and descent–ascent pattern; the latter shows traces of contact with heavenly enthronement as well. In early Christianity this "developing myth" was catalyzed by beliefs about Jesus.

JESUS CHRIST IN THE LETTER TO THE HEBREWS

In the ancient world, and among many "primitive" peoples today, sacrifices are offered for several purposes: to feed the gods while they are on earth, to cement relations between the gods and their worshippers by sharing food, to make gifts to the gods in return for their abundance, to atone for, or expiate, sins committed in the past, and to persuade the gods to be favorable in the future (to propitiate the gods). It is believed that the gods who make the land fertile are entitled to share its best produce, its "first fruits," or that the gods who make the animals fertile are entitled to share their best, their "firstborn." As a result, highly complicated systems for sacrificing crops and animals arise and are administered by especially holy persons, the priests. In the ancient world, the priests are sometimes kings. Certain rites of anointing set the priests aside to fulfill their functions, and their family genealogies are kept with care to ensure their purity; normally the High Priest is at their head. Sacrifices are carried out in holy places (usually temples), and in the religious practices of Israel the High Priest has the privilege of entering the most holy place of the Jerusalem Temple once a year to make sacrifice for the sins of the priests and the people (Lev 16; cp. Exod 28; Tractate Yoma [a tractate in the Talmud]). This is the Day of Atonement, Yom Kippur.[55]

In the Book of Genesis there is a short episode about a Canaanite king of Salem named Melchizedek (Hebrew: "My king is righteous"), who was also a priest of the God "Most High" (Gen 14:17–20). Melchizedek, whose family genealogy is not given, brought out bread and wine and blessed Abram in the name of "Most High," Maker of heaven and earth, for delivering Abram from his enemies. Abram responded by giving Melchizedek a tithe of his captive flocks and herds. Nothing else is said of Melchizedek in the Scriptures—with one exception: The Davidic king who sits at God's right hand (Ps 110:1) is told by Yahweh, "You are a priest forever, according to the order of Melchizedek" (Ps 110:4). From such passages arose the extremely high evaluation of Melchizedek in Judaism around the time of Jesus, namely, that he was a supernatural being with a mythical biography: begotten by the Word of God in his mother's womb; a priest forever and therefore immortal; and, at the End, an eschatological judge who would separate the angels and righteous people from the demons and wicked people.[56]

The Christological hymn in Hebrews 1:3 is set within the context of an interpretation of Jesus Christ as the Son of God (2 Sam 7:14; Ps 2:7; cp. Ps 110:3), who was humiliated on earth and exalted to the right hand of God as the heavenly high priest according to the order of Melchizedek (Ps 110:1, 4). The argument began with reference to Psalm 8:4–5 (Heb 2:6b–8):

6b) "What is man that thou art mindful of him,
  or the son of man, that thou carest for him?
 7) Thou didst make him for a little while lower than the angels,
  thou hast crowned him with glory and honor,
8a) putting everything in subjection under his feet."

For the author of Hebrews this was a specific prophecy of Jesus Christ, who, as God's Son, was superior to the angels, became a human being, and was subjected to all the temptations and sufferings of human beings, though without sin (Heb 2:10–18; 4:14–6). Sprung from the non-priestly tribe of Judah, David's tribe (Heb 7:14), the Son of the household became superior to Moses, the founder of the household, in his ministry (Heb 3:1–6); during his earthly life "he offered up prayers and petitions, with loud cries and tears, to God who was able to deliver him from the grave" (Heb 5:7). Thus the supreme, once-for-all sacrifice, his own death, was rewarded with resurrection to the status of the great high priest in heaven according to the order of Melchizedek (Heb 7:1–3):

> 1) For this Melchizedek, king of Salem, priest of the Most High God, met Abraham returning from the slaughter of the kings and blessed him;   2) and to him Abraham apportioned a tenth part of everything. He is first, by translation of his name, king of righteousness, and then he is also king of Salem, that is, king of peace.   3) He is without father or mother or genealogy, and has neither beginning of days nor end of life, but resembling the Son of God he continues a priest forever.

As the high priest in heaven seated at the right hand of God, Jesus Christ was also superior in every way to the legitimate Aaronic priesthood in the temple (Heb 9:11–14):

> 11) But when Christ appeared as a high priest of the good things that have come, then through the greater and more perfect tent (not made with hands, that is, not of this creation)   12) he entered once for all into the Holy Place, taking not the blood of goats and calves but his own blood, thus securing an eternal redemption.   13) For if the sprinkling of defiled persons with the blood of goats and bulls and with the ashes of a heifer sanctifies for the purification of the flesh,   14) how much more shall the blood of Christ, who through the eternal Spirit offered himself without blemish to God, purify your conscience from dead works to serve the living God.

Such a viewpoint for the author of Hebrews offered hope for those who waited for his return. In short (Heb 9:23–28):

> 23) Thus it was necessary for the copies of the heavenly things to be purified with these rites, but the heavenly things themselves with better sacrifices than these.   24) For Christ has entered, not into a sanctuary made with hands, a copy of the true one, but into heaven itself, now to appear in the presence of God on our behalf.   25) Nor was it to offer himself repeatedly, as the high priest enters the Holy Place yearly with blood not his own;   26) for then he would have had to suffer repeatedly since the foundation of the world. But as it is, he has appeared once for all at the end of the age to put away sin by the sacrifice of himself.   27) And just as it is appointed for men to die once, and after that comes judgment,   28) so Christ, having been offered once to bear the sins of many, will appear a second time, not to deal with sin but to save those who are eagerly waiting for him.

JESUS CHRIST IN THE THOUGHT OF PAUL[57]

The apostle Paul came to terms with an "emerging myth" about Jesus Christ, which he himself helped to preserve by incorporating Christological hymns in his letters. Yet Paul did not see it as a myth in the sense of something that happened in primordial time, that is, in the "time" prior to world-time. What happened, though it may have functioned as a primordial myth to many early Christians, also happened, for Paul, *in time*. It is true that he had no particular interest in a biographical "life" of Jesus—"even though we once regarded Christ from a human point of view, we regard him thus no longer" (2 Cor 5:16b)—but it is also true that he resisted every attempt to deny Jesus' actual suffering and death on the cross; thus he quickly added "the death of the cross" to the Philippians hymn (Phil 2:8). Paul accepted Jesus as the preexistent Son sent by God, but he was also "born of woman, born under the law" (Gal 4:4). In short, what Paul proposed was not a Gnostic Redeemer myth but a "paramyth" which, paradoxically (from the point of view of myth in archaic societies), was rooted in history.

This view emerged especially in Paul's controversies with his opponents. In 1 Corinthians 1–4 he found it necessary to speak against those ("proto-Gnostic") Corinthians who believed that they had a superior knowledge (Greek: *gnōsis*) and wisdom (Greek: *sophia*) about their heavenly origins and entrapment in fleshly bodies. Some of the Corinthians were apparently so proud that they were willing to say *anathema Iēsous*, "Jesus be damned" (1 Cor 12:3), referring to the earthly Jesus. Paul responded with the exclamation *Kyrios Iēsous*, "Jesus is Lord!" Paul did use "wisdom" as a way of talking about the special knowledge of the mature Christian (1 Cor 2:6–16), but that wisdom was the message of the "Christ crucified," a "cause for stumbling" (Greek: *skandalon*) to the Jews, and foolishness to the Greeks (1 Cor 1:18–25). He argued that it was God's wisdom to choose what is foolish, weak, low, and despised in the eyes of the world, not the worldly wise, powerful, and those of noble birth—thus he chose many of the Corinthians (1 Cor 1:26–31). Likewise, he chose the way of the cross, a criminal's suffering and death, and though the cross symbolized for Paul the whole meaning of salvation, it included the Jesus who lived, suffered, and died.

Paul had to face another kind of opposition at Corinth: wandering preachers from the outside who came in teaching that they were the powerful, spirit-filled heirs of a hero-Jesus who was a "divine man" (Greek: *theios anēr*):

> This concept must be seen within the framework of Hellenistic anthropology, for which man was not simply a given species of being. Man in this concept is not simply what he is, but he is a being hovering between his two possibilities, the divine (*theion*) and the animal (*theriodes*). Only the Divine Man is man in the full sense; then his humanity becomes the epiphany (manifestation) of the divine. He is exceptionally gifted and extraordinary in every respect. He is in command both of a higher, revelational wisdom and of the divine power (*dynamis*) to do miracles. Yet he is not identical with a deity, but can be called "a mixture of the human and the divine," "a higher being," or "superhuman."[58]

Thus, whereas the first group considered themselves special because they believed Christ was a mythical god, this group considered themselves special because they exhibited special divine powers such as speaking in tongues, visions, and miracle working (esp. 2 Cor 10–13) like the miracle working of Jesus. Against them, Paul claimed that the apostle of the *crucified* Jesus was characterized by suffering (2 Cor 4:17–18; 6:3–10; 11:22–33). Jesus was Christ, Lord, and Son of God, who is known "according to the Spirit," but he was also a man who suffered and died, and this is the correct model for the Christian.

Paul also faced opposition from the "Judaizers" at Galatia, who wanted Christians to hold to Jewish dietary and circumcision laws as a prerequisite for becoming Christian. Paul developed his views against adherence to the Jewish law in his letter to the Galatians and again in his letter to the Romans, for at Rome tensions had arisen between Jewish and gentile Christians. Whereas Paul's interpretation of the cross usually stressed a particular view of who Jesus Christ was, now he further interpreted who Jesus Christ was "for us." The key term for this interpretation of Jesus Christ was "justification" (Greek: *dikaiōsunē*). In a formula Paul passed on, he wrote that Jesus "was put to death for our trespasses and raised for our justification" (Rom 4:25); that is, the one who believes in Christ is acquitted even though guilty. That is God's justice. Paul summarized (Rom 1:16–17a):

> For I am not ashamed of the gospel: it is the power of God for salvation to every one who has faith, to the Jew first and also to the Greek.   17) For in it the righteousness of God is revealed through faith for faith; as it is written, "He who through faith is righteous shall live" [Hab 2:4].

It is probable that Paul added the italicized words in the following formula, thereby linking the atoning death of Christ with justification and faith (Rom 3:25–26):

> . . . whom God put forward as an expiation by his blood, *to be received by faith*. This was to show God's righteousness, because in his divine forbearance he had passed over former sins;   26) it was to prove at the present time that he himself is righteous *and that he justifies him who has faith in Jesus.*

Other, similar passages indicate that God made his Son to be a sacrifice for sinners (Rom 5:9; 2 Cor 5:21) and that by this redemption Christians receive the status of "sons of God" (Gal 4:4–7). Paul's view of Jesus Christ was elaborated by his conviction that the cross made salvation present for the believer.

Paul had a number of other notions about the identity and meaning of Jesus Christ. To be "in Christ" or "in Christ Jesus" was to be in the community of believers (Gal 3:27; Rom 12:5), to share the gift of salvation through faith (2 Cor 5:19; Rom 3:24), and to labor for the gospel (1 Cor 4:15; 2 Cor 12:19). It will be recalled that Philo had the conception that the First Adam was the Perfect Man (Gen 1) and that the Second Adam was the fallen, physical man (Gen 2, 3); however, Paul saw the

Genesis Adam as the First Adam, who sinned and died, and Christ as the "Last Adam," the eschatological Redeemer who created a new humanity (1 Cor 15:21–22; 45–50; Rom 5:12–21). He may have been correcting the early Gnostic belief that the spark of light in the one who has knowledge is from the Heavenly Man, while fallen man is the second man. In any case, Paul stressed that Christ was the "Last Adam," and in connection with that, Christ was the true image (*eikōn*) of God (1 Cor 15:49; 2 Cor 4:4), an image that transforms the redeemed (2 Cor 3:18; Rom 8:29). In loving relationship, service, and responsibility these redeemed are "the body of Christ" (1 Cor 12:12–31; Rom 12:4–8), or one body "in Christ" (Rom 12:5). Paul believed that Christians were "baptized into one body" (1 Cor 12:13) and sustained by breaking the bread that is the body of Christ (1 Cor 11:24), the act of which is participating in the body of Christ (1 Cor 10:17).

In short, Paul took over from the Christological hymns a myth that was in the process of formation but "corrected" it in the direction of the history and significance of the cross. Likewise, Jesus was in his humility more than a "divine man" transmitting visionary, spiritual, and miraculous powers. Through God's gift of grace—Jesus Christ—the believer was justified, even though guilty. Christ was the "Last Adam," the true "image" of God, and he reversed the sin of the First Adam. This new humanity brought about a new community of those "in Christ," or "in the body of Christ," which shared a mutual love and responsibility. The Christian was initiated into this community by baptism, and by it the Christian was sustained, sharing in the body, especially through participation in the Lord's Supper.

JESUS CHRIST AND THE GOSPELS

The English term *gospel* came from the Middle English *godspell*, which in turn went back to the Latin *evangelium* and the Greek *euangelion*, literally, "good tidings (communicated orally)." The Jewish Scriptures also had the term *bāsar*, a verbal form which meant "to proclaim glad tidings" (Isa 52:7). Since there are allusions to this reference in the New Testament (Acts 10:36; Rom 10:15; Eph 6:15) and the related noun *basarah* can be found in the rabbinic literature, perhaps the Greek term emerged from the Jewish usage. However, there was also a specifically Greek usage related to some of the ideas considered above. In the Calendar Inscription from Priene (9 B.C.E.), the Greek read, "The birthday of the god has occasioned for the world the glad tidings (*euangelia*) associated with him." Indeed, in the Roman Empire the events of the emperor's life and the news of his enthronement were

termed *euangelion*.[59] Both of the latter usages emerged in the New
Testament. The Gospel of Matthew used the term for little speeches
and sermons of Jesus (especially Mt 4:23; 9:35). For Paul, the term was
used frequently for the oral proclamation of the complete story of
Christ. This was also a crucial meaning for Mark where Jesus was the
content of what was proclaimed (Mark 8:35; 10:29; 13:9–10; 14:9), but
it could also include a summary of Jesus' teaching (Mark 1:14–15). Finally, Mark used the term "gospel" for what he wrote as a *literary document:* "The beginning of the gospel of Jesus Christ, the Son of God"
(Mark 1:1).

Did Mark create the literary genre gospel? If so, what was the significance of this way of portraying Jesus?[60] We noted above that Paul
opposed the divine man approach to Jesus Christ, in which Jesus was
pictured as a spirit-filled miracle worker. A study of the *forms* of the
miracle stories in the gospels has shown that in some cases the stories
passed through a phase in the early churches in which they were patterned after miracle stories of such divine men. In other words, Jesus
was sometimes pictured as a divine man. Furthermore, studies of the
gospels indicate that Mark and John had at their disposal collections of
miracle stories about Jesus. The question of literary genre, however,
emerges in its clearest form if one considers something more than a
collection of such stories, namely, a kind of ancient popular *biography*
of a divine man. This is the question of the aretalogy (Greek: *aretē,*
"virtue," referring in some contexts to miracle). One scholar has seen
the aretalogy of the divine man in this way:

> . . . a formal account of the remarkable career of an impressive teacher that
> was used as the basis for moral instruction. The preternatural gifts of the
> teacher often included power to work wonders; often his teaching brought
> him the hostility of a tyrant, whom he confronted with courage and at
> whose hands he suffered martyrdom. Often the circumstances of his birth
> or death involve elements of the miraculous.[61]

In the most general sense, the aretalogy provides a type of analogy to
the gospels; however, the more specific one requires the parallels to be,
the less one can see such "lives" as available models for the short, crisp,
episodic character of the gospels. Moreover, the Gospels of Mark and
John do not mention unusual circumstances for Christ's birth. Though
this discussion will undoubtedly continue, it is possible at present to
conclude the following: The divine man as miracle worker is a definite
enough conception to be employed constructively in the evaluation of
the miracle stories about Jesus in the gospels, but the aretalogy is prob-
lematic enough in its definition and variation to be considered insuf-
ficiently distinct as a model for the gospels. At least at the more precise
level of comparison, the "gospel" seems to be a unique Christian (and
therefore Markan) innovation.

Once this question is "resolved" in this manner, however, the question of the variation of the Christian gospels themselves must be

faced.[62] Just as there is a quest for the antecedents of the Christian gospel, so there is a continuing quest for the precise character and meaning of each gospel. A complete characterization of Jesus in the New Testament would certainly include a portrayal, or image, of Jesus Christ in each of the gospels. Without in any way suggesting that one should "harmonize" the accounts into one story, what can be said in general about this way of portraying Jesus?

The first and most obvious fact is that the gospels are not biographical lives of Jesus attempting to describe the historical person as we did in Ch. 1. Rather, they are interpretations of his life written in different situations by different authors to meet different needs. Thus they are combinations of many different types of episodes strung together like pearls on a string, only a few of which can with any certainty claim to be "historical." Though there is a good deal more similarity between the first three gospels (Matthew, Mark, and Luke), there is an increasing tendency today to see the first three as less historical, and therefore like John, that is, as "theological" tracts. Meanwhile, the quest for an analogy to the gospels continues.

But it is also clear that Christianity did not take up only apocalypses, letters, and quasi-historical narratives of the early church (as in Acts); it also wrote gospels. Why did it not rest content with its Christological hymns, its collections of miracles, its summaries of Jesus' teachings, its passion stories? Was there some "crisis of confidence" connected with the political world, such as the destruction of Judea, which was the prime motive for Mark's initial project? Or was the "crisis" internal to Christianity, that is, an attempt to correct false impressions of Jesus Christ when he did not return as expected? However one answers these questions—certainly both external and internal factors were involved—there was created a *narrative* form of the event of Jesus that to varying degrees had a beginning, a middle, and an end and to varying degrees was rooted in actual events. As with Paul's "theology of the cross," the gospels in the most general sense were attempts to say more about Jesus than either the ancient myths had said about life and death or the legends had said about divine heroes. Though time and place in the gospels are frequently interpretive, there are references to time and place. There need not have been. In short, the gospels provided a counterweight to any religious expression about Jesus that would not confront the actual world.

SUMMARY

The early Christians did not write a biography of Jesus like that reconstructed in Ch. 1. They wrote what they selectively believed, confessed, experienced, sang, and prayed about the one who had lived and died. Just as it is difficult to find the historical Jesus, it is also difficult to pinpoint the origins of belief about him. Certainly, one major factor was the belief that God had vindicated his life and death by the resurrection. Early Christians who searched the Scriptures came to think that his resurrection, as well as his life and death, fulfilled them. In short, the life, death, and resurrection of Jesus were according to God's plan of salvation.

Jesus' life, death, and especially his resurrection led to a reflective evaluation of who he was and what he did. Some early Christians believed that he had been raised up to become Messiah, Son of God, and Lord *in heaven*. By using the language and thought patterns of the ancient enthronement of the king, they came to think that Jesus had this status at the right hand of God. Thus it was *at his resurrection* that he became Messiah, Son of God, and Lord (Rom 1:3–4; Acts 2:36; 13:33).

A second perspective focused on Jesus as the coming heavenly Redeemer, a portrait connected especially with early apocalyptic Christianity and its beliefs about Jesus as Son of Man. He would come again to judge and save, and he would do so in accordance with each person's response to him. Again it appears that this belief was connected with Jesus' resurrection to the heavenly spheres.

While in some quarters, Jesus' past and present status were being worked out within the context of resurrection as enthronement, and in others his past and future status were being thought through in apocalyptic terms, the Wisdom–*Logos*–Anthropos themes were merging in a "developing myth" to provide a structure for thinking about his preexistence, earthly existence, and postearthly existence. In other words, early Christians came to consider that he had descended from God and had returned to God. Meanwhile, the Letter to the book of Hebrews spoke of God's Son who became a human being, was tempted, suffered, and, without sin, became the once-for-all sacrifice for which he was rewarded with resurrection to the status of high priest in heaven according to the order of Melchizedek.

The tendency to see Jesus in more and more divine, heavenly terms was paralleled in certain early forms of Christianity that saw him as a "Divine Man," that is, not a god come to earth but a human hero so endowed with the Spirit that he was capable of miraculous feats. The apostle Paul felt it necessary to counteract both tendencies by rooting beliefs about Christ in the cross and stressing the suffering humility of the true apostle. Likewise, the gospels—insofar as they were narratives—incorporated stories and legends about Jesus that were rooted in actual history. This was the case especially with the synoptic gospels, Matthew, Mark, and Luke (though John also maintained that "the Word became flesh"). Yet it was the Gospel of John which—by incorporating the *Logos* and reflecting on the intimate relation of the Father and the

Son—set the direction for the development of Christian belief in its first few centuries.

NOTES

1. T. H. Gaster, "Resurrection," in *The Interpreter's Dictionary of the Bible,* ed. George Arthur Buttrick *et al.,* 5 vols. (Nashville: Abingdon Press, 1962), vol. 4, pp. 39–43.

2. Reginald H. Fuller, *The Formation of the Resurrection Narratives* (New York: Macmillan Co., 1971), pp. 9–49.

3. Harvey K. McArthur, "On the Third Day," *New Testament Studies* 18 (1971), pp. 81–86.

4. The extent of this adaptation is debated. For example, contrast I. Engnell, *Studies in Divine Kingship* (Uppsala: Almqvist & Wiksell, 1943) with Martin Noth, "God, King, People in the Old Testament," in James M. Robinson et. al., *The Bultmann School of Biblical Interpretation: New Directions* (New York: Harper & Row, 1965), pp. 20–48, or G. Ernest Wright, *The Old Testament Against Its Environment,* Studies in Biblical Theology, no. 2 (London: SCM Press, 1950).

5. Dennis C. Duling, "The Promises to David and Their Entrance into Christianity—Nailing Down a Likely Hypothesis," *New Testament Studies* 20 (1973), pp. 55–77.

6. Ibid.; see also Helmer Ringgren, *Israelite Religion,* trans. David E. Green (Philadelphia: Fortress Press, 1966), pp. 220–38.

7. Duling, "Promises," pp. 61ff.; among others, G. Widengren, "Royal Ideology and the Testaments of the Twelve Patriarchs," in *Promise and Fulfillment,* ed. F. F. Bruce (Edinburgh: T. & T. Clark, 1963), pp. 202–12.

8. H. E. Ryle and M. R. James, *Psalms of the Pharisees* (Cambridge: Cambridge University Press, 1891); G. B. Gray, "The Psalms of Solomon," in *The Apocrypha and Pseudepigrapha of the Old Testament in English,* ed. in R. H. Charles, 2 vols. (Oxford: Clarendon Press, 1913), vol. 2, pp. 648–49.

9. R. H. Charles, "The Testaments of the Twelve Patriarchs," in Charles, *Pseudepigrapha,* p. 303.

10. Texts for messianic fragments in J. M. Allegro, "Further Messianic References in Qumran Literature," *Journal of Biblical Literature* 75 (1956), pp. 174–87; discussion in Duling, "Promises," pp. 64ff.; K. G. Kuhn, "The Two Messiahs of Aaron and Israel," *New Testament Studies* 1 (1954/1955), pp. 168–80, reprinted in Krister Stendahl, *The Scrolls and the New Testament* (New York: Harper & Bros., 1957), pp. 54–64.

11. Hendrikus Boers, "Psalm 16 and the Historical Origins of the Christian Faith," *Zeitschrift für die Neutestamentliche Wissenschaft* 60 (1969), pp. 106–10.

12. Duling, "Promises," pp. 72–73; an exception to this view is that of Reginald Fuller, *The Foundations of New Testament Christology* (New York: Charles Scribner's Sons, 1965), pp. 165–67.

13. Evald Lövestam, *Son and Savior: A Study of Acts 13, 32–37, With an Appendix: 'Son of God' in the Synoptic Gospels.* Coniectanea Neotestamentica Series, no. 18 (Lund: S. W. K. Gleerup; Copenhagen: Ejnar Munksgaard, 1961), ch. 3.

14. On the theme of Moses in Hellenistic and Jewish literature, see Wayne Meeks, *The Prophet–King: Moses Traditions and the Johannine Christology* (Leiden: E. J. Brill, 1967); on Acts 3:21, see John A. T. Robinson, "The Most Primitive Christology of All?" *Journal of Theological Studies,* N. S. (1956), pp. 177–89, reprinted in *Twelve New Testament Studies,* Studies in Biblical Theology, no. 34 (London: SCM Press, 1962), pp. 139–53.

15. H. E. Tödt, *The Son of Man in the Synoptic Tradition,* trans. D. M. Barton (Philadelphia: Westminster Press, 1965); Hans Conzelmann, *An Outline of the Theology of the New Testament,* trans. John Bowden (New York: Harper & Row, 1968), pp. 131–37.

16. Geza Vermes, "The Use of בר נשא/בר נש in Jewish Aramaic," in Matthew Black, *An Aramaic Approach to the Gospels and Acts* (Oxford: Clarendon Press, 1967), pp. 320–28.

17. R. H. Charles, "Book of Enoch," in Charles, *Pseudepigrapha,* pp. 163–277 (48:2–3; 62:7–11, 14; 69:27–29).

18. G. H. Box, "IV Ezra," in Charles, *Pseudepigrapha,* pp. 542–624.

19. Norman Perrin, "The Son of Man in Ancient Judaism and Primitive Christianity: A Suggestion," *Biblical Research* 11 (1966), pp. 17–28.

20. The point has a number of ramifications. If there was such a conception in Judaism, what it meant will be related to the New Testament meanings at several possible levels, for example, whether Jesus took it over, how he took it over, whether he changed its meaning, and whether he applied it to himself. If Jesus did not take it over, the same questions could be applied to the early church. However, if no such conception existed, then either Jesus or the early church created the Son of Man as an identifiable figure.

21. This theory, which went back to the turn of the century, was widely publicized by Rudolf Bultmann and, more recently, H. E. Tödt (see note 15).

22. Among those scholars who place them in the early church are Conzelmann (see note 15), Perrin (see note 19), and Ernst Käsemann, "The Problem of the Historical Jesus," in *Essays on New Testament Themes* (Naperville, Ill.: Allenson, 1964), pp. 15–47.

23. See especially Willi Marxsen, *Mark the Evangelist,* trans. J. Boyce, D. Juel and W. Poehlmann, with Roy A. Harrisville (Nashville: Abingdon Press, 1969), ch. 4; Lars Hartman, *Prophecy Interpreted,* trans. Neil Tomkinson, Coniectanea Biblica Series, no. 1 (Lund: C. W. K. Gleerup, 1966).

24. Norman Perrin, "Mark xiv.62: The End Product of a Christian Pesher Tradition?" *New Testament Studies* 12 (1966), pp. 150–55.

25. See pages 38 and 53 for the influence of Psalm 110:1 in other New Testament passages.

26. See Ferdinand Hahn, *The Titles of Jesus in Christology,* trans. Harold Knight and George Ogg (London: Lutterworth Press, 1969), pp. 244–46.

27. Henry Bettenson, ed., *Documents of the Christian Church* (New York: Oxford University Press, 1943), p. 6; Ralph P. Martin, *Carmen Christi: Philippians ii.5–11 in Recent Interpretation and in the Setting of Early Christian Worship* (Cambridge: University Press, 1967) gives a discussion of the problems of Christological hymns in his introductory chapter; for the criteria used to isolate such formulas, see Ethelbert Stauffer, *New Testament Theology,* trans. John Marsh (New York: Macmillan Co., 1955), pp. 338–39.

28. For examples of divine honors paid to kings, see Frederick C.

Grant, *Hellenistic Religions: The Age of Syncretism* (New York: Liberal
Arts Press, 1953) pp. 64–69; an example is found in the discussion of "gospel," pages 57–59.

29. For a discussion of Wisdom in relation to the New Testament
Christological hymns, see Jack T. Sanders, *The New Testament Christologi-
cal Hymns: Their Historical Religious Background* (Cambridge: University
Press, 1971), pp. 29–57, to which I am very much indebted in this section.

30. Helmer Ringgren, *Word and Wisdom: Studies in the Hypostatization of Divine Qualities and Functions in the Ancient Near East* (Lund:
Öhlsson, 1947).

31. George Foote Moore, *Judaism,* 2 vols. (New York: Schocken
Books, 1971), vol. 1, pp. 263–69 (originally published in 1930).

32. Sanders, *Christological Hymns,* pp. 29ff., develops scholarly opinion on Word and Wisdom.

33. See especially Wisd 7:7–14; 9:1–2.

34. E. R. Goodenough, *By Light, Light: The Mystic Gospel of Hellenistic Judaism* (New Haven: Yale University Press, 1935), p. 340.

35. Most recently, Frederick Houk Borsch, *The Son of Man in Myth
and History* (Philadelpha: Westminster Press, 1967), pp. 55–88.

36. On Philo's views of the Heavenly Man/First Adam and the Second
Adam, see Oscar Cullmann, *The Christology of the New Testament,* trans.
S. C. Guthrie and C. A. M. Hall (Philadelphia: Westminster Press, 1959),
pp. 142–52.

37. Borsch, *Son of Man,* pp. 68ff., gives various scholarly opinions.

38. On Zoroastrian myths, in addition to Borsch, *Son of Man,* see R. C.
Zaehner, *The Teachings of the Magi: A Compendium of Zoroastrian Beliefs*
(New York: Oxford University Press, 1976) (originally published in 1956;
on Mandaeism, see Borsch, *Son of Man,* pp. 206–16; Charles H. H. Scobie,
John the Baptist (Philadelphia; Fortress Press, 1964), pp. 23–31.

39. Rudolf Bultmann, *Primitive Christianity in Its Contemporary Setting,* trans. R. H. Fuller (New York: Meridian Books, 1956), pp. 163–64.

40. Sanders, *Christological Hymns,* pp. 9–12, 58–74; Martin, *Carmen
Christi.*

41. In Phil 2:8, "like a man" (*hōs anthrōpos*) is unique; the Greek
translation of the Hebrew Scriptures (the Septuagint, or LXX) has *hōs
huios anthrōpou;* the gospels usually have *ho huios tou anthrōpou;* Revelation 1:13 and 14:14 have *homoios huios anthrōpou.*

42. Thus Sanders, *Christological Hymns,* pp. 96–98.

43. Ibid., pp. 12–14, 75–87.

44. James M. Robinson, "A Formal Analysis of Colossians 1:15–20,"
Journal of Biblical Literature **76** (1957), 270–87.

45. On this hymn, as well as the Philippians hymn, linguistic consider-
ations are given in Fuller, *Foundations,* ch. 8.

46. Hippolytus, *Refutation of All Heresies* 8.12; cp. the discussion in
Sanders, *Christological Hymns,* pp. 75ff.

47. C. F. D. Moule, *The Epistle of Paul to the Colossians* (Cambridge:
University Press, 1957), pp. 164–69.

48. Sanders, *Christological Hymns,* pp. 20–24, 29–57; Fuller, *Foundations,* pp. 222–27; Raymond E. Brown, S.S., ed., *The Gospel According to
John,* 2 vols. (New York: Doubleday & Co., Anchor Books, 1966), vol. 1, pp.
3–37.

49. Brown, *The Gospel According to John,* pp. lxii–lxiv.

50. Sanders, *Christological Hymns,* pp. 15–17, 94–95; Fuller, *Foundations,* pp. 216–18.

51. Sanders, *Christological Hymns,* pp. 17–18, 95–96; Fuller, *Foundations,* pp. 218–20.

52. Sanders, *Christological Hymns,* pp. 19–20, 92–94; Fuller, *Foundations,* pp. 220–21.

53. Sanders, *Christological Hymns,* pp. 14–15, 88–92.

54. Based on Ibid., pp. 24–25.

55. T. H. Gaster, "Sacrifices and Offerings, OT," in *The Interpreter's Dictionary of the Bible,* ed. George Arthur Buttrick, 5 vols. (Nashville: Abingdon Press, 1976), vol. 4, pp. 147–59.

56. David Flusser, "Jesus in the Context of History," in *The Crucible of Christianity,* ed. Arnold Toynbee (New York: World Publishing Co., 1969), p. 230.

57. In this section I am indebted to Reginald H. Fuller, "Aspects of Pauline Christology," *Review and Expositor* **71** (1974), pp. 5–17.

58. Hans Dieter Betz, "Jesus as Divine Man," in *Jesus and the Historian: Written in Honor of Ernest Cadman Colwell,* ed. F. T. Trotter (Philadelphia: Westminster Press, 1968), p. 116.

59. On "gospel," see W. Schneemelcher, "Introduction," in Hennecke–Schneemelcher, *New Testament Apocrypha,* pp. 71–75.

60. Clyde Weber Votaw, *The Gospels and Contemporary Biographies in the Greco-Roman World* (Philadelphia: Fortress Press, 1970); Howard C. Kee, *Jesus in History,* 2nd ed. (New York: Harcourt Brace Jovanovich, 1977), pp. 133–40.

61. Paul J. Achtemeier, "Gospel Miracle Tradition and the Divine Man," *Interpretation* **26** (1972), p. 187.

62. Kee, *Jesus in History,* chs. 4–7, has good sketches of the thought of the individual evangelists.

III

Jesus Christ
in the Great Church

For most people, Christian or non-Christian, precise and sophisticated definitions of the identity and activity of Jesus Christ are not very important topics. Living religion, goes the argument, is not concerned with such intellectual matters. There is a great deal of truth to this point of view; yet it should not be forgotten that in some periods of Western history, precise definitions of who Jesus Christ was and what he did were matters of life and death. Even today such definitions are of vital importance to orthodox Christians. In this chapter we will gain an impression of the thinking about Jesus Christ that became the heart of the Great Church, that is, the church which came to represent the majority of Christians. (In the remainder of this book we will be discussing events of the Common Era almost exclusively. For this reason we will usually give Common Era dates without the abbreviation c.e.)

From the earliest period of the New Testament churches, there were confessions and creeds recited in worship, especially in connection with baptism. But the historical context in which such creeds were refined and developed was the conflict between orthodoxy and heresy. The term "heresy" (Greek: *hairesis*) at first referred to simply a "faction" or "sect" like that of the Sadducees (Acts 5:17) or Pharisees (Acts 15:5). Paul, however, used the term to refer to groups which he thought were destroying the unity and harmony of the Corinthian church (1 Cor

11:19). More and more, the term became centered on false beliefs as such. In contrast, correct beliefs were "orthodox" (Greek: *orthodokeō,* "I think straight"), and "orthodoxy," which began to take shape as the churches each sought an identity distinct from Judaism, eventually had to contend with heresies within the Church, a struggle that intensified with the legalization of the Church in 313.

In studying this phase of Christian thinking about Jesus Christ, four points should be kept in mind. First, whereas the varying portraits of Jesus in the New Testament arose in a syncretistic environment of many thought forms, from the "messianic" mythologies of the ancient Near East to the many Hellenistic cults and religious philosophies, doctrinal discussion about Jesus Christ was increasingly influenced by the more abstract rationality of the Greek "enlightened" philosophical tradition, which had emancipated itself from its own mythical religious heritage. We will see that the most characteristic movement in this period was the movement from "quasi-mythical" forms of thought to *philosophy.*

Second, there is a corresponding shift in *language.* Whereas the New Testament contained mythical and quasi-mythical images, titles, metaphors, and so on, the later discussions were characterized by such terms as "essence," "substance," and "person." Great debates arose about the meaning of such terms. These debates were further complicated because some thinkers spoke Greek and others spoke Latin.

A third important factor is that the biblical views about Jesus Christ were not reducible to a single, definitive, orthodox conception. This, of course, is a historical judgment in retrospect, for what the debates sought to do was determine *the* orthodox view from the New Testament. Nonetheless, the New Testament views of Jesus ranged from prophet, rabbi, and Davidic king on the human side to Son of God, heavenly high priest, and preexistent *Logos* on the divine side. This duality—human and divine—became the heart of the discussion as definitions became more precise.

Finally, it should be recalled that Christian doctrine about Jesus Christ and the canon of twenty-seven books in the New Testament emerged together. In other words, the limitation of authoritative sources for beliefs about Jesus Christ was accomplished by many of the same persons who formulated the creedal statements about him. Thus formation of the New Testament and formation of Christological creeds and confessions in the Great Church went hand in hand.

It is important to have these facts in mind when you examine the thoughts of the early Christians and their conceptions of Jesus Christ.

JESUS CHRIST IN THE THOUGHT OF EBIONITES, GNOSTICS, AND THE EARLIEST CHURCH FATHERS

Jesus was a Jew, and the earliest form of Christianity, as indicated in Ch. 2, was Jewish Christianity. Some of these Jewish Christians created problems for the apostle Paul (Gal 2:4; 2 Cor 3:1; cp. Acts 21:20). There are traditions that they fled from Jerusalem to Pella across the Jordan River prior to the onslaught of the Roman armies against Jerusalem in 70 c.e. and that Jesus' brother, James, was their leader and was succeeded by some of Jesus' relatives (Eusebius *E. H.* 3.5.2f; 3.11.1). These Jewish Christians were known as "the sect of the Nazarenes" (Acts 24:5) or *Nozrim* (in a Jewish prayer against the heretics, the Eighteen Benedictions) and (among the Church Fathers) as the Ebionites (Hebrew: *'ebiōnīm,* "poor [ones]"); the latter eventually became a term of abuse among the orthodox (meaning "poor in faith in Jesus Christ").[1]

One of the central Ebionite views about Jesus Christ was that he was "the prophet like Moses." This view of the Messiah was current among the Essenes, the Samaritans, and the rabbis and had influenced Christian ideas about Jesus (Acts 3:22–24; cp. John 3:14). Both Moses and Jesus were miracle workers, lawgivers, leaders of bands of disciples, and covenant makers; yet some Ebionites considered Jesus greater than Moses, for they believed an Adam myth that portrayed Adam not as the one who fell and brought sin into the world but as the True Prophet (sin did not come until later) who was also manifested later in such great figures as Enoch, Noah, Abraham, Isaac, Jacob, and Moses. These Ebionites regarded Jesus as, so to speak, the last and greatest prophet.

A second view among the Ebionites was that only Jesus had completely fulfilled the Jewish law and that God therefore "adopted" him as his Son. This dignity was bestowed on Jesus *as a man,* and it occurred at his baptism (Ps 2:7: "Thou art my son . . ."; cp. Mark 1:11). They also believed that Jesus was capable of sinning. Finally, they called Jesus "the Son of Man," which for them meant simply "a man"—but a man who was resurrected to become a supernatural angel, Christ, who then became the Lord of all creation, and who would return.

The basic view of the Jewish Ebionites was monotheistic: Jesus was a man, and one dared not think of him as a second God. In contrast, the basic view of the Gnostics was dualistic; that is to say, they considered this world of darkness the creation of a lower god who opposed the true God of light.[2] Likewise, the Redeemer was a supernatural figure from the world of light, and Gnostic Christians found it difficult to imagine him taking the form of sinful, bodily flesh. He might have "seemed" to be human, a view called *Docetism* (Greek: *dokeō,* "I seem"), but that was only an appearance. Rather, the heavenly being, the highest being next to God, descended, inhabited the "flesh" for a period, and returned to heaven. For example, a second-century Egyptian Gnostic Christian by the name of Basilides said that the "ungenerated, unbegotten, un-named Father" sent his firstborn Mind (the first in a series of "emana-tions," like rays of light from the sun) to free those who believed in him from the power of the evil creator god and his demons. He appeared on earth as a man and worked miracles. Yet because he was Mind without body and thus invisible to all, he did not suffer, but took the form of Simon of Cyrene, the man along the way impressed to carry the cross (Mark 15:21). Thus Simon was crucified while Jesus stood by and laughed at the mistake the powers of evil had made!

The Ebionites and Gnostics represented two alternative conceptions of Jesus Christ: as a human being become divine (Adoptionism), or as a divine being become (almost) human (Docetism). For the Church Fa-thers, those key and authoritative writers of early Christianity who were not canonical, the problem was how to assert the more-than-human na-ture of Jesus Christ while at the same time maintaining the oneness of God (monotheism).

A solution to this problem came from the *Logos* doctrine, which brought together speculation about God's Wisdom, the Stoic notion of the rational order in the universe, and the Son of God.[3] The Wisdom ori-entation had influenced the Gospel of John, a key text for the Church Fathers. It should also be recalled that Philo of Alexandria, a contempo-rary of Jesus, saw the *Logos* as God's Wisdom, God's Son and a "second God," a participant in the act of creation, and an intermediary between God and humanity.

Though there were earlier Christian thinkers, it was Justin Martyr who developed the *Logos* conception of Jesus Christ.[4] For Justin there was only one God, the Father, who was totally transcendent, beyond the world. Yet all people had knowledge of the remote and "totally other" God by means of "seeds of *logos,*" that is, the reason which is found in each individual (as in Stoicism). Reasonable people, therefore, already had a knowledge of God, and the great religious figures from the past were especially *logos*-filled people. The universal *Logos* became fully known only when it became a human being, an incarnate man, that is, Jesus Christ. This was the same Rational Principle who was with the Father and was begotten before other things and persons were created, shared in the act of creation, and was subordinate to God. Through the incarnate *Logos,* called Christ, perfect knowledge of God was possible for believers. In short, the *Logos* was a mediator between God and man, the extension of God's own creative activity, and incarnate as the Christ.

Also from Asia Minor came Irenaeus, who was a presbyter at

Lyons about 177.[5] In his major work, *Against Heresies,* which has become the source for understanding many of the religious ("heretical") movements of the later second century, he made the Gnostics his special target. His main purpose was to show that Christianity believed in *one* God, like Judaism, but that the human race would be redeemed through his only Son, Jesus Christ. As Paul stated, the new Adam, Christ, reversed the sin of the old Adam (Rom 5:11ff.); likewise, argued Irenaeus, Mary reversed the sin of Eve. Irenaeus also affirmed that the *Logos* existed before creation (that is, was preexistent with God) and that he became flesh, truly suffered, and was therefore completely human. Thus, for Irenaeus the Gnostics were wrong to think of the *Logos* as coming *after* God as his highest emanation; the *Logos* was *always* with God and identical with, yet distinguishable from, God from the very beginning (John 1:1), prior to creation. In both Justin and Irenaeus, then, the *Logos* doctrine made it possible to think of a divine being who was not God—thus monotheism was protected—but was so much identical with God that he had always been with God. The attempt was to find the middle ground with the concept of a divine *Logos* become human, not that of a man adopted and made divine. This tendency would persist in orthodox Christianity throughout the ages.

THE MONARCHIANS AND TERTULLIAN'S DEFENSE OF THE LOGOS–CHRIST

There were those who believed that the *Logos* conception, despite its attempt to protect monotheism, erred on the side of ditheism, that is, that it emphasized Christ's divinity to the point where he became a second God alongside God the Father. Thus opposition came from those who continued to assert that Jesus was a great man who was miraculously conceived by a virgin and "adopted" by God at his baptism. For Theodotus, a leather worker who came to Rome from Asia Minor in about 190, perhaps from the circle of the *Alogoi* ("non-*Logos* adherents"),[6] Christ received from the baptismal Spirit "powers" (Greek: *dynameis*) for his special vocation, but he was not God. If he became God at all, it was *after* his resurrection. This *Dynamic Monarchianism* [7] was enough of a challenge to the church at Rome that in 199 Theodotus was excommunicated by Pope Victor, and though there were other Dynamists at Rome, the view eventually lost ground.

A more serious challenge to the *Logos* view of Jesus Christ came from the *Modalistic Monarchians,* also known as *Sabellians* or *Patripassians.* Like the Dynamic Monarchians, they stressed the one, single, and unified Monarch as opposed to the deification of the *Logos* alongside God the Father; but they are termed "Modalistic" because they thought of the *one* God as appearing in three separate and successive "modes," Father, Son, and Holy Spirit. The third-century Roman writer Novatian succinctly summarized the Modalistic position with respect to Christ's relation to God:

> If God is one,
> and Christ is God,
> and the Father is God,
> then Christ and the Father are one
> and Christ must be called the Father.[8]

In Asia Minor, Modalism was associated with a certain Noetus, who argued on the basis of John 10:30 ("I and the Father are one") that "Christ was the Father himself, and the Father was born and suffered and died."[9] Because of the stress on the suffering passion of the *Father*, this view is sometimes called *Patripassianism*. Similar views were held in Rome by Sabellius, who said that "Father, Son, and Holy Spirit are one and the same being."[10] For Sabellius, God played the roles of law-giver (Father), the Incarnate One for man's salvation (Son), and, after returning to heaven, the inspirer of the apostles (Holy Spirit). As a result of the influence of Sabellius, Modalistic Monarchianism in Rome was called *Sabellianism*.

Though support of the *Logos* doctrine against Sabellianism came from Hippolytus of Rome (ca. 170–235?), who argued that the Gospel of John also distinguished between God and the *Logos* (John 10:30, "I *and* the Father *are* one" [italics added] implied the distinction),[11] it was in Carthage that the *Logos* conception found its greatest defense. Tertullian (ca. 160–220),[12] educated as a lawyer and subsequently converted to Christianity (he later became a Montanist), was the first great thinker of the Church to write in Latin. When the Modalist (Patripassian) Praxeas apparently claimed "that The Father himself descended into the virgin, was himself born of her, himself suffered; in fact that he himself was Jesus Christ" (Tertullian, *Against Praxeas* 1), Tertullian also sought to defend the unity of God, but he did so by speaking of God in terms of the legal notion of property, or possessions, called "substance" (Latin: *substantia*). As several people could own one piece of property, so one *substantia* could be jointly shared by "three persons" (Latin: *tres personae*), that is, Father, Son, and Holy Spirit. Thus the one *substantia* of God is found in three *personae*.

The Father and the Son were different *personae*. What, then, was their relationship if they were not exactly the same, as Praxeas said? Tertullian argued that Christ the *Logos,* who is also God's Reason, his Power, his Word—that by which God created everything—was the same *substantia* as the Father but that the *Logos* did not possess the same *amount* of deity as God the Father. One might suggest that Tertullian thought of God as the greatest shareholder of the property (though Tertullian himself did not say that!) At this point Tertullian used an analogy:

> When a ray is shot forth from the sun, a part is taken from the whole; but there will be sun in the ray because it is a sun ray; its nature is not separated, but extended. . . . Thus, too, what proceeds from God is God and the Son of God, and both are one . . .[13]

This strong statement of both the deity of the *Logos* and his subordination to God the Father was then balanced by a conception of the humanity of the *Logos*. Following John 1:14, Tertullian argued that the *Logos* became flesh, was truly human.

> This ray of God, then as was ever foretold in the past, descended into a certain virgin and, becoming flesh in her womb, was born as one who is man and God united. The flesh, provided with a soul, is nourished, matures, speaks, teaches, acts, and *is* Christ.[14]

For Tertullian, Jesus Christ as *Logos* was not only of the same substance (*substantia*) as the Father, though in lesser measure; he was also of the same substance (*substantia*) as man. The two substances did not merge into a third substance, as gold and silver combine to make up electrum; each remained distinct, yet united, in one person (Latin: *una persona*). Tertullian supported his view with Paul's writings:

> Thus also the apostle teaches of both his substances: "Who was made," he says, "of the seed of David"—here he will be man, and Son of Man: "Who was defined as Son of God according to the Spirit" (Rom 1:3–4)—here he will be God, and the Word, the Son of God: we observe a double quality, not confused but combined, Jesus in one Person (*persona*) God and man.[15]

Thus, Tertullian forged from Latin legal terminology a vocabulary that would be exceedingly important for later discussions. God was one *substantia* shared by three *personae*, Father, Son, and Holy Spirit; the Son was the preexistent *Logos*, a participant in creation, and of the same *substantia* as the Father, though in lesser measure (both a deity and subordinate to the Father); and the *Logos* became flesh, was truly human, and was thus of the same *substantia* as man, the two *substantiae*, divine and human, being united in one *persona*.

THE *LOGOS*–CHRIST IN THE SCHOOLS OF ALEXANDRIA (ORIGEN) AND ANTIOCH (PAUL OF SAMOSATA)

In Asia Minor, Rome, Gaul, and North Africa the conception of the divine *Logos* having become flesh was gaining ground over Adoptionist (Ebionite, Monarchian) and Docetic (Gnostic) views. In the Gnostic and

Neoplatonic environment of Alexandria the *Logos* view began to take a highly speculative form. There an Egyptian by the name of Pantaenus founded a school for Christian instruction, and out of it came two of the Church's leading thinkers, Clement of Alexandria and Origen. So strong was the former's stress on the divinity of Christ the *Logos* that he believed Christ did not really need food and drink; Clement's view therefore verged on Docetism.[16]

The greatest thinker of the Alexandrian School was Origen (186–255).[17] His father, apparently a convert to Christianity, instructed him in the Christian faith. Soon the brilliant young man became the most famous pupil of Clement in the School of Pantaenus. In 202 the Roman emperor, Septimus Severus, launched a persecution against those religious groups who sought to proselytize, the Jews and the Christians, and Origen's father was arrested and executed. So intense did Origen's zeal for Christianity become that he refused to associate with heretics, openly supported the cause of persecuted martyrs, and, most especially, became caught up with the growing ascetic movement at Alexandria. When as a result of the persecution many older leaders of the School at Pantaenus, including Clement, were driven from the city, the very young Origen was appointed by Bishop Demetrius to become head of the school.

Under Origen's leadership the school expanded and attracted many excellent students. Nonetheless, there developed increasing tensions between the popular Origen and his bishop, Demetrius. In 231–32, while on a trip to Greece, Origen was ordained a presbyter by the bishops at Caesarea, Palestine. To halt this unprecedented move, Demetrius publicized the story that in his youth the zealous ascetic had emasculated himself for the kingdom of God (cp. Mt 19:12). Whether this was true or not, Origen was denied the priesthood, was not permitted to return to Alexandria, and was disgraced in all the churches but those in Palestine, Phoenicia, Arabia, and Greece. Eventually he settled in Caesarea, where he began another school and again became a famous and highly influential teacher. One of the greatest expositors of the Bible, and perhaps second only to St. Augustine as an ancient theologian, Origen was chained and tortured severely under the persecution of Christians by the emperor Decius in 249, and, failing in health, he died, probably at Tyre, Palestine, in 255.

Origen's thinking (like that of his Jewish predecessor Philo of Alexandria and his Christian predecessor Clement) was a combination of his highly allegorical interpretation of the Bible and his thoroughly Hellenistic background, which was dominated by Stoic and Neoplatonic views of the spiritual nature of the universe.[18] For Origen the preexistent *Logos* is subordinate to the one, transcendent, invisible, incomprehensible God, but superior to the other external spirits—the archangels, angels, demons, and (above the demons) the souls imprisoned in human bodies. The *Logos* is a divine being who mediates between the supreme Deity and all the "deities" of the universe. Thus the *Logos* is the image of God, while the other "deities" are only copies of that image. But the *Logos* is also the Son of God, not by adoption but, like all spirits, by being given his unending existence by God from all eternity. The *Logos*-Son never existed as a being separate from God; in fact, because he was an agent in creation, there never was a time when the Son did not exist. In contrast to the other created spirits, the *Logos* is *monogenēs*, "only-begotten," that is, uniquely created. Though he is *a* God, he is not *the* God, and he is less than God the Father. Yet he possesses the same nature, or substance, as God the Father. Like Tertullian, Origen frequently expressed this relation in terms of light emanating from the Father's mind. In short, since all spiritual beings have existed eternally, so the *Logos,* which is a spiritual being, is eternally generated; and since God is the only absolutely transcendent being, the *Logos* is subordinate to God, yet superior to, and mediator of, all other beings.

What, then, is the relation of the *Logos* to Jesus, especially in the light of the fact that Hellenistic thought would not have imagined the *Logos* becoming flesh, suffering, and dying, as the Bible (specifically the Gospel of John) said? In some places Origen suggested that there were two separate natures in Christ, one divine, the other human, and he claimed that the human nature became the whole man Jesus in order that the whole man might be saved. In other places—and this is more characteristic—he thought of the preexistent soul, or spirit, of Jesus, which (unlike other souls) did not fall, as the preexistent soul of the *Logos,* or he suggested that there were two preexistent souls, those of the *Logos* and of Jesus, which became united. Thus Jesus had the soul of the divine *Logos*. At his resurrection and ascension, his humanity was given the glory of his divinity, and thus he became divine. Such divinity, moreover, is effected for those who follow him. Finally, Origen made much of Jesus' death as a sacrifice. He was an offering to God for others, and he was a ransom paid to the evil powers who had temporarily gained control of the creation.

Origen was the first thinker to attempt a highly systematic doctrine of Jesus Christ. However, because he tended to separate the divine and the human in Christ and to suggest that the soul of Christ was the soul of the *Logos,* and therefore not totally human like other souls, later orthodoxy came to see his views on the subordination of Jesus as heretical. This was especially notable at the Fifth General Council, held at Constantinople in 553.

In contrast to the School of Alexandria was the School of Antioch.[19] The latter was not as deeply involved in speculative thought as the School of Alexandria, because Antioch's Jewish majority was more closely connected with a literal adherence to the letter of the sacred texts, and because Gnostic and Greek speculative currents were less influential in the region around Antioch. As a result, the Christian thinkers of Antioch tended to begin with monotheism, to protect the unity and oneness of God, and thus to center on the humanity of Jesus Christ. If the School of Alexandria at times tended toward Docetism, the School of Antioch at times tended toward Adoptionism.

Though the School of Antioch had strong influence in the fourth century, it was already current in the third century and was especially represented by the bishop of Antioch, Paul of Samosata, who in 269 was dramatically excommunicated for Modalistic Monarchian views by Syrian bishops educated by Origen.[20] For Paul, the Jewish *Shema'* "Hear, O Israel, the Lord your God is one God . . ." meant that the *Logos*-Wisdom/Son was a power of God so unified with him that it became a distinct existence only periodically, by being uttered. Thus it had a very limited and temporary existence as anything separate from God. As a result the divine *Logos* was never fully a man, but from time to time it dwelt *in* various individuals—Abraham, Moses, David, the prophets, and finally (and to the greatest extent), Jesus Christ. Jesus Christ himself was not the *Logos* become flesh; rather, the human Jesus was "honored by God" because of his "life full of virtue" and therefore became, in a limited (nonsubstantive) way, united in will and by love to God, a moral union for the benefit of humanity.

Thus, for this early representative of the School of Antioch, the unity of God is preserved by stating that occasionally his *Logos*/Wisdom, which is an attribute of God less than himself, fills certain noteworthy persons, the last and greatest of whom is Jesus Christ. Paul of Samosata's view, as we noted, was judged heretical.

JESUS CHRIST IN THE NICENE CREED AND IN ATHANASIUS

In the third century, the beliefs of the Gnostics and the Alexandrian conception of *Logos* were heavily weighted on the side of Jesus Christ's divinity; in contrast, the Ebionites and the School of Antioch tended to stress Jesus' humanity, as had the Monarchians, who opposed the *Logos* view. Thinkers such as Justin, Irenaeus, and especially Tertullian attempted to resolve this division with the idea that the *Logos* became completely flesh. Tertullian's formula, that in one person were united both divine and human substances, provided a measure of unity for the West; in the East there was still controversy.

In 312 Constantine defeated the last of the opposition to his mastery of the Roman Empire, and the following year Christianity became an officially accepted religion of the Empire. Around the same time there emerged an internal conflict within the church at Alexandria.[21] About 320 a pious and learned preacher by the name of Arius, educated in Antioch, stressed that there was only one God, that the Son was subordinate to the Father, and that the Son had not existed from all eternity, as had God. For Arius, only God had existed from all eternity without a beginning. After God, but still prior to creation, there took place the creation of the Son, the only one whom God himself created (the Arian interpretation of "only-begotten"); "and before he was begotten or created or ordained or founded, he was not."[22] The Son had a beginning and he was created *out of nothing,* like other created beings. Christ the *Logos*/Son was therefore not the same substance as the Father, nor was he from all eternity. Unlike the Father, he was changeable, or alterable. Indeed, he did not have a complete knowledge of God, and his sinlessness was by choice. Whereas Origen had claimed that the *Logos* was subordinate to God and generated from eternity, Arius now claimed that the Logos was subordinate to God but *not* generated from eternity. Arius also said that the Logos dwelled in Jesus, so that Jesus had no human soul. For Arius, Christ was neither fully God nor fully man; he was a mixture somewhere between.

For Alexander, Arius's bishop, this denial of the eternal generation of the Son was intolerable. He reasoned that if there was a point at which the Son was not yet, there was a point at which God had no *Logos,* that is, no Reason or Wisdom. Alexander also affirmed that the Son's substance (Greek: *hypostasis,* cp. Heb 1:3) is the same as that of the Father, surpasses all the other creatures that he has participated in creating, and is not changeable. When Eusebius of Caesarea, a fellow student with Arius at Antioch, came to Arius's defense by arguing that a coeternal, uncreated Son would destroy monotheism (the old issue for the School of Antioch), Alexander replied that only the Father was the *Un*begotten, but the son is *only*-begotten (*Monogenes*), that is, uniquely created by the Father as the Father's exact image, yet still generated *from all eternity.* For Alexander, denial of the eternal generation of the *Logos* and the "same substance" doctrine meant denial of Christ's divinity; for Arius, affirmation of the same doctrines implied belief in two gods.

Constantine, viewing the unity of Christianity as a support for the unity of the Empire, attempted to heal the breach by summoning bishops and representatives of the Church to a General Council, the Council of Nicaea, in 325. Most of the bishops were from the East, and most were unfamiliar with the intricacies of the problem. At the opening of the Council, a creed proposed by the Arians was rejected; then one or more Eastern creeds was modified in the direction of the strongly anti-Arian Creed of Antioch. Since this creed was worded in terms of the Son

rather than the *Logos,* the term that had played such a crucial role in
the debates was totally omitted from the creed adopted at Nicaea, despite its heavily Johannine cast. The wording of the Nicene Creed was
as follows: [23]

> We believe in one God, the Father Almighty, Creator of all things visible
> and invisible;
>   And in one Lord Jesus Christ, the Son of God, begotten of the Father as
> only-begotten, that is, from the substance [Greek: *ousias*] of the Father,
> God from God, Light from Light, true God from true God, begotten not cre-
> ated, of the same substance as [Greek: *homoousion*] the Father, through
> whom all the things were made, both in heaven and on earth; Who for us
> men and our salvation came down and was made flesh, becoming human.
> He suffered and the third day he rose, and ascended into the heavens. And
> he will come to judge both the living and the dead.
> And we believe in the Holy Spirit.
> And those who say, "There was when he was not,"
> and, "Before he was begotten he was not,"
> and that, "He came into being out of nothing,"
> or who assert that, he, the Son of God, is
> "Of a different *hypostasis* or *ousia,*"
> or that, "He is a creature,"
> or, "changeable,"
> or, "alterable,"
> the Catholic and Apostolic Church anathematizes.

The central term in Greek, *homoousios,* which was equivalent to
the Latin *consubstantialis,* along with the denials that the Son was of a
different substance (*hypostasis*) or essence (*ousia*), stressed the closest
unity between Father and Son, the deity of the Son, and thus the inadequacy of the Arian position. The difficulty with the term *homoousios*
was that it had been suspect among eastern thinkers because the Adoptionist Paul of Samosata was said to have used it of the impersonal
Logos. The other denials, however, reinforced the anti-Arian stance of
the creed. Yet Arianism did not die; in fact, it grew for the next forty
years and might have been reestablished except for one figure, Athanasius of Alexandria.

Like Origen and Tertullian, Athanasius (298–373) was one of the
most important thinkers of the ancient Church.[24] Educated in the Cat-
echetical School at Alexandria, he experienced the martyrdom of acquaintances and teachers in the last and most severe persecution of the
Christians under Diocletian and Maximin, from 303 to 311. Probably in
the same period, young Athanasius became the attendant of the famous
Egyptian monastic Antony, whose biography he later wrote. The main
influences of Athanasius's younger years, therefore, were his education
in the Christianized Greek philosophical tradition, ascetic monasticism,
and the current atmosphere of persecution and martyrdom.

When Athanasius was about twenty years old, he composed two influential books, *Against the Heathen* and *On the Incarnation*. He wrote these before attending the Council of Nicaea in 325 as a private secretary to Bishop Alexander, whom he succeeded in 328. Athanasius held that post until 373, having survived five banishments. The third, which began in 356, was followed by a series of Synods in the East that challenged the *homoousios* formula of Nicaea as unscriptural (which it was) and Sabellian. Consequently, at Constantinople in 360, the Creed of Ariminum was adopted. This creed contained the statement, "The Son is like [*homoios*] the Father." In other words, a *homoiousios* ("of like substance") position replaced a *homoousios* ("of the same substance") position. This was a semi-Arian compromise.

Athanasius's little classic, *On the Incarnation,* was written before Nicaea, but it is a good illustration of the type of thinking that concurred with the Nicene faith. Athanasius claimed that God was a good, infinite God, and the Mind that created the universe and creatures out of nothing. The means of creation was the *Logos* (Gen 1:1; Heb 11:3), the Lord Jesus Christ. In the same manner, God created man in his own image, having given him a share of the reasonableness of his *Logos,* and intending that he should be immortal. Thus it was possible to know God through his image in man and in the works of his creation. However, by the deceit of the devil, man disobeyed the one prohibition (against eating from the tree of the knowledge of good and evil) and became increasingly evil, sinned, and as a result died. But God was good and consistent of character; he could not tolerate constant destruction and death. He gave man his law and sent the prophets to supplement knowledge of him through creation. Yet sin was too great, and single acts of repentance were not enough. Finally, God once again gave his incorporeal, incorruptible, and immaterial Word. Even though his Word, in union with himself, pervaded all creation, paradoxically it was necessary to re-create the world by entering it anew, this time by "stooping" to man's level in his love and self-revelation.

> You know what happens when a portrait that has been painted on a panel becomes obliterated through external stains. The artist does not throw away the panel, but the subject of the portrait has to come and sit for it again, and then the likeness is redrawn on the same material.[25]

Thus God formed for himself a *real* human body (not a Docetic appearance) from a "spotless, stainless . . . virgin . . . untainted by intercourse with man."[26] He was born and ate food; but he further showed himself to be the Son of God by miraculous deeds. With a truly human body, he was capable of death, and so surrendered himself as a pure sacrifice to God, as a sinless substitute for sinful man, as payment of the debt for sin, and as a payment of ransom to the devil. Having overcome sin, he overcame death and raised himself, thus making a new beginning of life by offering the hope of the resurrection. Finally, he would return in majesty to judge each person's deeds, giving the reward to those who imitated the saints and led a godly life, who loved God the Father in Christ Jesus the Lord and in the Holy Spirit.

In contrast to the Arians, Athanasius affirmed a loving God from the very beginning, and therefore an eternally generated Son from the very beginning, a Son who was of the same essence (*homoousios*) as the Father, uncreated though uniquely begotten, and unchangeable.

THE COUNCILS OF CONSTANTINOPLE AND EPHESUS

The Nicene Creed clarified the divinity of Jesus Christ as *homoousios* with the Father from all eternity; though it *asserted* the humanity of Jesus Christ, it did not clarify the sense in which his humanity was related to his divinity. In the West, Tertullian had claimed that the Godhead was one (*una substantia*) in three persons (*tres personae*) and that the Second Person not only shared God's *substantia* but also shared man's *substantia* in such a way that the two *substantiae* were united but distinct.

The first thinker in the East to tackle the relation of the human and the divine in Jesus Christ was Apollinaris (?–390), bishop of Laodicea in Syria.[27] For Apollinaris the crucial issue was the *unity* of the divine and human. He supported the Nicene solution as to the divinity of Jesus Christ; nonetheless, drawing on Aristotle's logic, he found it difficult to see how in one unified nature (Greek: *physis*) there could be two perfect and complete natures, divine and human, without at the same time affirming two Sons. Recall that Arius had suggested that a subordinate *Logos* dwelled in Jesus Christ and thus that Jesus had no human soul. For Apollinaris man was composed of three parts: the fleshly body, the lower, sensuous soul (Greek: *pseuchē*), and the higher spirit (Greek: *pneuma*) with its reasoning mind (Greek: *nous*). Apollinaris's solution was to think of the divine *Logos* or Reason as replacing the reasoning mind of the spirit of Jesus, that is, the higher self alone. Thus Jesus derived his fleshly body from the virgin and had a lower, human soul, but a divine mind that guided his thinking and willing. At the same time, the three parts of Jesus were, as in all human beings, united in one "nature." This more precise modification of Arius by Apollinaris was, however, viewed as denying the full and complete humanity of Jesus, and after being condemned at Rome and Antioch, it was decisively repudiated at the Second General Council, held at Constantinople in 381. The Council also continued to condemn Arianism and, in addition, affirmed the full deity of the Holy Spirit as "proceeding" from the Father. In short, Apollinaris's stress on the unity of Jesus Christ came close to the final orthodox solution; but his claim that God did not operate through the wholly human soul of Jesus was viewed as absorbing Jesus' humanity into his divinity, that is, as a denial of the full Incarnation.

The opposite tendency, to stress two distinct "natures" (Greek: *physikes*), divine and human, came from the School of Antioch. With its monotheistic tradition, this school wished to avoid confusing the immortal, indestructible, and unchangeable God with the mortal and changeable man, whose rational, moral will became corrupt through the Fall. These thinkers held that salvation implied a *morally* regenerated humanity and that to accomplish this, the *Logos* took the form of a servant, restored to persons the divine image (which has been distorted through Adam's Fall), and produced a new creation. The Antiochenes spoke of a "conjunction" of two *distinct* "natures" in Jesus Christ, and as noted above, confusion arose for Western thinkers when the Antiochenes referred to them with the term "substance" (*hypostasis*). To protect Jesus' humanity, they thought of the two "natures" as conjoined but continually "divided," and they often asked whether specific Scriptural texts were talking about his divinity or about his humanity.

The argument about Christ's two natures broke out in relation to what is called the *Theotokos* controversy.[28] In 428 Nestorius, a learned monk and bishop from the region of Antioch, became patriarch at Constantinople. There he encountered the widely popular but very un-Antiochene conception of Mary as the "bearer of God" (Greek: *Theotokos*) as well as the bearer of man. If she bore the flesh, it was said, she also bore the Word of God become flesh; the term was meant to preserve the unity of Jesus Christ's nature. But Nestorius found the term, at least in its commonly accepted interpretation, inappropriate, for he did not think it sufficiently distinguished the two natures. Nestorius's conception was actually closer than the Theotokos view to the correct view as understood in the West. However, a rival bishop from the School of Alexandria, the ambitious and politically minded Cyril, realizing that Constantinople was a growing rival of Rome, claimed that the views of Nestorius asserted two Sons, or two Persons, side by side. Cyril argued that there was only *one* "nature" (*physis*) of the *Logos* made flesh, a "hypostatic union" of divine and human. To him the term "nature" meant "person," a single individual. At the Council of Ephesus, in 431, Cyril succeeded in having Nestorius condemned—before the friends and supporters of Nestorius arrived. Though their coming brought about a counter condemnation of Cyril, imprisonment for both was followed by the release of Cyril, while Nestorius was banished to a monastery. Modern scholars have attempted to vindicate Nestorius and to see his views as closer to those of the solution that ultimately emerged; nonetheless, "Nestorianism" as a denial of the popular *Theotokos* view was placed alongside Arianism and Apollarianism as a Church heresy.

JESUS CHRIST IN THE THOUGHT OF AUGUSTINE

Augustine of Hippo (354–430)[29] had little direct influence on the great controversies about Jesus Christ in the East; nonetheless, he came after Tertullian (and Cyprian) as a product of North Africa, was influential in the thought of the great Pope Leo, and was considered the dominant theological influence on the medieval Church and the Protestant Reformation, so that he must be considered in this context.

Augustine was born in Tagaste to a pagan father, who converted late in life, and a Christian mother, Monica, who was a strong influence in his life. He was, as he recalled in his *Confessions,* an especially sensuous young man. At age 17, while studying rhetoric at Carthage, he took up with a concubine who bore him a much-loved son, Adeodatus. As a teacher less impressed with the Scriptures than with Cicero, Augustine sought spiritual and intellectual truth in a syncretisitic, Gnostic-type religion, Manichaeism. During this period, he recorded in his *Confessions* that he prayed, "Grant me chastity and continence—but not yet!"

Unsatisfied by Manichaeism, Augustine eventually became a skeptic. In 383 he was off to Rome and then to Milan to teach rhetoric. At the instigation of his mother, who had joined him, Augustine dismissed his concubine and became engaged to marry a young girl. Meanwhile, he took up with another concubine. Augustine now became depressed because of his life-style. He was encouraged by his study of Neoplatonism, the preaching of the great Latin theologian Ambrose, the study of the Scriptures, and the spirituality of the poor and unlearned monks. His spiritual struggle then led him to a garden next to his house, where he overheard the voice of a neighborhood child say, "Take up and read." He picked up his Bible, and his eyes fell on Romans 13:13: "Let us behave with decency as befits the day: no revelling or drunkenness, no debauchery or vice, no quarrels or jealousies!" Suddenly aware of a new peace of mind, he found the power to put his sinful life behind him, and soon he was baptized by Ambrose. Partly due to ill health, he resigned his post, and after a period of retreat and study and the death of his mother, he returned to Africa. After the death of his son in 391, he went to Hippo (modern Algeria), was ordained to the priesthood, became a cobishop and, at the death of his colleague, founded a monastery, established a Rule, and founded a training school for the clergy. After a fruitful career of writing, he died in 430, as the barbarian Vandals besieged the city.

Augustine began not with abstract speculation but with religious experience.[30] Yet he aligned his experience with Christian scripture, tradition, and dogma, and he usually placed his views in the framework of Neoplatonism. Augustine believed that the universe is one and God is one; sin is due to human free will, not God. In Adam, all sinned, forfeited freedom, became "a mass of perdition" incapable of saving itself, and fell into bondage to death (Original Sin). As a result, only God's free gift of grace, which no one deserves but which God grants by his own choice, made possible the forgiveness of sins. As Tertullian's successor, Cyprian had argued that the only means to this grace is through the one, holy, Catholic, and apostolic Church, which is an infallible, indestructible Kingdom of God on earth. The Church is therefore a visible institution; only members of this institution receive salvation, though the Church may contain sinners, too. There the Word is preached and the sacraments (including the Lord's Supper, exorcism, ordination, marriage, and baptism) administered. In his classic *City of God,* Augustine stressed that the hierarchically organized Church, in league with the peace-preserving state, would eventually rule the world, a notion that bore much fruit in the Medieval period.

It was Pelagius, a learned British (or possibly Irish) monk, who opposed Augustine and denied that Adam's sin was universally transmitted to the human race. He taught that after baptism it was possible to accomplish moral improvement by human freedom. By a bit of political maneuvering, the African church, spearheaded by Augustine, obtained the condemnation of Pelagius and his followers in 418.

For Augustine, then, God was above all the biblical God of grace, love, and mercy, and his supreme gift for the salvation of humanity was Jesus Christ. In *On the Trinity* Augustine stated that the one, unchangeable, and eternal God was also the triune God—Father, Son, and Holy Spirit. So strong was his view of the oneness of God that he spoke of the "three persons" (*tres personae*) almost as a concession to the tradition and to the inadequacy of human language. Yet he attempted to go into great depth to understand the three persons. Throughout eternity there has always been a Trinity of mutually related, equal, yet distinguishable persons. The unity was so strong that there could be no subordination of the Son (as Tertullian, Origen, and Athanasius said) or of the Spirit; though the latter "proceeded" from both Father and Son, it was not in a sense that implied subordination. There has eternally existed a Trinity of mutually related, equal, yet distinguishable persons. In attempting to understand this Trinity in unity,

Augustine sought human analogies, since analogies were to be found in that which reflects the image of God, however distorted they were due to the Fall. For example, reasoned Augustine, when the human soul, or mind, loves itself, one person is at the same time lover and object of love. This also implies the love of love itself; without loving love, the lover cannot love. In one essence, then, "lover, loved, and love: these are three."[31] In contrast to the mixture of water, wine, and honey, in which different substances become one new substance, with lover, love, and loved, "all are in all." By means of such abstractions Augustine sought to elucidate the triad that is at the same time one.[32]

Yet each person of the Trinity had a different mission. The Son, who as Word participated in the creation of the world and time, nevertheless chose the place and time for his mission as mediator between sinful man and the Father. While being the same (invisible) substance as the Father, the Son also had the same (visible) substance as a human being: Christ is one person of twofold substance (*una persona geminae substantiae*). He had a human, rational soul, which provided the point of union between Word and flesh, and a human body; yet, because he was born of the virgin Mary, he was free of Original Sin. Neither was he ignorant of anything. Drawing another human analogy, Augustine said that if it is possible to think of an incorporeal soul being joined to a corporeal body, how much more is it possible to think of an even more incorporeal Word of God being joined to an incorporeal human soul. Thus it was as a human being that Christ the mediator appeased God for all humanity, and as a divine being that he transformed the heart of man.

The heart of the redemptive act, for Augustine, was Christ's death on the cross. Sometimes Augustine suggested sacrificial analogies, such as that Christ was mediator–priest offering himself as mediator–victim, a sinless substitute for humanity, or a satisfaction due to God. Sometimes Augustine dramatized the event as setting a trap for the devil in which the body of Christ was the bait; thus the devil was deprived of his "right" to power over humanity. Finally, more than any of his predecessors, Augustine stressed the moral influence of the humble man Jesus Christ, whose humility was in direct contrast to the prideful sin of man.

THE CHALCEDONIAN CREED

As we have noted, the capable Cyril won the Nestorian controversy, for Nestorius was condemned. But at Cyril's death, in 444, the anti-Nestorian banner was taken up by the less capable monk Eutyches. Eutyches so radically stressed Cyril's doctrine of "one nature," according to which there were two natures prior to the union of the *Logos* with Jesus' human nature but only one nature afterward, that he claimed the human nature was totally absorbed by the divine nature. Though this was a deñial of Jesus' humanity and of the *Theotokos* doctrine, Eutyches persisted by appealing to Pope Leo I (440–461), to the new Patriarch of Alexandria, and to the emperor. In 449, a Council was called at Ephesus. Eutyches was upheld, while the judge who had condemned him earlier was mobbed to death before the altar! However, in 450 the emperor died, and Pope Leo agreed to a new ecumenical council if his *Tome* (an excellent Christological treatise in line with earlier positions in the West) would be accepted. Under strong encouragement by the new emperor, the Council of Chalcedon was called in 451 to settle the problems once and for all.

The statement of the Council of Chalcedon on Jesus Christ reaffirmed the statements of the previous general councils, especially that of Nicaea, but also those of Constantinople and Ephesus. It condemned Arianism, Apollinarianism, "Nestorianism," and Eutychianism, and it affirmed the position that had been originally forged in the West by Tertullian, had been made more precise by the Eastern thinkers Athanasius and Cyril (both of Alexandria) and, in part, by Nestorius (of the School of Antioch), and was finally stated by the Western pope, Leo the Great, in his *Tome*. The formula was as follows. (The bracketed insertions indicate which heresies the various statements were meant to repudiate.)

> Following, then, the holy Fathers, we all with one voice teach that it should be confessed that our Lord Jesus Christ is one and the same Son, the Same perfect in Godhead, the Same perfect in manhood, truly God and truly man, the Same consisting of a rational soul [anti-Apollinarian] and a body; the same essence (*homoousios*) with the Father as to his Godhead [anti-Arian], and the same essence (*homoousios*) with us as to his manhood [anti-Eutychian]; in all things like unto us, sin only excepted; begotten of the Father before ages as to his Godhead [anti-Arian], and in the last days, the Same, for us and for our salvation, of Mary the virgin, the God-bearer (*Theotokos*) as to his manhood [anti-Nestorian];
>
> One and the same Christ, Son, Lord, Only-begotten, made known in two natures (*physikes*) without confusion, without change, without division, without separation [anti-"Nestorian"]; the difference of the natures having been in no wise taken away by reason of the union [anti-Eutychian], but rather the properties of each being preserved, and (both) concurring into one person (*prosopon*) and one substance (*hypostasis*)—not parted or divided into two persons (*prosopa*) [anti-"Nestorian"], but one and the same Son and Only-begotten, the divine *Logos*, the Lord Jesus Christ; even as the prophets of old (have spoken) concerning him, and as the Lord Jesus Christ himself has taught us, and as the Symbol of the Father has delivered to us.[33]

The creed attempted to define an answer to the two problems that had arisen in Christianity: Jesus Christ's relation to God (the first paragraph) and the relation of divinity and humanity in Jesus Christ (the second paragraph). It stated that Jesus Christ was "truly God and truly man," a *hypostatic union* of two natures in one person.

The creed did not heal all of the divisions.[34] Many Easterners believed that the doctrine of "two natures" so "hypostatized" them as separate "persons" that it was Nestorian. The Fifth Ecumenical Council, held at Constantinople in 553, attempted to accommodate these Monophysites by making Cyril's Christology of "one nature" (*mono physis*) the basis for understanding Chalcedon, but by then the Monophysite churches were well established in Egypt, Armenia, and parts of Syria, and the Roman Empire was in decline. Nestorian churches still existed in the East, especially in Syria. Thus the East was developing its own thinking about Jesus Christ. Furthermore, after a good deal of inner controversy in the West, the Sixth Ecumenical Council, at Constantinople in 680–81, affirmed the two wills (human and divine) of Christ, thus supporting most of the Roman popes against the patriarchate of Constantinople.

Relations became increasingly strained, and the East soon retaliated by charging the West with heresy in such matters as adding the *filioque* clause to the creed (indicating that the Spirit also proceeds from the Son, a view Augustine held), priestly celibacy, and the use of unleavened bread in the Mass. Though at the Seventh Ecumenical Council (at Nicaea in 787) East and West were united in allowing the portrayal of the human Christ in images (which the Protestants later came to reject), the peace was not to last. As a result of the divisions, there was eventually a break between the Eastern and Western branches of Christendom. Though the East made important contributions to mysticism in succeeding centuries, speculative discussion about Jesus Christ by the East tended to fall back on the thought of the Church Fathers.

JESUS CHRIST IN WESTERN MONASTICISM

The founder of Christian monasticism[35] is usually considered to be the Egyptian Copt Antony, who about 270 decided to model his life on Jesus' command to the rich young ruler to give up his possessions and, after fifteen years of asceticism, became a hermit in the desert, denying himself, fasting, and praying to rid himself of the demons. This *hermitic* form of monasticism had numerous adherents, one of the innovators being Symeon Stylites, who lived for more than thirty years on top of a pillar in the midst of the Egyptian desert until his death in 459! The more dominant of the forms that emerged in the early period, however, was *cenobitism*, that is, following the pattern of the Egyptian Pachomius, who established the first Christian monastery at Tabennisi about 315–320; it organized like-minded individuals (men or women) into a spiritual community centering in the disciplined life without obligations to bishop or emperor. This, then, was a lay movement.

In the West, monasticism gradually became allied more closely with the institutional Church. It was most successfully developed in the early period by Benedict of Nursia, Italy (ca. 480–547), who tempered asceticism with communal labor, whose stress on learning made preservation of many important documents possible, and whose famous *Rule* became the foundation for order within and among the monasteries. The movement spread northward from Italy, and in the tenth century the Benedictines were reformed at Cluny, France, by stricter asceticism and the central authority of abbots. When it grew more worldly, it was in turn reformed by the Cistercians, who were less centrally organized but who made the *Rule* uniform, stressed the mystic contemplation of Christ, and began public preaching. Hermitic orders, such as the Carthusians, also arose (1084). In the thirteenth century came the great revolution in the direction of the wandering "friars" who, while holding to poverty, chastity, and obedience, went out into the world to preach the gospel and do good. Dominic of Castile (1170–1221) developed Augustine's *Rule* and, with Paul's preaching as a model, sent his preachers to such centers as Rome, Paris, and Bologna. With its strong stress on learning, the Dominican Order produced Albertus Magnus, Thomas Aquinas, the mystics Meister Eckhart and John Tauler, and the Italian reformer Girolamo Savonarola.

The most famous of all the medieval monks was the legend-provoking Francis of Assisi (1182–1226).[36] A mischievous, middle-class Italian youth, Francis came down with a fever while on a military expedition. Gradually he began to act more and more like a monk, renouncing his possessions and selling cloth from his father's warehouse to rebuild churches in and near Assisi. One day in 1208 in a church near Assisi, Francis heard the gospel for the day, which included Matthew 10:7–10:

> Wherever you go, preach, saying, "The Kingdom of God is at hand." Heal the sick, cleanse the lepers, cast out demons. Freely you have received, freely give. Provide neither gold nor silver, nor brass in your purses, nor pack for your journey, nor coats, nor shoes, nor staffs, for the laborer is worthy of his hire.

From this point on Francis wished to lead his life as an imitation of the life and poverty of Jesus Christ, as a means to mystical union with him, believing that Christ was literally God in the flesh. Gathering followers, he composed a simple *Rule*, which seems originally to have been a selection of Jesus' commands. In 1209 he gained official approval, and the brothers went about Europe two by two, preaching, singing, caring for the lepers and the sickly, and aiding peasants.

Francis was what might be called a nature mystic.[37] In his *Canticle of Brother Sun* he referred intimately to "Brother Sun," "Brother Fire,"

Giovanni Bellini, detail of *Saint Francis in Ecstasy*
COPYRIGHT, THE FRICK COLLECTION, NEW YORK

"Brother Wind," "Sister Moon," "Sister Fire," and "Mother Earth." He was also remembered for putting the lowly worms to the side of the road so no one would step on them, and for addressing the animals lovingly as "Brother Donkey" or "Sister Sparrow." He was especially fond of the larks, which, he believed, offered solace to Christ the night of his crucifixion and resurrection. His sermon to the birds, his "little sisters," telling them to love God, inspired paintings, murals, etchings, and church windows all over Europe. His little sermon to the turtledove went:

> Sister Turtle Dove, may I tell you how to serve the Lord. You repeat *Qua, qua* and not *La, la*, that is, "Here, here on earth" and not "There in heaven." Oh, my Sister Turtle Dove, how rightly you coo. But you, man-child, why do you not learn from the example of Sister Turtle Dove?[38]

The following quotation, which illustrates Francis's view of Jesus Christ, is taken from his revised *Rule* of 1223:[39]

1. This is the Rule and way of life of the brothers minor; to observe the holy Gospel of our Lord Jesus Christ, living in obedience, without personal possessions, and in chastity. . . . 2. If they wish to adopt this way of life, and shall come to our brothers, they shall send them to their provincial ministers; to whom alone, and to no others, permission is given to receive brothers. And the ministers shall carefully examine them in the Catholic faith and the sacraments of the Church. . . . Having already taken a vow of continence . . . the ministers shall tell them, in the words of the holy Gospel, to go and sell all that they have and carefully give it to the poor. . . . After that they shall be given the garments of probation: namely two gowns without cowls and a belt, and hose and a cape down to the belt . . . And, when the year of probation is over, they shall be received into obedience; promising always to observe this way of life and Rule. . . . And those who have now promised obedience shall have one gown with a cowl, and another, if they wish it, without a cowl. And those who really need them may wear shoes. And all the brothers shall wear humble garments, and may repair them with sack cloth and other remnants, with God's blessing. . . . 3. The clerical brothers shall perform divine service according to the order of the Holy Roman Church . . . And they shall fast from the feast of All Saints to the Nativity of the Lord; . . . Let them be gentle, peaceable, modest, merciful and humble, with honorable conversation towards all, as is fitting. They ought not to ride, save when necessity or infirmity clearly compels them so to do. . . . 4. I strictly command all the brothers never to receive coin or money either directly or through an intermediary. . . . 5. Those brothers, to whom God has given the ability to work, shall work faithfully and devotedly. . . . 6. The brothers shall possess nothing, neither a house, nor a place, nor anything. But, as pilgrims and strangers in this world, serving God in poverty and humility, they shall confidently seek alms, and not be ashamed, for the Lord made Himself poor in this world for us. . . . 8. All the brothers shall be bound always to have one of the brothers of the order as minister general and servant of the whole brotherhood, and shall be strictly bound to obey him. . . . 9. The brothers shall not preach in the dioceses of any bishop who has forbidden them to do so . . . and let their discourse be brief; for the words which the Lord spoke upon earth were brief. 10. . . . I warn and exhort, moreover, in Christ Jesus the Lord, that the brothers be on their guard against all pride, vainglory, envy, avarice, care and worldly anxiety, detraction and murmuring. And they shall not be concerned to teach those who are ignorant of letters . . . 11. I strictly charge all the brethren not to hold conversation with women so as to arouse suspicion, nor to take counsel with them. And, with the exception of those whom special permission has been given by the Apostolic Chair, let them not enter nunneries. . . . 12. . . . Furthermore, I charge the ministers on their obedience that they demand from the lord pope one of the cardinals of the Holy Roman Church, who shall be the governor, corrector and protector of the fraternity, so that, always submissive and lying at the feet of that same Holy Church, steadfast in the Catholic faith, we may observe poverty and humility, and the holy Gospel of our Lord Jesus Christ; as we have firmly promised.

JESUS CHRIST IN SCHOLASTICISM

In the eleventh and twelfth centuries there was a resurgence of learning in the cathedral schools of France (Chartres, Orleans, and Paris). In the next two centuries intellectual activity was renewed in Europe in the newly founded universities, notably at Paris and Oxford. This new "school" activity centered in a new breed of thinkers, the "schoolmen," otherwise known as *Scholastics,* and the whole movement, in both its earlier and its later phases, is referred to as *Scholasticism.*[40]

In general, the Scholastics attempted a new and creative synthesis of Christian theology and Greek philosophy, of faith and reason, of Christian themes (Trinity, Incarnation, and salvation) and philosophical ones (truth, freedom, and evil). Moreover, there now became available the writings of Aristotle, the ancient master of logic, literature, and ethics, whose works had been preserved by the Moslems and were now being gradually translated into Latin. In this new climate the philosophical issue that became dominant was that of *universals:* Do universals (such as humanity) exist *prior* to particulars (such as specific human beings), or only in connection with particulars, or only as abstract names attached by thought to particulars? Such "heady" issues affected every thinker, and the thinkers were the teachers of monks, priests, kings, and popes. Scholasticism thus had a profound impact on late medieval life and thought.

The Father of Scholasticism was Anselm (1033–1109), who was born in northern Italy, received his advanced education at the English monastery of Bec, was made a monk in 1060, and was elevated to the position of Archbishop of Canterbury in 1093.[41] Anselm's famous point of departure for Christian thought was *fides quaerens intellectum,* "faith in search of understanding"; this phrase meant that the Christian stands within faith and does not begin with reason. Though he did not think articles of faith could be proved by rational arguments, he attempted to show that what reason can discover on its own is not in contradiction with belief.

In his *Proslogion* (1075?) Anselm gave his classical argument for the existence of God. He first defined God as "a Being than which none greater can be thought."[42] To deny his existence, according to the definition, would involve one in a logical contradiction: To claim that God does not exist always implies a humanly conceived object—"God"—which by definition is not God. With this proof as a base, Anselm attempted to give rational arguments that God is a Trinity, thus supporting the orthodox "one substance, three persons" (*una substantia, tres personae*), Father, Son, and Holy Spirit. His conclusion about Jesus Christ as the Son was also orthodox: He is the same substance as God, truly God; yet he is also the same substance as man, one person in two natures and two natures in one person. His view of the Incarnation was that in Jesus Christ there is a "hypostatic union," unconfused, of two persons or natures, divine (of the substance of the Father) and human (of the substance of man). Likewise, it was necessary that the second person of the trinity, the Son and Word, "assume" a human nature (particular, not universal). The major question that arose in Anselm's day, however, was why God became man, that is, what the correct view of the atonement was. The creeds had affirmed that the reason for the Incarnation was "for our sins," and orthodox tradition generally accepted the view that Satan had gained power over the human race from Adam's Fall, that sin and death resulted, and that (as Augustine said) Christ's death was a ransom paid to Satan for "man's" release. To Anselm, however, the ransom theory suggested that something was justly *owed* Satan; in fact, Satan's hold on man was an illegitimate and illegal robbery. Should God be thought to strike a bargain with Satan?

In his classic *Cur Deus Homo* (*Why God Became Man*), Anselm attempted to rethink the question of the atonement. As a medieval person, he was influenced by the view that the serf owed due allegiance and proper honor to the feudal overlord. If the overlord was offended, the serf either could be punished or could render back due "satisfaction" by restoring the honor due his superior, not only by repayment, but by reparations greater than the offense. It was in this vein that Anselm reasoned about the atonement. Man ought to make satisfaction to God for his sin, but he is too sinful. Therefore God does it himself through a God–man, a sinless one who freely wills to die, thus making the proper repayment and reparations. The Son deserves the reward for overcoming Satan this way; yet because he lacks nothing, he transfers it to man. In short, Anselm sought to replace the ransom theory of the atonement with a satisfaction theory. Though other theories would come forth (such as that God's *justice* was satisfied by a sinless substitute [the penal substitutionary theory], or that Christ's suffering love on the cross offered a moral example [the moral theory]), it was the satisfaction theory that became most predominant among medieval and Reformation thinkers.

The greatest and most influential thinker among the Scholastics was Thomas Aquinas (1225–74).[43] Born at Roccasecca (between Rome and Naples), the son of the public official Landolfo of Aquino, Thomas studied first with the Benedictine monks at Monte Cassino (established by Benedict himself) and then at the University of Naples, where he encountered the thought of Aristotle. In 1243, against his family's wishes, he entered the still struggling order of the Dominicans. Because they recognized his intellectual potential, they sent him to study in the Dominican course at Paris. But he was abducted by his brothers and held prisoner in his father's castle for a year. With the help of his sister, he escaped and continued to Paris. After two years of study he went with his famous teacher Albertus Magnus to Cologne, and in 1248 he became Albertus's subordinate as a teacher.

In 1252 Thomas was summoned to Paris to prepare for his doctor's degree, which he received in 1256. By now he was already well known as an excellent teacher and scholar. After teaching the customary three years at Paris, Thomas returned to Italy. He resumed responsibilities in and about Rome among the Dominicans, and he was promoted to Preacher General. He taught, did research, and wrote, especially on Aristotle, whose works were becoming more readily available in translation. In 1268 Thomas received the distinguished honor of an appointment in theology at the University of Paris. There he found himself between those faculty members who interpreted Aristotle in ways that challenged many traditional Christian doctrines, and those in the city who felt that even Thomas's moderate Aristotelianism was too unorthodox. In fact, some of his views were among those condemned by Parisian bishops at the time. Nevertheless, Thomas published most of his philosophical and theological writings, including his *Summa Theologica,* in this period. Then, in 1272, he became master of theology at the University of Naples. On the way to a Church council at Lyons in 1274, he fell ill, and he died at a Cistercian monastery in Fossanova, Italy. Just before his death it was rumored that he was to have been made a cardinal. He was canonized a Saint in 1323; in 1879 Pope Leo XIII declared that Thomas's theology should be the basis of all seminary instruction for prospective priests.

We will not attempt to summarize a thinker as comprehensive as Thomas Aquinas, but several points will help to clarify his thought about Jesus Christ.[44] As an Aristotelian, Thomas was a Moderate Realist; that is, he held that universals are known only *in* particular things, in physical realities, through the five senses. *Human* knowing produces three speculative "sciences": physics, which reasons about the natural world or about bodies and their motions, principles, and qualities; mathematics, which reasons about the quantity of things; and metaphysics, which deals with what is beyond the physical world, the Cause behind the effects. The latter requires the supreme intellectual effort.

For Thomas, these three disciplines constituted the province of philosophy—what can be known by natural reason. He saw philosophy as "ascent" toward the divine by way of sense data and human recognition. Theology, in contrast, begins where philosophy must stop, with the "descent" of the divine to the human, with matters of faith. It is reflection about revealed knowledge, which is a gift of grace from God. Its channels are Scripture and the tradition of the Church, especially its creeds and sacraments. Though nature can prepare for grace, grace alone reveals *who* God is. One cannot arrive at revealed truth by philosophy, but neither is it contrary to philosophy, and philosophy can demonstrate the fallacies of those who object to revealed knowledge. Thus philosophy, inadequate by itself, comes to the aid of theology in its attempt to understand the data of faith. Whereas philosophy is limited to "externals" (effects, or "accidents"), theology can grasp the "essences," even of the First Cause, God himself. Philosophy can demonstrate *that* God exists, but only theology can know *who* he is and *what* he does. In short, there is natural knowledge, revealed knowledge, and the understanding of revealed knowledge by reason—theological knowledge.

> There is, then, in man a threefold knowledge of things divine. Of these, the first is that in which man, by the natural light of reason, ascends to a knowledge of God through creatures. The second is that by which the divine truth—exceeding the human intellect—descends on us in the manner of revelation, not, however, as something made clear to be seen, but as something spoken in words to be believed. The third is that by which the human mind will be elevated to gaze perfectly upon the things revealed.[45]

As Augustine and Anselm said, theology is "faith in search of understanding."

Thomas sought for revealed truth in Scripture and the Church's tradition. In characteristic medieval fashion, he interpreted Scripture both literally ("historically") and spiritually (morally, allegorically, and eschatologically). One product of his mature thought was his argument that God had revealed himself as a Trinity, one essence in three persons, Father, Son, and Holy Spirit; like Augustine and Anselm, he sought to provide some understanding of this revelation by analogy with the functions of the human mind.[46] He also argued, in line with orthodox tradition, that Christ is the same divine essence or substance as God. Nonetheless, due to Adam's sin and God's mercy, "it was fitting" (not necessary, as Anselm had argued) that the second person, the Son, become incarnate. Thus the mystery of the Incarnation is that divinity and humanity are "hypostatically" united in one essence. Man did not become God by "ascent"; rather, the fullness of God as the divine *Logos* descended deep within human nature, that is, "condescended" to become human. As a human being, the Son took to himself bodily sadness, hunger, thirst, pain, and death. He had a rational soul and human flesh. Thus Jesus Christ was truly God and truly man. Moreover, like Anselm, Thomas held to a satisfaction theory of atonement.

Most characteristic of Thomas was his *form* of logical argument, by the presentation of key objections, rebuttal, and response to the objections. The following is a sample from the *Summa Theologica:*

Article 6.   Is this statement true, "God was made a man"?

THE SIXTH POINT: 1. It seems that the statement, "God was made a man," is false. For since "a man" signifies an independently existing subject, to be made a man implies an absolute beginning of existence. But it is false to attribute an absolute beginning of existence to God. It is, then, false to say, "God was made a man."

2. Moreover to be made a man is to undergo change. Yet God cannot be the subject of change, *I am the Lord and I change not* (Mal 3:6). Consequently, it appears that the statement, God *was made a man,* is false.

3. Moreover, the term *a man,* when predicated of Christ, stands for the person of the Son of God. Now it is false to say, *God has been made the person of the Son of God;* hence it is also false to say, *God was made a man.*

ON THE OTHER HAND,   *The word was made flesh* (Jn 1:14). And Athanasius comments, *To say, "The Word was made flesh" is equivalent to saying, "was made a man."*

REPLY: Whenever a new predicate is attributed to a subject we speak of the subject's being made whatever it is that the predicate signifies. Now it has already been pointed out that "to be a man" is truly predicated of God; at the same time this is not an eternal attribute of God but one that arises in time, with the assumption of a human nature. Consequently, the statement, "God was made a man" is a true one. Nevertheless, different teachers understand it in different ways, as has already been noted regarding the statement, "God is a man."

HENCE: 1. To be made a man implies an absolute beginning of existence wherever a human nature begins to exist in a newly created subject. But when we say that God was made a man, we are referring to the fact that a human nature began to exist in a subject already subsisting from eternity in the divine nature. Consequently, that God was made a man does not imply an absolute beginning of existence in God.

2. . . . Whenever . . . new predication is accompanied by change in the subject, then "to be made" is equivalent to undergoing change. . . .

In the case, however, of predicates signifying relationships, it can happen that these are newly predicated of a subject without its being intrinsically changed. A man, for example, can be made to stand on the right-hand side without any change occurring in himself, simply because someone else moves to his left. . . .

Now, "to be a man" is attributed to God in virtue of the union; and this union is a form of relation. Accordingly, without any change in God being implied, we newly predicate of him that he is a man by reason of the change occurring in the human nature which is assumed to the divine person. Similarly, when we say, "God was made a man," there is no question of attributing any change to God, but exclusively to the human nature.

3. The term "a man" does not stand for the bare person of the Son of God but for that person as in a human nature. While, therefore, the statement, "God was made the person of the Son," is false, this other is true, "God was made a man," because he was united to a human nature.[47]

We conclude this section with a comment about Thomas Aquinas in relation to medieval piety and sacramentalism.[48] During the period just considered, the Church had become for most people a holy institution that cared for and watched over every phase of the Christian's life, and since ancient times the Church had taught that it was the sole source of salvation. Within the Church, the means to salvation was an elaborately developed sacramental system, that is, a system of liturgical and moral acts that accompanied doctrinal confessions and beliefs.

In the context of these ideas about Church and salvation, Thomas Aquinas elaborated a system of seven sacraments. A *sacrament* was a special sign or rite believed to have been instituted by Jesus Christ. It was tangible and was considered to confer grace by its very enactment. The Christian was initiated into the Church, usually as an infant, by *baptism*. (If the person became a Christian as an adult, regeneration and pardon of all previous sins took place.) At the age of discretion, the Christian underwent *confirmation* of faith. Still later, there was *marriage* within the Church. Finally, at the point of death, the Christian was anointed with oil for the health of soul and body (*extreme unction*). These four sacraments were ritual acts that took place (and still do) at crucial transitions from one phase of life to another.

The other three sacraments were penance, the Eucharist, and ordination. *Penance,* said Aquinas, was directed toward specific acts of sin, and it involved four parts: being sincerely sorry for sins committed, along with the will not to commit them again (contrition); confession privately to a priest; acts of satisfaction, that is, good works to atone for one's sins; and the priest's pronouncement of forgiveness (absolution). Without such a pardon from the priest, no one who was guilty of a special class of seven "deadly" sins after baptism could be sure of salvation.

All members of the Church were required to participate weekly in the *Eucharist,* the reenactment at the Mass of Jesus Christ's sacrifice. According to Christian belief, as given official sanction in 1215 and clarified by Aquinas, a miracle of God took place when the priest said the words of consecration: The "accidents," or outward and visible shape and taste, of the bread and wine remained the same, but the "essence" or "substance" of the bread and wine was transformed into the actual body and blood of Jesus Christ. This miracle was called transubstantiation. Aquinas's view was that both the body and the blood were in either element, and gradually it became customary for the laity not to take the cup, but only the bread. It is worth stressing that the Eucharist was the high point in medieval piety: As the repetition of Christ's passion and a sacrifice that pleased God, it represented the belief that God had become man and the conviction that all who participated ritually would receive God's special favor and spiritual strength.

The special status and power to administer these six sacraments lay in the seventh—the *ordination* of men (only) to the priesthood—an act that separated the priests as especially holy men from all other persons (the laity).

SUMMARY

From the second to the fifth centuries, early Christianity sought to determine the orthodox view of Jesus Christ. Strongly influenced by Greek philosophical tradition, it attempted to draw on the New Testament and to give precise definitions of (a) the relation of Jesus to God and (b) the relation of divinity and humanity in Jesus. The first definition had to affirm that Jesus Christ was divine without endangering the belief that God was one God. The solution of the Ebionites was to consider Jesus the last, greatest prophet ("like Moses"), who was "adopted" by God at his baptism; though this view protected monotheism, it avoided making Jesus a second God at the price of denying his eternal divinity. The Gnostics exhibited the opposite tendency: They regarded Christ the Redeemer as so "divine" that he could only "seem" to be a human being, for they found it unthinkable that a heavenly being should inhabit sinful flesh. This view, too, was unacceptable to orthodoxy, for it denied the humanity of Jesus. Thus both Adoptionism and Docetism were unacceptable, the former because it overstressed Christ's humanity, the latter because it overstressed his divinity.

The views of Justin Martyr and Irenaeus (in the second century) and Tertullian (in the third century) were considered more orthodox. Drawing especially on the Prologue to the Gospel of John, these thinkers elaborated the notion of the incarnate *Logos* as God's Rational Principle, which had its counterpart in human reason. The *Logos* was considered to be preexistent, a participant in creation, but also incarnate in the flesh as one who truly suffered and died. This high estimate of Jesus Christ encountered opposition from the Monarchians, whose beliefs were firmly rooted in the monotheistic tradition. The Dynamic Monarchians stressed that Jesus received special powers (*dynameis*) from God at his baptism and that he did not receive divine status until after his resurrection. The Modalistic Monarchians claimed that God appeared in three separate and successive "modes," Father, Son, and Holy Spirit. This view was also called *Sabellianism,* after Sabellius, who thought of God as playing three roles, and *Patripassianism,* after the belief that it was the Father himself who, playing the role of the Son, suffered in the passion. Defense of the *Logos* doctrine came from the North African Tertullian, the first Church thinker to write in Latin; he said that God was one "substance" shared by three "persons" and that the second person, the Son, was not only the same substance as the Father (though in lesser measure) but also the same substance as human beings.

The greatest thinker of the School of Alexandria, Origen, drew on Stoic and Neoplatonic thought and elaborated the *Logos* conception in terms of the eternal generation of the Son, the subordination of the Son to the Father, and the union of this preexistent *Logos* with the preexistent soul of Jesus; in other words, he believed that Jesus' soul was the *Logos* which existed from all eternity and had particpated in creation. In contrast, Paul of Samosata, from the monotheistically oriented School of Antioch, stated that God's *Logos*, a power of God, united from time to time with noteworthy persons, the last and greatest of which was Jesus. Whereas the School of Alexandria stressed the divinity of Jesus Christ, the School of Antioch stressed his humanity.

From the first General Council, the Council of Nicaea (325), emerged the formula that Jesus Christ was of the "same substance" (*homoousios*) as the Father. This repudiated the Arian view that the *Logos* in Christ's mind was created by God secondarily, as a subordinate creature of a different substance from the Father. The *homoousios* view was defended by Athanasius, Augustine, and Leo and was reaffirmed at the Councils of Constantinople (381), Ephesus (431), and Chalcedon (451).

The latter three councils also considered the relation of divinity and humanity in Christ. The Council of Constantinople condemned the view of Apollinaris that the *Logos* assumed only the highest part of Christ's threefold nature; this way of stressing the unity of his person threatened his full humanity. The Council of Ephesus stressed that the complete separation of Jesus Christ's human and divine nature, which rightly or wrongly was associated with Nestorius, was inaccurate; following Cyril, it spoke of the two natures as *hypostatically* united and, consequently, affirmed that Mary bore both divine and human natures (the view of Mary as *Theotokos*). Yet, when Eutyches stressed the divine nature so strongly that he saw the divinity as absorbing the humanity, the Council of Chalcedon condemned him and held to Christ's full humanity. Thus, the orthodox conclusion was that Jesus Christ was "truly God and truly man," a hypostatic union of two natures in one person, the second person of the Trinity.

The orthodox position, as mentioned, was supported by Augustine, whose Neoplatonic tendencies led him to stress the unity of the Trinity, as well as the two substances in one person, the Son. Augustine was also influenced by monasticism and founded his own monastery. In the West, monasticism became more and more absorbed into the institutional Church. The ideals of the monastic life were poverty, chastity, and obedience, which were considered the basis of the true Christian life as exemplified by Jesus. Moreover, the monasteries were highly influential in the development of many famous Scholastics, including the Father of Scholasticism, Anselm of Canterbury, and the most important Scholastic of all, Thomas Aquinas. Both were thinkers within the mainstream of orthodoxy, and both defended it ably, the latter with a logic increasingly influenced by Aristotle. Finally, we note that the means by which God conferred grace through Jesus Christ was deeply rooted in the sacramental system, the heart of medieval piety.

NOTES

1. Hans-Joachim Schoeps, *Jewish Christianity*, trans. Douglas R. A. Hare (Philadelphia: Fortress Press, 1969); P. Vielhauer, "Jewish Christian Gospels," in Hennecke–Schneemelcher, *New Testament Apocrypha*, vol. 1, ch. 3.
2. Hans Jonas, *The Gnostic Religion* (Boston: Beacon Press, 1963); Robert M. Grant, *Gnosticism and Early Christianity* (New York: Columbia University Press, 1959); for the account of Simon in Basilides, see Robert M. Grant, ed., *Gnosticism: A Source Book of Heretical Writings from the Early Christian Period* (New York: Harper & Row, 1961), pp. 33ff. On the Gnostic Marcion, see Adolph Harnack, *History of Dogma*, trans. Neil Buchanan, 7 vols. (New York: Dover Publications, 1961), vol. 1, pp. 267–86 (originally published in German in 1900); Grant, *Source Book*, pp. 45–46.
3. For a rather technical discussion of the *Logos* and its background, see C. H. Dodd, *The Interpretation of the Fourth Gospel* (Cambridge: University Press, 1960), pp. 263–85. Note also the *Logos* hymn discussed in Ch. 2.
4. Cyril C. Richardson, ed., "Introduction to *The First Apology of Justin, the Martyr*," in *Early Christian Fathers*, Library of Christian Classics, vol. 1 (Philadelphia: Westminster Press, 1963), pp. 225–41.
5. Richardson, ed., "Introduction to Selections from *Against Heresies*," in *Early Christian Fathers*, pp. 343–57.
6. Harnack, *History of Dogma*, vol. 3, pp. 14–19, gives the beliefs of the *Alogoi*.
7. Ibid., pp. 30–36.
8. Novatian, *On the Trinity* 26, quoted in T. E. Pollard, *Johannine Christology and the Early Church* (Cambridge: University Press, 1970), p. 73.
9. Hippolytus, *Against Noetus* 1. For a further sketch of Sabellianism and other heresies, see Harry Austryn Wolfson, *The Philosophy of the Church Fathers*, vol. 1, "Faith, Trinity, Incarnation" (Cambridge: Harvard University Press, 1956), pp. 575–608. I am also indebted in general to the collections in Vincent Zamoyta, *A Theology of Christ: Sources* (Milwaukee: Bruce Publishing Company, 1967) and Ralph J. Tapia, *The Theology of Christ: Commentary* (New York: Bruce Publishing Company, 1971) for orthodoxy and heresy in the early centuries of Christianity.
10. Epiphanius, *Against Heresies* 62.1. On Sabellianism, see von Harnack, *History of Dogma*, vol. 3, pp. 81–88.

11. Pollard, *Johannine Christology,* pp. 52–58; von Harnack, *History of Dogma,* vol. 2, pp. 247ff.

12. S. L. Greenslade, ed., "General Introduction to Tertullian," in *Early Latin Theology,* Library of Christian Classics, vol. 5 (Philadelphia: Westminster Press, 1956), pp. 21–24; von Harnack, *History of Dogma,* vol. 2, pp. 279–86; Tapia, *Commentary,* pp. 79–82, selected from R. Cantalamessa, *La Christologia di Tertulliano* (Freibourg: University of Freibourg, 1962), pp. 193–96; Robert V. Sellers, *The Council of Chalcedon* (London: SPCK, 1953), pp. 182–203 passim.

13. Tertullian, *The Apology,* in R. Arbesmann et al., *Tertullian: Apologetical Works* (New York: Father of the Church, Inc., 1950), pp. 63–65, as quoted in Zamoyta, *Sources,* p. 18.

14. Ibid.

15. Tertullian, *Against Praxeas,* in E. Evans, *Tertullian's Treatise Against Praxeas* (London: T. and A. Constable, 1948), pp. 173–75, as quoted in Zamoyta, *Sources,* p. 24.

16. A. Grillmeier, S. J., *Christ in Christian Tradition,* trans. J. S. Bowden, 2nd ed. (New York: Sheed and Ward, 1975), pp. 125ff.; parts of the first edition are reprinted in Tapia, *Commentary,* pp. 48–56; see also "General Introduction," in J. E. L. Oulton and Henry Chadwick, eds., *Alexandrian Christianity,* Library of Christian Classics, vol. 2 (Philadelphia: Westminster Press, 1954), pp. 15–39.

17. See "General Introduction to Origen," in Oulton and Chadwick, *Alexandrian Christianity,* pp. 171–79, and Bibliography pp. 456–58; Sellers, *Chalcedon,* pp. 132–57; Grillmeier, *Christ,* pp. 163–72.

18. See note 17; also Pollard, *Johannine Christology,* pp. 86–105.

19. Sellers, *Chalcedon,* pp. 158–81.

20. Pollard, *Johannine Christology,* pp. 113–16.

21. Letter of Arius to Eusebius of Nicomedia, in *Christology of the Later Fathers,* ed. Edward R. Hardy, Library of Christian Classics, vol. 3 (Philadelphia: Westminster Press, 1954), p. 330. The letter is reprinted in Zamoyta, *Sources,* pp. 30–32. See also Tapia, *Commentary,* pp. 100–105, taken from J. D. N. Kelly, *Early Christian Creeds* (London: Longmans, 1960), pp. 231–39; Pollard, *Johannine Christology,* pp. 141–64.

22. Letter of Arius to Eusebius of Nicomedia, in Zamoyta, *Sources,* p. 31.

23. John H. Leith, *Creeds of the Churches* (New York: Doubleday & Co., Anchor Books), pp. 28–31; Pollard, *Johannine Christology,* pp. 166–83.

24. "The Life of St. Athanasius," in *St. Athanasius on the Incarnation,* trans. and ed. A Religious of C. S. M. V. (London: A. R. Mowbray & Co., 1944); "Introduction to Athanasius," in Hardy, *Christology of the Later Fathers,* pp. 43–51.

25. *On the Incarnation* para. 14; in general, see Pollard, *Johannine Christology,* pp. 184–245, for Athanasius's refutation of Arianism.

26. Ibid. para. 8.

27. Karl Adam, *The Christ of Faith,* trans. Joyce Crick (New York: Pantheon Books, 1957), pp. 29–37, as quoted in Tapia, *Commentary,* pp. 105–9.

28. The First Letter of Nestorius to Celestine, and The Third Letter of Cyril to Nestorius, in Hardy, *Christology of the Later Fathers,* pp. 346–48; both reprinted (the latter, in part) in Zamoyta, *Sources,* pp. 48–52.

29. The basis for the summary of Augustine's life is his own autobiography, *The Confessions,* found in Whitney J. Oates, ed., *Basic Writings of Saint Augustine,* 2 vols. (New York: Random House, 1948), vol. I, pp.

3–256; see also "Introduction" by Whitney Oates, pp. ix–xl. For Augustine's thought, see Eugene Portalie, S.J., *A Guide to the Thought of Saint Augustine*, trans. Ralph J. Bastian, S.J. (Chicago: Henry Regnery Company, 1960), part 1; Williston Walker, *A History of the Christian Church*, 3rd ed., rev. by Cyril C. Richardson, Wilhelm Pauck, and Robert T. Handy (New York: Charles Scribner's Sons, 1970), pp. 160–70; Albert Cook Outler, ed., *Augustine: Confessions and Enchiridion*, Library of Christian Classics, vol. 7 (Philadelphia: Westminster Press, 1953); John H. S. Burleigh, ed., *Augustine: Earlier Writings*, Library of Christian Classics, vol. 6 (Philadelphia: Westminster Press, 1953); John Burnaby, ed., *Augustine: Later Works,* Library of Christian Classics, vol. 7 (Philadelphia: Westminster Press, 1955).

30. Adolf Harnack, *Outlines of the History of Dogma*, trans. Edwin Knox Mitchell (Boston: Beacon Press, 1957), p. 312.

31. *On the Trinity* para. 3, reprinted in Burnaby, *Later Works*, p. 58.

32. However, these abstractions were to have great influence on Christian thought about the Trinity.

33. Translation taken from Sellers, *Chalcedon*, pp. 210–11; see also Leith, *Creeds*, pp. 34–36; Henry Bettenson, *Documents of the Christian Church* (New York: Oxford University Press, 1960), pp. 72–73.

34. Walker, *History*, pp. 140–50, 157, 201–3.

35. Herbert B. Workman, *The Evolution of the Monastic Ideal* (Boston: Beacon Press, 1962) (originally published in 1913); Owen Chadwick, ed., *Western Asceticism*, Library of Christian Classics, vol. 12 (Philadelphia: Westminster Press, 1958); Walker, *History*, pp. 125–28, 232–38.

36. Lawrence S. Cunningham, *Saint Francis of Assisi* (Boston: Twayne Publishers, 1976), with bibliography. A popular edition of stories about St. Francis is *The Little Flowers of St. Francis, The Mirror of Perfection by Leo of Assisi, and The Life of St. Francis by St. Bonaventure* (New York: E. P. Dutton and Co., 1951).

37. Edward A. Armstrong, *Saint Francis: Nature Mystic* (Berkeley: University of California Press, 1973).

38. Ibid., p. 56.

39. Bettenson, *Documents*, pp. 181–87.

40. Eugene R. Fairweather, ed., "General Introduction: The Intellectual Achievement of Medieval Christendom," in *A Scholastic Miscellany: Anselm to Ockham*, Library of Christian Classics, vol. 10 (Philadelphia: Westminster Press, 1956), pp. 17–43 (includes bibliography).

41. Fairweather, "Introduction to Anselm of Canterbury," in Fairweather, *A Scholastic Miscellany*, pp. 47–68; Eadmer, *The Life of St. Anselm*, ed. R. W. Southern (London: Thomas Nelson and Sons, 1962). Eadmer (ca. 1060–1124) was an English historian and ecclesiastic; his biography of Anselm was written about 1100.

42. Anselm, *Proslogion* ch. 2, in Fairweather, *A Scholastic Miscellany*, p. 73; for Anselm's thought, see especially Jasper Hopkins, *A Companion to the Study of St. Anselm* (Minneapolis: University of Minnesota Press, 1972).

43. Walker, *History*, p. 245; Anton C. Pegis, ed., "Introduction," in *Introduction to Saint Thomas Aquinas* (New York: Modern Library, 1948); Josef Pieper, *The Silence of St. Thomas*, trans. John Murray, S.J., and Daniel O'Connor (New York: Pantheon Books, 1957), pp. 3–41.

44. Ibid.; A. M. Fairweather, ed., *Nature and Grace: Selections from the Summa Theologica of Thomas Aquinas*, Library of Christian Classics,

vol. 11 (Philadelphia: Westminster Press, 1955); Vernon J. Bourke, ed., *The Pocket Aquinas* (New York: Washington Square Press, 1969).

45. *Summa Against the Gentiles* 1.5, in *The Pocket Aquinas*, pp. 319–20.

46. *Summa Against the Gentiles* 26, in *The Pocket Aquinas*, pp. 324ff.

47. *Summa Theologica* part 3, ques. 15, article 6, from *St. Thomas Aquinas: Summa Theologiae*, trans. C. E. O'Neill (New York: McGraw-Hill Book Co., 1963), vol. 50, pp. 3ff., as quoted in Zamoyta, *Sources*, pp. 100–101.

48. Walker, *History*, pp. 274–79.

IV

Jesus Christ in the Protestant and Catholic Reformations

The fifteenth and sixteenth centuries in Christian Europe marked a crucial change in the thinking of the West and of Christians, and thus in ideas about Jesus Christ. On the one hand, traditional medieval views about Jesus continued to play an important part in Christian life and belief; on the other hand, there was a move in the direction of what moderns call "the historical consciousness." This move was characterized especially by interest in recovering the original, "pure" Christianity of the Bible.

We will consider how thinkers in the Renaissance and Reformation regarded the past and why some felt dissatisfaction with the medieval church. Then five central views of Jesus Christ will be described. Two of the views come from Martin Luther and John Calvin, who were key Protestant reformers; another will be that of the more radical "left wing" reformers; finally, we will consider two views that essentially continue certain strains in medieval thought: those of the Roman Catholic Jesuit Ignatius Loyola and of the Roman Catholic mystic Teresa of Ávila.

THE RENAISSANCE[1]

During the fifteenth century in Western Europe, certain intellectuals came to think that the 1000 or so years prior to their own time had been a period of cultural and religious inferiority. Wishing to return to (and surpass) the golden age of Graeco-Roman civilization and Christian antiquity, they began to study the past, which they divided into two distinct epochs: classical Greece and Rome and their civilizations, from about the fifth century B.C.E. to the fifth century C.E., and the "declining" cultural epoch of about 1000 years that followed, which they called the "dark" or "middle" ages (between classical antiquity and their own present). They thought of their own period as one of rebirth (French: *renaissance*). The belief of these thinkers that their own time was superior to the medieval era gave rise to certain judgmental terms that are now commonly accepted, such as "Renaissance," "Middle Ages," and even "Gothic" (referring to a style of architecture influenced by the barbarian Goths). Thus the new consciousness focused to a large degree on history and on evaluating ancient documents.

Accompanying this move in the direction of historical thinking was a new mood about those who made history—human beings. Renaissance thinkers did not turn away from reflections about God and his divine Son; yet their writings showed a new emphasis on reflection about "the dignity of man." The intellectual leaders and benefactors of this way of thinking came to be known as *Humanists*. Medieval thinkers had tended to think that man had a fixed and determined place in a hierarchy, with God at the top, then angels, man, animals, plants, and, finally, inanimate matter. In contrast, Pico della Mirandola stressed in his *Oration on the Dignity of Man* (1487) that man's place was not fixed and determined but that he had the free will to become either more godlike or more animallike. This meant that whereas medieval thinkers tended to stress man's separation from God as fallen and sinful, a being in need of repentance before an angry God and an avenging Christ, Renaissance thinkers tended to stress man's freedom, his potential, creativity, and progress before a merciful God and a compassionate Christ. The effect was to make man more the center of all thought, and this had repercussions in other traditionally accepted hierarchial orders of the Middle Ages. Most especially, the religious hierarchy from the pope down to the peasant, and the religious institutions that supported it, began to give way to more private forms of religious experience. Now a larger place was found for intuition and the individual Christian conscience.

This new way of thinking awakened a love of the classical Greek and Latin writers. This interest spread from Italy, where the Renaissance began, to northern universities, especially in Germany, where twelve universities were founded between 1409 and 1506. Gradually, Humanism made inroads into medieval Scholasticism. For example, Nicholas of Cues (1401–64), a scholar who leaned toward Humanism, was so universal in his thinking that in his comparison of Christianity with Judaism and Islam he concluded that the three were one religious truth in a variety of expressions. By 1440 he and Lorenzo Valla (1405–57) had demonstrated their facility at historical study by proving that the late eighth-century document called the *Donation of Constantine*, which required that all Church officials be subject to the pope and that the papacy be given control over Italy and the western sections of Constantine the Great's empire, was a forgery.

The historical interest exhibited by Renaissance Humanists laid the groundwork for new attitudes toward the development of the institutional Church over the centuries. You will recall from the previous chapter that the heart of the institutional Church's practice was the sacramental system, which was rooted in sacred tradition and clarified by Thomas Aquinas. But, some thinkers asked, was it rooted in Scripture? This was a question that demanded study of the Bible, which for the most part had been limited to the educated elite within the Church. The official Bible of the medieval Church had been the Latin Vulgate, in the common language of the Roman Empire. But by the sixteenth century Latin had become the language of the educated only; since most people were uneducated, the Church felt it necessary to protect the common people by carefully controlling biblical interpretation. However, the new humanistic learning was not simply in the service of the church, and one of the major concerns of the Humanists was that Christians should have access to the Bible in their own language so they could read it for themselves. When humanistic interest in ancient texts and vernacular translations of them, coupled with their rapid production by the newly developed printing press (1450), led to vernacular translations of the Bible, many could read and interpret for themselves. Now Christians could test the institutional Church by means of Scripture.

Renaissance interest in history and the human beings who made it, in the classical writers from the past, in historical criticism, and in the ancient Scriptures were among the volatile factors that led to the Protestant Reformation. This new mood was well represented by Desiderius Erasmus of Rotterdam (1466–1536),[2] whose work on the Greek text of the New Testament led to a second edition (1519), which became the foundation of most vernacular translations of the Bible, including Luther's Bible and the King James Version of 1611. Erasmus's famous satirical work, *In Praise of Folly*, illustrates the boldness with which some Humanists were willing to criticize the institutional Church on the basis of the Bible. His biting remarks about the clergy at Rome provide a typical example:

> . . . scarce any kind of men live more voluptuously or with less trouble; as believing that Christ will be well enough pleased if in their mystical and almost mimical pontificality, ceremonies, titles of holiness and the like, and blessing and cursing, they play the parts of bishops. To work miracles is old and antiquated, and not in fashion now; to instruct the people, troublesome; to interpret the scripture, pedantic; to pray, a sign one has little else to do; to shed tears, silly and womanish; to be poor, base; to be vanquished, dishonorable and little becoming him that scarce admits even kings to kiss his slippers; and to be stretched on a cross, infamous.[3]

Erasmus's *Paraphrases of the New Testament* (1520) went so far as to question the authority of the pope, which was based on Matthew 16:18 ("You are Peter, and upon this Rock I will build my Church"), and he referred to the gospel in terms of "justification by faith in Jesus," a phrase that Martin Luther would make famous.

JESUS CHRIST IN MARTIN LUTHER'S THOUGHT

Martin Luther (1483–1546) was born of an upward-bound, lower-middle class German mining family.[4] He received his early education at the University of Erfurt, where the curriculum was oriented to the new thought of William of Occam (died ca. 1349). Occam was critical of Aquinas's high estimate of reason as preparation for revelation and of his attempts to distinguish between "essences" of things and their outward manifestations, for Occam was a Nominalist, that is, he thought "essences" were simply an abstraction of the human mind. Occam also defended the independence of the state from Church authority, taught that Scripture, not councils and popes, was binding for Christians, and doubted the biblical basis for transubstantiation.

Luther graduated from Erfurt in 1505 and began to study law. Shortly thereafter, as he was returning to Erfurt after a visit with his parents, he was caught in a violent thunderstorm and struck to the ground by a bolt of lightning. Terrified for the salvation of his soul, he vowed to become a monk. Over his father's objections, he entered the Augustinian monastery at Erfurt. His further studies of Occam, Augustine, the German mystics, and the Bible deepened his piety, but they did not quiet his personal anguish. As part of his penance, Luther continually pestered his superiors with hours-long confessions about trivia. So great was his consciousness of sin that he felt unworthy to celebrate his first Mass and fled the altar.

By 1513 Luther was in Wittenberg, a professor of Scripture in the newly established university. It was probably soon thereafter that he underwent a conversion. In his later life he wrote that he had hated the righteousness of God which punishes sinners and that he was studying the Epistle to the Romans to find Paul's true meaning:

> At last, by the mercy of God, meditating day and night, I gave heed to the context of the words, namely, "In it the righteousness of God is revealed, as it is written, 'He who through faith is righteous shall live'" [Rom 1:17]. There I began to understand that the righteousness of God is that by which the righteous lives by a gift of God, namely by faith. And this is the meaning: the righteousness of God is revealed by the gospel, namely, the passive righteousness with which a merciful God justifies us by faith, as it is written, "He who through faith is righteous shall live." Here I felt that I was altogether born again and had entered paradise itself through open gates. . . .[5]

The solution for Luther's anguish lay in Scripture: It was "faith alone"—not works—that was the basis for forgiveness. Thus were born the bywords of the Protestant Reformation: *sola scriptura* ("Scripture alone") and *sola fide* ("faith alone").

Little by little, Luther's insight brought him into conflict with the abuses in the system, especially as they centered in the sacrament of

Portrait of Martin Luther by L. Cranach
COPYRIGHT, NATIONALMUSEUM, STOCKHOLM.

penance. When the Dominican friar John Tetzel came to Wittenberg selling for a fee the extra merits accumulated in a heavenly "bank" by the goodness of the Virgin Mary, Christ, and the saints, Luther penned his *Ninety-five Theses,* the heart of which was an attack on papal authority. In three important treatises of 1520 (*An Open Letter to the Christian Nobility of the German Nation, The Babylonian Captivity of the Church,* and *On Christian Liberty*) Luther attacked the "Roman tyranny," accepting only three sacraments (baptism, penance, and the Eucharist), and treating the pope as his equal. He also rejected the doctrine of transubstantiation as a philosophical perversion of biblical faith's simple trust that the body and blood of Christ were "really present" in the bread and wine. The authority of the priest to perform the rites of the Church was not totally condemned; yet Luther came to think that all Christians could hear one another's confessions and that all were priests ("the priesthood of all believers"), and eventually he would reject the sacrament of penance. In short, Luther attacked the authority of the Church by his judgments about its supreme leader, the pope, and its means of grace, the sacramental system. Like others of his period, Luther was reexamining the Bible and beginning to give it his own interpretation as a means of evaluating Church tradition.

At the Diet of Worms in 1521, Luther refused to recant and was charged with heresy by the emperor. Shortly thereafter he was excommunicated, and his supporters kidnapped him for his own safety and carried him off to Wartburg Castle. In 1522 he returned to take up the reform of Wittenberg. Three years later he married a former nun. After a long life of writing and activity as a Reformation leader, Luther died in 1546.

Luther's early view of Jesus Christ was focused on a highly judgmental image, a figure who required acts of penance. Without them, he thought, Christ sought revenge. Luther wrote in later years,

> I was often terrified at the name of Jesus. The sight of a crucifix was like lightning to me and when his name was spoken, I would rather have heard that of the devil, because I thought I must do good works until Christ, because of them, became friendly and gracious to me.[6]

After his discovery of "by faith alone" in the writings of Paul, Luther no longer feared Jesus Christ; he believed that the message in Scripture about Jesus Christ was that God's real righteousness was forgiveness of the sinner. To him, that was the transforming message of salvation. Faith that one was justified became, for Luther, the impetus to works.

Luther sought to maintain the orthodox doctrine of Jesus Christ as "truly God and truly man"; however, he did not find in Scripture what the Church's traditional interpretation said was there. He usually avoided using the Church's language and the philosophical language of

Aquinas, preferring to employ down-to-earth expressions and language taken directly from Scripture. Whereas the great Scholastic looked at his holy text with ahistorical, doctrinal spectacles, Luther's own glance was backward into the past, for it was the Jesus who lived that became the focus of his notion of Jesus' humanity and divinity. To the extent that Luther looked back, he shared the Renaissance attitude toward history.

What did Luther see in the Bible? His was not a "religion of the book" in the sense that the *words* themselves were holy; rather, he spoke of the *Logos,* or Word, contained *in* the words. But that Word was not limited simply to the *Logos* concept of the Fathers, nor was it identifiable with the words as they were written. For Luther the New Testament apostles were those who unlocked the Old Testament orally, and it was because of a "great failure and weakness of spirit" that books had to be written. The Word of God for Luther was an uncovering, a revelation that went beyond the written words of the Bible.

Luther was not directly in line with the classical *Logos* doctrine; neither did he accept the allegorical method of interpreting Scripture, which had dominated the Church through the influence of the School of Alexandria. Luther's view was that the Bible was a unity: Both Old and New Testaments should "drive home Christ." But that did not mean that the Old Testament was full of allegorical references to Christ. Luther stressed another traditional method of interpretation that was derived from the School of Antioch and Augustine: concentration on the *plain, literal sense* of the text and the use of clearer passages to illuminate more obscure ones. Luther believed that Scripture interprets itself: The Gospel (New Testament) is the plainest witness to Christ, and the law (Old Testament) is to be read in the light of it, but without reading into the text secret, symbolic references to Christ. One might compare the Roman Church's canon law, institution, and sacraments to Israel's law, institution, and cultic life; to the gospel of the New Testament one might compare justification by grace through faith. However, the "law–gospel" scheme was reproduced in every believing Christian: Salvation by works (law) is overcome by salvation by grace through faith (gospel). The movement from law to gospel included the perspective of the advance of the New Testament on the Old for Luther, but it included much more.

When Luther came to the New Testament itself, he concentrated on the humanness of Jesus. It was the weak, lowly, and beggarly Christ that attracted him most. Jesus Christ was born in lowliness, lived his life as a humble beggar, and suffered and died on the cross a weak man, the object of scorn and contempt:

> He had eyes, ears, mouth, nose, chest, stomach, hands, and feet, just as you and I have. He took the breast: his mother nursed him as any other child is nursed. . . .[7]

He ate, drank, slept, awoke, was tired. He was sad and happy. He wept and laughed; He hungered and thirsted, froze and perspired. He chatted and worked and prayed. In short, He required all the necessities and sustenance of this life, and died and suffered like any other man, sharing fortune and misfortune.[8]

For Aquinas, God can be known in his essence—in a preparatory way by natural reason, and completely by the revelation of God, which is then to be explained by natural reason; for Occam, God is unknowable in his essence; for the German mystics, God is known through the "imitation of Christ," a way of devotion leading to union with him. For Luther, God is known through the humble Jesus, a notion that is closer to Occam and the mystics than to Thomas Aquinas. Luther's conception is well expressed in the German term *Ausbund,* a mercantile expression for "the faultless sample bound to the outside of a bolt of cloth to indicate the quality of the merchandise within."[9] Jesus Christ is a visible, tangible manifestation of the God who is hidden from sight. He expresses the Father's will and heart; he is God's seal, standard, ensign, pledge, and especially beloved Son. He is "The Man," a term of authority for Luther somewhat analogous to the way government employees refer to the President as "The Man." For Luther, the Christian relies solely on "The Man" for salvation. Thus the most characteristic God-given task, or office, of "The Man" is that of preacher (or teacher, which is virtually synonymous). Jesus' literal words as preacher are the means through which God's Word comes, and they are spoken with childlike simplicity. He preached not law, but gospel; not rules, but life. In short, his spoken message was "by faith alone" (*sola fide*).

How is this salvation accomplished? Luther believed that the "popish rabble" had falsely stressed pilgrimates, monkery, private masses, holy orders, and ascetic lives. Instead of these Luther wished to stress Jesus Christ alone, especially the Jesus who suffers, dies, is raised, and ascends; he saw these events not simply as something that happened, but as something that mysteriously and unexplainably happened "for me." "The words OUR, US, FOR US, ought to be written in golden letters—the man who does not believe them is not a Christian."[10] Thus Christ is a continual mediator who speaks for us at God's right hand in heaven, requests the Holy Spirit for us, and mediates our prayers.

Christ's role as mediator involved several conceptions for Luther. As Messiah, he came not to liberate Israel, but to be the universal Savior, king, and priest. Christ is true king, although his kingdom is not of this world (John 18:36), and as such he reigns over heavenly and spiritual things. He is true priest, interceding in heaven on behalf of believers and offering himself as a sacrifice. It is especially this priesthood conception that interests Luther. As mediator between God and the people, Christ is the great high priest "after the order of Melchizedek" (Heb 7) who offers himself as a sacrifice on the cross. He is also the true pass-over lamb, the Lamb of God (John 1:29) who is sacrificed for our sins. Like Anselm, Luther held to a satisfaction theory of atonement, but unlike Anselm, he was suspicious of reason. Whereas reason attempts to atone by the performance of good works, ceremonies, the invocation of the saints and the Virgin Mary (of Mary, Luther sarcastically re-marked, "Intercede for me before your Son, show Him your breasts"[11]), faith understands that "One has sinned, another has made satisfaction. The one who sins does not make satisfaction; the one who makes satis-faction does not sin. It is an amazing doctrine!"[12] Finally, Christ not only overcomes sin; he also defeats death.

If Jesus Christ and justification are inseparable, so are Jesus Christ and sanctification. How does one become holy before God? The piety of the monks and mystics of the period, based on the "imitation of Christ," stressed that one becomes better and better, progressing to higher stages of perfection. Although Luther apparently was influenced by the mystics and apparently thought that the Christian emulates Christ in his faith, love, and suffering, he also believed that the Christian does not do so *in order to* progress to higher stages of perfection. It is not the believer's holiness that makes him acceptable (see the discussion of Ig-natius Loyola, on pages 121–24). Just as works proceed from faith—not the reverse—so sanctification results from justification. Moral acts are not a means to salvation; rather, they result from salvation as a gift to the believer. The Left Wing of the Reformation and John Wesley, the Father of Methodism, would alter this belief.

Luther's different perspective on Jesus Christ was accompanied by a different accent on the rites of the Church. As noted, he reduced the seven sacraments to two. He regarded the sacraments as visible signs of God's invisible grace, and each had to have grounding in Scripture. On the basis of Romans 6, baptism (in which the visible sign was water) signified beginning to die to this world in order to live in the world to come. "Thus, you have been once baptized in the sacrament, but you need continually to be baptized by faith, continually to die and con-tinually to live."[13] Because the most important aspect of baptism was not the holiness of the rite or the ordination of the priest, Luther ac-cepted the baptism of infants. What matters in this case is the faith of the sponsors and of all members of the Church.

In his ideas about the Eucharist, or the Lord's Supper (in which the visible sign was bread and wine), Luther departed from tradition on three significant points: (1) He claimed that Scripture asserts the uni-versality of the cup (Mark 14:23); that is, all participants—not just the priests—are to drink it. (2) He rejected the Thomistic conception that while the "accidents" remain the same, the essence (or substance) is transformed into the body and blood of Christ (transubstantiation); this was because what he found in Scripture was not this "scholastic perversion" but the simple conviction that the body of Christ is "in, with, and under" the elements of bread and wine as a special manifestation of the Christ who is everywhere. (3) He rejected the celebration of the Mass as a sacrifice, as a rite whose proper performance would ensure grace, in favor of its character as a promise established and fulfilled through faith. Thus the administration of the sacraments is to be accomplished not by a "holy priest" with special powers but by a "minister" whose special calling and gifts include preaching and teaching, gifts Luther believed were characteristic of Jesus Christ but sadly missing in the Roman clergy. Though the minister is commissioned by the community or his superior, he is in principle not uniquely holy: *All* believers are priests to each other.

In summary, Luther attempted to be orthodox, but he did not present Jesus Christ in the orthodox manner, that is, with a systematic and well formulated doctrinal position. Rather, he looked back and took up the simple language and simple ideas of the Bible, only occasionally interspersing them with the language of orthodox doctrine. Just as the New Testament had no unified, consistent view of Jesus Christ, so Luther emphasized no Christ doctrine in the traditional way. Thus it is possible to say that Luther had no Christology. He did not begin with "who Jesus is" in his essence and then proceed to "what he does"; rather, Jesus is who he is because of what he does and who he says he is—better, who he said he *was*. At times, Luther appeared simply to take over a more cosmic and ahistorical Jesus Christ from the creeds, but that is because he looked back behind the Church's tradition and dogma at the Christ found in the New Testament—especially in the Gospel of John. But even more, he turned to the poor, weak, beggarly Christ he found in the synoptic gospels. There he saw Jesus primarily as preacher and teacher, just as he himself was preacher and teacher. His Christ was really present in the sacrament of the Eucharist, but not in the philosophical sense of Scholastic philosophy. Baptism was the rite of participating in the death and resurrection of Christ, the beginning of understanding what is to become a continual life-and-death struggle. Believing that God mercifully justifies sinners, Luther saw in the Scriptures not the Jesus who was the terrifying judge, but the humble preacher and teacher who offered salvation to those he met. Luther saw a Jesus who was destroying the myths of his own time—a figure who challenged the way in which concentration upon the sacred traditions and rites themselves could obscure the true intention of those traditions and rites. Thus Luther's own look at the past was a small but definite step in the direction of affirming that the profane world is also sacred—for the one who believes.

JESUS CHRIST IN THE LEFT WING
OF THE REFORMATION [14]

There were those who believed that Luther had not gone far enough. In Germany, they were the Saxon radicals, Karlstadt and Müntzer (Wittenberg was in the province of Saxony). In Switzerland, certain of Huldrich Zwingli's followers (Zwingli himself was a somewhat more radical reformer than Luther) also believed that Luther had not gone far enough. These radicals made up the left wing of the Reformation. Some statement of their views of Jesus Christ is in order, since they are the ancestors of the Mennonites, the Amish, and (more remotely), the Church of the Brethren, the English Baptists, and the Quakers.

Andreas Bodenstein of Karlstadt (1480–1541) [15] was initially a scholastic Thomist who opposed Luther at Wittenberg. After being challenged by Luther to an intense study of Augustine, he took his colleague's side and adopted Luther's teaching on Scripture, justification by faith, and the priesthood of all believers. Karlstadt eventually came to believe that the central issue was not law and gospel, but *law and spirit:* He thought anything physical or sensory impedes the spirit and should be discarded. On Christmas Day, 1521, while Luther was in hiding a Wartburg Castle, Karlstadt celebrated the Mass in German without priestly attire, thinking that he was in concert with Luther's views. He addressed his listeners as fellow laymen, stated that it was not necessary to have had confession before Mass, read a simplified Mass that omitted all references to sacrifice, did not elevate the bread and wine (contrary to custom), and offered both bread and cup into the hands of the laity. The next day he announced his engagement to marry and wrote a letter inviting the Elector of Saxony to his January 19 wedding, stating that he hoped to encourage priests to marry their "cooks"! He then went on a campaign to remove images, crucifixes, and organs from Wittenberg churches and pressured the city council to act in order to avoid rioting, which had broken out in the city. However, upon Luther's return on March 6, 1522, Karlstadt was checked as being too radical. He then underwent a further transformation, set aside his doctor's degree, donned a gray peasant's coat, occupied himself with heavy farm labor, and requested that he be addressed as "Brother Andreas" or "Neighbor Andreas." For Karlstadt, the priesthood of all believers now meant complete social egalitarianism and the removal of all titles, including those of the minister. Luther thought that this program would mean the end of the educated clergy altogether and that it encouraged violence and insurrection against the princes, whom he saw as crucial to his stand against Rome. With Luther's approval, Karlstadt was banished from Saxony in 1523. Karlstadt took another parish at Orlamünde and continued to gather a large following. Luther was then forced to write against Karlstadt's innovations.

At Orlamünde, from 1523 to 1525, Karlstadt shifted his focus from justification to "regeneration," that is, the rebirth to a new life, and "sanctification," that is, the process whereby a person becomes holier. As preparation for regeneration, Karlstadt emphasized Jesus' demands for renunciation of family, life, money, and possessions. The egocentric (or sinful) self had to deny itself in order to achieve supernatural rebirth as a new self (salvation). The pattern for life, thought Karlstadt, was Jesus Christ:

> Our spiritual birth occurs with a fundamental death of our self-will. . . .
> For just as Christ arose with a renewed life and the mortal life was changed
> into an immortal one, so too the old Adam in us with all its desires and
> lusts, self-will and disobedience must die and lie in the grave and our life
> must become new in obedience to God's will.[16]

Karlstadt's favorite text was Galatians 2:20a: "I have been crucified with Christ; it is no longer I who live but Christ who lives in me. . . ."

> He who wants to be fundamentally renounced . . . must freely surrender
> his "I-ness" or "self-ness"; then this renounced self or "self-ness" becomes
> a Christ-like I . . . where one discovers and perceives that his life is not a
> human but a divine life. *And he does not live but Christ lives in him. . . .*[17]

In line with such renunciation, he stressed that though a person did not become a Christian by works, good works were a sign of "faith rich in love," and he mocked what he thought was Luther's laxness on works. Karlstadt also had a stronger focus on the Old Testament and law than Luther, and from the Old Testament he derived his demand that images be removed from the churches.

We see, then, that Karlstadt's view of Jesus Christ had essential differences from Luther's. First, as the quotations above show, the concepts of "Christ in me" (Gal 2:20a) and of the transformation of believers by Christ's death and resurrection (Rom 6:1ff.) were much more central to Karlstadt's view than to Luther's. Second—and this has been strongly emphasized by modern scholars—Karlstadt saw Christ as an example for the Christian: Christ's renunciation was to be imitated. From Luther's point of view Karlstadt had retreated to the "works-righteousness" of medieval piety and had destroyed Christian freedom; however, Karlstadt attempted to show that one does not imitate Christ *in order to* become regenerated, but only *after* being born into Christ. Yet Karlstadt did believe that renunciation prepares one for regeneration. Third, Christ had died for the Christian's sins, and through his death the Christian was forgiven. Karlstadt's view came through in his Eucharistic tracts, in which he "spiritualized" the sacraments, especially the Eucharist. Whereas for Luther, Christ was really present in the meal, Karlstadt saw the meal simply a *memorial* ("Do this in remembrance of me," 1 Cor 11:24–25), or a spiritual communion, in which the elements were only symbolic.

Karlstadt was banished from Saxony in part because he was (somewhat unfairly) associated with Thomas Müntzer (1468?–1525).[18] Whereas Karlstadt's radicalism was modified by his Lutheranism, Müntzer's views were quite radical and had a strongly political orientation.

Müntzer was a well-educated monk who had come to believe that the Word of God was present more through direct spiritual enlightenment and visionary experiences than through Scripture. For Müntzer, justification was not as important as the "imitation of Christ," even if that meant literally following in his footsteps to the cross. Müntzer himself was a powerful prophetic figure who combined his spiritual religion with a radical eschatology (expectation of the imminent return of Jesus Christ) and a revolutionary bent that led him to wish to root out the ungodly from the elect. For Müntzer, the elect were visibly identifiable by a highly emotional conversion. Bound together in a covenant, they would bring in the kingdom of justice and love with the sword; that is, they would put down priestly injustices with bloody revolution, if necessary. Since election is visible, baptism is for adults only. Müntzer's views of Christ were typified by the gospel statements "Do not think that I have come to bring peace on earth; I have not come to bring peace, but a sword" (Mt 10:34) and "But as for these enemies of mine, who did not want me to reign over them, bring them here and slay them before me" (Luke 19:27). He wrote, "Preaching of a sweet Christ to a carnal world is the worst poison. . . . He who will not have a bitter Christ will kill himself on honey."[19] Müntzer took part in the Peasant's Revolt against the German princes in 1525 and was captured and executed. Luther, who had come to oppose the anarchy and social chaos of the revolt, saw Müntzer's execution as the judgment of God.

Perhaps most characteristic of the left wing of the Reformation were the Anabaptists (Greek: *anabaptizō,* "I baptize again," referring not literally to a second baptism but to adult baptism), most of whom were originally followers of the humanist reformer Huldrich Zwingli (1484–1531).[20] Zwingli himself was a more radical thinker than Luther, permitting only what the Bible commanded rather than simply discarding what the Bible did not command. He eliminated fast days, images, statues, the crucifix, and music; his churches in Zurich were characterized by whitewashed walls, hard benches, and a simple wooden table and cup for the Lord's Supper. Like Karlstadt, Zwingli considered the Lord's Supper to be purely spiritual, and he came to Germany to debate the matter with Luther at Marburg, Hesse, in October 1529.

The Anabaptists believed that even Zwingli had not gone far enough. Some were political revolutionaries like Müntzer; some were quietist mystics; some were apocalypticists who expected the 1000-year reign of Christ predicted in Ch. 20 of the Book of Revelation to begin immediately; some were spirit-filled prophets and preachers; some were biblical literalists to the extent of organizing new crusades and establishing polygamy; some were dedicated to communal living; and some were simply humanistic scholars. All believed in the radical separation of church and state and considered the church a voluntary society of the disinherited elect (which they rapidly became!); all thought of religion as the individual's direct relation to God; and all affirmed the necessity of free choice in becoming a Christian—and hence of adult baptism. Although the most radical Anabaptists were fanatical in their beliefs, it was the more moderate groups that grew rapidly. They were strictly disciplined, highly moralistic, socially oriented, and largely pacifist. As a result of their views, they were frequently persecuted by princes, Catholics, and other Protestants.

A typical example of Anabaptist thinking came from the Dutch Anabaptist Menno Simons (1492–1559), after whom the Mennonites were named. His "imitation of Christ" view is illustrated by the following passage, reflecting the prefacing statement of the Christ hymn in Philippians 2:

> My little children, for whom I travail in birth again until Christ be formed in you, "let this mind be in you which was also in Christ Jesus" [Phil 2:5], for Christ is the image of God to whom we must conform. For whom he did foreknow, he also did predestinate to be conformed to the image of his Son. Those, therefore, who have become conformed to the image of Christ Jesus are the truly regenerate children of God, having put off the old man, and having put on the new which is created after God in true righteousness and holiness.[21]

According to Simons, those who are predestined to conform to the image of Christ become pacifists:

> How can Christians fight with the implements of war? Paul plainly said, "Let this mind be in you, which was also in Christ Jesus" [Phil 2:5]. Now Christ Jesus was minded to suffer; and in the same way all Christians must be minded. . . .
> Christ did not want to be defended with Peter's sword. How can a Christian then defend himself with it? Christ wanted to drink the cup which the Father had given Him; how then can a Christian avoid it?[22]

JESUS CHRIST IN JOHN CALVIN'S THOUGHT

As compared with the beliefs of the Saxon radicals or the Anabaptists, Calvin's views were fairly close to Luther's. Yet Calvin was a more systematic radical, and his ideas deserve to be considered because they became important for the German and Swiss Reformed churches, the

French Huguenot Protestants, the Dutch Reformed churches, Scottish and English Presbyterians, and New England Puritans.

John Calvin (1509–64) was born at Noyon, France, about sixty miles northeast of Paris, where his father had become a respected state and ecclesiastical bureaucrat.[23] Supported by the Church, his father obtained the best possible education for his five children, and Calvin excelled scholastically. At age fourteen he began to study for the priesthood at the University of Paris, where he also became an excellent Latinist. He changed his area of concentration to law in 1528 and entered the University of Orléans, pursuing Greek on the side. With the death of his father in 1531, Calvin decided to leave his legal career and return to Paris to take up classics and beginning Hebrew. There he wrote his first book, a commentary on Seneca's *Treatise on Clemency*.

It is probable that soon thereafter Calvin had what he later called his "sudden conversion," although the precise moment is unknown. What is certain is that Calvin's friend Nicholas Cop, the newly appointed rector of the university, gave an address defending Marguerite d'Angoulême, a sister of the king who supported the famous but controversial Humanist and biblical translator Jacques Lefevre. When Cop had to flee to Basel, Switzerland, on a charge of heresy, Calvin became anxious for his own life and hastily departed from Paris, leaving his possessions for the police. After a visit with Lefevre, Calvin returned to Noyon in May 1534, gave up his financial support by the church, was jailed twice (we are not sure why), and made his way to Basel to live under an assumed name. There he made friends with a number of reformers and, in 1536, published the first edition of his *Institutes of the Christian Religion*. After a trip to Italy, Calvin was persuaded by the reformer Guillaume Farel to help reform the city of Geneva. Along with Farel, Calvin was at first banished for his zealous attempts at reform, and he went to Strasbourg; in 1541, however, he was invited to return and put his beliefs into practice, which he did until his death in 1564.

Calvin is especially famous for two things: the well reasoned and well written *Institutes* and the transformation of Geneva into a Christian theocracy. In the *Institutes* Calvin reasserted the main tenets of Lutheran Protestantism, but without Luther's stress on the soul-searching quest for salvation. Rather, Calvin stressed the absolute sovereignty of God the Creator: He maintained that human effort was of no consequence for salvation whatever and that, in fact, God had predestined the elect to salvation and sinners to damnation (though his final choice of the elect is unknown). Influenced by his legal studies, Calvin also stressed the value of law and order; yet he went further than Luther in his conviction that the state has no right to force one away from obedience to God.

Such ideas were put into effect in Calvin's reorganization of Geneva as a theocracy. When asked to return in 1541, Calvin immediately had a

Portrait of John Calvin by L. Cranach
THE BETTMANN ARCHIVE.

constitution put into effect that was based on the Bible as interpreted by local pastors and enforced by the civil magistrates. Regulations of life among the citizens of Geneva included prohibitions against fighting, swearing, fornication, promiscuous bathing, card playing, dancing, and laughing and sleeping in church. They were enforced by banishment from the city and excommunication.[24]

John Calvin had never been ordained to the priesthood. He was first a lawyer and then a Humanist who, like Luther, had come to view the Bible as the sole criterion of religious truth. The *Institutes* were written, as he said, "to prepare candidates in sacred theology for the reading of the divine word," and he called the *Institutes* his "Christian philosophy," a phrase borrowed from the humanist Erasmus.[25]

The *Institutes* began with a section on the knowledge of God the creator (Book 1). If one looks at the marvelous world in which we live, thought Calvin, or the human creatures in the world, one can perceive God. This knowledge of God makes people conscious of responsibility for evil, but it is not enough knowledge for salvation. Salvation requires the additional knowledge of God the Redeemer, which comes only through the Scriptures.

Like Luther, Calvin thought that Scripture as a whole was infallibly inspired by what he called "the inner witness of the Spirit," that is, a conviction not totally demonstrable by rational argument. Though the authority of Scripture lay not in the teaching of the Church or in the words themselves, God's truth was nevertheless to be derived from the words studied grammatically, in context, and with due attention to the authors' point of view. Like Luther, then, Calvin looked back to the past, stressed the natural and obvious interpretation, and believed that Scripture should be read with the purpose of finding Christ there. Thus Calvin had a historical orientation in the tradition of Renaissance Humanism.

Calvin questioned allegorical interpretations even more than Luther did, and this led him to value the Old Testament highly. Instead of maintaining Luther's sharp law—gospel emphasis, he sought to relate the testaments by means of *typology* (the principle that people, events, and institutions in the Old Testament anticipate similar but greater people, events, and institutions in the New Testament). Thus, for example, one should not think *only* Christ when one reads about Moses, but Moses is nonetheless a *type* of his greater counterpart, Jesus. Calvin believed that the Old and New Testaments were also related by means of prophecy and fulfillment.

In Scripture, Calvin found his understanding of humanity, and that was the backdrop for his view of Jesus Christ. Scripture made it clear that everyone has inherited Original Sin, that is, that each person is fundamentally contaminated, has feelings of guilt, and is not free. Therefore God promised to his people a messiah, and in his Gospel he fulfilled that promise. Since people could not save themselves, they had to rely on a mediator who descended, became like them except for sin, and reascended to the Father. Calvin put it in orthodox terms: Christ was both divine and human.

In Book 1 of the *Institutes* Calvin concentrated on the divinity of Christ. Christ existed prior to the creation of the world and participated in it as God's "Word" or eternal Wisdom (John 1:1; Col 1:17). Calvin then looked at Old Testament prophecies that name the Messiah "God" (Isa 9:6) and noted New Testament passages where Old Testament "God language" is applied to Christ (Heb 1:10; John 20:28). Jesus' divinity is proved in his power to forgive sins (Mt 9:6), his ability to penetrate the silent thoughts and hearts of people (Mt 9:4; John 2:23), and his performance of miracles by his own power.

In Book 2 Calvin developed scriptural proof for Christ's full humanity. Directing his proofs against the Marcionite and Manichaean positions (and against Menno Simons), he wrote that Jesus was born of woman (Gal 4:4), was descended from Abraham and David (Matt 1:1; Rom 1:3), and referred constantly to his humanity by means of the title "Son of Man," which in Hebrew, Calvin argued, meant true man (he cited Ps 8:4 and Heb 2:6). Calvin drew on Philippians 2 to show that "Christ emptied himself in a nature truly human," and on Romans 5 to indicate that "as sin came in . . . through one man (Adam), and death through sin . . . so through the righteousness of one man (Christ) grace abounded."

> Here is something marvelous: the Son of God descended from heaven in such a way that, without leaving heaven, he willed to be borne in the virgin's womb, to go about the earth, and to hang upon the cross; yet he continuously filled the world even as he had done from the beginning.[26]

Book 2 also developed the theme of Christ's "threefold office" (as king, priest, and prophet). Like Luther, Calvin was aware that the two most important Old Testament figures to be anointed with oil were the priest and the king. When he came to passages that refer to priests and kings, he thought of either the provisional revelation to Israel or of "types" of Christ, or he was led further to suggest that Christ himself was the true priest and king. The New Testament takes up some of the same themes. Jesus Christ is already king during his life, for the penitent thief on the cross "adores Christ as a king." But he is king also at the resurrection and the ascension to heaven, and he will be king when he returns: Past, present, and future are included. Furthermore, in a "spiritual" sense *every* believer shares in Christ's kingship.

> Thus it is that we may patiently pass through this life with its misery, hunger, cold, contempt, reproaches, and other troubles—content with this one thing: that our King will never leave us destitute, but will provide for our needs until, our warfare ended, we are called to triumph. Such is the nature of his rule, that he shares with us all that he has received from the Father. Now he arms and equips us with his power, adorns us with his beauty and magnificence, enriches us with his wealth.[27]

Christ's kingly rule also includes present and future judgment.

Christ is also priest. Recall that in ancient times priests functioned as uniquely holy men in charge of the cult, the main purpose of which was to offer specifically prescribed sacrifices to atone for the sins of the people and ward off the anger of God. Drawing especially on Hebrews 7–10, Calvin sees Christ as the great and holy high priest whose holiness is acceptable in place of the believer's unholiness, who sacrifices himself on the cross as the victim to blot out the believer's guilt and make satisfaction for sins committed. Thus God's wrath is offset by his measureless love in the sacrifice of his holy son. (Atonement theories related to God's justice are frequently called penal theories.) Calvin did not believe that Jesus' sacrifice is repeated in the Mass (as the Church claims), but that Jesus continually defends the believer in heaven before God. That priestly role (as in Luther's view) is shared with the believer through the church.

In the first edition of his *Institutes* (1536) Calvin followed most of the early Christian, medieval, and Lutheran interpretations in speaking of a *twofold* office of Jesus Christ: kingship and priesthood. By the 1539 edition, hints of a third, prophetic office began to appear. (The prophet is also anointed with oil in the Old Testament.) In the 1559 edition, a whole chapter was devoted to the *threefold* office. Calvin referred to the Old Testament passage, "The Spirit of the Lord Jehovah is upon me, because Jehovah has anointed me to preach to the humble . . . to bring healing to the brokenhearted, to proclaim liberation of the captives . . . , to proclaim the year of the Lord's good pleasure" (Isa 61:1–2) and noted that Jesus applied this prophecy to himself in Luke 4:18–19. The prophetic office was part of his perfect wisdom, but Calvin indicated that it is also passed on to the church. As Jesus was inspired to preach, so is every preacher.

How did Calvin view the significance of Jesus Christ for the sacrament of the Lord's Supper? For Luther the words "This is my body" were mysteriously, but literally, true, and the sacrament involved the real presence of Christ; this was a matter of *faith*. Karlstadt, Zwingli, and the Anabaptists believed in the symbolic presence of Christ in the sacrament; this was a matter of the *spirit*. For Calvin there was no real presence of Christ in the bread and wine of the Supper (which were "signs"), yet there was a real "spiritual" presence. The elements were said to be outward and visible "signs" of inward and spiritual grace. One might say that Calvin attempted to stand midway between Luther and Zwingli on the presence of Christ in the sacrament, neither purely realistic nor purely symbolic. Like Luther, Calvin also accepted the baptism of infants.

The humanistically trained Calvin stressed the sovereignty of God, the uselessness of human struggle for salvation, and a typological (or prophecy–fulfillment) interpretation of the Old Testament. What is most distinctive in his view is the threefold office of Jesus Christ, as king, priest, and prophet. As king, Christ provides for his people; as priest, he makes satisfaction for sinful believers and shares his priesthood with them; as prophet, he receives the Spirit, heals, and preaches—roles that he passes on to the leaders in the church. Calvin also accepted two sacraments and interpreted them especially with respect to Christ's spiritual presence in the community.

THE CATHOLIC REFORMATION AND CHRISTIAN MYSTICISM

The reformation of the Church was not limited to the Protestant movement.[28] Prior to Luther, there had been attempts to curb papal authority by means of ecumenical councils; but such attempts had failed, and the symbol of their failure, the burning of the reform-minded John Huss in 1415, was still remembered. There had also been monastic reform in Italy and the critiques by Catholic Humanists such as Erasmus. In Spain, King Ferdinand, Queen Isabella, and Cardinal Ximines had carried out extensive reforms (better education for the clergy, including study of the Bible, combined with strict orthodoxy), which had been backed by the Spanish Inquisition. Pope Adrian VI (1522–23) also attempted reforms of the Spanish type, but they were ineffective. Early reforms within the Church were either local or unsuccessful, and no widespread, successful reform was made from Rome until the Protestants had gained a great deal of momentum. But the seeds were sown.

Already in 1517, a group of prominent clerics in Rome were calling for reform on the Spanish model, but without the political methods employed in that country. Calling themselves the Oratory of Divine Love, they were led by men such as Gian Pietro Caraffa (1476–1559). By 1536 Pope Paul III had curbed sexual license and reformed financial matters in Rome, and by 1542, under Caraffa's urging, he organized an inquisition throughout Christendom to repress heresy and to enforce administrative and moral reforms. In Italy those who leaned toward the Protestant pattern of reform or were "Erasmian" in the eyes of the papacy were silenced.

By 1545 papal power was again strong in Catholicism. In that year, with urging from the emperor, the first session of the Council of Trent met. (Its third and final session was not completed until 1563.) With much moral reform already accomplished, the Council turned first to doctrine. The Council was controlled by papal nuncios, Dominican theologians, and Italian clergy and heads of monastic orders. It leaned toward Scholastic theology and a repudiation of the Protestant (specifically, Lutheran) doctrinal views: A doctrine of justification by faith was defined to allow a larger place for works of merit; tradition was declared equal to Scripture as a source of truth, and Scripture, with the Latin Vulgate as the authoritative text, was to be interpreted only by the Church; the belief in all seven sacraments was reaffirmed, and transubstantiation was reasserted; the importance of free will in attaining salvation was supported; and a number of reforms were set into motion, including educational reform for the clergy, prohibition of secret marriages, and the establishment of the Congregation of the Index to determine which books should be forbidden for Catholics to read. When Caraffa assumed the papacy (as Pope Paul IV) in 1555, strenuously religious Catholicism had returned to Rome.

The establishment of the Inquisition and the reforms of Trent had precedents in Spain, where neither the Renaissance nor the Protestant Reformation had ever gained a foothold. It was also in Spain that Christian mysticism became strong in the sixteenth century. Since the two thinkers we have chosen as representative of Catholic Christianity in this period were both Spanish and mystical, we will first consider mysticism briefly.

In general, mysticism is the view that the possibilities for the perfected life lie *within* the self: By controlling one's mind in concentration or contemplation, or in highly disciplined physical exercise, one can detach oneself from the usual cares and concerns about the self and the world and reach an ecstatic (and sometimes visionary) state of heightened consciousness, of unity with the Ultimate.[29] The classical forms of Far Eastern mysticism are Hindu and Buddhist Yoga and Zen Buddhism, both of which foster extensive learning periods with "enlightened" teachers (the Hindu *Guru* or the Zen *Roshi*), either privately or in a monastery. In the most characteristic Western forms of mysticism, the view that ultimate reality lies in a purified inner self is usually tempered by Jewish and Christian notions that ultimate reality—God—is also an external being who created the world and his people as *distinct* from himself, who makes himself known by *unexpected* revelation, and who demands an active response from people, who are by nature *sinners*. Moreover, the means to unity with the divine is not only mental discipline and self-renunciation, but also prayer directed to this external God (though often silent prayer was encouraged). In short, Western mysticism is primarily a search for direct, immediate union with God through a self-renouncing, world-renouncing asceticism combined with the discipline of contemplation and prayer life. It is characterized by ecstatic love of the inner revelation. Though usually quietistic, it can also be combined with a more active life.

The roots of Western mystical tradition lay in the Neoplatonic idea of the "spark of the divine" in the human soul and in monastic asceticism. Mysticism emerged again among the Scholastics, some of whom were educated in the monasteries, and all of whom were familiar with Neoplatonism, especially through the writings of Augustine. The most famous representatives of Western mysticism were the German Dominicans "Meister" Eckhart (1260–1327), whose views were ultimately condemned by the Church as "pantheistic" ("God is all, all is God"), and John Tauler (1300?–61), Eckhart's disciple. In Switzerland there emerged a group of mystics called the Friends of God, who produced the widely read *Theologica Germanica;* from the Netherlands there arose the Brethren of the Common Life, the most famous of whom was Thomas à Kempis (1380?–1471), who may have been the author of the most widely circulated book of the late medieval period, *Imitation of Christ*. There were more extreme representatives of mysticism, who claimed that God could become incarnate in every believer, or that they could become sinless, or that prayer and the sacraments were superfluous because union with God was direct. However, these mystics were usually judged to be heretical; the more moderate mysticism was normally tolerated and had a profound effect not only on medieval Catholics but also on such Protestant reformers as Martin Luther and John Wesley.

As we said, mysticism was especially strong in sixteenth-century Spain, and Spanish Christianity was a vital force in the Catholic Reformation. One important figure influenced by the mystical tradition was Ignatius Loyola (1491–1556), founder of the Society of Jesus (the Jesuits), which became the leader in Catholic Christian missions. A second was Teresa de Jesus of Ávila (1515–82), a more visionary mystic, but also a reformer of the Carmelite nuns and a literary figure of some distinction. It should be noted that these two, along with Ignatius's follower Francis Xavier (1506–52) and one influenced by Teresa, Juan de la Cruz (1542–91), were all Spaniards who were later canonized as saints by the Church.

JESUS CHRIST IN THE THOUGHT
OF IGNATIUS LOYOLA

Born of a noble family in northern Spain, Ignatius became a page at the Spanish court of Ferdinand and Isabella, and then entered military service with the expectation of becoming a professional soldier.[30] In contrast to Luther, Ignatius was a man of the world and not plagued by his sins. In 1521, the year Luther stood before emperor, prince, and prelate at Worms and was spirited away to safety at Wartburg Castle, Ignatius was severely wounded defending the fortress of Pamplona against the French. He then had to face the reality that he was crippled for life. During a slow recovery at his father's castle, the worldly Ignatius read the lives of Christ, St. Dominic, and St. Francis. These readings awakened in him a desire to become a saint himself. He learned to overcome his worldliness, sin, and Satan by meditating on holy things, especially the life of Christ. When he had somewhat recovered from his wounds, he journeyed to Montserrat, where he placed his officer's sword on the altar and dedicated himself to becoming a soldier for Christ.

Ignatius then went to Manresa, where he had contact with the Dominicans. He began to work out a series of meditations which were later to become the basis for his *Spiritual Exercises,* the most influential devotional guide of the age. In 1528 he entered the University of Paris, where he developed a circle of friends and followers, mostly young Spaniards, who practiced his spiritual exercises. By 1536 this group had taken the name "Society of Jesus." They took an oath to bind themselves strictly to obedience to the pope and to make war on sin and heresy. Armed with the discipline of the *Spiritual Exercises,* the Jesuits

Saint Ignatius Loyola
BROWN BROTHERS PHOTO

rapidly spread to become the pope's official shock troops and the leaders of the Catholic Reformation in the 1540s. Ignatius himself was their absolute leader, or "general." After a long and fruitful service, Ignatius Loyola died in 1556.

The most important source for understanding Ignatius's view of Jesus is his *Spiritual Exercises*. The mystical tradition is aptly set forth in the section entitled "Purpose of the Exercises":

> The purpose of these Exercises is to help the exercitant to conquer himself, and to regulate his life so that he will not be influenced in his decisions by any inordinate attachment.[31]

The *Spiritual Exercises* is a four-week retreat guide designed to overcome the self's attachment to the values of the world and to mold the self to the pattern of Christ's life by the examination of conscience and by meditation, contemplation, prayer, and various other spiritual disciplines. By performing them, one should come to a state of indifference to fame, wealth, and love of security and develop an appreciation for lowliness and poverty, and an aversion to security. For example, one should, on arising in the morning, resolve to correct a particular sin; after lunch one should consider how many times one has fallen into the sin hour by hour, and do the same again in the evening, keeping all the while a record of one's defects. Each time the sin occurs, one should repent it. One should also undertake a general examination of conscience with regard to sins of word and deed. In all this, there is a great battle for the individual between Christ and Satan, and true peace comes with the gradual process of meditating on sin and overcoming it by *conforming with the life of Christ.*

> The *Exercises* are never simply a series of meditations, nor even a summary of the spiritual life. Their meaning emerges only in the light of their ultimate purpose: to present the exercitant with a choice which transforms his life and in which he must find in peace the will of God for him by conforming himself, as far as he possibly can in his particular situation, to the law of life laid down by Christ. Hence the very heart of the Exercises is the contemplation of the call of Christ the King, in which we are called upon to take part in the battle between Christ and Satan which is still going on in the Church today . . . the *Exercises* in their entirety are aimed ultimately towards the "glory" of God the Father, whose Divine Majesty receives greater glorification every time a person conforms himself more nearly to "Christ poor and despised."[32]

The first week of the *Exercises* is designed to purge the person of sins by a general examination of conscience, reflection on one's sins, and confession. The modern scholar Hugo Rahner suggests that it involves meditation on the "history of sin," the "psychology of sin," and the "eschatology of sin"; that is, one contemplates those who have fallen (angels, Adam and Eve, oneself), examines one's whole life in the light of the question whether sin has become a reality in it, and reflects on the "mystery of hell."[33] Ignatius stressed in this week a "colloquy" at the end of the first exercise:

> Imagine Christ our Lord before you, hanging upon the cross. Speak with Him of how, being the Creator, He then became a man, and how, possessing eternal life, He submitted to temporal death to die for our sins. Then I shall meditate upon myself and ask "What have I done for Christ? What am I now doing for Christ? What ought I do for Christ?" As I see Him in this condition, hanging upon the cross, I shall meditate on the thoughts that come to my mind.[34]

After this week of purgation from sin come the second and third weeks, which are weeks of illumination. They attempt to answer the questions above, which center in the question, What shall I do for Christ? Beginning with a contemplation about Christ, the eternal king, and his kingdom, Ignatius went on to stress the contemplation of the Incarnation, birth in Bethlehem, the "hidden years" of Christ as a boy at Nazareth, the young Jesus in the temple, and the poverty, shame, and disgrace of Christ. For Ignatius, the divine essence was hidden in Jesus' humanity; the "radiance" of the Godhead was concealed—yet revealed—in the lowliness of Christ's human nature. In the meditation on "the Call of the King," one faces not the political Redeemer, but the Suffering Servant who overcame Satan through his crucifixion. In the meditation of "the Two Standards" (that of Christ and that of Lucifer), the former brings about inner joy through what is hard and bitter, while the latter promises gratification but leads to "eternal exile." This is reinforced by reflection on the temptation stories of the gospels, which illustrate the "desire for possession" (stones into bread), the "desire for self-affirmation" (the offer on the pinnacle of the Temple), and the eternal perversion of Christ's nature by Satan (the request that Christ worship Satan). The second week also includes stress on the three modes of humility: (1) ". . . that I humble and abase myself as much as is possible for me, in order that I may obey in all things the law of God our Lord. . . ."; (2) that ". . . I am in possession of it if my state of mind is such that I neither desire nor even prefer to have riches rather than poverty, to seek honor rather than dishonor, to have a long life rather than a short one. . . ."; and (3) that ". . . I desire and choose poverty with Christ poor rather than riches, in order to be more like Christ our Lord. . . ."[35]

All of this points to the cross, the more specific center of the third week. Now the contemplation follows Christ's sufferings during the passion in order that one may be cleansed from worldly attachments and be conformed more totally to Christ. Again the divinity is mysteriously hidden in "the most sacred humanity." In this section there are also rules to be observed for eating food; for example, one should occupy one's mind with Christ at the Last Supper while eating, thus never being occupied with the food itself, always eating in moderation.

The fourth week then leads to the highest attainment, unity with Christ, God, and the Trinity by contemplation of the resurrection of Christ. During this week it is important to consider further Christ's divinity, which up to now has been hidden in his humanity, and to meditate on his return. The goal here is to attain the love of God, and finally to surrender the self completely.

For Ignatius Loyola, who stressed that religious orders are superior to the matrimonial state, spiritual exercises should include frequent hearing of the Mass, extended prayers, confession to a priest, veneration of saints, relics, and images, pilgrimages, indulgences, fasting and strict observance of holy days, vows, maintaining obedience to superiors, and study of Scholastic theology, especially that of Thomas Aquinas. He was concerned that too much talk about predestination, grace, or justification by faith—all of which in varying measure denied the ability of works or pious acts to accomplish anything for salvation—would not bring about the kind of willed spiritual discipline required for the vows of poverty, chastity, and obedience.

In short, the first week of purgation, the second and third weeks of illumination, and the fourth week of unity are to lead to the transformation of a person into greater spiritual perfection, a true soldier of Christ, who by imitating Christ's life overcomes the sinful attitude that wishes to be attached primarily to worldly affairs.

JESUS CHRIST IN THE THOUGHT
OF TERESA OF ÁVILA

Teresa de Cepeda y Ahumada was born on March 28, 1515, the third of twelve children of a Spanish noble family.[36] Teresa's mother instilled in her children exciting and heroic legends of the saints, to the point that Teresa and her brother one day attempted to run away to die martyrs' deaths fighting the Moors, and had to be fetched back. Teresa was so devout that when her mother died, in 1528, the thirteen-year-old threw herself down before a statue of the Blessed Virgin and vowed to be her daughter from that day on.

At age sixteen Teresa was sent by her virtuous and God-fearing father to a finishing school, and while there, she roomed at an Augustinian convent outside Ávila. After a severe two-year illness, during which she pondered the letters of St. Jerome, she concluded that a nun's life could not be worse than purgatory, and in 1536 she entered the Carmelite order at the Incarnation Convent of Ávila. The following year she took her final vows. Disturbed by her lack of ability at concentrated prayer, and forced to leave the cloister for medical treatment, she sought and found aid reading the *Third Spiritual Primer* of the Franciscan mystic Francisco de Osuna, who had been influenced by the German and Dutch mystics and by Sufism, the mystical form of Islam. Teresa learned from Osuna how to move from the active discipline of self-denying asceticism and concentrated prayer to the passive contemplation and quietistic prayer in which rational thought passes into the intuitive state and, finally, into union with God. Meanwhile, Teresa's physical state deteriorated so much that she was on the point of death and received the Last Rites of the Church.

In 1540, after eight months in bed, the partially paralyzed, suffering nun returned to the convent, where she gradually improved. She began to have frequent visions of a gigantic toad, which she identified with the devil. In the years following her father's death (in 1543), Teresa struggled to find a higher form of mystical contemplation, but now with the aid of more capable Jesuit confessors. In 1555, when she was forty years old, she chanced to see a painting of the wounded, suffering Christ; deeply disturbed at the cost of salvation, she underwent a "second conversion" in which she experienced the love of God, felt Christ to be a close personal friend, and discovered that she had passed beyond passive contemplation to a higher state.

Teresa had her first "ecstatic rapture" in 1558. Despite her well founded fears that the Inquisition would persecute her as an *alumbrada*

Gianlorenzo Bernini, *The Ecstasy
of Saint Theresa,* Cornaro Chapel, Rome
ANDERSON-ART REFERENCE BUREAU.

(an "illusionist"), she continued to have visions and to speak divine utterances. The most famous was her ecstatic experience in 1559 of being
pierced in the heart with a golden spear by a little Cherub:

> I saw in his hands a long golden spear and at the end of its iron head it
> seemed to have some fire. The angel seemed to put the spear through my
> heart several times so that it reached my very innermost parts. As the spear
> was removed, it seemed to me that it took my entrails out with it and left
> me burning with a great love for God. The pain was so great that it caused
> me some moaning but the sweetness caused by this great pain was also so
> superlative that there was no desire to lose it, since the soul is not satisfied
> by anything less than God. This pain is not corporeal but spiritual, although
> the body cannot help participating in some manner and even a great deal. It
> is a loving communication so sweet between the soul and God that I entreat
> His bounty to give a taste of it to whoever may think I am not telling the
> truth.[37]

In the following period, Teresa had many experiences of what she
believed were diabolical temptations, but also many visions, and she

now founded her first reformed (more austere) convent of Carmelites (San José, or St. Joseph), formally authorized in 1562. Out of it came many more convents and even her reform of her own Incarnation Convent. In 1567 the final form of her autobiographical *Life* appeared. Five years later she achieved the highest mystical state, a "spiritual marriage," a union with God completely detached from the world. In 1572 she completed her masterpiece, *The Interior Castle*, a report on her more advanced mystical experiences. She died in 1582, author of poetic works, describer of mystical experiences, and foundress of many reformed Carmelite convents. She was canonized in 1622.

For Teresa the ultimate goal was ecstatic communion with God, the means being the purified and loving soul's progress in prayer. In her *Life* she expressed the four stages of prayer in the mystic's road to God by means of the allegory of watering the garden:

> It seems to me that one may water a garden in four ways, [1] either by getting the water from the well, which means a great effort for us, [2] or by means of a chain, pump and buckets, which is done with a wheel (I myself have drawn water that way several times): this means less work than the other way, and one also gets more water; [3] or directly from a river or brook; this kind of irrigation is still much better, because the earth is better filled with water, need not be watered so often and makes much less work for the gardener, [4] or by means of much rain so that our Lord waters the garden without any effort of course and this is uncomparably much better than anything mentioned before.[38]

Teresa found meditation on the passion of Christ a special aid in the first hurdle. The gardening allegory developed the notion that God was the gardener and spiritual dryness was the cross of Christ. If the Christian would help carry Christ's cross—accept spiritual dryness—Christ would eventually help carry the Christian's cross. In doing so, the Christian should imitate the knights who desire to serve their sovereign without reward.

A similar theme is found in Teresa's masterpiece, *The Interior Castle* (1577), which is centered on the allegory of a crystal or diamond with seven mansions, each with many rooms (cp. John 14:1–6). The outer mansions are full of dangers such as snakes, vipers, and toads, but as one passes to the interior of the crystal, the mansions are more comfortable until finally, in the center, there is the mansion of the Lord. At the sixth mansion the soul finds itself bearing the slime of sin, which is a cross to bear. To remove this burden, one must meditate again and again on the humanity of Jesus Christ, for he is the way and the light that leads one on. Then, by effort one may attain raptures, including visions of Christ as flashes of light.

A third major work, *The Way of Perfection* (1562), was a testament to the nuns at Teresa's newly founded convent. Essentially, it took the form of an extended elaboration of the Lord's Prayer. In her interpretations Teresa stressed fighting for Catholic Christianity against (especially Protestant) schism and heresy; the need for poverty in the Carmelite's life style, dress, and speech; perfect love as the goal in the Carmelite community; an uncomplaining and perfect humility, imitating the great humility of the Blessed Virgin, "whose habit we wear and whose nuns we call ourselves with confession"; humility, resolution, concentration, and love as the way of progress in prayer; and, in an exposition of the seven petitions of the Lord's Prayer, the idea of the "brides of Christ" becoming one with Christ the Groom by the Bread of the Communion. Such a "bride of Christ" view was also expressed in one of Teresa's many pithy and sometimes witty poems:

> Since our Bridegroom
> Loves our captivity,
> Up, take the wedding gown
> Of cloistered activity.[39]

Teresa records in rather stereotyped patterns numerous visions, especially in the *Reports,* and it is here that her image of Jesus Christ shines most clearly. In the following vision, which in its recording is careful not to conflict with orthodox views about the ascended Christ and the Eucharist, she sees Christ repeating for her the act toward the disciple Thomas (John 20:24–29):

> A certain day (of 1571), I believe it was after Communion, our Lord resplendent, took His place beside me and began to console me . . . and told me . . . : Show me your hands, and it seemed to me He took them, put them into his side and said: Look at my wounds . . . From other things which He told me I understand that since His ascension to heaven, He never came down to earth, except in the Blessed Sacrament, to communicate with anybody.[40]

A second example is striking in its focus on the blood of Christ, a theme which also occurs in other mystics such as Catherine of Sienna:

> On Palm Sunday (1571) having just received Communion, I fell into such an ecstasy that I was not able to swallow the host and thus holding it in my mouth, it really seemed to me, when I returned somewhat to my senses, that my whole mouth had been filled with blood, and also my face and my whole body were covered with it, just as once the Lord himself shed it. It seems to me, it was hot and the sweetness which I felt was excessive and the Lord told me: Daughter, I wish that my blood may taste well to you and don't fear that my compassion may be lacking for you. . . . I want to return the invitation you extended to me the other day.[41]

Teresa of Ávila is a representative of the form of mysticism so dominant in the Spanish Christianity of the sixteenth century. Because she was reared in a pious atmosphere, it was natural that she should eventually take the cloister as her way of life. She became an ecstatic visionary, an austere reformer of the Carmelite order, and a literary figure of note. Her view of Jesus Christ is best illustrated in the visions that stress her close, personal relationship with, and love of, her Lord.

SUMMARY

The fifteenth and sixteenth centuries were the centuries of the Renaissance and the Reformation. The Renaissance period saw its own time as an advance on the previous age and came to have a higher respect for the potential of human beings than the medieval era did. There also arose an interest in Greek and Roman classics and early Christian sources, and thus in the Bible and the Jesus Christ who actually lived.

The Protestant Reformation leveled various criticisms at the institutional Church and its Christ. For Martin Luther, Jesus Christ was not the remote, divine Jesus Christ of Christian dogma and tradition, but a figure whose divinity was most apparent in the poor, weak, beggarly figure of the gospels. In Scripture—the holy book of the past—Luther found the way to salvation through God's justification of the sinner. All could receive the benefits of Jesus Christ by being priests to each other. Calvin's views were similar: He saw the Jesus Christ of Scripture especially in the roles of prophet, priest, and king, each of which was available to the believer through the church. The left wing of the Reformation went further, for it tended to stress Jesus Christ as a direct influence on the believer almost to the exclusion of the institution. Karlstadt found the Jesus Christ of self-renunciation, and he saw the imitation of Christ as virtually a preparation for regenerating the self. Müntzer combined this emphasis with emotional conversion and political revolution. For him, Jesus was a radical and the kingdom of God would even be brought in with the sword, if necessary. The Anabaptists also came into conflict with the institutional means of appropriating Jesus Christ and his benefits. Finally, the Catholic Reformation was more institutional and concentrated on the practical. Its right arm was the Jesuit order, founded by Ignatius Loyola, whose piety was in the best Catholic mystical tradition. Teresa of Ávila was also in the mystical tradition, in this case characterized by the visionary experience. Nevertheless, a new appreciation for the historical, human Jesus had been developed by Humanists and Protestants. If Jesus Christ was human, he was more "of the world." The next major transformation in thinking about Jesus Christ would be influenced by the scientific and philosophical views of the Enlightenment, which would alter the Western view of the world and of humanity's place in it.

NOTES

1. Joseph A. Mazzeo, *Rennaissance and Revolution: The Remaking of European Thought* (New York: Pantheon Books, 1965).

2. A standard work in this area is J. Huizinga, *Erasmus and the Age of the Reformation* (New York: Phaidon Press, 1952).

3. Desiderius Erasmus, *In Praise of Folly*, trans. John Wilson (Ann Arbor: University of Michigan Press, 1958), pp. 117–18. For Erasmus's overall contributions, see also Preserved Smith, *Erasmus: A Study of His Life, Ideals, and Place in History* (New York: Frederick Unger, 1923), ch. 7.

4. On the life of Martin Luther, see especially Roland H. Bainton, *Here I Stand: A Life of Martin Luther* (New York: Abingdon-Cokesbury, 1950; Mentor Books, 1955); Gordon E. Rupp, *Luther's Progress to the Diet of Worms* (London: SCM Press, 1951); Oskar Thulin, *A Life of Luther: Told in Pictures and Narrative by the Reformer and His Contemporaries*, trans. Martin O. Dietrich (Philadelphia: Fortress Press, 1966).

5. Quoted from Luther's 1545 "Preface to the Latin Writings," in *Luther's Works*, a translation of most sections of the Weimar edition, ed. Jaroslav Pelican (Philadelphia: Fortress Press, 1960), vol. 34, ed. Lewis W. Spitz, p. 337.

6. Roland H. Bainton, *The Age of the Reformation* (Princeton: D. van Nostrand Co., 1956), p. 94, translated from the Weimar edition of *Luther's Works*, vol. 4, p. 43. In general, the following discussion is highly indebted to Jan D. Kingston Siggins, *Martin Luther's Doctrine of Christ* (New Haven: Yale University Press, 1970).

7. Translated from *Luther's Works* (Weimar edition), vol. 33, p. 115, as quoted in Siggins, *Doctrine of Christ*, p. 199.

8. Translated from *Luther's Works* (Weimar edition), vol. 46, p. 598, as quoted in Siggins, *Doctrine of Christ*, p. 200.

9. Siggins, *Doctrine of Christ*, p. 86.

10. Translated from *Luther's Works* (Weimar edition), vol. 31/II, p. 432, as quoted in Siggins, *Doctrine of Christ*, p. 110.

11. Translated from *Luther's Works* (Weimar edition), vol. 20, p. 623, as quoted in Siggins, *Doctrine of Christ*, p. 131.

12. Translated from *Luther's Works* (Weimar edition), vol. 31/II, p. 339, as quoted in Siggins, *Doctrine of Christ*, p. 136.

13. From *The Babylonian Captivity of the Church*, in *Luther's Works*, vol. 36, trans. A. T. W. Steinhäuser and rev. F. C. Ahrens and A. R. Wentz. Available in Martin Luther, *Three Treaties* (Philadelphia: Muhlenberg Press, 1960), p. 190.

14. Harry Loewen, *Luther and the Radicals* (Waterloo, Ont.: Wilfred Laurier University, 1974).

15. Gordon Rupp, "Andrew Karlstadt" in *Patterns of Reformation* (Philadelphia: Fortress Press, 1969), pp. 49–156; Ronald J. Sider, *Andreas Bodenstein von Karlstadt: The Development of His Thought, 1517–1525* (Leiden: E. J. Brill, 1974).

16. Translated from Karlstadt, *Von manigfeltigkeit*, CiiiV, as quoted in Sider, *Karlstadt*, p. 223.

17. Translated from Karlstadt, *Sich Gelassen,* diii-div, as quoted in Sider, *Karlstadt,* p. 227.

18. Rupp, "Thomas Müntzer," in *Patterns,* pp. 157–356.

19. Translated from Müntzer, *Schriften und Briefe,* ed. Günter Franz with Paul Kirn, Quellen und Forschungen zur Reformationsgeschichte, no. 33 (Gütersloh: G. Mohn, 1968), p. 222, as quoted in Rupp, *Patterns,* p. 290.

20. John Dillenberger and Claude Welch, *Protestant Christianity* (New York: Charles Scribner's Sons, 1954), pp. 58–67; Bainton, *Reformation,* ch. 3; George H. Williams, *The Radical Reformation,* ch. 3; George H. Williams, *The Radical Reformation* (Philadelphia: Westminster Press, 1962); G. H. Williams, ed., *Spiritual and Anabaptist Writers,* Library of Christian Classics, vol. 25 (Philadelphia: Westminster Press, 1962); G. W. Bromiley, ed., *Zwingli and Bullinger,* Library of Christian Classics, vol. 24 (Philadelphia: Westminster Press, 1957); Jean Rilliet, *Zwingli· Third Man of the Reformation,* trans. Harold Knight (Philadelphia: Westminster Press, 1964).

21. Menno Simons, "The Blasphemy of John of Leiden" (1535), in *The Complete Writings of Menno Simons,* trans. Leonard Verduin, ed. John Christian Wenger (Scottdale, Pa.: Harald Press, 1956), p. 56.

22. Ibid., p. 45.

23. Williston Walker, *John Calvin: The Organizer of Reformed Protestantism, 1509–1564* (New York: Schocken Books, 1969) (originally published in 1906); Walker, *A History of the Christian Church,* pp. 348–57.

24. *Calvin: Theological Treatises,* trans. J. K. S. Reid, Library of Christian Classics, vol. 22 (Philadelphia: Westminster Press, 1954), pp. 76–82; also reprinted in Clyde L. Manschreck, *A History of Christianity* (Englewood Cliffs, N.J.: Prentice-Hall, 1964), pp. 93–95.

25. The primary source is John Calvin, *Institutes of the Christian Religion,* Library of Christian Classics, vols. 20 and 21, ed. John T. McNeill, trans. F. L. Battles (Philadelphia: Westminster Press, 1960); for interpretation, see Edward A. Dowey, Jr., *The Knowledge of God in Calvin's Theology* (New York: Columbia University Press, 1952); Wilhelm Neisel, *The Theology of Calvin,* trans. Harold Knight (Philadelphia: Fortress Press, 1956).

26. Calvin, *Institutes* 2.13.4 (ed. John T. McNeill), vol. 1, p. 481.

27. Calvin, *Institutes* 2.15.4 (ed. John T. McNeill), vol. 1, p. 499.

28. Walker, *History,* pp. 374–80; P. Janelle, *The Catholic Reformation* (Milwaukee: Bruce Publishing Co., 1949); Jubert Jedin, *History of the Council of Trent* (St. Louis: Herder & Herder, 1957).

29. Though there are some similarities between mystical states and drug-induced experiences, most contemporary mystics renounce the chemical artificiality and psychophysical dependence of the individual on drugs; see Huston Smith, "Do Drugs Have Religious Import?" *Journal of Philosophy* 61 (1964), pp. 517–30; on Christian mysticism, see especially Ray C. Petry, ed., *Late Medieval Mysticism,* Library of Christian Classics, vol. 13 (Philadelphia: Westminster Press, 1957); Walker, *History,* pp. 252–5.

30. Paul van Dyke, *Ignatius Loyola* (New York: Charles Scribner's Sons, 1927); Joseph de Guibert, S.J., *The Jesuits: Their Spiritual Doctrine and Practice: A Historical Study,* trans. W. J. Young, S.J., and G. E. Ganss, S.J. (Chicago: Loyola University Press, 1964); Robert W. Gleason, S.J., ed., "Introduction," in *The Spiritual Exercises of St. Ignatius,* trans. Anthony Mottola (New York: Doubleday & Co., Image Books, 1964), pp. 11–31; Hugo Rahner, *Ignatius the Theologian* (London: G. Chapman, 1968); see also the edition *The Spiritual Exercises of St. Ignatius,* trans. T. Corbishley (New York: P. J. Kennedy & Sons, 1963).

31. *Exercises* (Gleason edition), p. 46.

32. Rahner, *Ignatius the Theologian,* pp. 55–56.

33. Ibid., pp. 67ff.

34. *Exercises* (Gleason edition), p. 56.

35. Ibid., pp. 81–82.

36. Helmut A. Hatzfeld, *Santa Teresa de Ávila* (New York: Twayne Publishers, 1969), pp. 11–22. The standard edition of Teresa's works is *Obras de Santa Teresa de Jesús,* ed. R. P. Silverio, 9 vols. (Burgos: El Monte Carmelo, 1915–1924), revised as *Obras completas: Nueva revision del texto original,* 3 vols. (Madrid: Biblioteca de Autores Cristianos, 1951–1959). The quotations that follow are translated from the Madrid edition by Hatzfeld with attention to the English version of the original edition in Edgar Allison Peers, ed., *The Complete Works of Saint Teresa of Jesus,* 3 vols. (London: Sheed and Ward, 1944–1946).

37. Teresa of Ávila, *Life* 29, p. 121, quoted in Hatzfeld, *Teresa,* p. 82. This classic vision was sculpted by Bernini in the Cornaro Chapel of the Santa Maria della Vittoria church in Rome, shown first in 1651; see Robert T. Petersson, *The Art of Ecstasy: Teresa, Bernini, and Crashaw* (New York: Atheneum, 1970).

38. *Life* 11, p. 38, as quoted in Hatzfeld, *Teresa,* p. 25.

39. Poem 30, as quoted in Hatzfeld, *Teresa,* p. 95.

40. *Reports,* 15, p. 216, as quoted in Hatzfeld, *Teresa,* p. 77.

41. *Reports* 26, p. 219, quoted in Hatzfeld, *Teresa,* p. 78.

V

Jesus Christ in Rationalism, Pietism, and Romanticism

The period of the Renaissance and the Reformation produced intellectual revolutions in Western thinking in general and Christian views about Jesus Christ in particular. Even more significant, perhaps, were the intellectual revolutions that took place during the period of the Enlightenment (the seventeenth and eighteenth centuries). Progressive thinkers during the Enlightenment sought freedom from all traditional authorities, that is, from the persons, institutions, writings, and ideas that had held Western civilization together for centuries: the kings and popes, the Holy Scriptures, the creeds, and the Church. They saw reason as the attempt of the human mind to understand the universe and the self *apart* from these authorities. Reason had had a central place in Scholasticism, but it was thought not to conflict with revelation. The Protestants had been more suspicious of reason than the Scholastics. For the Enlightenment, reason was supreme whether it was in accord with revelation or not. James Hastings Nichols described this period in terms of "the secularization of the West":

> The opening of our period of "modern" church history is defined by the end of the medieval and Reformation pattern of a church-dominated state and society. It is easier to begin with the negative definition of modern culture as a culture emancipated from Christian control and integration. In the seventeenth century, for the first time in a thousand years in Western history,

a deliberate attempt was made on a grand scale to organize a religiously neutral civilization—a political, economic, ethical, and intellectual structure independent of Christianity. This great transformation was effected in the seventeenth and eighteenth centuries by the movement sometimes described as the *Enlightenment*. And although the positive dogmas of the Enlightenment were themselves to undergo radical criticism and often rejection in the nineteenth and twentieth centuries, nevertheless by and large the negative side of the work of the Enlightenment endured.[1]

In this chapter we will show how Enlightenment thought challenged a number of basic Christian convictions, including many about Jesus Christ. One outcome was the rationalists' portrait, especially in Germany, of a nonmiraculous, human Jesus. Then we will describe the Protestant Pietist alternative to rationalism, especially as worked out by John Wesley in his view of Jesus Christ. Finally, we will discuss the romantic reaction to rationalism, concluding with the German Protestant Friedrich Schleiermacher.

THE ENLIGHTENMENT CHALLENGE TO TRADITIONAL CHRISTIAN THOUGHT

Most Western Christians in the seventeenth century would probably have made the following claims:

1. Christianity is a revealed religion; that is, the full Christian truth goes beyond what can be discovered by means of human reason alone. (For Roman Catholics, reason had its rightful place and did not conflict with revelation; Protestants allowed for conflict, were more suspicious of reason, and trusted revelation over reason.)
2. Revelation is based on Scripture and interpreted in the church's teaching as expressed in the creeds of the Ecumenical Councils. (In the West, Catholics preferred to stress that tradition was the source of the authoritative interpretation of Scripture; Protestants attempted to test tradition by the norm of Scripture.)
3. Scripture indicates, and the church's teaching defines, the belief that there is a Trinity, one God in three persons—Father, Son, and Holy Spirit.
4. God is the creator who, according to the first chapter in Genesis, created the world out of nothing. The creator is not identical with creation. Yet both God and his created world are good.

5. Adam, the first man, was created good with an immortal soul. But Adam sinned and therefore died, and such sin and death have been inherited by the human race (as Original Sin). (Catholic tradition continued to stress that Mary, the mother of Jesus, was conceived without Original Sin; this belief in the *Immaculate Conception* of Mary became official doctrine in 1854.)

6. The Mother of Jesus Christ was a virgin who conceived him miraculously by the Holy Spirit. (Especially in Catholic tradition, Mary's virginity was considered "perpetual"; that is, Jesus had no brothers or sisters. Mary was also to be called "the Mother of God," *Theotokos*.)

7. Jesus Christ is truly God and truly man, two distinct natures in one person, the Mediator between God and humanity, the one who atoned for humanity's sins as the gift of God's grace.

8. Not only was Jesus born miraculously, but his divinity can be proved by his miracles, by his literal fulfillment of prophecy, and by the miracle of his resurrection from the dead and ascension to heaven.

9. Jesus Christ will come again, will be judge of the living and the dead, and will establish his eternal kingdom.

10. Finally, the Bible is a book of revelation to be trusted, including its view that Moses wrote the first five books (the Pentateuch) and that Matthew, Mark, Luke, and John wrote the gospels. (The Protestant stress on the authority of Scripture made this belief extremely central to its position, not only in its debates with Catholics, but also in its confrontation with the emergent secular world.)

In time, every one of these convictions was challenged by scientific, philosophical, or political thinkers of the seventeenth and eighteenth centuries.

Medieval views of the created universe were based on the biblical account of the creation, combined with Aristotelian physics and the astronomical theories of Claudius Ptolemy of Alexandria (127–151 C.E.), who postulated that the heavenly bodies revolved around a stationary earth, the center of the cosmos, at uniform speeds and in complex orbits. However, this *geocentric* theory of the universe, though supported by biblical revelation, gave way before a series of astronomical discoveries by the Polish priest Nicolaus Copernicus (1473–1543), the German Johannes Kepler (1571–1639), the Italian Galileo Galilei (1564–1642), and the British Sir Isaac Newton (1642–1727). It was replaced by the *heliocentric* theory, according to which the planets revolved around a moving sun. By the time of the Enlightenment, the universe was seen as a great machine run by *natural laws,* without divine interference. It was discovered through the exploration and experiments of the human mind, often despite the resistance of the Church. In fact, Galileo's defense of the Copernican system led to his being compelled to recant before a Church Inquisition; he was imprisoned for a term, but later he returned to his theories.[2]

Now that reason held sway in science, it was inevitable that reason would make its appearance in philosophy.[3] The new philosophies were to a large extent the application of "laws" to the universe and/or the mind. Each in its own way used some form of science as the model for reflection, and each affirmed human reason, not divine revelation, as the basis for all knowledge. The central problem was this: What, if any, is the relation of human reason to the laws of the universe, that is, of mind to matter: The philosophical *rationalists*, best represented by René Descartes (1596–1650), used abstract mathematics as a model. Descartes believed there were clear and distinct universal ideas (which he referred to as a priori ideas) in the mind: the doubting/thinking self ("I think, therefore I am"), cause and effect, perfection, God, human free will, and the perfection of geometric figures. He sought to find their connection to what he regarded as distorted knowledge of matter obtained through the five senses. However, his major legacy to Western thinking was the contrast of inner and outer worlds, the thinking "subject" (mind) and the material "object" (matter). This is the famous *Cartesian dualism*.

Whereas rationalism thought that the only true knowledge was found in abstract ideas of the thinking mind, *empiricism* began with matter as known through the senses (experience) and moved only gradually to the mind and its ideas. This was the experimental or inductive method, launched by the Englishman Francis Bacon (1561–1626). Empiricism was further developed by Thomas Hobbes (1588–1679), who came to think of the mind as a machine that operated according to laws, like the universe; he regarded ideas as simply "motions" in the brain and the heart. According to Hobbes there is only matter; "spirit" does not exist. This *mechanistic materialism* eventually led Hobbes to militant atheism. Other famous British empiricists were John Locke (1632–1704), George Berkeley (1685–1753), and David Hume (1711–76). For Locke, the mind is originally a "piece of blank paper" (*tabula rasa*), to which the senses relay simple ideas about external matter and in which there is built up the act of reflection. There is a connection, said Locke, between certain "primary" qualities of matter and the ideas in the mind. Berkeley challenged Locke by saying that even the existence of the external world could not be proved by logic alone, but that ideas do have reference to a Reality beyond the mind that continually thinks all ideas—a Spirit, or God. However, David Hume was led further, to *skepticism*, the position that external reality *may* exist but cannot be *proved* to exist and that no "God hypothesis" may be brought in to make it exist. In Hume the medieval concern for thinking about God, humanity, and the universe *all together* (classical metaphysics) is absent; it is replaced by a radically empiricist concern with the immediate impressions and ideas of human beings.

In France, Voltaire (1694–1778) and the French Encyclopedists emerged, notably Denis Diderot (1713–84). Voltaire was a friend of monarchs, an archenemy of the institutional churches, and a novelist, poet, amateur scientist, historian, and philosopher. A literary genius, he demoralized with a turn of the phrase what he could not demolish with logic. Diderot was the editor of the *Encyclopedia or Reasoned Dictionary of Sciences,* the first volume of which appeared in 1751, in cooperation with Voltaire and Jean Jacques Rousseau. The Introduction to the *Encyclopedia,* by Jean le Rond D'Alembert, stressed that philosophy based on reason had replaced medieval theology and revelation. Diderot himself was a mechanistic materialist like Hobbes; he held that the universe is matter, that it runs by physical, not mental or spiritual laws, that the body is a machine, that thought is simply the mechanism of the brain, and that there is no ultimate design and no ultimate Designer.

In philosophy, the Enlightenment had moved from Cartesian rationalism to empiricism, through skepticism, and finally to materialism, none of which was based on the Bible and revelation. In politics,[4] the theory of the "divine right of kings" no longer held sway; instead, political theorists held that laws were contracts made among *reasonable men,* either to avoid destroying each other (as in Hobbes's *Leviathan* [1651]) or to preserve freedom for the common good (as in Locke's *Two Treatises on Civil Government* [1690]) or to express the collective will which reflects the common interest (Rousseau's *Social Contract* [1762]). Such thinking would be translated into dramatic political action in the American Revolution (1776) and the French Revolution (1793). As stated in the American Declaration of Independence, written largely by Thomas Jefferson, such action was based on the "Laws of Nature," "Nature's God," and "self-evident" truths: a combination of ideas influenced by the new thinking.

Such a combination was characteristic of the "new religion." Between more traditional forms of Christian orthodoxy and Pietism on the one hand and growing numbers of anti-Christian atheists on the other stood a group of thinkers who attempted to find a compromise between religion and the new thought.[5] Some of these were known as *deists* (literally, "God-ists"), and to them true religion was reasonable and universal. Though early English and Irish deists such as John Locke himself (*The Reasonableness of Christianity* [1695]) and John Toland (*Christianity Not Mysterious* [1695]) allowed for revelation, one of the earliest, Lord Herbert of Cherbury (1583–1648), summarized his views without resorting to revelation. The "Bible" of deism, Matthew Tindal's

Christianity as Old as the Creation (1730), claimed that anything known by revelation could be known by reason alone.

Though there were philosophical and theological reactions against deism—Hume was, as usual, skeptical, while theologians such as William Law and Joseph Butler tried to argue the limits of reason—the "new religion" spread to thinkers such as Voltaire on the continent and Benjamin Franklin, Thomas Jefferson, and Thomas Paine in the American colonies. Benjamin Franklin, for example, indicated that he had already begun to doubt his Calvinistic heritage at age fifteen; in the following statement, he offered a good summary of the major beliefs of many deists:

> I had been religiously educated as a Presbyterian; and though some of the dogmas of that persuasion, such as the eternal decrees of God, election, reprobation, etc., appeared to me unintelligible, others doubtful, and I early absented myself from the public assemblies of the sect, Sunday being my studying day, I never was without religious principles. I never doubted, for instance, the existence of the Deity; that He made the world, and governed it by his Providence; that the most acceptable service of God was the doing good to man; that our souls are immortal; and that all crime will be punished, and virtue rewarded either here or hereafter.[6]

Franklin was then led to develop his own set of "virtues" as a means of arriving at moral perfection and to work at each virtue one week at a time by marking black spots on a chart to indicate his moral shortcomings. He thought that his own creed contained "the essentials of every known religion . . . being free of everything that might shock the professors of any religion."[7]

Thomas Paine went further. He believed that it is *only* by the exercise of reason that one can discover God, and he disavowed all appeals to revelation. God is the "final cause," known only through the creation.

> It is not Moses and the prophets, nor Jesus Christ, nor his apostles, that have done it. The Almighty is the great mechanic of the creation; the first philosopher and original teacher of all science.[8]

> Great objects inspire great thoughts; great magnificence excites great gratitude; but the groveling tales and doctrines of the Bible and the Testament are fit only to excite contempt.[9]

As for religious institutions:

> I do not believe in the creed professed by the Jewish church, by the Roman church, by the Greek church, by the Turkish church, by the Protestant church, nor by any church that I know of. My own mind is my own church.
>
> All national institutions of churches, whether Jewish, Christian, or Turkish, appear to me no other than human inventions, set up to terrify and enslave mankind, and monopolize power and profit.[10]

Such statements show clearly that to the "new religion," orthodoxy with its creeds, dogmas, institutions, Virgin, and Christ could only obscure the universal morality known to all by human reason. The human Jesus' teaching *might* be one expression of that morality, but it was a morality that all religions had in common, and to many Deists its association with one person missed the point.

NEW VIEWS OF HISTORY AND THE RISE OF BIBLICAL CRITICISM

With the notable exceptions of Giovanni Battista Vico, Edward Gibbon, and Rousseau, most of the great minds of the Enlightenment did not think there was much to be learned from the historical past.[11] This followed naturally from their belief that humanity had not really advanced much in the past. The peoples of the past, like the aboriginal peoples of the New World and other recently "discovered" areas, had created fantastic myths rather than be guided by reason. Nonetheless, though historical knowledge was inferior to rationalistic or empirical knowledge, it *was* a type of knowledge. The historical documents might be untrustworthy, either by accident or design, but perhaps there was some actual history behind the legends, stories, and myths. The skeptical attitude toward ancient documents, given its initial impulse by Renaissance humanists, became stronger. But with it came one of the ingredients of the modern historical consciousness: the critical evaluation of sources. Gradually, but persistently, this critical scrutiny was turned on the major source for understanding Jesus Christ, the Bible.

Some Enlightenment thinkers, such as Descartes, simply dismissed history as useless. They regarded historians as people who had romantic fantasies about the past and were no longer in touch with reality.[12] Voltaire wrote two excellent historical works, *The Age of Louis XIV* (1752) and *Essay on the Manners and Mind of Nations* (1756), in which he rebelled against the Christian belief that history was guided by *God's providence* and substituted for it a secular and naturalistic view of history guided by *human progress*. These writings express the dominant Enlightenment attitude toward history: that the past is inferior to the present because the past is subject to all manner of irrationality and superstition. Voltaire's motto was *écrasez l'infâme* ("crush the infamy," that is, superstition).

Contemporary primitive peoples were regarded in similar ways and frequently were compared to the ancients. Pierre Bayle, in his *Historical and Critical Dictionary* (1697), often compared what he thought were the barbaric myths of primitives with the equally barbaric myths of Graeco-Roman antiquity and Christian Europe. He saw them all as expressions of immature people who deified their kings—even their kings' immoralities. Moreover, he claimed, many contemporary Christians were more interested in living with their superstitious myths and performing their long-established rites than in correcting the impurity of their own lives.[13] In his *Discourse on the Origin of Fable* (1724), Bernard le Bovier Fontenelle compared the ancient Greeks, the American Indians, simple peasants, and children, suggesting that all peoples passed through stages of progressively more rational belief. In his *Digression into the Ancients and Moderns* (1715), he revived Augustine's theory that the history of humanity was like the history of individual human beings, from childhood to maturity: Myth was characteristic of childlike minds, whereas abstract reasoning was characteristic of adult minds. Hume put forth a similar view in his *The Natural History of Religion* (1757), claiming that religion and myth were born in primitive passion and feeling.[14]

The empiricist philosophical tradition produced other views of ancient religion. The Frenchman Charles de Brosses (1709–77) attempted to subsume what he regarded as the primitive's childish, mad, mentally ill, and fear-ridden emotionalism under the idea of *fetishism*, the belief that all objects, animate or inanimate (from rocks, springs, rivers, groves, weapons, and trees to birds and beasts) contained special divine powers. Nicolas-Antoine Boulanger attemped to trace all religious superstition to the fears accompanied by the universal flood. Antoine Court de Gebelin moved closer to the deist position by suggesting that all ancient myths were allegories of the great cosmic order. One of the most extreme claims was Charles Dupuis's thesis that the eroticism of much primitive religion went back to the worship of the Phallus.[15]

Perhaps the strongest attack on the "primitive" came from the Baron d'Holbach (1723–89), who combined many of the standard Enlightenment views into one great hodgepodge theory. To Holbach, religion was a highly contagious disease, born of fear and nurtured by tyrants and priests who exploited the sick imaginations of the masses; Christianity was certainly no exception.

> Tell several painters to represent a chimera. Each one of them having a different idea will paint it differently. All the theologians in the world, do they paint for us anything but one great chimera?[16]

> These chimeras adopted without examination by the fathers were transmitted with variations to their civilized children who often reason no better than their fathers did.[17]

In the matter of religion people are generally much like infants.[18] Holbach even anticipated Sigmund Freud in his view that painful experiences and sensations in childhood, brought about by unsatisfied needs, gave rise to anxiousness in primitive minds. Reinforced by plague, famine, and disease, this anxiousness (or fear, since this general explanation is frequently referred to as the "fear theory" of the origin of religion) led to the creation of gods for protection. Such gods were simply imitations of human beings. Thus Holbach explained the myths about the gods as "projections" of human needs.

Thomas Paine's *The Age of Reason* applied such theories to belief in Jesus Christ's divinity:

> It is, however, not difficult to account for the credit that was given to the story of Jesus Christ being the son of God. He was born when the heathen mythology had still some fashion and repute in the world, and that mythology had prepared the people for the belief of such a story. Almost all the extraordinary men that lived under the heathen mythology were reputed to be the sons of some of their gods. It was not a new thing, at that time, to believe a man to have been celestially begotten; the intercourse of gods with women was then a matter of familiar opinion. Their Jupiter, according to their accounts, had cohabited with hundreds; the story therefore had nothing in it either new, wonderful or obscene; it was conformable to the opinions that then prevailed among the people called Gentiles, or Mythologists, and it was those people only that believed it. The Jews, who had kept strictly to the belief in one God, and no more, and who had always rejected the heathen mythology, never credited the story.[19]

From similar mythologies sprang the Trinity, the veneration of Mary, and the canonization of saints, until the "gods" were as numerous as before.

> The Christian theory is little else than the idolatry of the ancient Mythologists, accommodated to the purposes of power revenue; and it yet remains to reason and philosophy to abolish the amphibious fraud.[20]

How did such attitudes affect thinkers' regard for the Bible?[21] Primarily, thinkers came to see the Bible not simply as a holy book of inspiration for Christians, but as a book written by human beings from ancient times and therefore subject to the same critical scrutiny as all other ancient books. It followed that one should not automatically trust the reports of other people when they speak about revelation. Hobbes had already pinpointed this issue in his *Leviathan:*

> When God speaketh to man, it must be either immediately; or by mediation of another man, to whom he had formerly spoken by himself immediately. How God speaketh to a man immediately, may be understood by those well enough, to whom he hath so spoken; but how the same should be understood by another, is hard, if not impossible to know. For if a man pretend to me, that God hath spoken to him supernaturally, and immediately, and I make doubt of it, I cannot easily perceive what argument he can produce, to oblige me to believe it. . . . For to say that God hath spoken to him in the Holy Scripture, is not to say God hath spoken to him immediately, but by mediation of the Prophets, or of the Apostles, or of the Church, in such manner as he speaks to all other Christian men. . . . How then can he, to whom God hath never revealed his Will immediately (saving by the way of natural reason) know when he is to obey, or not to obey his Word, delivered by him, that says he is a Prophet?[22]

Hobbes's skepticism about mediated revelation led him to question one of the main tenets of orthodoxy, the belief that Moses wrote the Pentateuch. In this he was followed by Baruch Spinoza (1632–77), who analyzed the Pentateuch in great detail in his *Tractatus Theologico-Politicus* (1670).

Biblical criticism of the New Testament first gained impetus from those who sought to recover the original wording from the mass of manuscripts that were becoming available. A growing recognition that the original wording might not be absolutely attainable began to undercut the notion of an authority for inspired words; for some, this even weakened the authority of the Bible itself. How could one be sure that the words were inspired if there was no absolute assurance what those words were?

Once the New Testament was considered to be a human book subject to error, it was possible to advance in a number of different directions. Christian critics such as J. S. Semler (1725–88) and J. D. Michaelis (1717–91) tried to separate the Word of God from the words of Scripture (Luther's distinction) so that the former could be set aside when analyzing the latter. As a result, historical criticism of the Bible was beginning to occur without the supervision of the churches. Individual books were studied separately so that the traditional Protestant view of the *unity* of the inspiration of the Bible—that one book could be used to interpret another ("Scripture interprets Scripture")—began to break down.

But of all the fundamental beliefs of traditional Christianity, the two that were most devastated by the new scientific, philosophical, and critical perspective were the beliefs in Jesus' miracles and in his fulfillment of prophecy. In 1777 Gotthold Lessing wrote *On the Proof of the Spirit and of Power:*

> Fulfilled prophecies, which I myself experience, are one thing; fulfilled prophecies, of which I know only from history that others say they have experienced them, are another. Miracles, which I see with my own eyes, and which I have the opportunity to verify for myself, are one thing; miracles, of which I know only from history that others say they have seen them and verified them, are another.[23]

Thomas Paine referred to this mediated type of knowledge as "hearsay" knowledge, or "hearsay" revelation—which, of course, was to be judged by reason. Lessing focused on the central issue of miracles:

> . . . I live in the Eighteenth Century, in which miracles no longer happen. If I even now hesitate to believe anything on the proof of the spirit and of power [to perform miracles], which I can believe on other arguments more appropriate to my age, what is the problem?
> The problem is that this proof of the spirit and of power no longer has any spirit of power, but has sunk to the level of *human testimonies* of spirit and power.[24]

Lessing's famous philosophical axiom to express this problem is: "Accidental truths of history can never become the proof of necessary truths of reason." Thus it is impossible to jump from historical truths to truths of the heart or to moral and metaphysical truths. History cannot prove that Jesus is the divine Son of God. For Lessing, all such historical arguments fail; there is an "ugly, broad ditch" between historical information and the necessary truths of reason. Since miracles and prophecy could not be proved, they were not convincing. Only Jesus' simple teaching could have such spirit and power.

It is apparent that the Enlightenment was not sympathetic to accepting the past on its own terms, and this judgment included the mythmaking of ancient peoples—Greeks, Romans, *and* Christians. The new scientific view of the universe as a unified set of causes and effects could not tolerate noncausal views of the world. In the earlier stages of history, it was held, the capacity for a reasoned view of the world had not yet been fully developed. Perception of the true nature of reality was distorted. This "primitive" mentality viewed the world primarily in terms of feeling, emotion, and imagination; its forms of expression were not deduction or induction, but poetry, art, and especially myth. Enlightenment thought saw primitive myth within the context of a developmental view of history, analogous to the growth from childhood (or infancy) to adulthood (or maturity): Children make myths; adults reason.

These ideas brought almost every belief of orthodox Christianity under attack. The deists believed that reason was superior to revelation, or at least that revelation must not contradict reason; that Scripture and tradition had to be viewed critically because they claimed to be based on revelation; that the creation story in Genesis was an unscientific myth and thus untrue; that Moses did not write the Pentateuch; that sin was not so much a problem of Adam as of universal human morality; that both sin and morality were discoverable on the basis of human reason; that the virginity of Mary and the divinity of Christ were (as Paine suggested) adaptations to pagan myths; that the belief in the early return of Jesus was obviously in error; and that miracles and fulfillment of prophecy were not provable and therefore not evidence for the divinity of Christ.

RATIONALIST VIEWS OF CHRIST[25]

The typical rationalist approach to Jesus Christ has already been exemplified by Thomas Paine's deism: The supernatural elements, especially the miracles, were seen as common superstitious beliefs of ancient peoples, and Christianity had simply borrowed such beliefs as the virgin birth and the divinity of Christ. Basically, the rationalists were impressed by parts of Jesus' moral teaching. Indeed, Thomas Jefferson wrote *The Life and Morals of Jesus* in order to "save" the simple teaching of Jesus from the "religion of the priests." But if Jesus was a simple teacher of morals, what of the miracle stories? This was the heart of the matter. Miracles were contrary to the "new science," for, it was thought, God does not stop the Great Machine of the Universe.

The rationalists explained orthodox Christian acceptance of miracles by means of two basic theses, which may be further subdivided:

1. Some *conscious deception* is involved:
   a. Founders of religions lied about their feats.
   b. Followers lied about their founders, whether the founders lied or not. (Variation: "priests" deceived the masses.)
2. *Unconscious misperception* by prerational mentalities is involved:
   a. Unusual or misperceived events are given miraculous explanations by eyewitnesses who also write the literature.
   b. Events are gradually, over a period of time, embellished with the miraculous.

The first three explanations deal only with the texts in which eyewitness material is apparently involved; either the eyewitnesses were deceived by founders or followers (or priests), or they simply did not understand the natural order of the universe and its laws. In examining the thought of the German critics Hermann Reimarus and Heinrich Paulus, we will see that the theories of Reimarus combined the "disciple deception" theory (1b) with the theories of gradual miraculous embellishment (2b) and priestly ecclesiastical deception (1b), whereas Paulus used the misperception theory (2a) in combination with the theory of gradual miraculous embellishment (2b).

Knowledge of Hermann Reimarus's life is somewhat obscure, partly because his name was first made famous by David Strauss in the nineteenth century, long after Reimarus's death in 1768.[26] He was born in 1694 in Hamburg. After his education, he became a Rector in Wismar for five years and then, in 1728, a teacher of Oriental languages at the advanced high school (*Gymnasium*) in Hamburg. In 1754 he published a number of deistic works, among them *Die vornehmsten Wahrheiten der natürlichen Religion (The Most Distinctive Truths of Natural Religion)*. All of these works asserted the truth of rational religion against the claims of the churches. His greatest work, *Apologie oder Schutzschrift für die vernünftigen Verehrer Gottes (Apology or Defense in Behalf of the Rational Worshippers of God)*, circulated among friends during his lifetime, and was published in part (seven fragments) by Lessing as *Fragmente eines Ungenannten (Fragments by an Unknown Author)* in 1774–78. (Lessing did not agree with Reimarus, but he saw his writings as fuel for the rationalist fire and was himself criticized for publishing them.)

One of the seven fragments of Reimarus published by Lessing was called "The Aim of Jesus and His Disciples."[27] Reimarus considered it necessary to reconstruct Jesus' life and teaching in the Framework of his Jewish background. His first step was to deny that such orthodox Christian dogmas as the Divine Sonship of Christ and the Trinity could be documented in Jesus' words. For the Jews such ideas as sonship and spirit had no such metaphysical connotations; therefore, he claimed, the Son and Spirit, in the sense of the second and third persons of the Trinity, are not directly derived from Scripture. Having dispensed with such metaphysical conceptions, Reimarus also followed John Locke in separating the "apostles" (presumably, Peter, James, and especially Paul) from the four Evangelists because the apostles, too, developed mysteries and articles of faith *that were not Jewish*. The proper records for learning about Jesus, then, were the four Evangelists. But even they did not present Jesus as he actually lived and taught, as a *Jew among Jews*. This is because the Evangelists did not write during Jesus' lifetime, but only later, when their doctrines had changed. Moreover, Reimarus believed, later copyists added some doctrinal statements, such as the command to baptize in the name of the Father, the Son, and the Holy Spirit in Matthew 28:16ff.

Reimarus did not consider Jesus' teaching essentially new to the Jews. Jesus proclaimed that they should repent, for the kingdom of heaven was at hand, and by "the kingdom of heaven" he meant what all Jews meant: the kingdom of the Messiah, who was to be "a great temporal king" and who "would establish a powerful kingdom in Jerusalem, whereby he would free them of all servitude and make them masters over other peoples."[28] Thus Jesus' purpose was to establish the *political* kingdom of God, to deliver the Jews from *political* oppression. So much for the aims of Jesus.

What happened when all of this did not take place? The followers of Jesus were disappointed; they had not expected his death. Reimarus thought it entirely possible that they then stole Jesus' body from the tomb and, as the many contradictions in the resurrection stories seemed to indicate, invented the resurrection story, waiting about fifty days so that there could be no examination of the body. Seizing then upon the minority view of Jews that the Messiah would appear first in suffering and misery and a second time in power and glory, they further invented the second coming of Jesus. The new system of belief was this:

> . . . that Christ or the Messiah was bound to die in order to obtain forgiveness for mankind, and consequently to achieve his own glory; that upon the strength of this he arose alive from death out of his tomb upon the third day as he had prophesied, and ascended into heaven, from whence he would soon return in the clouds of heaven with great power and glory to judge the

believers and the unbelievers, the good and the bad, and that then the kingdom of glory would commence.[29]

Thus Reimarus thought the earliest disciples had replaced the historical Jesus with an unbelievable myth. What could have been their motive? They had learned that the wandering life of an apostle would keep them (that is, they would have abundant friends, food, and clothing), and they would participate in the power and glory of Jesus as well! Eventually, the deception of the early disciples would be transferred to the priests and the institutional church.

What then of the miracles? Reimarus realized that if his thesis was correct, belief in miracles could in no way save the orthodox faith. The miracles found in Moses' stories are the product of a "most childish" writer, and "to believe them one would have to abandon all the maxims of a healthy mind."[30] As to the New Testament miracles, he thought that most of them are probably inventions. Even if Jesus did heal a few blind and sick, that does not prove he was a God.

Reimarus's evaluation of prophecy was similar: If one applies the canons of strict and accurate prediction or asks whether the prophecy was clearly formulated after the claim of its fulfillment, one will conclude that the prophecy is doubtful. In fact, he found the Old Testament prophecies "worthless and false."[31] Jesus' prophecies of his own suffering, death, and resurrection fell under the same judgment: They are obvious attempts to superimpose the new doctrine of the apostles on Jesus' life after the fact of its invention.

The second major rationalist whose views of Jesus we will consider is Heinrich Eberhard Gottlob Paulus (1761–1851).[32] Paulus was born in Leonberg, Germany, where his father was a deacon. Paulus's father, though at times rationalistic in his views, became absorbed with spiritualism and made his wife promise as she was dying that if it were possible she would appear to him in bodily form. This, he hoped, would help him understand the doctrine of immortality. When he thought he saw her sit up after she died, he became convinced that he was able to communicate with the spirit world—so much so that his superiors removed him from office in 1771. Young Heinrich, in order to keep peace with his father's beliefs, pretended that he, too, was in communication with the spirit of his mother.

It was perhaps natural that Paulus took the opposite course. After attending the Theological Institute at Tübingen, where he absorbed the ideas of the more rationalistic biblical critics Semler and Michaelis, he eventually became an assistant pastor and was appointed to the University of Jena as a professor of oriental languages in 1789. In 1793 he became professor of theology. Between 1800 and 1802 he produced a commentary on the synoptic gospels in which he gave a rationalistic interpretation of the miracles; as a result, ecclesiastical pressure was brought to bear to have him removed. The attempt was unsuccessful, but only because he was protected by the important biblical scholar Johann Gottfried Herder (see pages 158–59), who was then president of the ecclesiastical group that attempted his removal. In this period Paulus and his wife were also close friends with a number of romantic thinkers, including Immanuel von Fichte (whom he unsuccessfully defended against a charge of atheism), Goethe, and Schiller. Nevertheless, his philosophical position was more sedate, and in 1803 he produced a study of the life and writings of Spinoza.

Paulus accepted the position of professor of theology at the University of Würzburg in 1803, but his participation in the abortive attempt to establish a new curriculum for Catholic students led to his resignation. Thereafter he worked four years attempting to reorganize the school system in the southern German province of Bavaria. In 1811 he went to the University of Heidelberg to accept a post as professor of theology, a position he held until his retirement. Despite his earlier friendship with certain romantics, Paulus was fearful of mysticism and attacked it wherever he found it, especially in the writings of Friedrich Schelling, whose resignation he succeeded in forcing at the University of Berlin. He was also indiscreet in his political views, espousing a strong anti-Semitism. At Heidelberg he had a long and productive life. He was known especially for his biblical commentaries and his rationalistic *Life of Jesus as the Basis of a Purely Historical Account of Early Christianity* (1828).

Paulus's *The Life of Jesus* is a fitting conclusion to the age of rationalism. He believed that spiritual truths could be neither proved nor disproved by unexplained interruptions of the natural order and that the supreme power of God stood behind everything which happened in nature. Nonetheless, he did not believe that the events related in the New Testament were actual miracles. Miracles for Paulus were explanations by simple peoples of certain puzzling but *natural* events. If one understood the laws of nature, one could discern the natural event behind the miracle.

The *healing miracles* are not difficult to explain in this way. Paulus hypothesizes that Jesus was knowledgeable about medicines, sedatives, and the effect of spiritual power on the central nervous system and that he was aware of the importance of special diet and care after a healing (Mark 9:29: "this kind [of demon] goes out only by prayer [and fasting]"). The *nature miracles* are more difficult to explain, but Paulus makes the attempt. To explain the accounts of Jesus' walking on water, Paulus proposes a kind of sandbar theory: Jesus was walking along the shore and in the mist he was taken for a ghost by the excited disciples. The feeding of the five thousand is explained with the theory that the rich shared their lunches with the poor. The transfiguration of Jesus on the mountain can best be explained by the hypothesis that it was early in the morning, the disciples were not yet fully awake, and they saw

Jesus illuminated by the rising sun. Paulus calls the stories about risings of the dead "deliverances from premature burial," for they were not really dead but only in a coma. A similar theory is applied to Jesus' resurrection: Jesus was only in a deathlike trance; the lance thrust, a mere surface wound, had the same effect as the ancient practice of bleeding, which was thought to have healing value; the cool grave and aromatic spices continued the process of resuscitation; the storm and earthquake rolled away the stone and aroused Jesus to full consciousness; Jesus then stripped away his own clothes and put on the gardener's clothes, and was mistaken for the gardener; though sometimes weak from suffering, he then ate with his disciples and for a period of about forty days appeared in both Galilee and Jerusalem; finally, on the Mount of Olives, as he was speaking to the disciples for the last time (again in the early morning!), a cloud came between them and he disappeared, never to return again, an event the disciples came to call the "ascension."

CONTINENTAL PIETISM [33]

To the "enlightened" person of the eighteenth century, reason had finally won its battle over all the superstitions, myths, and creeds of the past. Nonetheless, many Christians found rationalism and deism insufficient. What was missing? In a word, *feeling*. For the rationalists, feeling, emotion, and imagination were characteristic of the superstitious, religious savages who did not use their reason to benefit humanity and foster progress. But for others, especially the Pietists, the heart of religion was feeling, not reason. Like the rationalists, the Pietists believed in liberty, equality, fraternity, social reform, and education, and many of them were familiar with the new thinking. In stressing feeling over reason, however, they believed that they were revitalizing the inwardness of Luther's religion and the ministry of the laity as an interpretation of the priesthood of all believers. Indeed, they considered themselves heirs of the belief in justification by faith, though in practice they leaned toward sanctification, as had certain representatives of the left wing of the Reformation. This is evident in their stress on a deeply personal (devotional) study of the Bible, the struggle of the soul, and a sudden conversion followed by gradual perfection (holiness) as a way of life. They came to stress good and simple preaching, education of the young, and a denial of worldly pleasures (theater, card playing, dancing).

There were many anticipations of Pietism in Ignatius Loyola, Luther, the left wing reformed groups, Puritanism, and mysticism, but Pietism as a distinct movement is usually associated with three figures who emerged within German Lutheranism: Jacob Spener (1635–1705), August Hermann Francke (1663–1727), and Count Ludwig von Zinzendorf (1700–60).

In 1670, after four years as head pastor of Frankfurt, Jacob Spener began his attempt to reform what he considered to be a barren, doctrinaire, institutionalized orthodoxy. Wishing to strengthen the spiritual life of his congregation, he gathered small groups in his home for Bible study, prayer, and discussion of Sunday sermons. These "little churches within the church" (*ecclesiolae in ecclesia*) multiplied and were given the name "associations of piety" (*collegia pietatis*).

Spener's book *Pia Desideria,* published in 1675, put forth his program for the renewal of the church. It stressed most of the ideas and practices by which Pietism was characterized at the beginning of this section. In addition, it recommended the formation of *collegia pietatis* with a stress on mutual love and care in the fellowship. The response to Spener's innovations was overwhelming. Some of his followers, against his wishes, wanted to separate from the orthodox Lutheran church. Partly as a result of such inclinations, Spener encountered much opposition, so much so that he was forced to take a new pastorate at Dresden. When the opposition followed him there, he finally settled as a successful pastor in Berlin from 1691 until his death in 1705.

Meanwhile, Pietism spread throughout Germany and into various parts of Europe, notably Scandinavia. In Leipzig a young university professor by the name of August Hermann Francke, after a short visit with Spener at Dresden, began to preach and teach Pietism. Soon he gained a strong following among both Leipzig townspeople and students. The city was in a dither. Like Spener, Francke was forced to take another pastorate, at Erfurt. When trouble pursued him there, Spener helped him obtain a professorship at the University of Halle, which rapidly became the center of the German Pietistic movement. Here Francke launched many new programs, including a school for poor children, a Latin school, an orphanage, a home for the poor, and a seminary for teachers. A friend influenced by Francke established a Bible Institute committed to the publication of inexpensive Bibles and tracts. There also emerged an interest in foreign missions, a relatively new phenomenon for Protestant Christians.

Still another phase of the Pietistic movement was the Unity of the Brethren (*Unitas Fratrum*), known eventually as the Renewed Moravian Church (Moravia is today in central Czechoslovakia). Originally a pre-Lutheran reform movement, the Brethren had often been persecuted by the Catholic majority in Moravia and Bohemia. In 1722, still suffering oppression, they were invited by Count Nicholas von Zinzendorf of Saxony to his estate at Berthelsdorf, called *Herrnhut*. Eventually, there emerged at *Herrnhut* a kind of Protestant monastic community which, though without vows of celibacy, placed Christian service above marriage, separated young men and young women, and reared children apart from their parents. At first the community maintained close connections with the Saxon Lutheran church; despite Zinzendorf's efforts, however, the Moravians tended toward separatism. Eventually, opposition arose from both orthodox Lutherans and Pietists. Zinzendorf was banished from Saxony; he became a world-traveling missionary, especially famous for his work among the American Indians. In 1747 he was permitted to return to Saxony. He successfully defended his orthodoxy and eventually became a Lutheran bishop.

In summary, Protestant Pietists stressed the inwardness of spiritual experience, the emotional component of religion, without which they believed religion was in danger of becoming cold, dry, formal, and too intellectual. Small groups of Pietists gathered together for Bible study, prayer, and discussion of sermons and dedicated themselves to spiritual growth. In addition, they established many educational agencies and organizations for the betterment of community conditions, published Bibles and tracts, and launched missions.

JESUS CHRIST IN THE THOUGHT OF JOHN WESLEY [34]

Pietism and Moravianism grew vigorously in seventeenth-century continental Europe. In England, where the lower classes were depressed economically, spiritually, and morally during the beginnings of the Industrial Revolution, the time was ripe for religious renewal.

John Wesley (1703–91) was the fifteenth of nineteen children (eight died in infancy). His father, Samuel Wesley, a priest of the Anglican church (in America this is the Protestant Episcopal church) priest, bequeathed to him both Anglican and Pietistic impulses. His mother, Susannah, though at times domineering, was very religious and influenced him greatly. After his early schooling, John became a student at Christ Church, Oxford, in 1720. About 1725 he began studying two books that helped shape his ideas about Christian piety: Bishop Jeremy Taylor's *Rules for Holy Living and Dying,* essentially a biblically oriented handbook of spiritual discipline that stressed progress in inner holiness and external rules of behavior, and the *Imitation of Christ.* Wesley then developed his own program of strict spiritual discipline and morality. Following Taylor's lead, he chose to enter the Anglican priesthood as a voluntary celibate.

The following year Wesley began his study of William Law's *Christian Perfection,* which presented an "imitation of Christ" ideal centering on daily self-denial, for example, by moderate fasting, leaving home and

Portrait of John Wesley by Nathaniel Hone
NATIONAL PORTRAIT GALLERY, LONDON

family for the sake of Jesus, and abstinence from improper books, dramas, plays, and conversation. By 1729 Wesley was also beginning to emerge as a leader of an Oxford student group formed by his brother Charles and eventually nicknamed the Methodists because of the group's dedication to a way of disciplining one's life and study called the "rule and method." In this period Wesley studied the Bible and the medieval mystical document *Theologica Germanica*.

In 1735, accompanied by his brother Charles, John Wesley set out to become a missionary among the Indians of Georgia in order to "save his own soul." On board ship, he became friends with some Moravians. Once in Georgia, Wesley took temporary charge of a parish in Savannah and met the young niece of the chief magistrate of the city, Sophy Hopkie. Though Wesley was determined to keep his commitment to remain single, and Sophy claimed that she wished to return to England

to avoid marrying a disreputable suitor, Wesley's frequent and occasionally intimate associations with her led to love and he vaguely
hinted at marriage. For the moment, Sophy avoided Wesley's restrained
overtures and told him she had resolved never to marry. Wesley consulted his Moravian friends. As was his custom in difficult decisions, he
drew lots. The lot said: "Think of it no more." Though Sophy gave him
ample opportunities, Wesley made no further advances. But to his con-
sternation, Sophy announced her engagement to still another suitor and
quickly married him. Later, when Wesley refused her communion on
the technicality that she had not given legal notification to communicate after her absence for a period, he encountered great opposition from supporters of the newlyweds and, after being indicted by a
grand jury (the trial never occurred) he decided to leave Georgia.

Unsuccessful and demoralized in all his efforts, in 1737–38 John
Wesley returned to England where religious revival was well under way.
Both Wesleys now came under Moravian influence, and both had conversion experiences. For John, the famous event occurred in 1738 while
he listened to a reading from Luther's *Preface to the Commentary on
Romans* at a Methodist society meeting at Aldersgate Street, London.
Wesley later wrote about his Aldersgate experience in his *Journal:* "I
felt my heart strangely warmed. I felt I did trust in Christ, Christ alone
for salvation. . . ."[35]

After a visit to Germany to learn more about the Moravians, Wesley
returned to preach at the many societies in and about London and,
finally, at George Whitefield's urging, even in an open field near Bristol.
By the 1740s Wesley found relations with the Calvinist wing of the revival (led by Whitefield) strained, and because the Moravians showed an
increasing tendency toward mystical quietism and separation from the
church, he decided to split with them. His own group centered in the
rapidly growing "societies." With a tremendous talent for organization,
Wesley developed smaller support groups within the "societies" (classes
and bands) and, to the chagrin of the Anglicans, developed the office of
"lay preacher." Organized for mutual support, discipline, and pastoral
care, these groups became the context for the practical implementation
of Wesley's view of Jesus Christ among the Methodists. Despite
Wesley's wishes, the Methodists separated from the Anglicans by 1795,
four years after his death.

Because Wesley wrote no treatise about Jesus Christ, his views on
this subject must be gleaned from various places in his writings.[36] The
difficulty of systematizing his views is compounded by the fact that
such a systematic statement was not as important to Wesley as the
Christian life itself.

In theory, Wesley followed the Reformers' stress on salvation by

Scripture alone (*sola scriptura*); in practice, he was also highly influenced by books about spiritual discipline and mysticism. This meant that he read the Scriptures from the perspective of human, personal, quasi-mystical, quasi-ascetic, Pietistic, and evangelical movements. To Wesley, Scripture was to be interpreted in the light of experience and experience in the light of Scripture. Thus he frequently used biblical characters as models for interpreting particular events in his own life, especially in times of great crisis, and he was not beyond opening a Bible to find a random passage to solve a problem. The *sola* in *sola scriptura* meant, then, not "solely," but "primarily." We will see that was true of *sola fide,* that is, not "by faith alone," but "primarily by faith."

Wesley's specific method of biblical interpretation stressed the Reformation principles that one should look for the plain, literal sense of a passage and that "Scripture interprets Scripture." But he had a higher estimation of human reason than Luther's, and he criticized Luther and the mystics on this very point. His Pietistic inclination is reflected in his belief that the result of interpretation should be "plain truth for plain people," free from "all nice and philosophical speculations; from all perplexed and intricate reasonings." Wesley also differed from the Reformation thinkers in being somewhat more concerned with maintaining Christian orthodoxy. Drawing on his Anglican background, he believed that Scripture should be interpreted in relation to tradition.

This overall perspective is crucial to Wesley's view of Jesus Christ. Like Calvin, he came to believe that all persons share in Adam's sin, are totally without merit (Original Sin), and therefore are dependent on God's totally free gift of grace through the sacrifice of his Son, Jesus Christ (justification by faith). At least, these were his views by the time of his conversion in 1738. However, Wesley went on to state that God's gift of grace is continually available and that a person is continually free to accept or reject it. This perspective on human freedom took the sharp edge off Calvinist predestination. For the Calvinists, including Whitefield, Wesley's focus on continual free choice was in danger of stressing human effort so strongly that a doctrine of works would result—shades of Catholicism! Wesley did not go that far, but his interest in works of love as part of the Christian life was not characteristic of either Luther or Calvin. At one point, he suggested that faith was only the "handmaid of love." Again, *sola fide* meant "primarily by faith."

We can obtain a clearer impression of Wesley's overall view by considering the *stages* of salvation that sometimes appeared in his writings. Though these stages were distinct, Wesley did not think of them as static or irreversible. The first stage is *prevenient grace.* This is the working of God in such a way that one experiences the feeling of having done something wrong and an increasing desire for God. Next comes *convincing grace,* the strong knowledge of sin and guilt, a poverty of spirit, accompanied by the desire and readiness to amend one's ways. This stage involves "works of repentance" *before* one attains mature, justifying faith, a view Luther and Calvin would not have accepted because of their fear of works of righteousness. For Wesley such works did not "buy" salvation. Third comes *justifying faith,* accompanied by sudden *new birth.* Justifying faith is a feeling of being liberated from sin (Wesley saw this as "a relative change"); new birth is an assurance that one is freed from the power of sin by the gift of the Spirit of God ("a real change"). Again, we should note that for Wesley, justification is not just "bare assent," but acting out the gift with works of love, that is, works of piety (prayer and meditation) and of mercy (love of neighbor). This, then, is the fourth stage, the gradual *progress* of the Christian life in the light of one's knowledge of sin. Fifth, though some imperfection may remain, it is possible to gain inward and outward purity and holiness. This is the stage of *Christian perfection,* a goal to which one may come closest at "a moment before death." The final stage of complete sanctification is the *glorification* that comes beyond the grave.

The view that the experience of salvation was just this sort of *gradual process* stands out in Wesley's life and thought. Yet, true to his 1738 Aldersgate experience, he held to the importance of *sudden conversion.* It seems probable that this tension between sudden conversion and gradual progress toward perfection (Wesley spoke of "going on to perfection") provides a basis for understanding Wesley's view of Christ. The conversion experience and justification apart from human effort corresponded to the Christ who accomplished what is impossible for sinful persons to accomplish, while the stages of perfection (sanctification) corresponded to Wesley's modified concept of piety based on the imitation of Christ.

Though Wesley was attracted to the simple view of Christ and avoided metaphysical speculation, he continued to draw on orthodox conceptions. Christ was a representative person, the mediator of a new relationship between God and his people. When speaking of Jesus Christ directly, Wesley tended to stress his divinity: Christ is the Son of God from the beginning of time; he was eternally generated; he is the same substance (*homoousios*) as the Father; he is the second person of the Trinity; he is truly God and truly man; he is Messiah and the savior of the world; he is prophet, priest, and king; and he will return at the End. Likewise, Wesley accepted traditional views on the atonement, that is, on the question of *how* Christ effected salvation for Christians. Augustine had suggested a ransom theory; Anselm was famous for the satisfaction theory; and Reformers had moved toward a penal theory. Wesley held all three: Jesus Christ paid the debt for sin (ransom theory), satisfied God's justice (satisfaction theory), and became a substitute for sinful human beings on the cross (penal substitution theory).

Wesley made the atonement central to his view of justification by faith alone:

> The sole cause of our acceptance with God (or, that for the sake of which, on the account of which, we are accepted) is the righteousness and the death of Christ, who fulfilled God's law, and died in our stead.[37]

Yet Wesley's views on sanctification as the process of Christian perfection led him to develop a moral influence theory of the atonement. To be sure, he was cautious. His former spiritual mentor, William Law, appeared to him to have taken the doctrine of sanctification in the direction of a legalism centered on works that did not take into account the depth of sin. At this point, Wesley agreed with the Reformers that one was not justified by imitating Christ. Nonetheless, Wesley believed that *after* justification and new birth, progress toward perfection could take the form of the imitation of Christ. Given justification, there was a form of sanctification in which Christ had a moral influence on the believer. Jesus Christ was not only a sinless substitute and in that regard impossible to imitate; he was also an example to be followed. Christ is therefore the pattern of the Christian life, the revealer of true holiness, a holiness not of resignation or of quietism, but a holiness in the world. Thus Wesley's moral influence theory of the atonement led to a view of ethical behavior as the proper expression of love.

Wesley's attempt to explain his view of sanctification and his theory of Christ's moral influence can be observed in his interpretation of the Sermon on the Mount (Mt 5–7), the source of many of his sermons. The Sermon on the Mount described, for Wesley, the way of salvation:

> The Son of God, who came from heaven, is here showing us the way to heaven; to the place which He hath prepared for us; the glory He had before the world began. He is teaching us the true way of life everlasting; the royal way which leads to the kingdom; and the only true way—for there is none besides: all other paths lead to destruction. From the character of the Speaker, we are well assured that He hath declared the full and perfect will of God.[38]

Wesley came close to a conception of the "mystical way" of salvation when he discussed the beatitudes of the Sermon. These were like the mystical ladder of ascent, that is, they were progressive steps to be followed. Following them, "real Christianity always begins in poverty of spirit, and goes on in the order here set down, till the 'man of God is made perfect.' "[39] But unlike many mystics, he never lost sight of sin and justification. "Poor in spirit" referred to the Christian who "sees himself . . . utterly helpless with regard to atoning for his past sins; utterly unable to make any amends to God, to pay any ransom for his own soul."[40] Yet there remained the cross of Christ as the path to follow:

> "Blessed are ye when men shall revile you and persecute you"—shall persecute by reviling you—"and say all manner of evil against you falsely, for My sake." This cannot fail; it is the very badge of our discipleship; it is one of the seals of our calling; it is a sure portion entailed on all the children of God. . . . Rejoice, because by this mark also ye know unto whom ye belong; and "because great is your reward in heaven"—the reward purchased by the blood of the covenant, and freely bestowed in proportion to your sufferings, as well as to your holiness of heart and life.[41]

If, then, "going on to perfection" does not mean going on without sin, it is nevertheless a sincere goal, the basis of which is the *pattern of Christ's life:*

> But whom then do you mean by "one that is perfect?" We mean one in whom is "the mind which was in Christ," and who so "walketh as Christ also walked;" a man "that hath clean hands and a pure heart," or that is "cleansed from all filthiness of flesh and spirit;" one in whom is "no occasion of stumbling," and who accordingly, "does not commit sin." [!] . . . We understand hereby, one whom God hath "sanctified throughout in body, soul and spirit." . . .
> This man can now testify to all mankind, "I am crucified with Christ: Nevertheless I live; yet not I, but Christ liveth in me."[42]

In summary, John Wesley's view of Jesus Christ stressed the Lutheran tradition that God's act in Jesus Christ was accomplished apart from all merit on the part of sinful humanity. Yet it also emphasized the importance of human merit in the process of "going on to perfection" (sanctification). The stress on justification by faith, which emerged especially in connection with Wesley's Aldersgate experience in 1738, made it difficult for him to maintain consistent relations with English Pietists and Moravians. The emphasis on a process of sanctification, which emerged through his reading of the mystics and Pietists and through the influence of the Moravians, tended to conflict with the Calvinist denial of free will. His synthesis of justification by faith and sanctification was made by drawing on the age-old notion of *stages* of salvation. Justifying faith and new birth were placed between preparatory stages of grace ("prevenient" and "convincing" grace) and resultant acts of piety, which progressively lead one toward perfection. In this way, the view that Jesus Christ has done all for the sinner was combined with the view that Jesus Christ is the model for imitation. What the view lacked in consistency it gained in completeness.

ROMANTICISM AND HISTORY

The religious movements we have just considered—Pietism, Moravianism, and Methodism—were reactions against the dryness and coldness of rationalism, which dominated eighteenth-century thought in the West from orthodoxy to deism. This reorientation toward feeling and religious experience was accompanied by broader but parallel changes in many aspects of European culture. Generally, these changes were characterized by a reaffirmation of the value of feeling, individualism, and nature. The *romantic movement,* which received its impetus from these changes, profoundly altered attitudes toward history and myth, and thus toward Jesus Christ.

The factors that led to the romantic movement are not easily isolated.[43] One was the French Revolution, which fostered *nationalism* throughout Europe. With national identity came a longing to discover the past, the history and folklore of "the people." This was a romantic trend.

Another factor that led to the romantic movement was the new stress on human *feeling.* Perhaps because of this stress, the leaders of romanticism were not philosophers or scientists, but literary figures, musicians, and artists. For example, the *Sturm und Drang* ("storm and stress") movement in German literature, typified by Lessing, Herder (1744–1803), Schiller (1759–1805), and Goethe (1749–1832), emphasized individualism, rebellion against the establishment, a vague sense of uneasiness in the modern world, a love of nature, and the inadequacy of Enlightenment poetic form (the neoclassic form).

Even a cursory survey of romantic art would be beyond the scope of this book. However, one can trace the strands we have mentioned in literature and music throughout Europe in the late eighteenth and early to middle nineteenth centuries: preoccupation with personal, interior feeling, interest in the folk life of one's country or in its heritage of folk art and mythology, love of nature and use of both its beneficent and its destructive sides as symbols of human experience, fascination with the rebellious or "alienated" individual, and the development of more flexible and more loosely structured artistic forms. When Keats found himself deeply moved by Chapman's translation of Homer or by the Elgin Marbles, he was inspired to write poems not about these masterpieces themselves, but about his own very personal reactions to them. Rebellious or world-weary romantic figures such as Goethe's Young Werther, Byron's Childe Harold, Melville's Captain Ahab, and Emily Brontë's Heathcliff were not mere misfits; they struck a responsive chord in many readers. In music, the gloomy yearning of a Tchaikovsky symphony, the intimacy of a Schubert song, the mythical settings and passionate intensity of Wagner's operas were all expressions of different facets of the romantic awareness. Joseph Kerman writes of romantic music:

> That a special affinity exists between Romanticism and music was an article of faith with the Romantics themselves. All the arts, they believed, have one essential function: not the praise of God, or the imitation of the

external world, or the gratification of the senses—as might have been claimed at earlier times—but the expression of human feeling and inner experience. And of all the arts, music was the one that could fulfill this function most deeply and freely.[44]

How did the romantics regard the subject of history? Romanticism was much more interested in the historical past than the Enlightenment had been.[45] Jean Jacques Rousseau (1712–78), who was highly influential among romantics, differed from other philosophers of his time in suggesting that civilization had corrupted the innocence of children.[46] He showed a positive appreciation for the primitive mentality. Giovanni Battista Vico (1668–1744)[47] has been called the first modern historian. For Vico, history is apparently irrational, cruel, and passionate, but it has its own law. Though each period has its own distinct languages, warfare, customs, laws, governments, religions, myths, and so on, there are general patterns or cycles in history: a heroic period (characterized by an agricultural economy, imagination, morality based on prowess in war, and poetry and ballad literature), a classical period (characterized by an industrial economy, abstract thought, morality based on peace, and prose literature), and a period of decline (when the creative power of the classical period is exhausted). For Vico, the past came into view not simply as inferior to the present, but as a stage on which the drama of the historian's search for truth was played.

Sensitivity to the historical past was also developed in German romanticism. Johann Georg Hamaan (1730–88),[48] "the prophet of German romanticism," believed that feeling was of divine origin, and his student, Johann Gottfried von Herder (1744–1803), became the central figure in the transition from Rationalism to romanticism in Germany.[49] Herder's romantic temperament was unsuited to removing himself from his sources and asking about the historical facts behind them, as many Enlightenment critics had attempted. Rather, he was interested in letting the past speak on its own terms and attempted to assimilate its mystery himself. Herder's study ranged from Near Eastern languages and poetry, which deepened his appreciation for myth, to the accomplishments of the Middle Ages and the Reformation, those "religious" ages that had been virtually ignored by the Enlightenment thinkers. In his studies of myth, he held to a romantic view of the people (*Volk*), which in its early stages of development attempted to answer questions about the origins of the universe and of humanity. The *Volk* also developed notions of good and evil and of its own origins through mythical heroes. The language of such myths was concrete, emotional, and poetic, and in such primitive language, a nation's true soul was embedded.

As a result of his studies, Herder did not believe that the Judaeo-Christian religion was unique, for every religion had its own complete revelation. Yet, he did think that it was especially revelatory, partly because of its beautiful pictorial language, Hebrew. Moreover, though

Herder read the Bible as a human book, he read it with affection and delight, attempting to find in it the course of history and the spirit of God working through a great and chosen people. As a result of his appreciation for things mythical, Herder anticipated Harnack (see pages 205–11) in his view that the doctrinal Christology of the early church was a corruption of the human Jesus of history which speaks to the human in everyone. Of Jesus he wrote:

> A divine phantom walking upon earth is something I dare not imitate in thought or deed . . . thus for every Christian and for every Christian theologian the human Christ is not some image in the clouds to be gazed at in wonder, but a perfect example upon earth for our imitation and instruction. Every written work which develops historically and represents morally this perfect example, the figure of the purest man on earth, is an evangelical book. On the other hand, all scholastic sophistry which contrives to turn it into something calculated to dazzle, something devoid of humanity, is diametrically opposed to the spirit of the writings of the New Testament and harmful to it.[50]

We will see that the romantic view of history had great influence on writers about Jesus in early nineteenth century historical thought (see Ch. 6). Before taking up these early historians, however, it will be necessary to consider one of the most important Protestant thinkers influenced by romanticism, Friedrich Schleiermacher.

JESUS CHRIST IN THE THOUGHT OF FRIEDRICH SCHLEIERMACHER

Friedrich Schleiermacher (1768–1834)[51] is an especially appropriate representative of this period for two reasons: A number of the movements just described converge in his thought, and his later writings focus on Jesus Christ. Schleiermacher's early years were spent in Moravian schools, where he absorbed the Bible, the classics, and Jesus piety. He then entered the University of Halle and, after passing his examinations in 1790, spent three years as a private tutor, preacher, and writer in Schlobetten and Berlin. He passed his second theological examinations in 1794, became an assistant Reformed pastor at Landsberg for two years and, by 1796, returned to Berlin as a poorly paid chaplain at the Charité Hospital.

Schleiermacher next entered the first really productive period in his life. Though at first friendly with the Reformed (Calvinist) clergy, he gradually developed a close intellectual relationship with his highly educated Jewish landlady, Frau Herz, and her circle of Berlin avant-gardists; he also became acquainted with a group of young romantic poets and philosophers spearheaded by Friedrich Schlegel. In 1799, away from his friends on a commission at Potsdam, Schleiermacher wrote *On Religion: Speeches to Its Cultured Despisors,* a controversial bombshell in which he sought to defend the reality of religion as rooted in feeling as opposed to the views of those enlightened sophisticates who sought to reduce it to thought (metaphysics) or action (ethics). In his *Confidential Letters on Lucinde,* he defended Schlegel's haphazard, erotic, and highly criticized *Lucinde.* He also created a stir by courting Eleonore Grunow, the unloved and unhappily married wife of a Berlin clergyman. In 1802 Schleiermacher left Berlin to become pastor at Stolp in order to force a decision on Eleonore Grunow. She decided to return to her unhappy marriage.

In 1804 Schleiermacher accepted a professorship at the University of Halle. As a Reformed pastor and scholar among Lutherans, and as a romantic, he was given a cool reception by the Halle rationalists, biblical critics, supernaturalists, and Pietists. He now published *Christmas Eve,* a Platonic-type dialogue, setting forth his views on Jesus Christ. After Halle was closed in 1806 as a result of Napoleon's victories, Schleiermacher went to Berlin, lectured, and became involved in Prussian attempts to assert national independence.

In 1809 he married the young widow of a former friend. The same year he became the pastor of the highly influential Trinity Church, a post he held until his death. As result of his writing on education, he was named professor of theology and dean of the faculty at the newly opened University of Berlin in 1810. When Napoleon was finally defeated in 1814, the aristocracy in Prussia returned and men of liberal persuasion, including Schleiermacher, came under suspicion. He himself was denied his political appointment, though he continued to teach. In 1820 he entered into open conflict with an increasingly influential member of the faculty, the philosopher Hegel, over another colleague who had been imprisoned. In 1821–22 his mature work, *The Christian Faith,* appeared. In contrast to the *Speeches,* it was more ordered and exact, was intended for Christian believers rather than "cultured despisors," and was focused not on religion in general but on Christianity and Jesus Christ in particular. In this period, Schleiermacher also lectured on the life of Jesus. At his death in 1834 nearly 30,000 mourners thronged the streets of Berlin, a testimony to his breadth of learning and widespread popularity.

In contrast to his earlier (romantic) period, when he focused on religion in general (*Speeches*), Schleiermacher's later writings were much more centered around Christianity and Jesus Christ. The sources for this period are primarily the *Christmas Eve Celebration: A Dialogue* (1804), his mature work *The Christian Faith* (1821–22), and the posthumous reconstruction of his lectures on *The Life of Jesus* from his students' notes.[52]

Christmas Eve is a dialogue among friends about the meaning of celebrating Christmas Eve and the biblical story of Jesus' birth. The participants represent several approaches to the Scriptures and Jesus. Leonhardt, an Enlightenment type, thinks that the Jesus of history is scarcely recoverable, that his true meaning centers around the death and resurrection, and that in any case, the historical Jesus is irrelevant to Christian faith. He suggests that the story of Jesus' birth in the Bible is simply a legend about the night; hence, that is when Christmas Eve is celebrated! Ernst responds with less skepticism about recovering the Jesus of history. He believes that it is more important to participate in the joy and selflessness of the new life symbolized by Christmas. Such a new life emanates from one who possessed this life in its highest perfection, Jesus. Eduard, in a similar vein, states that he likes the most mystical gospel, John. This gospel is concerned with the spiritual meaning of Christ for all people, but it continues to connect the Christ with the Jesus who actually lived. Finally, the Pietistic *Herrnhuter* Joseph rejects all scholarly criticism in the name of *feeling*. Such views may reflect various moods of Schleiermacher himself, or at least various notions at different points in his life, Ernst perhaps representing Schleiermacher's most recent view at the time (his full name was Friedrich Daniel Ernst).

This early statement already indicates that for Schleiermacher *it is not the historical Jesus of the past that counts, but the Christ who gives new life to the Christian in the present.* In 1817 Schleiermacher attempted his own solution to the problem of the literary relationship of the gospels. He suggested that between the early oral stories about Jesus and the written gospels there were written "fragments" that the evangelists received in differing combinations. Though his solution was not widely accepted, his adventure with historical research convinced him that a connected biography of the historical Jesus was impossible. This result fitted well with his own personal views on Jesus Christ. It was impossible to reconstruct the Jesus of history, but his significance was not in the past anyhow; it was in the present. This becomes clearer in *The Christian Faith* and his lectures on *The Life of Jesus*.

Drawing on Plato and Kant, Schleiermacher saw the Christ as an ideal archetype, that is, a model for the self-consciousness that is filled with consciousness of God. That ideal archetype is approximated by the individual Christian consciousness in the corporate life of the living community, the church. Where Schleiermacher differed from the idealist philosophers was in his view that the archetype was completely expressed in a historical person, Jesus of Nazareth. To put it simply, he affirmed that *Jesus was the pure expression of the immediate feeling of absolute dependence on God.*

Schleiermacher recognized that the language of the Bible was mythical and metaphorical; he also knew that the language of the creeds was derived from Greek philosophy, that is, built on a (metaphysical) view of the universe in which God was external to the world and humanity. This, of course, meant that if time and space were never interrupted from "without" by some supernatural force, as the Enlightenment believed, miracles were difficult to explain. Either one had to assert the supernatural view of miracle in the face of the new science, or one had to avoid or explain away the miraculous and then present Jesus as a simple human teacher. But, said Schleiermacher, what if God is *not* perceived as an external, supernatural force who transcends nature and history and reveals himself by miracle? Schleiermacher's alternative was to view revelation not from without, but from within. God reveals himself in humans as *the immediate feeling of absolute dependence*. The archetype of Schleiermacher's view of revelation was Jesus' consciousness of being dependent on God. Moreover, Jesus was absolute perfection; he had the creative power to save people; he was original and unique in history.

In Schleiermacher's thought, the classical view of Christ's two natures, the divine and human, is put in the form of an ideal archetype and its realization in history.[53] God placed in the human Jesus the archetypal consciousness of God that was superior to every other form of consciousness of God. No connected biography of the historical Jesus is necessary. When one encounters Jesus' teaching, the teaching of the nearness of the kingdom of God, one also encounters Jesus himself, specifically, Jesus' consciousness of God. Further, Jesus drew and draws believers into the power of his consciousness of God, giving them a new life in the present. They are, so to speak, the incarnation of Jesus' consciousness of God. They experience this salvation in the community; this is their "grace," or gift from God. Here, Christians are forgiven, reborn, made holy. The relation with Jesus Christ is quasi-mystical: mystical not in the sense of self-denying unity with God but in the sense that it cannot be understood without experiencing it firsthand. It cannot, therefore, be rationally explained, for it lies in the realm of *feeling*.

Schleiermacher interpreted the traditional theories of atonement in a similar way. He rejected the Moravian "blood and wounds" stress in his background. He did not accept the classical formulation of substitutionary atonement, that is, Christ as a sinless substitute for sinful humanity. Rather, as Jesus overcame suffering and death, so his faithful followers do not experience suffering and death as punishment for sin; in fact, prayer in the name of Jesus makes it possible to be accepted by God. In the light of God's love as experienced in the community, sin is reduced to virtual insignificance. This is an obvious softening of the Reformation emphasis on a radical distinction between a righteous God and sinful humanity, and subsequent critics blasted Schleiermacher for what appeared to them a watered-down view of humanity. For Schleiermacher, however, the Christian became an adopted child of God, received a new life (conversion and regeneration), was forgiven (justification), and was made holy (sanctification). As the divine *Logos* united with the man Jesus, so the ideal Christ was "mystically" united with the Christian.

Schleiermacher also reinterpreted other traditional views. He rejected the whole concept of "sacrament." He criticized infant baptism. He interpreted eschatology in terms of the gradual progress of the spirit over the flesh in this world, the final completion of new life in the kingdom of God, which is beyond, and personal immortality. Speculation about what will happen in particular, he thought, was beyond the human imagination. In this respect, New Testament representations of the End were "simply" symbolic and mythic visions and prophecies of a beyond that has been already intuited.

Schleiermacher's later thought was dominated by Christ as the archetype for a true consciousness of God, which he understood as the feeling of absolute dependence. This archetype was realized in the historical Jesus and through him extended to the faithful in the community. For Schleiermacher the biblical myths and metaphysical doctrines of the church should be understood in nonobjectified, nonphysical, experiential, and personal ways. Revelation is from within. His biblical roots lay mostly in the Gospel of John, where Jesus came into history but was given a highly spiritual casting. With this view of Christ, Schleiermacher reinterpreted the whole of Christian thought, and judgments on him vary from the claim that he severely altered the Christian view to the claim that he saved Christ for the modern world.

SUMMARY

The period from about 1650 to 1800 was the period of the Enlightenment in Western culture. Modern secularism overtook Christianity. The heart of this transformation was a shift in authority: Human reason upstaged divine revelation as contained in the major Christian creeds. The Newtonian universe with its natural law challenged long-held views based on the Bible and Aristotle. In its wake came philosophies that rested not on medieval metaphysics but on human modes of thinking. The rationalists, taking mathematics as their model, sought true knowledge in clear and distinct ideas which they claimed were innate and *a priori*. The empiricists, taking as their model testing and verification in the physical sciences, sought knowledge through the data received by the five senses. Some, like David Hume, were left primarily with the mind itself (skepticism); others became materialists, viewing the mind as a machine like the universe itself. Thinking about the state took a course parallel to these movements. It no longer took its departure from God's revealed will about the organization of the community, but instead began with self-evident laws based on reasonable relationships among human beings, regardless of whether they were considered basically evil or basically good.

Thinking about the historical past, which had received a boost during the Renaissance and Reformation, tended to be more negative. Those who had come before were considered childish or were compared to the mentally ill, or European peasants, or the American Indian. It was now thought that such savages were driven by emotion and imagination, were frequently duped by their religious leaders, and were incapable of understanding real causes and effects or of thinking in abstractions. They dabbled in art, poetry, and myth-making. The mature, rational, enlightened European, however, had advanced beyond such childish thinking.

Many of those who wanted to be both enlightened and religious in Europe and America became deists; they believed in a God who created the universe as a Great Machine, a morality discoverable by human reason, and in immortality inferred from human limitations. Deism did not normally believe in the divinity of Jesus Christ or in the Holy Spirit (it was not Trinitarian), though Jesus was evaluated highly as an example of practical morality. In Germany, where rationalistic biblical criticism began to take hold, the problem was how the human Jesus became the divine Jesus Christ, an unbelievable myth. With as yet somewhat limited access to the history of Jesus' times and to cultural analogies for the transmission of religious traditions in oral cultures, frequently the theories about Jesus' miracles involved some kind of conscious deception on the part of Jesus' followers or, at best, misapprehensions of natural law which might be understood by some reasonable event.

In contrast to the enlightened rationalists, the Pietists, drawing on the Lutheran tradition of the individual's relationship to God, on the left-wing Reformation focus on the Spirit, and in some cases on medieval mysticism and Puritanism, sought to arouse the Christian from a cold, intellectualistic sleep to the warm, fresh sunlight of feeling and emotion. They stressed small-group study of the Bible, mutual support, strict morality, and education. A sudden conversion followed by a life of gradual perfection (sanctification) made them reborn Christians.

The major impulses from the Continent were Spener and Francke's movement within German Lutheranism and the Moravians who made their way from what is now Czechoslavakia to Zinzendorf's estate in Saxony. Within the Anglican church in England a similar movement influenced John Wesley, who also absorbed himself in medieval mystical literature and pietistic writers who stressed the imitation of Christ. This produced a modification of the Lutheran–Calvinist stress on the once-for-all act of God in Jesus Christ as the basis for justification by faith. For Wesley, it was also important to "go on to perfection," that is, to imitate Christ in the secure knowledge that one is assured of salvation. The conversion gave one a feeling of assurance that became the basis for the Christian life modeled on Jesus Christ.

The romantic movement also became disillusioned with the abstract generalizations and the orientation toward natural law among Enlightenment philosophers and scientists. They sought truth in the concrete, the particular, the exotic, the emotional, and the imaginative. They exhibited a renewed interest in individuals and nations in history, along with a general appreciation for art, poetry, music, and religion— things that remained suspicious to the rationalist. This mood, along with Kant's location of religion within the realm of practical reason (that is, ethics), greatly influenced thinking about Jesus Christ.

A writer about Jesus Christ who was especially oriented toward romanticism was Friedrich Schleiermacher. He was reared among Pietists and as a student was associated with the romantics. In his *Speeches* he located religion in the realm of "feeling," and in his later works he thought of Jesus as the purest expression of the "immediate feeling of absolute dependence on God," that is, the religious consciousness. In Jesus the myths of the Son of God, the Son of Man, and *Logos* became history. Moreover, the Christian could experience God's love in the community in such a way that sin was virtually nullified—as in Wesley's views, there was some sense of assurance.

NOTES

1. James Hastings Nichols, *History of Christianity, 1650–1950: Secularization of the West* (New York: Ronald Press Co., 1956), p. 6.

2. For a brief sketch see Ernest Nagel, "The Scientific Revolution," in *The Columbia History of the World,* ed. John A. Garraty and Peter Gay (New York: Harper & Row, 1972), pp. 681–92; a standard work is Thomas S. Kuhn, *The Copernican Revolution* (Cambridge, Mass.: Harvard University Press, 1957).

3. The Mentor philosophy series is always accessible. See Stuart Hamshire, *The Age of Reason* (New York: New American Library, Mentor Books, 1956); Sir Isaiah Berlin, *The Age of Enlightenment* (New York: New American Library, Mentor Books, 1956); W. T. Jones, *A History of Western Philosophy,* 2nd ed. (New York: Harcourt Brace Jovanovich, 1969), vol. 3, "Hobbes to Hume"; John Herman Randall, Jr., *The Career of Philosophy,* 2 vols. (New York: Columbia University Press, 1962).

4. Jacques Barzun, "Society and Politics," in Garraty and Gay, *Columbia History,* pp. 692–707; Thomas Hobbes, *Leviathan,* parts 1 and 2 (New York: Bobbs-Merrill Co., 1958); John Locke, *The Second Treatise of Government* (New York: Bobbs-Merrill Co., 1952).

5. In general, see Manuel, *The Eighteenth Century Confronts the Gods* (Cambridge, Mass.: Harvard University Press, 1959), ch. 2; Paul Hazard, *European Thought in the Eighteenth Century* (Cleveland: World Publishing Co., 1967), part 3, book 3; G. Adolf Koch, *Religion of the American Enlightenment* (New York: Thomas Y. Crowell Co., 1968) (originally published in 1933); Franklin L. Baumer, *Religion and the Rise of Scepticism* (New York: Harcourt Brace Jovanovich, Harbinger Books, 1969), ch. 1; Jacques Barzun, "Science versus Theology," in Garraty and Gay, *Columbia History,* pp. 707–21; Sydney E. Ahlstrom, *A Religious History of the American People,* 2 vols. (New York: Doubleday & Co., Image Books, 1975), vol 1, chs. 22 and 23.

6. *The Autobiography of Benjamin Franklin,* ed. Leonard W. Labaree et al. (New Haven: Yale University Press, 1964), pp. 145–46.

7. Ibid., p. 162.

8. Paine, *Age of Reason,* p. 254.

9. Ibid., p. 252.

10. Ibid., p. 6.

11. In general, see R. G. Collingwood, *The Idea of History* (New York: Oxford University Press, 1956), pp. 69–85; Karl Löwith, *Meaning in History* (Chicago: University of Chicago Press, 1949), pp. 104–44; Nicholas Capaldi, ed., *The Enlightenment: The Proper Study of Mankind,* Spirit of Western Civilization Series (New York: G. P. Putnam's Sons, Capricorn Books, 1967), vol. 5, ch. 3, "The New Import of History"; Frank E. Manuel, *Eighteenth Century;* Jan de Vries, *The Study of Religion, A Historical Approach,* trans. and intro. Kees W. Bolle (New York: Harcourt Brace Jovanovich, 1967), ch. 5, "The Eighteenth Century." See also Peter Gay, *The Enlightenment: An Interpretation,* vol. 1, "The Rise of Modern Paganism" (New York: Alfred A. Knopf, 1969), book 2, "The Tension with Christianity."

12. Collingwood, *The Idea of History,* p. 59.

13. Ibid., p. 76; Löwith, *Meaning,* pp. 104–14.

14. David Hume, *The Natural History of Religion,* ed. H. E. Root (Stanford, Cal.: Stanford University Press, 1956); Manuel, *Eighteenth Century,* ch. 4, part 3.

15. Ibid., ch. 6, parts 4 and 5.

16. Holbach, *Le Bon Sens ou Idées naturelles opposées aux idées surnaturelles* (1772), p. 125, as trans. in Manuel, *Eighteenth Century,* p. 232.

17. Holbach, *Le Bons Sens,* p. 9, as trans. in Manuel, *Eighteenth Century,* p. 235.

18. Ibid., p. 8.

19. Thomas Paine, *The Age of Reason,* in *Basic Writings of Thomas Paine* (New York: Wiley Book Co., 1942), pp. 10–11.

20. Ibid., p. 11.

21. R. M. Grant, *A Short History of the Interpretation of the Bible* (New York: Macmillan Co., 1963), ch. 11 (originally published in 1948); Werner Georg Kümmel, *The New Testament: The History of the Investigation of Its Problems,* trans. S. McLean Gilmore and Howard C. Kee (Nashville: Abingdon Press, 1972), pp. 40–73; S. L. Greenslade, ed., *The Cambridge History of the Bible: The West from the Reformation to the Present Day* (Cambridge: University Press, 1963), pp. 238–55; Samuel Terrien, "History of the Interpretation of the Bible III: Modern Period," in *The Interpreter's Bible,* vol 1, pp. 127–32.

22. Thomas Hobbes, *Leviathan* (Oxford: Clarendon Press, 1909), pp. 287–88 (originally published in 1651).

23. G. E. Lessing, "On the Proof of the Spirit and of Power," in *Lessing's Theological Writings,* trans. Henry Chadwick, A Library of Modern Religious Thought (Stanford, Cal.: Stanford University Press, 1957), p. 51.

24. Ibid., p. 52.

25. Kümmel, *New Testament,* pp. 89–97; Albert Schweitzer, *The Quest of the Historical Jesus,* chs. 2, 3, and 5.

26. Schweitzer, *Quest,* ch. 2; Charles H. Talbert, ed., "Introduction," in *Reimarus: Fragments,* trans. Ralph S. Fraser (Philadelphia: Fortress Press, 1970), pp. 1–18.

27. Reimarus, "The Intention of Jesus and His Teaching," in Talbert, *Reimarus: Fragments,* pp. 61–269.

28. Ibid., p. 126.

29. Ibid., p. 151–52.

30. Ibid., p. 232.

31. Ibid., p. 236.

32. Schweitzer, *Quest,* pp. 48ff.

33. John T. McNeill, *Modern Christian Movements* (Philadelphia: Westminster Press, 1954), pp. 15–103; Dillenberger and Welch, *Protestant Christianity,* ch. 6; John R. Wienlick, *Count Zinzendorf* (Nashville: Abingdon Press, 1956); Theodore G. Tappert, "Introduction," in Philip Jacob Spener, *Pia Desideria,* trans. Theodore G. Tappert (Philadelphia: Fortress Press, 1964), pp. 1–28; Manschreck, *A History of Christianity,* ch. 6; F. W. Stoeffler, *The Rise of Evangelical Pietism,* Studies in the History of Religions, No. 9 (Leiden: E. J. Brill, 1956); Walker, *History,* chs. 6 and 7.

34. Richard M. Cameron, *The Rise of Methodism: A Source Book* (New York: Philosophical Library, 1954); Albert C. Outler, *John Wesley* (New York: Oxford University Press, 1964); Martin Schmidt, *John Wesley: A Theological Biography,* 3 vols., vols. 1 and 2 trans. Norman P Goldhawk, vol. 3 trans. Denis Inman (Nashville: Abingdon Press, 1962–1966); Frank Baker, *John Wesley and the Church of England* (Nashville: Abingdon Press, 1970); Thorvald Källstad, *John Wesley and the Bible: A Psychological Study,* Acta Universitatis Upsaliensis Psychologia Religionum, no. 1 (Uppsala, 1974); Walker, *History,* ch. 7.

35. The account is given in *The Journal of the Rev. John Wesley, M. S.,* ed. Nehemiah Curnock, 8 vols. (London: Epworth Press, 1938), vol. 1, pp. 465ff. It is dated May 24, 1738.

36. In addition to note 34, see Robert W. Burtner and Robert E. Chiles, *A Compend of Wesley's Theology* (Nashville: Abingdon Press, 1954); Colin W. Williams, *John Wesley's Theology Today* (Nashville: Abingdon Press, 1960); John Deschner, *Wesley's Christology: An Interpretation* (Dallas: Southern Methodist University Press, 1960); Harald Lindström, *Wesley and Sanctification* (London: Epworth Press, 1946).

37. Lindström, *Wesley,* p. 89.

38. *The Standard Sermons of John Wesley,* annotated E. H. Sugden, 2 vols. (London: Epworth Press, 1956), vol. 1, p. 316.

39. Ibid., p. 321.

40. Ibid., p. 324.

41. Ibid., pp. 326–27.

42. Thomas Jackson, ed., *The Works of John Wesley, A.M.,* 3rd ed., 14 vols. (London: John Mason, 1829), vol. 11, p. 324.

43. Oskar Walzel, *German Romanticism,* trans. Alma Elise Lussky (New York: G. P. Putnam's Sons, Capricorn Books, 1966) (originally published in 1932); Bruce Wilshire, *Romanticism and Evolution,* Spirit of Western Civilization, no. 6 (New York: G. P. Putnam's Sons, Capricorn

Books, 1968); Rene Wellek, *Confrontations: Studies in the Intellectual and Literary Relations between Germany, England, and the United States During the Nineteenth Century* (Princeton: Princeton University Press, 1965); H. G. Schenk, *The Mind of the European Romantics* (New York: Doubleday & Co., Anchor Books), 1969; Jacques Barzun, *Classic, Romantic and Modern* (London: Secker & Warburg, 1961); Norman Foerster, *Image of America* (Notre Dame: University of Notre Dame Press, 1962), ch. 3; Lilian T. Furst, *Romanticism in Perspective* (New York: Humanities Press, 1970).

44. Joseph Kerman, "Music," in H. W. Janson and Joseph Kerman, *A History of Art & Music* (New York: Harry N. Abrams, n.d.) pp. 270–71.

45. Collingwood, *The Idea of History*, pp. 86–88; Schenk, *European Romantics*, pp. 31–46.

46. Jean Jacques Rousseau, *Émile*, trans. Barbara Foxley (New York: E. P. Dutton & Co., Everyman's Library, 1957), p. 5.

47. Collingwood, *The Idea of History*, pp. 63–71; Löwith, *Meaning in History*, pp. 115–36; Manuel, *Eighteenth Century*, ch. 4, part 2. See Giambattista Vico, *The New Science*, trans. T. G. Bergin and M. H. Fisch (Ithaca, N.Y.: Cornell University Press, Cornell Paperbacks, 1970).

48. Manual, *Eighteenth Century*, ch. 4, part 1; Berlin, *Age of Enlightenment*, pp. 271–75.

49. Manuel, *Eighteenth Century*, ch. 4, parts 2 and 3; Johann Gottfried von Herder, *Reflections on the Philosophy of the History of Mankind*, abridged and introduced by Frank E. Manuel, Classic European Historians Series (Chicago: University of Chicago Press, 1969); Karl Barth, *Protestant Thought: From Rousseau to Ritschl*, trans. Brian Cozens (New York: Harper & Brothers, 1959), pp. 197–224; de Vries, *The Study of Religion*, pp. 43–45. On the question of thinking about myth in general, see Christian Hartlich and Walter Sachs, *Der Ursprung des Mythosbegriffs in der Modernen Bibelwissenschaft* (Tübingen: J. C. B. Mohr [Paul Siebeck], 1952).

50. J. G. Herder, *Briefe d. Stud. Theol. betr.*, ed. B. Sulphan (Berlin, 1877), pp. 238–39, in Barth, *Protestant Thought*, p. 221.

51. Barth, *Protestant Thought*, pp. 306–54; Martin Redeker, *Schleiermacher: Life and Thought*, trans. John Wallhausser (Philadelphia: Fortress Press, 1973); Stephen Sykes, *Friedrich Schleiermacher*, Makers of Contemporary Theology Series (Richmond, Va.: John Knox Press, 1971).

52. Ibid.; Hugh Ross Mackintosh, *Types of Modern Theology* (New York: Charles Scribner's Sons, 1937), chs. 1 and 2; Richard R. Niebuhr, *Schleiermacher on Christ and Religion: A New Introduction* (New York: Charles Scribner's Sons, 1964); Gerhard Spiegler, *The Eternal Covenant: Schleiermacher's Experiment in Cultural Theology*, Makers of Modern Theology Series (New York: Harper & Row, 1967); Robert W. Funk, ed., *Schleiermacher as Contemporary*, Journal for Theology and the Church, vol. 7 (New York: Herder & Herder, 1970); Friedrich Schleiermacher, *Christmas Eve: Dialogue on the Incarnation*, trans. Terrence N. Tice (Richmond, Va.: John Knox Press, 1967); Schleiermacher, *On Religion: Speeches to Its Cultured Despisers*, trans. John Oman (New York: Harper & Row, Harper Torchbooks, 1958 [originally translated 1893]); *The Christian Faith*, trans. H. R. Macintosh and J. S. Stewart (New York: Harper & Row, Harper Torchbooks, 1963).

53. Redeker, *Schleiermacher*, p. 135.

VI

Jesus Christ in Early Nineteenth-Century Historical Thought

We have suggested above that Renaissance and Reformation thinkers took steps in the direction of the modern "historical consciousness" in their study of ancient languages and original sources, and in their view that the medieval period was inferior culturally and religiously. This was accompanied by a stronger focus on the human Jesus of the Bible and on his importance for the *individual's* religion, which tended to diminish the importance of the Church. During the Enlightenment, history took a back seat to reason. There was a strong awareness that historical sources about Jesus might be untrustworthy, especially when they attested what seemed contrary to the laws of the physical world (the problem of miracles). Jesus Christ began to be looked on as a nonmiraculous, human Jesus, who had been a teacher of high ethical principles. In the view of the Protestant Pietist movement Jesus Christ not only had justified the sinner but also had set the *example* to be imitated, much in the same way as he had been looked on in a legendary and mystical way by Catholic pietists. With the romantic movement, there emerged the Jesus Christ who was the true religious man, the archetype for the feeling of absolute dependence on God.

In this chapter we look at some of the most dominant advances in thought about history: idealism, materialism, positivism, and evolutionism. Then three of the most important thinkers about Jesus Christ will be considered: David Friedrich Strauss, who is frequently considered a historical skeptic; Ferdinand Christian Baur, who is usually considered the "father of historical theology"; and Ernest Renan, who, influenced by both romanticism and the German critics, is usually regarded as the author of the first historical biography of Jesus.

HEGEL AND THE IDEALIST VIEW OF HISTORY

The most important philosopher after the great ethical theorist Immanuel Kant (1724–1804) was Georg Wilhelm Friedrich Hegel (1779–1831).[1] For medieval thought, especially influenced by Plato and Aristotle, True Reality was fixed and unchanging, and for Kant, the categories of the mind, which order human experience, were fixed and unchanging. In contrast, Hegel believed that all reality involved constant change. For him the universe was like a great living organism that has desires, aims, intentions, and purposes; it was a spiritual and thinking being. This constantly changing reality he termed Absolute Mind, Absolute Idea, or World Spirit.

How did this notion of World Spirit relate to history? Hegel acknowledged the practical side to writing history, such as the evaluation of eyewitness observations and the reconstruction of events, but he was more concerned with change and movement in history. Hegel did not rest easily with what appeared to be the injustices of history, that is, human misery in war, the suffering of the innocent, insanity among humans, and the inevitability of death. Was history the product of irrational passions, a series of unique, unrepeatable events with no particular meaning? Hegel decided it was not; on the contrary, he saw a rational plan in history. For Hegel, God was perhaps subtle, but not malevolent. What appeared to be irrational was, in fact, the "cunning of reason," or Absolute Mind expressing itself in action, in human events. Hegel came to think that history was working itself out by resolving contradictions. Johann Gottlieb Fichte (1762–1814) had spoken of thesis, antithesis, and synthesis. Though Hegel usually did not use these precise terms, he did develop his philosophy around triads, that is, the tendency of one idea (thesis) to generate its opposite (antithesis), resulting in some further idea (synthesis). As change occurs, conflicts and contradictions lead to resolutions or compromises which, through further changes, become poles of new contradictions. This eternal process is the Hegelian *dialectic*. It is the process of Absolute Mind, or World Spirit, working within the world. World history, said Hegel, is the unfolding of "World Reason," the Absolute Mind working itself out in the conflicts of empires and nations, each with its own national-ethnic spirit

(*Volksgeist*). In each successive period, moreover, one nation will be dominant because its time as a special representative of World Spirit has arrived. Through this process, said Hegel, humankind is moving closer and closer to human freedom. He saw history not simply as a series of unrelated, irrational, empirical events, but as a series of events reflecting opposing ideas (dialectic) in the subtle unfolding of the World Spirit.

Hegel wrote a *Life of Jesus* (1795), but it took an Enlightenment form and suggested that Jesus was a moral teacher whose views had been wrongly transformed by the institutional Church. His more enduring contribution was his philosophy of history. His idealistic approach to history gave it meaning and direction. Such a view had profound effects on nineteenth-century historical thinking in general, most notably on the left-wing Karl Marx and the right-wing F. C. Baur.

LEFT-WING HEGELIANISM AND THE MATERIALIST VIEW OF HISTORY

At the University of Berlin there emerged a young, rather radical group of Hegelian thinkers who took Hegel's tendency to see the progressive development of human freedom as a program leading to philosophical materialism and atheism. In contrast to right-wing Hegelians, the left wing considered orthodox Christianity and philosophy incompatible. One left-wing Hegelian was Ludwig Feuerbach (1804–72), whose major point is the claim that knowledge is limited to the material world: All religion, according to Feuerbach, arises from the objectification of human (material) needs, wishes, or desires. In Feuerbach's words, "Religion is the dream of the human mind."[2]

The key left-wing thinker influenced by Hegel and Feuerbach was Karl Marx (1813–83).[3] For Marx, Hegel's idealism had to be modified in the direction of Feuerbach's atheistic materialism. Thus the Hegelian conflict of *ideas* as the basis for conflict in material history is turned upside down: Marx declared that material (economic) conflicts are the driving forces in history; ideas follow only later. Through Feuerbach's materialism, combined with a view of class struggle put forth by the French thinker Saint-Simon, Marx transformed Hegel's dialectic of abstract ideas, or *dialectical idealism,* into a dialectic of concrete conflict between those of different economic status, or *dialectical materialism.*

Marx believed, as did Hegel, that history was the story of human freedom; the battle to attain that freedom was the conflict between the social classes that control economic production and the workers. For Marx, there were five major periods in history: (1) primitive communism, (2) the slave system of ancient Greece and Rome, (3) the feudal system of medieval Europe, (4) the modern capitalist system with its industrial technology, and (5) the system of the future, communism. In each period, changes in the *quantity* of production converged to inspire an eventual revolution that changed the *quality* of society as a whole. For Marx there was a law of history: he saw history as *economically determined*. The control of property is the key. In the slave period, the slave was less free than were people in the primitive period, but in this case the move was necessary to accommodate society's production to the invention of tools. Then, in the medieval phase, the serf was more free than the slave, for he had some share in owning the means of production. In the capitalist phase the modern worker became more free than the serf but still did not own the means of production. This, of course, was Marx's own period, and he reasoned that the owners of production (the *bourgeoisie*) and the workers (the *proletariat*) were engaging in a conflict that would lead to a dictatorship of the proletariat as a transition to the final stage of the classless society, the communist phase. The problem of the capitalist system for Marx was that whereas a product ought to be sold for what it cost the laborer to produce it (the "labor theory of value"), the capitalist was able to sell it for more, pocket the profit, and keep the laborer at the subsistence level. As a result of his views, Marx saw religion as a tool of the bourgeoisie to keep the proletariat in its place; religion was "the opiate of the people," a drug to keep them happy under oppressive conditions.

A left-wing Hegelian who was more directly involved in study of the life of Jesus was Bruno Bauer (1809–82).[4] Bauer at first became a right-wing Hegelian and criticized Strauss's *Life of Jesus* (1835 [see pages 177–84]) from the perspective of orthodoxy. A noticeable turn to the left appeared in Bauer's writings from the 1840s on. In two anonymous publications (1840 and 1841) he argued that the atheism of the young Hegelian left was rooted in Hegel himself. Bauer decided in an analysis of the Gospel of John that it was purely a work of art, with no historical basis. What if Mark, now believed by some to be the earliest gospel, were also a (fictional) *literary* production, a piece of art? In his study of the gospels (1841–42) Bauer began with the assumption that the personality of the historical Jesus had evoked the *Christian* version of the idea of the Messiah. As Bauer proceeded in his analyses, his views became increasingly radical. *His historical study was now throwing doubt on the very historicity of Jesus.*

It was hardly surprising that in 1842 Bauer was forbidden by the Prussian minister of culture to continue lecturing. In his "Christianity Exposed" (1843) he made a devastating critique of all religions and defended a humanistic self-consciousness as the new form of thought. This work was confiscated, but a few copies survived to influence Marx and Engels. Bauer also wrote on secular history, became involved in politics—ironically, as a conservative—and in the 1850s again took up an analysis of the gospels, Acts, and the Pauline letters. By 1874 he had come to the view that Philo's fusion of Greek speculation with Judaism had anticipated primitive Christianity. Three years later his book *Christ and the Caesars: The Origin of Christianity from Greco-Roman Civilization,* which was highly influential among socialists and Marxists, attempted to argue that the Christ, in effect, was a cultural idea with no real root in a historical personality. Bauer had become anti-Christian, anti-Semitic, and antireligious altogether. His works remained standard reading for communists long after his death in 1882.

POSITIVISM AND HISTORY

Positivism had certain antecedents in the British empiricist denial of a priori ideas in the mind. However, its more immediate precursors were the French thinkers.[5] In 1750 Anne Robert Jacques Turgot (1727–81) put forth his view of history as a three-stage development of the human race and mind: first, idolatrous paganism; second, civilizing and humanizing Christian love and justice; and third, the ideal society characterized by justice, rights of work and property, increasing wealth, and pleasure and happiness for all. The Christian view of *God's providence over history* here begins to be replaced by a view of *human progress through history.* Such a view was carried farther, though in a more markedly atheistic form, by Marie Jean Nicholas Caritat, the Marquis de Condorcet (1743–94), who was condemned and executed by the Jacobins during the French Revolution. There were other exponents of historical progress, such as Saint-Simon (who, it will be recalled, influenced Karl Marx). But above all, positivism in France was associated with one great thinker, Auguste Comte (1798–1857), whose classic work on positivism was *Cours de Philosophie positive* (*Course on Positive Philosophy* [1830–42]).

Like Hegel, Comte was a *historical* thinker, deeply concerned with the purpose of history, especially as seen in connection with the evolution of Western culture. Whereas Hegel believed that historical movement in Western culture was superior because of the West's Christian orientation, the secular thinker Comte thought that the West was superior because of the physical, chemical, and biological conditions of Caucasians. He sought to discover a discernible order in history, and he found it in the progress of the human mind as it moved toward maturity. Not only Western history, but all classes of thinking, he reasoned, move through three stages:[6]

1. *Childhood:* a "theological" stage that searches for the origin and ultimate purpose of things, explaining them by *divine powers,*

first within things (fetishism), then outside things (polytheism), and finally by a single Divine Power (monotheism).

2. *Youth:* a "metaphysical" stage that seeks the absolute "essence" of things, explaining them by *impersonal and abstract forces.*

3. *Manhood:* a "positivistic" (that is, scientific) stage that does not seek origins, ultimate purposes, essences, or final causes of things, but simply wishes to *describe* things as they are, explaining them by a set of constant cause-and-effect relations that are *relative* only to each other, and to apply such knowledge to the material and social life of humanity.

As the third stage indicates, Comte's positivism was concerned to explicate the constant order, the invariable law, of the world and history, *whether or not a universal intelligence is behind it.* In true Enlightenment fashion, he wished to think of religion in terms of the natural sciences, to study it with scientific methods (beginning, however, with deduction and moving to induction), and to make observations about it that would lead to scientific knowledge about the *human being* as an intellectual, moral, and social being. John Stuart Mill summarized Comte's positivism as follows:

> We have no knowledge of anything but phaenomena; and our knowledge of phaenomena is relative, not absolute. We know not the essence, nor the real mode of production, of any fact, but only its relations to other facts in the way of succession or of similitude. These relations are constant; that is, always the same in the same circumstances. The constant resemblances which link phaenomena together, and the constant sequences which unite them as antecedent and consequent, are termed their laws. The laws of phaenomena are all we know respecting them. Their essential nature, and their ultimate causes, either efficient or final, are unknown and inscrutable to us.[7]

Comte's application of positivism to human beings led him to develop an early form of "sociology" that included reflections on group behavior, family life, and the division of labor. Thinking in terms of a society that resembled a secularized medieval community, he theorized about the total reorganization of society along the lines of a humanized religion that included a Supreme Being, renowned scientists as saints, and a set of "social" sacraments ("rites of passage" along life's way: presentation, initiation, admission, destination or choice of career, marriage, and retirement). Comte believed that as other sciences had gone through the three stages, so now it was the turn of sociology, and he as the philosopher would lead the way. He would be the first high priest who would attract groups of followers from every quarter! Historical progress for Comte did not lead to perfection, as in the thought of Condorcet, but it did lead to total reorganization of society along the lines of a secularized religious model. No traditional God was necessary.

EVOLUTION AND HISTORY

Though Charles Darwin (1809–82) was not the first to propose a theory of evolution, he is usually recognized as the first to develop a full-blown theory with the support of scientifically acceptable data.[8] On a voyage around the world (1831–36), Darwin abandoned the Genesis creation story after reading in Charles Lyell's *Principles of Geology* that the formation of the earth's surface had taken place over great spans of time. In September 1832 Darwin was surprised to find, about 300 miles south of Buenos Aires, fossils of extinct animals much larger than their surviving counterparts. Had God created two like species of radically different size? How had they been transformed? How had they evolved?

In 1837 he finished compiling his notes from his journal of the trip (published in 1839 and revised in 1845 as *The Voyage of the Beagle*). Then he set about counteracting the orthodox Christian belief that each species had been created *at one time* by God, a view he called "creationism." It was also necessary to overcome previous and inadequate theories of evolution. Taking up Lyell's view that the physical environment and climate had changed over the years, Darwin argued that those which were weaklings in one environment might be the survivors in a changed environment, and that in the competition for survival a favorable variation would then be preserved. In 1838 he read Malthus's *Essay on the Principle of Population* (1798), which stressed the amazing rapidity of population growth and the scarcity of food that makes it impossible for every living being to survive. This confirmed Darwin's view that the struggle for survival was intense and that as a result of this struggle there occurred a mutability, or transformation, of species by *natural selection*. Darwin now had a plausible theory that would fit his information: In the intensely competitive struggle for survival by rapidly multiplying species over great expanses of time and through diverse environments, there is a tendency for the species that are better adapted to new environments to perpetuate themselves through inheritance. Evolution could be explained by "natural selection."

By 1844 Darwin had sketched out his theory of evolution, but he did not publish it until a rival, Alfred Russell Wallace, developed the same theory and wrote him about it in 1858. Persuaded by Lyell and his friend, the botanist Thomas Hooker, to publish his ideas along with those of Wallace in that same year, he then set about rapidly elaborating his theory in a book that rocked the Western world, *The Origin of Species by Means of Natural Selection* (1859). In his *Descent of Man* (1871) Darwin developed the view that man came from a lower order of primates (Darwin himself disliked thinking in "lower–higher" categories). This led his opponents to say he believed man had evolved from the apes, a view which many considered an attack on cherished biblical beliefs. The fallout from Darwin's views was amazing. Those who already believed in evolution could now point to Darwin's study as proof; many others began to apply evolution to other fields; and those who opposed theories of evolution now faced a growing body of adherents.

It is impossible to discuss Darwin's vast influence fully here; it is enough to mention the views of the most important evolutionary philosopher of the period, Herbert Spencer (1820–1903).[9] In 1851 Spencer combined a number of viewpoints, including Malthus's theory of population, and argued that those in whom the power of self-preservation is greatest will tend to survive. From this he concluded that "higher" forms will evolve from "lower" ones. Spencer's phrase to describe this evolution was "survival of the fittest," a phrase he sought to popularize, along with the theory of evolution in general. His view was that everything—including history and society—evolves from lower to higher forms. Like Comte, he believed that there is progress in three stages, from simple societies (those with little political organization) to compound societies (those that are politically elaborate) to more compound societies (those that are industrialized). Unlike Comte, however, Spencer employed a model that was biological and all-encompassing, and it included an ultimate (metaphysical) purpose. Finally, Spencer's biological basis for social–historical evolution had several political and social ramifications that influenced historical theory in the late nineteenth and twentieth centuries—some of which in their racial implications were unfortunate.

Major thinkers of the early and middle nineteenth century—Hegel, Marx, Comte, Darwin, Spencer—revolutionized Western attitudes toward history. For Hegel, there was a kind of divine rationality through history, moving it forward by a dialectic of ideas; for Marx, the movement was brought about by purely human class conflict with the vision of a classless society in the future; for Comte, history had passed through definable stages following its own laws without regard to ultimate causes or designs; for Darwin, history had evolved over great expanses of time by natural selection, thus proving that a literal view of biblical creation was inaccurate; for Spencer there were three stages of evolution from lower to higher forms, the basis being survival of the fittest. They all saw history as having been somewhere or as going somewhere—as movement. Though Hegel had a concept of the World Spirit, none of their theories supported the orthodox view of a God external to the universe whose providence guides history or whose self-revelation can interrupt it. Only Hegel's theory allowed room for a deity (as usually conceived), and we will see in the next chapter that his views were held in less regard than those of Marx, Comte, Darwin, and Spencer in the late nineteenth century.

JESUS CHRIST IN THE THOUGHT
OF DAVID FRIEDRICH STRAUSS

Albert Schweitzer opened his chapter on the life of David Friedrich Strauss (1808–74) in the following way:

> In order to understand Strauss one must love him. He was not the greatest, and not the deepest, of theologians, but he was the most absolutely sincere. His insight and his errors were alike the insight and errors of a prophet. And he had a prophet's fate. Disappointment and suffering gave his life its consecration. It unrolls itself before us like a tragedy, in which, in the end, the gloom is lightened by the mild radiance which shines forth from the nobility of the sufferer.[10]

The suffering prophet, David Friedrich Strauss, was born the third of four children in 1808 in the little village of Ludwigsburg, near Stuttgart in southern Germany.[11] His mother, Christiane, was only moderately educated, but she knew the Bible well and had developed her own form of rationalism. His father, Johann Friederich Strauss, was a struggling businessman, an excellent Latinist, and a good poet. He also spoke fluent French. From this modest family, the bright young Fritz went to the theological seminary at Blaubeuren in 1821, partly because it was the least expensive route for entrance to the university. One of his teachers was the (eventually) famous Hegelian church historian F. C. Baur.

In 1825 Strauss and a number of his Blaubeuren friends, notably Märklin and Vischer, matriculated at the University of Tübingen. Faced with several uninteresting professors in philosophy, the group enthusiastically embraced the romantics on their own. Strauss also became absorbed in the mystics and developed a fascination for local occult practices.

Strauss entered the theological phase of his education at Tübingen in 1827. Baur, who had become a professor at Tübingen the previous year, directed Strauss and his friends to the writings of Schleiermacher. Though the latter's views helped to shift the group away from the romantics and the occult, they were not yet intellectually satisfied. With Hegel it was different. Though the Berlin philosopher was viewed with suspicion at Tübingen, Strauss's group eagerly devoured *The Phenomenology of Spirit.* By now Strauss was as much a philosopher as a theologian; when he graduated with a first in 1830, he no longer held to traditional orthodox beliefs.

In 1831, after nine months in the parish, Strauss was excitedly off to Berlin, which was the capital of Prussia, a great cultural center, and a mecca for young theologians. Among other things, Strauss was eager to hear the lectures of the great Hegel. After Strauss had heard two of Hegel's lectures, Schleiermacher had the unpleasant task of informing him that Hegel had suddenly died of cholera. Strauss was crushed. He disappointedly blurted out, "But it was for his sake that I came here!" This so offended the now famous Schleiermacher that relations between him and Strauss became strained, though Strauss grew to like Schleiermacher's spontaneous classroom style in his course on the life of Jesus.

In May 1832 Strauss was back in Tübingen among friends, lecturing on logic, metaphysics, Kant, and ethics, but he was now beginning to encounter opposition because of his Hegelian philosophical views. After a year and a half of teaching, he retired to work on his *Life of Jesus*. Showing the inadequacy of both the supernaturalist and the rationalist views, he proposed as an alternative a "mythical" interpretation of the texts. This placed them in question as accurate historical sources. When the first volume appeared, on June 1, 1835, extremely strong reaction flared up, first on the part of the seminary, and then from all quarters, including the Hegelians. The momentum carried to the remotest corners of German church life, and things were never again the same for German theology or for Strauss.

The rest of Strauss's life corresponds to Schweitzer's description. He was dismissed from Tübingen as a bad influence on the seminary students, and though a second edition of the *Life* was quickly printed, he was limited by the authorities to teaching Latin at Ludwigsburg. Back in Stuttgart, he began to write defenses of his views (*Polemical Writings*). Slowly three friends from Tübingen—but only three—came to his support. Even F. C. Baur, his teacher and manuscript reader, remained silent and cautiously sought to diminish the importance of the book (it appeared before Baur's major works) and to stress that Strauss's method was negative (destructively critical) whereas his own was positive (constructively critical). In 1838 Strauss was appointed to a position at Zürich. The third edition of his *Life of Jesus* appeared, greatly modified. But opposition also mounted against him at Zürich, and he was pensioned off before assuming his responsibilities. Never again would he be appointed to a church or a university position. It is scarcely surprising that in the fourth edition of his book (1840) he returned to his original views. Strauss now made an all-out attack against the orthodox theologians (1840/1841). He married an opera star in 1842, but shortly after the birth of two children, they were separated. Strauss was elected to the provincial parliament in 1848 but soon encountered opposition from his own constituency. From 1842 to 1862 he moved from town to town, partly to avoid his estranged wife, who sought reconciliation. During this period he wrote about politics, biography, literature, and history, but not theology.

In 1864 Strauss reentered the battle and wrote his *Life of Jesus for the German People,* an attempt to communicate with the masses in the way that Renan's recent *Life of Jesus* had communicated in France. In contrast to the *Life* of 1835, this new book explicitly sketched a "life of Jesus" and dealt with the origins and dates of the gospels. At times, Jesus appeared as an exceptional religious personality and great ethical teacher, but sometimes he seemed to be a deluded fanatic. After more polemics (1865) and preoccupation with the Franco-Prussian War (1870–71), Strauss wrote his last work, *The Old and New Faith* (1872). He confessed that though religious feeling still exists, "we are no longer Christians." He regarded the church as a worthless institution to be replaced by the arts, as he turned to Darwin's and Ernst Haeckel's theories of evolution, espoused a conservative morality, and claimed Jesus was a deluded fanatic. In the book his final words were, "The time of vindication will come, as it came for the *Life of Jesus:* only this time I shall not live to see it." He returned to Ludwigsburg in November. Now his lifelong friend Vischer could not agree with his position. The book was also attacked by Friedrich Nietzsche. Strauss was ill. In February 1874 he died, requesting that there be no church funeral, no music from the church tower, no cross on the pall, and no clergyman.

Strauss became known for his mythical view of the New Testament. There is a certain irony in this characterization, because Strauss did not himself believe in a Christ myth, nor did he propose an intellectual understanding of myth with anything like the modern sensitivity to primitive myth. In fact, in his classic *Life of Jesus* of 1835 he scarcely wrote anything about Jesus as an identifiable entity!

Did his mythical view come from the romantic interest in the past and in primitive myth? He had read Herder. He had devoured the romantics, especially Schelling, at Tübingen. Moreover, F. C. Baur, who had been influenced by the early Schelling's view of myth (1792), had lectured to Strauss and his friends on this subject in 1828–29. Strauss had also studied the once romantically inclined Schleiermacher and was, himself, a sensitive poet of feeling. He may have known of the later Schelling's lectures on myth, which began in 1828 at Berlin. Yet the romantic approach to myth did not shine through—at least not directly. You will remember from our discussion on page 158 that Herder's romantic spirit was not inclined to more rationalistic historical-critical precision. However, C. G. Heyne's was. It was Heyne (1729–1812) who in many respects was still deeply rooted in the Enlightenment. And it is especially Heyne whom Strauss cites in his *Life of Jesus;* it would not be accurate to think of the *Life* as an epitome of romanticism or of Strauss's Jesus as a romantic's Jesus.

Neither was Strauss's view of myth rooted in Hegelian idealism. It is true that Strauss was deeply absorbed in Hegel's thought; in fact, he presented his material in "dialectical" fashion, that is, he discussed the orthodox supernaturalist interpretations of Jesus (thesis), then the rationalist interpretations (antithesis), thus clearing the ground for his own "mythical" interpretation (synthesis). His thinking was the product of conflicting ideas. Yet the *form* of his presentation, or argumentation, did not mean that Strauss thought of myth simply as an *idea* of the "God–man" that made contact with history in Jesus of Nazareth. Strauss accepted Hegel's distinction between abstract "concept" and concrete "image," but to Strauss thinking in concepts was an *advance* over thinking in images, and the two types of thinking remained separate. Though the idea or "concept" of the God–man was important to him, it was not necessary that it be linked to the biblical images, such as Jesus' power over the demons, resurrection, and ascension. Strauss viewed the biblical images critically because he could *move on* to abstract ideas—in this case, the concept of the God–man—without them. Furthermore—and this is the major point—myth for Strauss was not the Hegelian "idea" or "concept" which became concrete, as Schleiermacher's notion of consciousness of God became concrete in Jesus; on the contrary, myth was the concrete image, that beyond which the philosopher should move.

What Strauss called "myth" came from a somewhat different direction. The notion of myth in Heyne's thought was applied to Judaism by J. S. Semler (1725–88) and to the Old Testament by J. G. Eichhorn (1752–1827). To Eichhorn, myths in both Hebrew and pagan history were not the product of deceit and falsehood, but the way primitives spontaneously expressed events and unseen realities in sensuous, pictorial, visual, and dramatic imagery characteristic of their times. The older the sources, the more they were pervaded with "myths." Such views began to be applied to the New Testament by Eichhorn and J. P. Gabler (1753–1826), but only in a limited sense, especially to infancy stories which seemed to have a long oral tradition. Similar views were held by G. L. Bauer (1755–1806), who claimed that if a narrative deals with matters which cannot have been witnessed, or if it explains events through the direct intervention of personal gods rather than natural causes and laws of nature, or describes everything in a sensuous way, one is in the realm of myth. For Bauer there were "philosophical myths" (stories about the origins of the world, the human race, or future life), "historical myths" (stories about the oldest histories of peoples, their founders, benefactors, and inventions, with quasi-historical events behind them), and "poetical myths" (stories invented or embellished by poets and embellished over time with multiple layers). Among the New

Testament "myths" Bauer included narratives of angels and demons, the virgin birth, and the transfiguration.

There was reason for caution in all this: The historicity of the gospels was now at stake. Strauss pointed, for example, to some important anonymous articles. In Henke's *Magazine* in 1796, a certain "E. F." had anticipated Bauer by explaining the virgin birth as simply a popular Jewish belief from Old Testament prophecy (Isa 7:14) applied to Jesus' birth. In 1799 an anonymous book entitled *Concerning Revelation and Mythology* (possibly written by J. C. A. Grohmann, professor of philosophy at Wittenberg) argued that Jesus' life was interpreted in the pattern of the Old Testament Messiah current in popular Jewish belief at the time, though Jesus' actual life had been quite different. Another anonymous article in Bertholdt's *Critical Journal of the Most Recent Theological Literature* (1816) attacked both the rationalists' and the mediators' explanations and proposed that the "mythical" view be carried out in interpreting the *whole* New Testament; to illustrate his point he drew parallels between the Old Testament Elijah–Elisha miracles and New Testament stories about Jesus' miracles.

Strauss himself built on this tradition and attempted to do two things: to define his terms and to carry out his mythical interpretation on the whole life of Jesus. He distinguished the terms as follows:

(1) *Evangelical myth:* ". . . narrative relating directly or indirectly to Jesus which may be considered not as the expression of a fact, but as *the product of an idea* (in this context, "idea" means "religious image") of his earliest followers." It has two sources:
   (a) Jewish *messianic* ideas and expectations, before or independent of Jesus (for example, the transfiguration).
   (b) The *general* impact of Jesus' personal character, actions, and fate, which modified the messianic idea (for example, Jesus' hostility to temple worship gave rise to the story of the rending of the veil in the temple). The latter, however, verges on the next type.
(2) *Historical myth:* a specific historical fact which religious enthusiasm has enveloped with ideas (religious images) of the Christ, such as the baptism, or a saying (such as the cursing of the fig tree) that has become a miraculous story.
(3) *Legend:* ". . . those parts of the history which are characterized by indefiniteness and want of connection, by misconstruction and transformation, by strange combinations and confusion—the natural results of a *long course of oral transmission;* or which, on the contrary, are distinguished by highly colored and pictorial representatives, which also seem to point to a traditionary origin."
(4) *Additions of the author:* ". . . *purely individual,* and designed

> merely to give clearness, connexion, and climax, to the presenta-
> tion." [12]

As we have said, Strauss's application of myth to the whole story of Jesus involved rejecting both the supernatural and the rationalist interpretations. In the process he pointed out again and again the discrepancies among the various versions of a story, frequently interpreting it as a pure "evangelical myth" with its origin in an Old Testament story. In direct contrast to Schleiermacher, he concluded that the Gospel of John was, by definition, the most "mythical" and hence the least historical. In short, Strauss did openly and completely what had heretofore been done only anonymously or partially: He cast doubt on the historical credibility of much of the life of Jesus.

Strauss's method is best observed by taking an example, the story of Jesus' baptism. Strauss noted that the orthodox interpreters said (thesis) that Jesus was conscious of being Messiah already, but that he refrained from assuming his Messianic prerogatives until he was acclaimed publicly. However, the rationalists pointed (antithesis) to the problems in the text such as the opening of the heavens, the descent of the dove, and the voice of God. Was there originally a flash of lightning, a clap of thunder and, at the same time, a dove hovering overhead? After noting the divergences of the various interpretations, Strauss pointed (synthesis) to God's speaking in Isaiah 42:1 ("Here is my servant whom I uphold, my chosen one in whom my soul delights"), which Matthew 12:17ff. says was applied to Jesus as the Messiah. On the basis of the Old Testament it was believed that God would speak to the Messiah this way. Strauss also pointed to Psalm 2:7 ("Thou art my son; today I have begotten thee"), which was considered messianic by Jewish interpreters. The two Old Testament texts were combined in the Gospel of Hebrews (apocryphal) and Luke's version of the baptism (Luke 3:1ff.). This explains the origin of the voice in the account: The popular mind believed it would happen that way and so portrayed it. Similarly, the dove as the image of the spirit was based on the view that the spirit would come in messianic times (Joel 3:1; Isa 11:1ff.), that the spirit was presented in concrete images in the Old Testament (for example, a fire) and spoken of as "hovering" like a bird (Gen 1:2). In the East, the dove was considered a sacred bird, was given special significance in the Noah–flood story, and was esteemed in Jewish writings. It would therefore have been natural to associate the dove with baptism by water and the Spirit, which comes from the heavens. For it to come, the heavens, of course, had to be opened. These items were therefore not factual (that is, historical), but "mythical." Was the baptism itself historical or mythical? Interestingly, Strauss believed that it was probably historical, for it would have provided a reason for Jesus' messianic project. That point, however, was lost. What had been an occasion for Jesus' condescension, or a set of natural events given a misunderstood significance, now became only a probable event colored by myth.[13]

We have pointed out that Strauss was really interested in analyzing the mythical character of the gospels, not in portraying the Jesus who was the product of his critical study. Yet he did make occasional statements about Jesus, and his view of Jesus can be reconstructed from them.[14] For Strauss, little could be known about the birth, infancy, and childhood of Jesus, for they were the product of myth. Certainly, Jesus was a disciple of John the Baptist and continued John's preaching about the coming Messianic kingdom after John was imprisoned. At first, Jesus spoke of the Son of Man as someone different from himself. Gradually, however, he came to think of himself as that coming Son of Man, and referred to himself also as the Son of God and the Messiah. Thus it was not the resurrection of Jesus that caused the early church to identify him with such titles (see Ch. 2), but Jesus' own teaching. For Strauss, Jesus did not consider these titles in the Jewish nationalist or political (Zealot) sense; rather, he viewed them as *religious* images related to the apocalyptic expectations of the Jews about the coming supernatural kingdom.

Strauss found little history in the *narratives* about Jesus. Though Jesus' *teachings* were historically based, they had passed through interpretive elaboration in the oral tradition, had been placed in a new context by the synoptists, and furthermore offered little that was new or unique in comparison with Jesus' contemporaries. Strauss concluded that Jesus did not intend to sever connections with Judaism. Despite his messianic claims, Jesus simply presented himself as a correct interpreter of the Mosaic law in contrast to the traditional interpretations of the Scribes and Pharisees, with the addition that the Mosaic law would come to an end with his glorious return to the regenerated earth at the End. Jesus also spoke many of the parables attributed to him, though the settings were different, and possibly Jesus spoke some of the "woe unto you" sayings against his opponents and the rich, but these were also characteristic Ebionite teaching in this period.

Strauss claimed that as Jesus' life moved toward its completion, Jesus predicted that after the destruction of Jerusalem and the temple he would come on the clouds of heaven as the supernatural Son of Man, thus bringing to end the present age. Though he might have considered this role without his intervening death at first, he later came to see that suffering and death were part of his messianic vocation, and he sought to prepare his followers for that possibility. Not political revolution, but the supernatural power of God would be the means for ushering in the End. Thus Jesus was in fact wrong in his predictions. Though Strauss saw most of the details of the passion story as "myth," he thought it probable that Jesus became afraid in the garden and prayed for release from his sufferings; that he publicly claimed to be the Messiah before the Sanhedrin and Pilate; and that he met an actual death. Strauss nonetheless doubted the resurrection of Jesus and believed that the empty tomb stories were legendary myths and that the appearances were the product of the disciples' hallucinations.

Strauss analyzed the gospels as a whole as being a product of myth, thus casting much doubt on their historical character. Jesus might have been a highly distinguished personality who made some impact on human history, but Strauss had difficulty in accepting even that conclusion. Ultimately, the "myths" of the gospels should be replaced by philosophical speculation about the God–man.

JESUS CHRIST IN THE THOUGHT OF FERDINAND CHRISTIAN BAUR

Ferdinand Christian Baur (1792–1860) was born in the southern German town of Schmiden, near Stuttgart.[15] His father, Christian Jakob Baur, a Lutheran pastor, and his mother, Eberhardine Rigine Gross, were serious, industrious, hard-working, and pious Christians. Little is known of F. C. Baur's childhood. He was educated in his early years by his father until, at age 13, he entered the "lower" theological seminary at Blaubeuren, where his father had taken a pastorate. A normal course of languages, biblical interpretation, history, and philosophy for two years was followed by two more at Maulbronn Kloster and then five with the supernaturally oriented faculty of the seminary at the University of Tübingen. Despite the faculty's orientation, Baur encountered Kant's philosophy and rationalist historical criticism through the teaching of the moderate G. E. Bengel and by studying G. G. Niebuhr's *Roman History*. He may also have read the romantics Fichte and Schelling at this time.

After serving two parishes for short periods, he became an assistant in the lower theological seminary at Schönthal, a lecturer at Tübingen in 1816, and then a professor at the seminary at Blaubeuren in 1817. For the next ten years, he broadened his study with ancient history, classical philosophy, linguistics, mythology, and history of religions. The most important influences on him seem to have been Plato and the romantics—and especially Schleiermacher. Baur's first major work, *Symbolism and Mythology* (1824/1825), abandoned the old Tübingen supernaturalism, developed ideas of religion based on the romantics and Schleiermacher, and drew contrasts between nature religions and historical religions, *one* of which was Christianity.

In 1826, after the death of Bengel, the Tübingen faculty underwent reform, thus permitting Baur to be appointed to teach Church history,

Ferdinand Christian Baur

as well as the history of Christian dogma, and various New Testament subjects. His inaugural dissertation of 1827 criticized Schleiermacher's view of the ideal Christ, which Baur thought was not rooted enough in history. This strongly *historical* bent also appeared in his famous and highly influential article "The Christ Party in the Corinthian Church" (1831), in which he developed the view that in Corinth, the hellenistic (Gentile) adherents of Paul had as their opponents the more Jewish adherents of Peter, and that these opposing parties could be traced further in other New Testament writings. The point emerged that primitive Christian history, like all human history, was played out on the stage of human conflicts. After a brief departure into discussions about Catholicism and Protestantism, in which he constructively compared Protestantism to nonhistorically oriented Gnosticism (1834), he elaborated the latter theme in *Die Christliche Gnosis (Christian Gnosticism* [1835]), which showed the direct influence of Hegel for the first time.

When Strauss was dismissed in 1835 from Tübingen after the publication of his controversial *Life of Jesus,* Baur's response was mixed. Never did Baur deny the "heinous charge" of their friendship. Yet, partly for political reasons, he never explicitly defended his former pupil; gradually, he came more and more into conflict with Strauss's method. In a series of publications from 1836 to 1853, Baur dissociated himself from what he believed was Strauss's "negative" criticism, claiming that his use of myth did not do justice to the historicity of the gospels. Strauss, however, believed that Baur was refusing to take sides in order not to rile the conservatives and that he, Strauss, had become too famous too fast for his teacher. By 1846 Strauss had severed the relationship, and a year later Baur wrote that Strauss not only was too negative but did not take the tendencies of New Testament writings *as a whole* into account (Baur's famous "tendency criticism"). Finally, in 1853 Baur put forth his own view of Jesus.

From 1835 on, Baur was a highly productive scholar, especially on the history of dogma, early church history, and the New Testament. He and his "Tübingen School" are especially famous for several interlocking contributions: interpreting history by means at Hegel's thought, "tendency criticism," and the dating of a number of New Testament books. From Hegel came the idea of a dialectic that led to certain conflicts and turning points in history; "tendency criticism" sought to analyze documents *as a whole* according to their literary–theological tendencies. With an understanding of the documents and the turning points, Baur then placed the documents at their appropriate position in the chronological framework according to their tendencies. Baur's attempt to interpret early Christian history in terms of conflicts is still influential in New Testament study, though today's scholars would hold that he dated some of the New Testament literature much too late, that he was too critical in concluding that there were only four authentic letters from Paul, and that his view of Paul's opponents as exclusively Jews was oversimplified. He is considered one of the foremost New Testament historians of the nineteenth century.

Ferdinand Christian Baur was above all a historian.[16] One lasting contribution was his interpretation of early Christian literature in the context of an overall perspective on the development of early Christianity. In this respect he might even be called the first modern Christian historian. Baur's historical consciousness also led to his quest for the historical Jesus. He believed, in fact, that the particular character of Christianity—its very essence and content—had always and everywhere been directly related to its founder. The personality of Jesus was, for Baur, the starting point and foundation for all that followed.

Because of the critical importance of the historical Jesus for understanding the essence of Christianity, it is important to see what Baur said about the sources. His studies, privately in 1838 and publicly in 1844, led him to the conclusion that the Gospel of John, though important for its own quasi-Gnostic Christ figure, was not composed by John the disciple and was of little historical worth for the Jesus he sought. Thus he concurred with Strauss's 1835 position on John as opposed to that of Schleiermacher, and he criticized Strauss for vacillating later. With regard to the synoptic gospels, let us recall that several theories had by this time been proposed, all of which were unacceptable to the orthodox because of the element of human error that such theories saw in the Bible. Basically, these theories held that the synoptics went back to a primitive Aramaic gospel (now lost), originally in either written or oral form, or to the collection of originally isolated stories. Otherwise, some form of dependence of one of both later gospels on the earliest was suggested, and this was also Baur's view. He accepted J. J. Griesbach's theory (1789) that Matthew was the earliest gospel, that Luke had used Matthew, and that Mark had abridged both. But literary dependence was not enough for Baur; it was also important to establish the "tendency" of each gospel and place it historically according to that tendency. The tendency of the Gospel of Mark was to produce a clearly arranged, nonrepetitive portrayal of the essential facts without much teaching material. The original (lost) Lukan gospel was an attempt to move Matthew's narrower Jewish gospel toward the universalistic Paul, and this was then revised in part to avoid the totally anti-Jewish attitude of the Marcionite Gnostics. The Gospel of Matthew, which Baur dated about 130–134 C.E. in connection with the revolt of Bar Cochba against the Romans, likewise went back to an earlier gospel in the form of a collection of sayings (the Gospel of the Hebrews mentioned by some of the early Church Fathers). Though it also had a theological "tendency" toward Judaism, Baur believed it contained the most credible traditions about Jesus. It was here, after many years of historical study, that Baur sought the true historical Jesus, the original and substantial essence of Christianity.

Baur's focus on the founder of Christianity meant that Jesus' teaching was behind every subsequent formulation of Christian consciousness. At the same time, he thought that what Jesus said (and did) was inseparable from who he was—or, to use more customary language, that Jesus' message and work were inseparable from his person. That person was best expressed by his messianic consciousness, not by the creedal formulations.

Jesus' teaching, said Baur, was somewhat like that of his Jewish background, but he went beyond that background in an original and radical way. Whereas the kingdom of God for Jews stressed God's rule breaking in from without to reestablish the nation of Israel, Jesus' radical transformation led to a *spiritual and inward kingdom for all people*. The heart of Jesus' teaching about the kingdom of God was found in the Sermon on the Mount (Mt 5–7), and within that, in the Beatitudes (Mt 5:3–10). In this teaching Jesus brought out the great tension human beings felt between the world as it is, full of anxiety, separation, incompleteness, sinfulness, and death, and the world as it might be, full of peace, reconciliation, perfection, salvation, and life with God. This tension, primarily expressed by Jesus in language about *time*—present and future, this world and the world to come—is for Jesus (says Baur) a *qualitative relationship* between God and persons, and it is more clearly present in Jesus' parables. The more a person is tied to the cares of the "present" world, the less that person is committed to the "future" world, and vice versa.

> The true greatness and dignity of the Christian consists in the fact that he does not merely see the visible but the invisible. Even now, as long as he is still engaged in his temporal pilgrimage, he lives not so much in the present world but much more in the future, to which everything present must be connected. . . . The whole content of his teaching consists in contrasting present and future so sharply that it becomes clear to us that to the extent to which a man possesses the one he does not possess the other.[17]

This statement makes it appear that there is a radical break between one mode of existence and another, between the "present" and the "future." Actually, Baur thought that such a break would have implied a miraculous or supernatural intervention of God's kingdom from without. His own theological position did not permit that; thus, to the extent that the will of God is realized in love of him and in moral relationships, the "future" kingdom is already "present."

This last point gives an especially moral focus to Jesus' kingdom. In the Sermon on the Mount, the stress is on purity and sincerity of intentions. There is a moral "ought" (as in Kant), but it is not to be obeyed simply by external acts, but by conforming one's will to it. In this Jesus affirmed the Law of the Old Testament, but, says Baur, went beyond it.

> The inner is opposed to the outer, the intention to the act, the letter to the spirit. This is the essential, fundamental principle of Christianity; and it is insistence on the intention as the sole factor wherein the absolute moral value of man consists, it is an essentially new principle.[18]

This is an ethic of self-determination, of moral freedom, and in that regard it is primarily an individual ethic; but Baur believed that it had social implications, too, for it was intended for all. Again, Jesus went beyond the national boundaries of Judaism.

In addition to the tension between two modes of existence and the moral thrust to Jesus' teaching, the third theme that runs through the Sermon on the Mount is the especially religious one, the call to righteous perfection. Fulfilling the law is important, but the law must be fulfilled by *internalizing* it. This form of righteousness overcomes the separation between God and persons.

Hodgson writes:

> The radically original and underived element in Jesus' teaching can be summarized as follows: it is the expression of a religious consciousness penetrated by the deepest sense of both the antithesis and unity between earth ("present") and heaven ("future"); it demands a radical moral inwardness, obedience, and universality of intention; and it calls for an absolute relation to God, corresponding to the righteousness of God, as the foundation of the religious consciousness. In each of these respects Jesus transcends his environmental context—especially that of Judaism—in a radical and unexpected way. His teaching might be summarized as the spiritual-

izing, inwardizing, universalizing, and radicalizing of the idea of the kingdom of heaven.[19]

As we have said, the personality of Jesus was crucial for Baur. He closely associated Jesus' teaching with Jesus' identity, what he said with who he was. The critical questions are: Did Jesus believe himself to be the Messiah, or is that impression the result of the faith of the early church? If he did believe it, was his view the same or different from that of his Jewish contemporaries? Again, Baur's basic document was the Gospel of Matthew.

Baur attacked the problem of Jesus' identity by taking up the issue of Jesus' "messianic consciousness" in relation to the kingdom teaching and the meaning of the Christological title "Son of Man," especially in Matthew. Christological titles, you will remember, are religious-cultural names that carry certain meanings to those who use them, though such meanings may shift depending on time, place, and individual or group use. "Son of Man," the most frequent title in the synoptics (occurs 68 times), is used only by Jesus. Did he mean it to refer to himself?

Baur notes that the gospels contain different meanings for the title: There are sayings of Jesus that speak about an exalted figure who will sit at the right hand of God and/or will come on the clouds of heaven as in Daniel 7:13–14 (future-apocalyptic sayings); there are sayings about the Son of Man's fate or authority on earth (no place to lay his head; forgiving sins; Lord of the sabbath), which refer to him as human (present, earthly sayings); and there are sayings about the coming passion, death, and resurrection of the Son of Man (passion prediction sayings). Baur questioned whether there was really a crystalized Jewish apocalyptic conception of the Son of Man for Jesus to take over, but he acknowledged that Jesus might have spoken of the Son of Man's judgment of the world which early Christians after Jesus' death apocalypticized. *Jesus' own emphasis was not apocalyptic.* Rather, he spoke of the present, earthly Son of Man as a human figure—himself—with the intent that such sayings would imply, without specifically stating, something of his mission on earth. This, of course, was to proclaim the kingdom and *bring about* the reconciliation between God and persons which is part of that proclamation. Jesus as Son of Man is an authoritative, authentic human being who makes the moral demand that he himself fulfills. He *is* what he *demands.* His teaching is the standard of judgment, and he will so judge. In his moral-religious consciousness and by his suffering and death (though he did not predict it of himself as Son of Man in the explicit way it is found in those sayings), he became the standard of judgment, the moral exemplar of his claim on his followers.

There is much in Baur's view of Jesus Christ that is derived through Immanuel Kant. Thus Baur admitted that Jesus' ethic was

a formal principle of action which in its essentials coincides with the Kantian imperative: so act that the maxim of your action can be the universal law of action.[20]

Yet Kant did not think that there was any *necessary* connection between the ideal of moral consciousness of mankind and the historicity of a particular individual. For the historian Baur, Kantian idealism was too "subjective," too unrelated to history, at that point. Similar critiques were leveled at Schleiermacher and Hegel. Schleiermacher asserted that the ideal consciousness of God was realized in Jesus, but Baur argued that this was a dogmatic *belief* of Schleiermacher's, a kind of unprovable miracle lacking in historical verifiability, and the historical Jesus was in fact unnecessary to this dogmatic belief. For the historian, *one must start with the historical Jesus.* Likewise, Baur thought Hegel's view absorbed the historical Jesus into a speculative idea. Once again, it is important to realize that Baur was primarily a historian; he combined critical historical research with a speculative philosophy of history, always maintaining that the historical Jesus and his personality must be the basis for Christian belief.

JESUS CHRIST IN THE THOUGHT OF ERNEST RENAN

Joseph-Ernest Renan (1823–92), the third child of Philibert and Magdelaine Renan, was born on February 28, 1823, in Treguier, Brittany.[21] His father, a grocer and merchant-mariner, drowned mysteriously when Ernest was only five, leaving the family in poverty. His mother, docile and good-natured, wanted him to become a parish priest in the Catholic Church, whereas his sister Henriette was aggressively anticlerical. These were strong influences on Renan, as he had a close relationship with both women.

The early part of Renan's life was directed by his mother. At age nine Ernest was placed in the Ecclesiastical School in his home town. Six years later he began his preparation for the priesthood near Paris at the minor seminary at Saint-Nicholas du Chardonnet. Here he began to have intellectual doubts and to feel the strain of his growing lack of piety. Despite his hesitations he entered the major seminary Issy-les-Moulineaux (near Paris) when he was 18, to study philosophy. After two years, he began his final course of study in theology at Saint-Sulpice, also near Paris. Renan decided for intellectual reasons not to enter the parish priesthood but to remain a scholarly priest and to keep his unorthodox views to himself. Finding Scholastic theology at the seminary "somewhat dry," he diverted himself with the study of Hebrew. That, however, only led him further toward the historical criticism that eventually replaced his Scholastic theology altogether. By the spring of 1845, Renan's desire for free intellectual pursuits apart from his Catholicism was making him feel as if he were "trapped in a net." To the dismay of others, he began to speak of abandoning Jesus in order to follow Jesus better. His moment of truth came in April 1845: He knew he did not believe enough. His sister, who was then in Poland, wrote him that she was pleased that he was no longer an infant!

Renan's full energies were now spent in his shift from the life of an unknown but financially secure cleric to that of a well known (but poor) and satisfied scholar. He worked feverishly on two additional degrees, tutored, wrote a series of nine notebooks (published posthumously), and most important, won the coveted Volney prize for his first scholarly work, an essay on Semitic languages, in 1847. From 1848 on, his life was filled with scholarly activity and the writing of romantic novels. After a two-year appointment in Italy surveying manuscript collections, he became an *attaché* to the manuscript division of the prestigious Bibliothèque Nationale, earned his *Docteur-des-lettres,* was elected to the Council of the Societé Asiatique, wrote and revised several pieces, and in 1856 was elected to the Academy of Inscription and Belles-Lettres.

In 1856 Renan married Cornélie Scheffer, daughter of the painter Ary Scheffer, and they had three children. Renan's vast scholarly productivity and honors went forward. In 1860 he was sent on a learned mission (partly archeological) to Syria, and while there he visited Palestine. Deeply inspired, Renan composed the first draft of what was to become his most famous study, *Vie de Jésus,* or *Life of Jesus.* When he returned in 1862, he received the position he had long coveted, the imperial appointment as professor of Hebrew, Aramaic, and Syriac languages at the Collège de France.

Renan's *Life of Jesus* appeared in 1863 as Volume 1 of a projected multivolume series on *The Origins of Christianity.* It was a smashing success and went through ten editions before the year was out, eventually being translated into eleven languages. Yet, because of it, Renan was removed from his position and appointed Assistant Director of the Department of Manuscripts in the Imperial Library. Meanwhile his scholarly activity and honors still continued. An unsuccessful attempt at political office in 1869 was followed by travel with Prince Napoleon during the Franco-Prussian War, and an exchange of letters with Strauss over the war, published in 1871. At the end of the war, Renan was reinstated at the Collège and continued to publish voluminously. In addition, he ran unsuccessfully for political office, was appointed to several important positions in academic societies, and gave the prestigious Hibbert Lectures in England (1880). A man of astonishing abilities and ambitious motivations, Renan finally died of pneumonia and heart trouble in his apartment at the Collège de France in 1892.

Ernest Renan's Jesus Christ was above all a romantic historian's portrayal of the human, historical Jesus.[22] He was less skeptical about the historical worth of the gospel texts than were Strauss (see page 184) and liberal French Protesants but was not dominated by the traditional and creedal Christ of French Roman Catholics; he sought within the texts, especially the synoptics, the history behind the "legend," or better, the reality behind the miraculous. What emerged was a wise (though formally uneducated) Jewish prophet who, to Renan's mind, was a simple, gentle, handsome, delightful, and even charming Galilean living among the pastoral beauties of the Galilean countryside. A superior person, to be sure, but nevertheless a real, historical, human person who became the object of veneration only gradually, and especially after his death.

Renan's universally recognized poetic charm can best be seen by letting him speak for himself. Awed and inspired by his visit to Syria and Palestine, Renan graphically drew on his own experience and nostalgic memories to portray the world of nature he believed Jesus loved. To him, Galilee

> was a very green, shady, smiling district, the true home of the Song of Songs [an Old Testament love poem], and the songs of the well-beloved. During the two months of March and April, the country forms a carpet of flowers of an incomparable variety of colors. The animals are small and extremely gentle—delicate and lively turtle doves, blue-birds so light that they rest on a blade of grass without bending it, crested larks which venture almost under the feet of the traveller, little river tortoises with mild and lively eyes, storks with grave and modest mien, which, laying aside all timidity, allow man to come quite near them and seem almost to invite his approach.[23]

Though Jesus was aware of "culture" (Herod's building projects were in evidence here and there), he had no real knowledge, said Renan, of the general state of the world and its powers: What he loved most were "his Galilean villages, confused mixtures of huts, of nests and holes cut in the rocks, of wells, of tombs, of fig trees, and of olives."[24] So striking was the Galilee where Jesus had his ministry that Renan wrote,

> The whole history of infant Christianity has become in this manner a delightful pastoral. . . . Greece has drawn pictures of human life by sculpture and by charming poetry, but always without backgrounds or distant receding perspectives. In Galilee were wanting the marble, the practiced workmen, the exquisite and refined language. But Galilee has created the most sublime ideal for the popular imagination; for behind its idyl moves the fate of humanity, and the light which illumines its pictures is the sun of the kingdom of God.[25]

The beauty with which Renan portrayed Galilee as the backdrop for his Jesus contrasts sharply with the place where Jesus met his fate, Jerusalem. One can hear the passion in Renan's description:

> The parched appearance of Nature in the neighborhood of Jerusalem must have added to the dislike Jesus had for the place. The valleys are without water; the soil arid and stony. Looking into the valley of the Dead Sea, the view is somewhat striking; elsewhere it is monotonous. The hill of Mizpeh,

around which cluster the most ancient historical remembrances of Israel, alone relieves the eye.[26]

Jesus was a stranger at Jerusalem. He felt that there was a wall of resistance he could not penetrate. . . .
    The city, as we have already said, displeased Jesus. Until then he had always avoided great centres, preferring for his action the country and the towns of small importance. Many of the precepts which he gave to his apostles were absolutely inapplicable, except in a simple society of humble men. Having no idea of the world, and accustomed to the kindly communism of Galilee, remarks continually escaped him, whose simplicity would at Jerusalem appear very singular. His imagination and his love of Nature found themselves constrained within these walls. True religion does not proceed from the tumult of towns, but from the tranquil serenity of the fields.[27]

Renan emphasized that Jerusalem represented a religion opposed to Jesus' nature; it was seething with Zealot revolutionaries and was "the true home of that obstinate Judaism which, founded by the Pharisees, and fixed by the Talmud, has traversed the Middle Ages, and come down to us."[28]

Renan's romantic elaborations of Jesus' environment were matched by his creative imagination in reconstructing Jesus' life. In Nazareth ("no place in the world was so well adapted for dreams of perfect happiness. . . . The people are amiable and cheerful; the gardens fresh and green. . . .")[29] Jesus and his "little comrades" were inspired by the lyrics of the Psalms, the prophet Isaiah's "brilliant dreams of the future," and Daniel's vision that the world empires would ultimately be subordinate to the destinies of the Jewish people. The miracle of Cana in John 2 led Renan to think that Jesus spent part of his youth there. Jesus did not marry; yet, Renan notes, he did have an "extremely delicate feeling toward women" and, though his relations with them were of "an entirely moral kind," his "freedom and intimacy," his "infinite sweetness," and his "universal charm" made him especially attractive to them.

Certainly, Jesus made many pilgrimages to Jerusalem. But he always returned

    . . . into his beloved Galilee, and found again his heavenly Father in the midst of the green hills and the clear fountains—and among the crowds of women and children, who, with joyous soul and the song of angels in their hearts, awaited the salvation of Israel.[30]

Unlike many of his Galilean contemporaries, Jesus was not concerned with the political overthrow of Rome. He was no Zealot revolutionary. Neither did he follow in the footsteps of his ascetic, Yogi-like mentor John the Baptist, great though John was in Jesus' eyes. In contrast, Jesus considered his role to be that of a prophet—but a prophet with an unusually high consciousness of his own divinity. Renan noted in passing that Scholasticism, Descartes, and the eighteenth century had produced deists and pantheists who had suppressed the very notion of the divine personality in Western culture. To the ancients, however, all this development had no meaning. They felt the divine within themselves. So it was with Jesus, who believed himself to be a true Son of God. Jesus did not have visions of a God outside himself, nor did God speak to him that way. God was within, and when he spoke of his Father, he drew on the message of his own heart. In a typical, nontraditional, romantic flourish, Renan indicated his view of Jesus' divinity:

> It was then for some months, perhaps a year, that God truly dwelt upon the earth. The voice of the young carpenter suddenly acquired an extraordinary sweetness. An infinite charm was exhaled from his person, and those who had seen him up to that time no longer recognized him. He had not yet many disciples, and the group which gathered around him was neither a sect nor a school; but a common spirit, a sweet and penetrating influence was felt. His amiable character, accompanied doubtless by one of those lovely faces which sometimes appear in the Jewish race, threw around him a fascination from which no one in the midst of these kindly and simple populations could escape.[31]

What did the "young master" say with such "exquisite feeling"? The heart of Jesus' teaching was the kingdom of God. For Jewish thought, said Renan, the kingdom was Judaism itself—its true religion, its monotheistic belief, its worship and piety. Some of the fringe of Jewish thinking, of course, took up the apocalyptic view of Daniel—that God's kingdom, or reign, would be realized in material form by a sudden catastrophe at the end of the world. Renan believed that Jesus moved in the direction of the latter view toward the end of his life. But Jesus' first (and most basic) idea was the nonpolitical, nonapocalyptic kingdom *within,* the kingdom for children and those like them, the kingdom for humble outcasts, heretics, schismatics, tax collectors, Samaritans, and pagans. Jesus' kingdom for Renan was a kingdom for the poor; his goal was not political, but moral, social, and religious revolution. This, then, was a kingdom for the perpetually living: "The kingdom of God is *within* you" (Luke 17:21, interpreting Greek *entos* as "within").

Thus it was that Jesus gathered around him a small band composed mainly of fishermen and common folk, teaching them his enjoyment of the simple life and its pleasures, his contempt for the strivings of power and prestige in the "world" by means of his beatitudes ("Blessed are the poor . . ."), his common sense proverbs, and his masterful parables. The social revolutionary Jesus who taught these things also taught a simple worship, free of priests and external observances, "resting entirely on the feelings of the heart, on the imitation of God, on the direct relation of the conscience with the heavenly Father"[32] and on human brotherhood. This was Jesus' style and his lasting contribution: "It has been by the power of a religion, free from all external forms, that Christianity has attracted elevated minds."[33] Again, Renan the romantic spoke:

> His preaching was gentle and pleasing, breathing Nature and the perfume of the fields. He loved the flowers, and took from them his most charming lessons. The birds of heaven, the sea, the mountains, and the games of children, furnished in turn the subject of his instructions.[34]

While Jesus' life and teaching was his true contribution, it was also clear that a perceptible change came over him in the strange, arid, scholastic, priest-infested capital, Jerusalem. Jesus' debates with the law-bound Jewish scribes of the Jewish temple made him realize that there could be no compromise between his views and those of official Judaism. Jesus' Father was not a god of the Holy Place, but a god to be worshipped "in spirit and in truth" (John 4:21–24). His was not a religion of the book, but a religion of the heart. For Jesus, Renan believed, the issue was now clear: "Jesus was no longer a Jew."[35]

Henceforth, the distance between him and official Judaism increased. He now allowed himself to yield to public opinion and allowed his quest for success to result in his being called "Son of David," a traditional title for the Jewish Messiah. His simple notion of sonship now took the traditional notion of power associated with "Son of God." He also accepted the designation "Son of Man" from the apocalypticist Daniel, to express his character as judge. (Renan noted that here were the seeds of the later church's ascription of supernatural divinity to him.) Samaritans and Gentiles were increasingly in his company. Alongside his view of the kingdom of God as inward and spiritual, directed to the poor, he also accepted—Renan politely pardoned him for this—the vain apocalyptic view of his day, however limited it might be in Jesus' own thought. Jesus believed that the prophets had written in reference to him (though his followers first applied the prophecies to him in great detail), and, like the miracle worker of any period, he performed many miracles, especially exorcisms and healings, though with some reluctance. The Twelve were in a privileged position, and they imitated him and formed the close association that was the germ of the church. His only sacrament was the meal which, after his death, became the Eucharist.

Jesus' final journey to the dreaded city of Jerusalem, of course, led to his decisive confrontation with the authorities. After the Last Supper, events were set into motion whereby the social-religious reformer's enemies accomplished the task of portraying him as a political revolutionary involved in sedition against the state. Then came his crucifixion and death. The epilogue to Renan's drama is that this Jesus, who was "at the highest summit of human greatness," was—with the cooperation of *all* humanity—the one who gave birth to *true religion, the religion of the heart*. Though he attempted to give Judaism its proper due, Renan believed that Jesus of Nazareth was the one, more than anyone else, who "caused his fellow-men to make the greatest step toward the divinity." [36]

> . . . whatever may be the unexpected phenomena of the future, Jesus will not be surpassed. His worship will constantly renew its youth, the tale of his life will cause ceaseless tears, his sufferings will soften the best hearts; all the ages will proclaim that, among the sons of men, there is none born who is greater than Jesus. [37]

SUMMARY

Some of the most important thinkers of the first three quarters of the nineteenth century were absorbed in reflection about history. For the German idealist G. F. W. Hegel, the apparent irrationality of history is actually a rational process of the Absolute Mind (God) working itself out through the clash of ideas (dialectic), which results in the clash of empires and nations in the empirical world but ultimately leads to progress toward human freedom. For Marx, who drew on Feuerbach's "materialistic" view that the idea of God is the projection of *human* needs, wishes, and desires, history has moved through five stages of "materialistic" conflict, that is, warfare between different economic classes, in which religion has been used by the upper classes to keep the lower classes in their place. Here the dialectic of Idea or Spirit, which in Hegel's theory gave rise to the dialectic of political and economic struggle, is turned upside down: In dialectical materialism, political-economic struggle precedes ideas in history. Another left-wing Hegelian, Bruno Bauer, is interesting in this connection, partly because he cast doubt on the historicity of Jesus by his view of the Gospel of Mark as a work of art.

The heightening of historical consciousness fostered by Hegelian idealism and Marxist materialism was paralleled in France by Comte's positivism, which viewed history as moving through stages and following describable laws without, however, any necessity for ultimate causes or designs, and culminating in a positivist, or scientific, age. Charles Darwin, influenced especially by Lyell's studies of the great age of the earth and Malthus's theories of rapid population growth, as well as his own discoveries of fossils and varying species of animals and birds, put forth the theory that rapidly multiplying species in an intensely competitive struggle for survival had, by "natural selection," evolved into better adapted species over great expanses of time. Meanwhile, Herbert Spencer had popularized the general theory of evolution and extended it in such a way that all of history and society had evolved through three stages, from "lower" to "higher" and more complex forms, the basis being "survival of the fittest."

None of these views require a transcendent God "out there" to direct history, though Hegel himself did think of Absolute Mind as operating *within* history. On the other hand, all of them did think that history had been somewhere or was going somewhere, and the impact of these thinkers on nineteenth-century ideas was tremendous.

One effect of the historical approach to the study of the Bible can be seen in the highly controversial *Life of Jesus* published by David Friedrich Strauss in 1835. Drawing upon writers, most of whom were anonymous, who began to think of certain New Testament stories as imaginative "myths" with little, uncertain, or no historical value, and others who began to interpret the life of Jesus as recast in the mold of ancient Jewish messianic beliefs, Strauss attempted to apply such perspectives to the *whole* life of Jesus. His real interest was to present his "mythical" interpretation of the gospels as an alternative to both the supernaturalist and rationalist interpretations; however, the net effect of his razor-edged analysis was that the gospels contained very little historical information about Jesus. In 1835, this position brought such reactions that Strauss was dismissed from his seminary teaching position at Tübingen; from that point forward, his life was one of disappointment and suffering.

Ferdinand Christian Baur was a right-wing Hegelian, considered by many to be the father of historical thinking in Christianity. His concern for the historical basis of Christianity in the teaching and life of Jesus Christ led him to reject as too "subjective" both Schleiermacher's view of Jesus as the exemplar of God-consciousness passed on through the church and Hegel's view of Jesus as the point at which the "God–man" made contact with history; that is, Jesus Christ was still too much of an "idea." Despite his debt to Hegel in viewing the early history of Christianity in terms of dialectic conflict, Baur believed that one must start with the historical Jesus. Taking the gospel of Matthew as the earliest and most reliable, he interpreted Jesus' teaching about the kingdom as unlike the Jewish apocalyptic, as inward, spiritual, present, and universal. With echoes of Kant, he said that Jesus' kingdom is a moral kingdom and that Jesus proclaimed self-determination and moral freedom. Jesus believed himself, thought Baur, to be an earthly Son of Man who *is* the moral being he demands that others be. With his belief that the historical Jesus is the starting point and foundation for all that follows, Baur's view of the ethical teacher of an inward, spiritual, present, and universal kingdom in contrast to Judaism would have many followers.

Renan's view of Jesus was influenced by both romanticism and new approaches to history. His *Life of Jesus*, published in 1863 during the period when liberal Protestants were beginning their quest for the historical Jesus, reflects the influence of Strauss and Baur as well as his own experience of the beautiful Galilean countryside, which he believed had affected Jesus. Renan had been there as an archaeologist. His heroic, human Jesus was an attractive, amiable character. He was a prophet who rejected the pleasures of the "world" and all institutional religion for the religion of the heart, the imitation of God, and the direct relation of the conscience to the heavenly Father. In this Jesus one could find true religion—and by implication, one's own true religion.

NOTES

1. Georg Wilhelm Friedrich Hegel, *Reason in History*, trans. Robert S. Hartman (New York: Liberal Arts Press, 1953); *The Philosophy of History*, trans. J. Sibree (New York: Dover Publications, 1956); Henry D. Aiken, *The Age of Ideology*, Mentor Philosophers Series (New York: New American Library, Mentor Books, 1956), pp. 71–97; Collingwood, *The Idea of History*, pp. 113–22; Löwith, *Meaning in History*, pp. 52–59; Barth, *Protestant Thought*, pp. 268–305; Stumpf, *Philosophy*, pp. 327–44; Walter Kaufmann, *Hegel: A Reinterpretation* (New York: Doubleday & Co., Anchor Books, 1966), pp. 249–97. For his views on Jesus Christ and Christianity, see Friedrich Hegel, *On Christianity*, trans. T. M. Knox (Gloucester, Mass.: Peter Smith, n.d.).

2. Ludwig Feuerbach, *The Essence of Christianity*, trans. George Eliot (New York: Harper & Row, Torchbooks, 1957), p. xxxix; an abridged version was edited by E. Graham Waring and F. W. Strothmann (New York: Ungar Publishing Co., 1957); Barth, *Protestant Thought*, pp. 355–61.

3. Collingwood, *The Idea of History*, pp. 122–26; Löwith, *Meaning in History*, pp. 33–51; M. M. Bober, *Karl Marx's Interpretation of History*, 2nd ed. (New York: W. W. Norton & Co., 1948); Stumpf, *Philosophy*, pp. 421–36. The major source is vol. 1 of *Capital* (*Das Kapital*), written in 1867.

4. Schweitzer, *Quest*, pp. 137–60; Stephen D. Crites, "Bauer, Bruno," in *The Encyclopedia of Philosophy*, 8 vols. (New York: Macmillan Co., 1967), vol. 1, pp. 554–56, with bibliography.

5. Collingwood, *The Idea of History*, pp. 126–30; Löwith, *Meaning in History*, pp. 60–103, which includes sketches of the thought of Proudhon, Condorcet, and Turgot; Stumpf, *Philosophy*, pp. 345–54; John Stuart Mill, *August Comte and Positivism* (Ann Arbor: University of Michigan Press, 1961 (originally published in 1865).

6. August Comte, *Introduction to Positive Philosophy* (the first two chapters of *Cours de philosophie positive*, 1857), Library of Liberal Arts (New York: Bobbs-Merrill Co., 1970), especially "Introduction," p. 2; Mill, *Positivism*, pp. 10ff.; Aiken, *The Age of Ideology*, p. 125. The wording is mine.

7. Mill, *Positivism*, pp. 7–8.

8. Charles Darwin, *The Voyage of the Beagle*, ed. Leonard Engel (New York: Doubleday & Co., Anchor Book, 1962), "Introduction"; Darwin, *The Origin of Species by Means of Natural Selection* (New York: New American Library, Mentor Books, 1958); Darwin, *The Descent of Man* (New York: P. F. Collier & Son, 1902); George Gaylord Simpson, *This View of Life: The*

World of an Evolutionist (New York: Harcourt Brace Jovanovich, 1964); Walter Karp, *Charles Darwin and the Origin of Species* (New York: Harper & Row, Horizon Caravel Books, 1968).

9. Henry D. Aiken, *The Age of Ideology,* Mentor Philosophers Series (New York: New American Library, Mentor Books, 1956), pp. 161–82.

10. Schweitzer, *Quest,* p. 68.

11. Schweitzer, *Quest,* pp. 68–120; Barth, *Protestant Thought,* pp. 362–89; Horton Harris, *David Friedrich Strauss* (Cambridge: University Press, 1973); Richard S. Cromwell, *David Friedrich Strauss and His Place in Modern Thought* (Fair Lawn, N.J.: R. E. Burdick, 1974); the major source is David Friedrich Strauss, *The Life of Jesus Critically Examined,* ed. Peter C. Hodgson, trans. George Elliot, Lives of Jesus Series (Philadelphia: Fortress Press, 1972); also Strauss, *The Christ of Faith and the Jesus of History: A Critique of Schleiermacher's The Life of Jesus,* trans. Leander E. Keck (Philadelphia: Fortress Press, 1977). See also Kümmel, *The New Testament,* pp. 120–26; Peter C. Hodgson, *The Formation of Historical Theology: A Study of Ferdinand Christian Baur* (New York: Harper & Row, 1966), pp. 73–86; Horton Harris, *The Tübingen School* (Oxford: Clarendon Press, 1975).

12. Summarized from Strauss, *Life of Jesus* (trans. George Elliot), pp. 86–87.

13. Ibid., pp. 237–49.

14. Ibid., passim; see also the Introduction by Peter C. Hodgson, pp. xxxi–xxxvi.

15. Hodgson, *Ferdinand Christian Baur* (above, n.11); *Ferdinand Christian Baur on the Writing of Church History,* ed. and trans. Peter C. Hodgson (New York: Harper & Row, 1968).

16. My major source is Hodgson, *Ferdinand Christian Baur.*

17. From a sermon of Baur's in Hodgson, *Ferdinand Christian Baur,* p. 114.

18. From *Das Christentum,* p. 29, in Hodgson, *Ferdinand Christian Baur,* p. 225.

19. Hodgson, *Ferdinand Christian Baur,* p. 224.

20. From *Neutestamentliche Theologie,* pp. 61–62, in Hodgson, *Ferdinand Christian Baur,* p. 226.

21. Richard M. Chadbourne, *Ernest Renan* (New York: Twayne Publishers, 1968).

22. Ernest Renan, *The Life of Jesus* (New York: Modern Library, 1955).

23. Ibid., p. 114.
24. Ibid., p. 96.
25. Ibid., p. 116.
26. Ibid., p. 216.
27. Ibid., p. 306.
28. Ibid., p. 113.
29. Ibid., p. 86.
30. Ibid., p. 118.
31. Ibid., pp. 125–26.
32. Ibid., p. 132.
33. Ibid., p. 149.
34. Ibid., p. 186.
35. Ibid., p. 225.
36. Ibid., p. 392.
37. Ibid., p. 393.

VII

Jesus Christ in Protestant Liberal Historical Thought

In the previous chapter we discussed the emergence of the historical consciousness in the nineteenth century. In the early part of the century, Hegel was especially influential. By the latter part of the century, Hegel's idealism was being attacked from all quarters, and the historical theories influenced by materialism (Marx), positivism (Comte), and evolutionism (Darwin, Spencer) were predominant. Moreover, scholars set out to uncover the past with hard-nosed, concrete historical research into the empirical *data* of history. Thought about Jesus Christ was no exception to this trend. Before considering the positions on Jesus that were characteristic of historical thought in that period, we must sketch two important developments: the progress in the historical evaluation of the sources for Jesus' life and teachings, which so far has been mentioned only in passing, and the movement called Protestant Liberalism. Then we will examine the classical European Protestant Liberal, Adolf Harnack, and his views of Jesus. We will also examine the American counterpart to European Liberalism, the Social Gospel movement, and one of its most significant writers on Jesus, Shailer Mathews. Finally, we will briefly sketch the direction taken by certain liberal-historical thinkers in late nineteenth- and early twentieth-century Germany. These were the thinkers of the *Religionsgeschichtliche Schule* ("History-of-Religions Schools"), one of its chief representatives being Wilhelm

Bousset. What unites these views is their historical orientation and their denial of traditional orthodox views, even though their evaluations and emphases vary.

THE HISTORICAL CRITICISM OF SOURCES

We suggested in Ch. 5 that one of the Enlightenment's lasting contributions to biblical study was the attempt to evaluate the sources for Jesus' life and teachings. In the nineteenth century, with the development of the historical consciousness, the problem of the historical worth of the gospels became increasingly important. One could be an orthodox scholar who accepted the ancient tradition, or one could abandon orthodoxy and look further for historical data and historical interpretation. In this case, what would happen if the gospels were considered to be full of myths, as Strauss suggested, or of extremely late origin, as Baur suggested? Could one ever find the historical Jesus as Renan, for example, proposed? Before going further into the quest for the historical Jesus in the nineteenth century, we must see how this problem of sources was resolved—at least to the satisfaction of some.[1]

There was no serious problem of sources as long as one believed that the gospels were written by authoritative disciples of Jesus (Matthew and John) or followers of Paul (Mark and Luke) who were divinely inspired and who, therefore, did not basically disagree with each other (Augustine's "gospel harmony" view of about 400). This approach, however, was not easy to sustain when, in true rationalistic spirit, people began to stress the *differences* among the four gospels. In 1774–75 J. J. Griesbach published only the first *three* gospels, Matthew, Mark, and Luke, in parallel columns, noting a few passages from John where there were similarities. This synopsis implied that John was a very different gospel from the other three and that only the three ought to be compared. Despite the general agreement in chronological order, there were clearly a host of smaller differences in wording and order. In 1783 Griesbach proposed an alternative to the traditional Augustinian view to explain the problems: Matthew was written first, but *Luke* (not Mark) was second. This direct dependence of Luke on Matthew, he thought, would account for the passages in these two gospels that were alike but were not found in Mark. Mark, then, omitted some passages from both Matthew and Luke. The theory had the advantage of being limited to the known, canonical gospels. Though the orthodox objected to placing Luke before Mark chronologically, the theory was well received by many scholars.

These two theories of progressive *literary* use of extant gospels—

Matthew–Mark–Luke–John (the Augustinian synthesis) and Matthew–Luke–Mark (Griesbach)—were accompanied by the emergence of other points of view, which eventually merged to form an alternative hypothesis. In 1778 G. E. Lessing, partly in reaction against Reimarus's notion that the gospel writers were intentionally devious (see pages 144–46), suggested that the three were different because each was using a variant Greek translation of a lost Aramaic gospel, or "proto-gospel." Furthermore, each modified the Greek translation from his own perspective. Lessing's theory of different uses of the "proto-Gospel" had some advantages: It suggested a period of oral tradition, then a written Aramaic gospel, and then the movement from Aramaic (the language of Jesus and of the earliest Christians) to Greek. It also made it possible to think of an original gospel that was very close to the actual life of Jesus (though it was not one of the extant gospels), and it explained the likenesses and differences.

Though there were other theories (in 1817 Schleiermacher suggested that the gospels were variant accounts of compilations of miracle stories, discourses, and perhaps a passion and resurrection account, which grew out of notes taken by Jesus' followers) it was Herder's view that gave further impetus to the "proto-Gospel" hypothesis. Herder, interested in things primitive, suggested that there was an *oral* gospel which became fixed in oral tradition very early and was passed on in that form by tenacious oral memory. More important, he believed that the Gospel of Mark was the best representative of the oral gospel because Mark was simpler, more primitive sounding, and fresher and because Mark's shorter gospel, beginning with the public life of Jesus and ending with his death and resurrection, accorded with the simple view of Jesus' life sketched in Acts 1:22. In Herder's view, then, the Gospel of Mark best approximated the "proto-Gospel."

Gradually more skepticism arose about the earliness of the Gospel of Matthew. If the Gospel of Matthew was not written by the eyewitness, disciple, and tax collector Matthew (Mt 10:3) who followed Jesus, and if Mark was a more primitive gospel than Matthew, as Herder suggested, how could one explain the agreements between Matthew and Luke, which the Griesbach hypothesis had explained so well?

The answer seemed to be a hypothetical "sayings source" used by Matthew and Luke but not by Mark; this solution was first proposed by H. Marsh in 1798 and again by Schleiermacher in 1832. In 1835 the classicist and text critic Karl Lachmann argued that the order of events in all three synoptics is based on the Gospel of Mark; he showed that when the Gospels of Matthew and Luke depart from the Gospel of Mark, they depart at different places: The common thread is Mark. Lachmann further proposed that the Gospel of Matthew was based on a "sayings source" with the material from Mark inserted into it. In 1838 C. H. Weisse proposed that the Gospels of Matthew and Luke were based on the "proto-Gospel" that underlay Mark (Herder's hypothesis) combined with the "sayings source." In the same year, C. G. Wilke gave a similar argument based on the Gospel of Mark itself, though he further believed that Matthew was based on both Mark and Luke. In short, when Matthew was no longer considered early, scholars eventually reached the alternative solution that either a now lost "proto-Mark" or the Gospel of Mark itself was combined with a now lost "sayings source" plus some other materials to form Matthew and/or Luke. Whereas Matthew was the chief gospel for Jesus' life traditionally (Augustine) and in Griesbach's theory, those who followed Weisse or Wilke relied more heavily on Mark. One can diagram the theories in this period as follows:

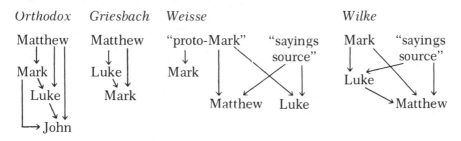

In 1863, H. J. Holtzmann's *Die synoptischen Evangelien* summed up the research to date and opted for the Weisse solution. Holtzmann's arguments convinced most late nineteenth-century scholars in Germany that the two-source theory was correct: Some form of Mark was the earliest gospel (the priority of Mark), and it and the "sayings source" (known as Q by the 1890s) were the sources for Matthew and Luke. By the twentieth century, many critics followed Wilke in maintaining that the Gospel of Mark itself lay behind Matthew and Luke (cp. B. H. Streeter's *The Four Gospels* [1924]).

It is important to understand that for many scholars the Gospel of Mark, or some form of it, provided an answer to Strauss's historical skepticism. Holtzmann regarded the story told in Mark as fairly reliable history in its detail, and from it he developed a rather definite picture of the historical Jesus. Since Harnack's view was similar, this portrait of Jesus will be considered along with the thought of the Protestant Liberal Adolf Harnack.

PROTESTANT LIBERALISM

Many Protestant scholars of the eighteenth and nineteenth centuries reinterpreted, neutralized, or almost totally ignored the orthodox Christ of the creeds. Instead, they saw Jesus as a human prophet, or a teacher of morality, or at most as the pattern for true religious thinking, acting, or feeling. The modern mind sought a modern Jesus Christ discovered by modern scientific-historical methods.

This was a redirection in Christian thinking away from metaphysics toward subjective experience (Schleiermacher), ethical action (Kant), and the activity of the Divine Spirit within the world and within human beings (Hegel). God was *immanent* in the world, nature, and humanity, working out his purpose. This was an essentially *optimistic* reorientation, for its stress was on human endeavor. The mood received further support, of course, from the evolutionists. Was not science moving toward the utopia for which human beings for centuries had dreamed? Was not humanity on the path to perfection, steadily approaching the establishment of equality in the political and social spheres? Was not humanity basically good, and was not Western civilization on the march toward ever higher possibilities, progressing technically, morally, and esthetically? It appeared that if God existed, he was after all a good God, full of love, and the Christian doctrine of Original Sin did not correspond either to human nature or to God's judgment. For the thinker, the obvious path was openmindedness, tolerance of others, truth wherever one finds it, congenial reasonableness, and the authority of personal, inner experience expressing itself in one's dealings with the world.

This is fundamentally the heritage of Protestant Liberalism.[2] To illustrate the mood in the late nineteenth century, we will take a brief look at one of its chief representatives, Albrecht Ritschl (1882–89).[3] Ritschl rooted his thinking in the Bible and the Protestant Reformation, but he understood them through the tradition of Schleiermacher and Kant. For Ritschl, God was not so much a God "out there" who judges sinful people—he rejected the doctrine of Original Sin in its usual sense—but a God of love who works within the world and its people. Jesus Christ so represented that love that he inspired people to live according to his high moral ideals. The kingdom he established was an earthly one in which people were organized to carry out this idea, and its successor is the Christian church. The divinity of Jesus Christ is based not on his metaphysical "essence"—Ritschl rejected metaphysical thinking—but on his moral influence. In traditional terms, this was the "moral influence" theory of atonement. Doctrines such as Original Sin, the virgin birth, and the preexistence of Christ are, like miracles, not the heart of the Christian religion. Rather, the Christian religion is to be found in the individual's religious experience of the love of God expressing itself in ethical behavior. Religion, then, is more of a general outlook on life than a system of beliefs. Being reconciled to one's neighbor overcomes selfishness and the lack of trust in, and reverence for, God. This reconciliation between persons is paralleled by *justification,* that is, the guarantee and realization, through faith, of the ideal of life (within human limits). There is no real conflict between science and religion, for they operate in different spheres. Science establishes facts; religion makes value judgments. True religion, unlike mystical religion, is constantly involved in the world through ethical activity; yet, in contrast to pietistic religion, it does not lead ultimately to perfection in this world based on a certain kind of experience. Yet the heart of religion is morality, and for Ritschl theology is, in the final analysis, the theology of moral values.

Two movements, historical criticism of sources (resulting in the Markan hypothesis) and Liberalism, went hand in hand in the late nineteenth and early twentieth centuries to create an ethos in which one of the central questions was the quest of the historical Jesus. The movement produced literally thousands of "lives of Jesus." One of the greatest of these Liberals was the German Adolf Harnack.

JESUS CHRIST IN THE THOUGHT OF ADOLF HARNACK

Adolf Harnack (1851–1930) was born in the university town of Dorpat, Estonia (now part of the Soviet Union.[4]) He was one of four sons of Theodosius von Harnack, a pietistically inclined professor of practical and systematic theology, who moved to the University of Erlangen in 1853 and back to Dorpat in 1866. Young Adolf also studied at both these universities, but he finished his studies at the University of Leipzig in 1873. There, as a result of his doctoral dissertation on Gnosticism, he was appointed university lecturer in 1874 and professor extraordinarius (assistant professor) in 1876. In this period he and his circle of friends came under the influence of the Liberal, moral-values oriented theology of Albrecht Ritschl. In 1875 he became one of the editors of an edition of the Apostolic Fathers. The following year he cofounded a periodical, *Theologische Literaturzeitung* (*News of Theological Literature*), still one of the best organs in Germany for reviewing German theological publications. Next came seven years at the University of Giessen (1879–86), during which he initiated the scholarly series *Texte und Untersuchungen* (*Texts and Investigations* [1882]) and published the first of three volumes of his monumental *History of Dogma* (1886). Though he was denied official recognition by the Lutheran church, he nevertheless gained a position at the University of Berlin in 1888 with the backing of Otto von Bismarck and the emperor, William II.

While at Berlin, Harnack showed himself to be a broadly based, far-ranging scholar. In 1890 the Evangelical-Social Congress, a church-oriented group concerned with social and political responsibility, was formed; Harnack's increasing involvement with the group led to his presidency from 1903–11. In 1890 he was elected to the Prussian Academy of Science and was invited by it to write its history as part of a hundredth anniversary celebration. At his urging, it established a commission on the early Church Fathers, which Harnack headed from 1893 to the end of his life. He also became rector of the University of Berlin, director of the Prussian Royal Library from 1905 to 1921 (a kind of second profession), and in 1911 founded the Kaiser Wilhelm Institute for the Advancement of Science (today called the Max Planck Institute), of which he was the first president. In all these endeavors he was recognized as a fine administrator, an expert fund raiser, and a strong builder of prestige. Indeed, Harnack was invited to be friends with the emperor and was made a nobleman in 1914. He guided the Kaiser Wilhelm Institute through Germany's military defeat in World War I, and he continued to do so through the troubled Weimar Republic. In 1929 he held his last seminar, having been an emeritus since 1921, when he had declined an offer to become ambassador to the United States. He died suddenly in 1930 at Heidelberg.

Harnack was above all a historian and a teacher. His extremely active and productive life was an expression of his vocation as a historian. To be sure, history for Harnack involved the technical, hard-nosed analysis of sources; in fact, a number of his works have become classic, most notably his *History of Dogma* (1886–89; 4th ed. 1909), his *Mission and Expansion of Christianity During the First Three Centuries* (1902; 4th ed. 1924), his *History of Ancient Christian Literature* (1893–1904), and his popular *What Is Christianity?* (1900; 15th ed. 1950). But history to Harnack was not just the technical and interpretive attempt to uncover past events. His ultimate goal was to replace theological dogmatism with "historical understanding," to substitute for creedal orthodoxy a total historical perspective. Experts have noted many influences on Harnack (the Enlightenment, the romantics, Hegel, F. C. Baur, Kant, Ritschl), but it is perhaps best to hear what Harnack himself said:

> We study history in order to intervene in the course of history, and it is our right and duty that we do this, for if we lack historical insight we either permit ourselves to be mere objects put in the historical process or we shall have the tendency to lead people down the wrong way. To intervene in history—this means that we must reject the past when it reaches into the present only in order to block us. It means also that we must do the right thing in the present, that is, anticipate the future and be prepared for it in a circumspect manner. There is no doubt that, with respect to the past, the historian assumes the royal function of a judge, for in order to decide what of the past shall continue to be in effect and what must be done away with or transformed, the historian must judge like a king. Everything must be designed to furnish a preparation for the future, for only that discipline of learning has a right to exist which lays the foundation for what is to be.[5]

Harnack was perceived by everyone as an unusually talented teacher. His students knew they were in the presence of genius, but he never made them feel inferior. One of the many testimonies to this fact reads:

> We had the feeling that a new world was dawning upon us. . . . here we were touched by the aura of genius. Harnack combined in himself in a unique way the qualities required of a scholar with the gifts of a born teacher: concentrated inquisitiveness; tireless industry; the ability of ordering and forming his materials; a comprehensive memory; critical astuteness; a clear and considered judgment, and, together with all this, a wonderful gift of intuition and combination and, at the same time, a marvelously simple, lucid, and appealing manner of presentation. And, to top it all, he also had not infrequently the good fortune of finding and discovering something new. To every subject and field of study he gave light and warmth, life and significance. In both theory and practice he was a master of the teaching method.
>   . . . He made the past live through the present and let the present explain the past.[6]

In short, Adolf Harnack is truly the exemplar of the late nineteenth- and early twentieth-century Liberal Protestant historian.

Harnack's most popular book was called in English *What Is Christianity?*[7] Such a translation misses the point of the book. Strictly translated, the title is *The Essence of Christianity*. In general terms, the "essence" for Harnack is "the gospel": the teaching of Jesus and the application of that teaching to several concrete ethical and theological issues. Building on this foundation, the second half of the book takes up "the Christian religion" in its major historical expressions. These are Paul and apostolic Christianity, Greek Catholicism, Latin Catholicism, and Protestantism.

You will recall that Harnack was primarily a historian of dogma and that his special subject matter was early Christianity. The basic problem with which the book as a whole wrestles can be put in the form of a question: Is the Church, with its hierarchical institution, its ministry and sacraments, its dogma and liturgy, its Virgin and supernatural Christ, its saints and angels and relics, the *legitimate evolutionary outgrowth* of the primitive gospel of Jesus, or is it in the final analysis a *distortion* of that primitive gospel? His answer was that it is a distortion that preserved the essence of Christianity almost by accident.

Of the influence of Greek religion and Greek civilization Harnack judged harshly: "*It was to destroy this sort of religion that Jesus Christ suffered himself to be nailed to the cross,* and now we find it reestablished under his name and authority!"[8] He was also severely critical of Greek and oriental-monastic "deviations," for, he said, the monks as a rule were ". . . the instruments of the lowest and worst functions of the Church, of the worship of pictures and relics, of the crassest superstition and the most imbecile sorcery."[9]

Roman or Western Catholicism moved away from the gospel to an even greater extent: ". . . the whole outward and visible institution of a Church claiming divine dignity has no foundation whatever in the Gospel. It is a case, not of distortion, but of total perversion."[10] Fortunately, Harnack believed, the Church preserved the potential for correction in the essence of the gospel—partly rediscovered in the Protestant Reformation, more completely captured in nineteenth-century historical reconstruction. The vocation of the historian, as contrasted with the theologian, is to recover that essence for the modern world.

When he turned to the sources for the gospel, Harnack followed the (by then) conventional judgment that the Gospel of John should be set aside and that the two-source theory would best explain gospel origins. Thus he accepted the Markan priority and with it a modified Markan hypothesis. Though the gospels were insufficient for a biography of Jesus, they did offer a clear picture of the main outlines of Jesus' teaching and its specific applications, the way Jesus' life was oriented to the service of his vocation, and the impression Jesus made on his disciples, which they passed on. Harnack did not consider miracles a central issue for the historian, as they had been for the rationalists a century earlier. He compared his more optimistic view with that of Strauss:

> Sixty years ago David Friedrich Strauss thought that he had almost entirely destroyed the historical credibility not only of the fourth but also of the first three Gospels as well. The historical criticism of two generations has succeeded in restoring that credibility in its main outlines.[11]

Thus, Harnack believed that the historian could isolate from the gospels a reliable basis for understanding Jesus' teaching and life. The "essence" of Christianity so obtained should be the norm for all subsequent developments. In the language of the Protestant Reformation: Scripture, historically interpreted, is the guardian of tradition.

Harnack believed that the essence of Christianity is to be found in *the religious experience of the historical Jesus, indeed, in religious experience itself.* The important thing is not the religion *about* Jesus, but the religion *of* Jesus, just as in the great Liberal tradition religious experience of the individual is the heart of religion.

Jesus' religion, for Harnack, had certain roots in Old Testament prophecy, but essentially it was an isolated and unique phenomenon in the midst of Old Testament tradition and Jewish religion. Jesus did not stress the nation; he did not teach strict observance of the Mosaic law; he subordinated thinking about the future; he did not separate himself from the world, as the Essenes did; he was not educated, as the rabbis were; in contrast to John the Baptist, he focused more on joy than on judgment. He was also unique in that he had no relation to the Greek outlook. His teaching could be summarized in three items, which Harnack made famous:

> *Firstly, the kingdom of God and its coming.*
> *Secondly, God the Father and the infinite value of the human soul.*
> *Thirdly, the higher righteousness and the commandment of love.*[12]

Concerning the kingdom of God and its coming, Harnack recognized that the *future* kingdom was an idea Jesus shared with his contemporaries, but it was only the *husk* of Jewish eschatology; the *kernel,* the eternally valid teaching, Jesus' own unique view, was the "rule of God in the hearts of individuals," the kingdom within, the *present* kingdom, which enters the soul through Jesus' healing and forgiving of sin. As Harnack put it, "Eternal light came in and made the world look new."[13]

The second item of Jesus' teaching is "God the Father and the infinite value of the human soul." Belief in the fatherhood of God is accompanied by the conviction of being a child of God. As one who prays the Lord's Prayer knows, God is Father and his children feel safe. Even the very hairs of one's head are numbered (Mt 10:30). Harnack thought that Jesus was the first to give the individual human soul such value ("What shall it profit a man if he gain the whole world and lose his own soul?" [Mark 8:36]), for other religions gave more emphasis to the nation, as did Israel.

The theme of "higher righteousness and the commandment of love," the center of Jesus' ethical teaching, embraced the whole gospel for Harnack. The "higher righteousness" is the righteousness demanded by the Sermon on the Mount, which is superior to conventional externals of religious worship and technical observance. "You have heard it said . . . but I say to you . . ." (Mt 5:27, 31, etc.) What counts is the inner disposition and intention to love God and to love one's neighbor as oneself with all humility, as is illustrated by the Beatitudes and parables such as the Good Samaritan parable. Whereas the Old Testament God, for Harnack, was a capricious God of fear and judgment, Jesus taught about a God of mercy and love. The result is a golden rule ethic of tremendous civilizing power. (Mt 7:12; Luke 6:31).

Harnack worked out the specific implications of his Liberal, ethical, civilizing Jesus in four practical areas (the Christian's relation to the world, to poverty, to public order, and to civilization) and two doctrinal areas (the Christian's relation to Christology and to creed).[14] In contrast to the view exemplified by monasticism (and praised by the philosopher Schopenhauer and the novelist Tolstoi), Jesus opposed the renunciation of the world. It is true that he countenanced self-denial when he spoke out against riches (Mk 10:17–31), excessive attachment to material things (Mt 6:25ff.), and egoism; but he was accused of being a glutton and a winebibber (Mt 11:19), he refrained from organizing his disciples

into a monastic order, and he encouraged them to continue their oc-
cupations and not to leave their wives! Self-denial and asceticism were
two different things to Harnack, and Jesus did not teach asceticism as
the Church was later to do.

The social question, too, was handled gently by Jesus. Harnack
argued that Jesus was not a social reformer, did not lay down a social
program for relief of the poor, spoke more of being "poor in spirit" (Mt
5:3) than of actual economic poverty, and established no foundation for
monastic vows of poverty. "The poor you always have with you," said
Jesus (Mk 14:7). Yet Jesus did indicate that the rich would have difficulty entering the kingdom of God, and there were social implications
to Jesus' more individualistic love ethic: Love of God and neighbor leads
to a *spiritual brotherhood* that cannot help but benefit the poor.

On the question of public order, or law, Harnack was convinced
that Jesus was not a political revolutionary and developed no political
program. The realm of God was distinct from the realm of Caesar. Jesus
was concerned with the *individual's* relation to God, not the nation's.
The attempt of the oppressed to achieve rights was ultimately futile, and
one was called on to disarm one's enemies by one's gentleness. In the
end, God would be just.

Similarly, civilization (science and the arts) was not of primary concern to Jesus, for that implies the notion of progress. Moreover, it can
become of such concern that it is seen as a "work," or "law," and that
was not the thrust of Jesus' teaching. One of the errors of Catholicism,
thought Harnack, was that it tied itself to medieval civilization!

In the realm of Christology, Harnack did not think of Jesus as the
political-national Messiah of Jewish hopes. Jesus' own "messianic consciousness" centered in self-subjection to God as Son and Jesus' authoritative request to keep his own commandments. God is Father; Jesus is
Son: "No man knows the Son but the Father; neither does any man
know the Father, save the Son, and he to whomsoever the Son will
reveal him," said Jesus (Mt 11:27). The evangelists say that Jesus had
an inner experience which became the foundation for his consciousness
as Son at his baptism. He was tempted as Son. Jesus had transferred
this to a more spiritual conception of the Messiah, current in some
quarters of Judaism, by the time of Peter's confession at Caesarea Philippi. His public declaration occurred at the entry to Jerusalem and the
cleansing of the Temple. Yet Jesus did not *proclaim* himself to be the
Son: *"The Gospel, as Jesus proclaimed it, has to do with the Father only
and not with the Son."* [15] In other words, Jesus was the way to the Father, appointed by the Father, and the Judge—but by virtue of what he
said, what he was, what he did, and what he suffered. The usual eschatological conception of the Messiah (expressed by the apocalyptic Son of
Man) was the *husk;* the experience of being a child of God was the *kernel.*

Finally, what is the relation between the gospel and doctrine? The gospel, said Harnack, is no theoretical system of doctrine, no philosophy of the universe, no theory of nature; rather, it is religion and morality, the inward experience of the living God along with its confession and practice. Already with early Christianity and Paul, the shift began to take place from inwardness toward doctrine. Harnack's judgment was:

> . . . we are reminded of the fact that, so far as history is concerned, as soon as we leave the sphere of pure inwardness, there is no progress, no achievement, no advantage of any sort, that has not its dark side, and does not bring its disadvantages with it.[16]

It is important to see the profound influence that Harnack's views of Jesus had on Protestant Christianity in the early twentieth century. Though the orthodox suspected him of heresy, most Liberal Protestant Christians have been in some way indebted to Harnack, whether in their historical consciousness, their basic distrust of an overly institutionalized religion, their focus on ethics rather than on ritual or discipline, or their notion that the individual's religious experience is the heart of religion. When a Liberal Protestant claims, "Jesus said . . . ," what usually follows is an echo of Harnack's views.

THE SOCIAL GOSPEL IN THE UNITED STATES

Adolf Harnack is a superb example of the nineteenth-century German Protestant Liberal thinker. In the United States, the Liberal-Modernist movement took a somewhat different form. Whereas the Europeans tended to develop Jesus' social message out of their understanding of his concern for individuals, the Americans—faced with a young, sprawling, industrial nation of cities, depressions, sweatshops, unemployment, and bankruptcies—moved somewhat more quickly to apply Jesus' teaching to the social situation. Karl Marx had challenged Christians with his view that religion was merely a tool of the upper classes and the industrialists to keep the lower classes and workers in their places. For Marx religion was used to drug the masses; it was "the opiate of the people." For the American who wanted to be "an intelligent modern and a serious Christian" (as Harry Emerson Fosdick put it), it was imperative that the social message of Jesus be brought forward and applied, where possible, to social conditions in the new industrial technocracy. In this context, many saw the message of Jesus as the Social Gospel.[17]

The intellectual tradition behind the movement that stressed the Social Gospel was the Liberal Protestant view of history and culture. The acknowledged classic of the movement was *Christianity and the*

Social Crisis (1907), by Walter Rauschenbusch, who had been reared in the pietistic tradition and had studied in Germany, where he had come under the influence of the writings of Schleiermacher and Ritschl, and more directly, Harnack. In Rauschenbusch, "evangelical Christianity" and Liberalism were wedded. But whatever the orientation, the American thinkers of the Social Gospel movement sought to apply Jesus' "timeless" teachings to the social problems of the day.

JESUS CHRIST IN THE THOUGHT
OF SHAILER MATHEWS

A key member of the Social Gospel movement was Shailer Mathews (1863–1941).[18] Mathews was born in 1863 in Portland, Maine, the heir to a long line of preachers and teachers. In his home he breathed the air of a rigid, evangelical, Baptist piety; he was required to avoid dancing, card-playing, and the theater. Eventually, Mathews attended Colby University (Colby College) in Maine, where he became close friends with one of his young teachers, Albion Small. Here his piety was somewhat modified by his study of the theory of evolution. After college he attended Newton Theological Institution (now Andover Newton) in Massachusetts. Like most seminaries of the period, Newton was orthodox and oriented to the Bible as the divine Word. Mathews, though still very orthodox in his views, nevertheless began to explore the "dangerous" view that the Bible might have been conditioned by certain social and historical factors.

After leaving Newton, Mathews accepted a teaching position in rhetoric and public speaking at Colby, where his friend Small was now President. Then, for a period, he returned to Newton to teach the New Testament. In preparation for his return to Colby to teach history and political economy, he went to Berlin to study history and economics. There he became acquainted with the thought of the great nineteenth-century positivist historian Leopold von Ranke, who is known for his view that history is a totally objective science, that is, a science of gathering and relating data without regard to theories or presuppositions. Mathews' economics teacher was Adolf Wagner, one of the organizers of the "Union for Social Politics," which repudiated the injustices of *laissez faire* capitalism and advocated government-supported social welfare. What a different world from his rural New England evangelical piety!

In 1892 Mathews returned to Colby University, but he no longer felt at home in the small New England town. His friend Albion Small, who had left Colby to establish the first graduate department in the field

of sociology at the newly opened University of Chicago, encouraged him
to become competent in the field, and he immediately set about reading.
By 1894, beckoned by Small and by Ernest DeWitt Burton, a former
teacher at Newton, he began teaching the New Testament at the University of Chicago Divinity School.

From 1895 to 1898 he published articles on "Christian sociology"
and then compiled them in a book, *The Social Teaching of Jesus* (1897).
Some twenty-three books, eight essays, eighty-nine articles, and ten
critical reviews were to follow. In 1906 Mathews shifted to the field of
historical and comparative theology, in 1926 he became professor of historical theology, and from 1908 to 1933 he was dean of the Divinity
School. This period was the heyday of the "Chicago School," a distinguished group of theologians oriented toward the empiricism and positivism of the natural sciences, the pragmatism and humanism of
philosophers such as John Dewey, and the sometimes relativistic sociohistorical approach to the Bible and Christian history. In this environment, the career of Mathews moved from evangelical Christianity to
evangelical Liberalism and then toward the views of his more materialistic and relativistic colleagues. But Mathews never gave up his quest
for the normative element in Christianity.

Mathews retired from the University of Chicago in 1933. He had
had a prolific career of publishing, had held the position of professor of
historical theology and chairman of the Department of Theology and
Ethics, and had been dean for twenty-five years. His death came eight
years later, in 1941.

Mathews' views on Jesus Christ were related to his general sociohistorical method of thought.[19] In line with the mainstream of nineteenth-century Liberalism, Mathews did not base Christianity on a set
of doctrines. He was critical of philosophy, especially of traditional metaphysics, and he understood Truth as grounded in mundane human experience, which he believed was expressed in particular modes of
thinking at particular periods of history. Doctrine was therefore a product of "the social mind"—in this case, of the way the Christian community formulated its beliefs in a particular cultural epoch. The *social
mind* of a particular cultural epoch he defined as "a more or less general
community of conscious states, processes, ideas, interests, and ambitions which to a greater or lesser degree repeats itself in the experience
of individuals belonging to the group and characterized by the community of consciousness."[20] Mathews noted seven such "social minds" in
the history of Western culture: the Semitic, the Greco-Roman, the im-
perialistic, the feudal, the nationalistic, the bourgeois, and the modern,
or scientific-democratic. The object of the "theologian" is to undertake a
sociohistorical investigation into the way Christian beliefs have been

formulated in their successive social environments in order to determine what is common to them all. This common element, then, would be (in Harnack's terms) the "essence" of Christianity (Mathews tended to think of the Christian "attitude" or "ideal"). The "essence" must then be interpreted further for the present, which for Mathews was the seventh epoch, the epoch of modern science and democracy.

Mathews' criticism was both unlike and like that of his European counterparts. Unlike them, he did not defend a particular critical view of the gospels such as the Matthean priority or the Markan hypothesis, and he cited the Gospel of John alongside the synoptics. In general, he trusted the chronological account of Jesus' life and the narrative setting of his teachings. Yet Mathews was very much like his liberal counterparts in believing that his sociohistorical *method* was objective and therefore not subject to the "social mind" of his own epoch. Thus he considered himself capable of finding the historical Jesus, at least in general. Moreover, the "essence" of Christianity, the "Christian ideal" or "Christian attitude" toward society in the successive cultural epochs, was based on the eternally valid life, message, and *personal example* of Jesus as the source and norm for spiritual renewal among believers. Who was this Jesus, and how did Mathews view him in relation to his own cultural epoch? To answer this we must turn to the final revision of his classic work, *The Social Teachings of Jesus* (1897), retitled in 1928 *Jesus on Social Institutions*.

The cultural epoch of Judaism in first-century Palestine was what Mathews called "the revolutionary spirit." When Jesus "closed the door of his shop in Nazareth and stepped into history,"[21] he wrote, Jesus entered a world seething with the psychology of political revolution: the yoke of Roman taxes enforced by the military presence; cooperation of the upper-class Sadducees; political, economic, and social inequalities experienced by the poor masses; a desire for revenge backed by revolutionary propaganda; and idealized hope centering in the coming of a Messiah who would reestablish the Davidic empire. The Pharisees fed such a spirit by their stress on the Jewish law for the Jewish people; the more radical Zealots fomented political revolution. The revolutionary literature of the day was apocalyptic, for its hope was expressed in terms of a kingdom both earthly (political) and heavenly (supernatural); that is, the war with Rome would also be a cosmic war with the forces of Satan. The Jews believed that God loved their nation, hated the foreign oppressors, and would eventually deliver them.

How did Jesus fit into this revolutionary spirit? Jesus was sympathetic with it and part of it, but he transformed it. As a member of the artisan class, he understood the position of the masses. The wing of the revolutionary movement to which he first gave adherence, however, was that of John the Baptist, which focused on nonviolence, ethics, and the spirit. Jesus eventually surpassed John, but he continued John's modified revolutionary-apocalyptic view. What this meant for Mathews' later views of Jesus (after 1897), influenced by Weiss and Schweitzer, was that Jesus taught in the *form* of an apocalyptic (cp. Harnack's "husk"), but the *content* was something more universal and permanent (cp. Harnack's "kernel"). Eschatology was therefore part of the Semitic "social mind." Jesus taught a kingdom that was not limited to the Jewish nation, a loving God, and a Messiah who would suffer, die, and be raised from the dead. Jesus' life embodied this teaching: He had a divine self-consciousness in which love, self-sacrifice, and the hope of immortality would be severely tested. He and his teaching were *preparation for the kingdom.* This resulted in certain social ideals, or "attitudes," the most fundamental of which was that all people, despite physical, mental, or political inequalities, were *equal in their obligation to express love.* The love ethic was therefore not an ethic of political revolution. "His gospel was not a new Declaration of Rights, but a Declaration of Duties." [22]

Mathews developed four special areas in which Jesus' attitudes became the foundation for lasting Christian attitudes—if not for social programs. These were the family, wealth, the state, and the church.[23] Judaism said little about the family *as an institution.* However, Jesus recognized that though marriage could stand in the way of the blessings of the kingdom (so that some would prefer to live in celibacy, like Jesus himself), monogamous marriage was a divine creative act and the only basis for family life (Mt 19:5, 6; Mark 10:6–8). Reaffirming this on the basis of Moses' social teachings, Jesus then proceeded to counteract Mosaic law by rejecting divorce (Mark 10:9). But this prohibition could not be the basis for social law, even among Christians, since Jesus' view of love also would require protection of the victims of bad marriages. What Jesus taught was the *ideal* for those who are not celibate but wish to enter the kingdom: Love in marriage means that the individuals involved will protect the family as a social unit, and this love will supersede any indiscriminate sexual urges. Otherwise, human beings would be reduced to animals and the love ethic forgotten. "If all families embodied the love of the Heavenly Father, who would think of divorce or of sexual irregularity?" [24] Thus Jesus taught not a law but an attitude, an ideal that has permanent validity.

Jesus' attitude toward *wealth* was similar. Jesus himself was poor, apparently gave to the poor (John 13:29), and asked others to do the same (Luke 12:33; Mt 6:19–21). When Jesus prepared people for the kingdom, the moral ideal of brotherhood appeared to be a renunciation of private property and individual wealth, or *socialism.* Yet the small-town artisan was not an economist and had nothing to say about intricate economic matters such as the means of production or the moral aspects of trade. He did not actually advocate socialism; giving up property, suggested Mathews, places a "premium on beggary" and runs the risk of putting economic power in the hands of those least likely to follow the ethic of love. Jesus' ideal was part of his apocalyptic world view. What was of lasting value in the ideal was the necessity to base "economic processes on a true recognition of personal values, cease to think of labor as a commodity, and endeavor to use whatever wealth he has morally gained in the interest of human welfare."[25]

Jesus' teaching about the *state* is an especially good illustration of his approach, which was to put forth an ideal rather than a law. Jesus both limited his mission to one nation, Israel, and saw the weaknesses of national chauvinism. Yet he nowhere gives explicit political teaching. The well-known passage "Render to Caesar the things that are Caesar's, and to God the things that are God's" (Mark 12:17) is an ambiguous answer to opponents that admits of various interpretations, depending on whether one is convinced that Caesar really owned the coins. The passage traditionally used to support the divine right of kings in the medieval period was Jesus' answer to Pilate, "Thou wouldst have no authority against me, except it were given thee from above" (John 19:11). But this, Mathews claimed, really expresses Jesus' view of God's providence. Was he then an anarchist? Not in the usual sense. Neither was he a monarchist, a socialist, or a democrat. One cannot even say that in every instance Jesus' views lead to pacifism. Sometimes war is necessary, but only after arbitration. "The bearing of the teaching of Jesus upon political affairs is thus the same as in the case of other social institutions. It contains no directions for social legislation. The supreme duty of man is to embody the principle of love in whatever social groupings he may be."[26]

The fourth special interest of Mathews is the *church*. Jesus, of course, did not establish the institutional church with its rites, priesthood, theology, and creeds. Nonetheless, that was its natural evolution. The purpose of the church is to perpetuate and socialize the original community's spirit by adjusting the attitudes of Jesus to the present. Many social agencies of a secular nature have arisen, and in some cases their experts are better equipped to carry on the social functions once reserved to the church. The church, however, is not simply another social agency but is called on to embody Jesus' ideal of love, to proclaim the Social Gospel.

In summary, Shailer Mathews, a leading figure in "the Chicago School," thought of the Social Gospel as an attitude of love and good will rather than a philosophy, a system, or a creed. Such a view excludes Marxism or any comparable mechanistic or deterministic point of view. The "Social Gospel" is a force that unifies the personality and provides a functional basis out of which to consider social relations. Mathews wrote:

> At all events, whether men dare accept it or not, whether the church makes it central or not, Jesus taught that *love is a practicable basis upon which to build human relations*. Once let humanity actually believe this

and the perspective of values will be changed. Giving justice will replace the manipulation of social advantages; the humanizing of necessary economic processes will replace the exploiting of human life in the interests of wealth of pleasure. . . .

. . . Within that movement there will be education, art, philosophy, and scientific research; there will be social institutions and ambitious altruism; but these will be controlled by that central attitude which Jesus described and so uncompromisingly embodied. His followers will possess the zest of the revolutionist, the painstaking method of the technician, the goodwill of the Heavenly Father. *But the greatest of these will be goodwill.* [italics added][27]

THE HISTORY-OF-RELIGIONS SCHOOL

The term "history of religions" today refers most often to the *general* science of religions, that is, the broad-ranging study of religious phenomena, from primitive religions past and present to the world religions, frequently including the insights of a variety of standpoints. In contrast, the term *Religionsgeschichte* ("history of religions") and its cognates (*Religionsgeschichtler*, "Historians of Religion"; *die religionsgeschichtliche Schule*, "the History-of-Religions School") in Germany referred primarily to the history of a particular religion in relation to the immediate religions of its environment, though at points it was influenced by the movement that became "history of religions."[28]

Religionsgeschichtler began to look at the history of primitive Christianity in the context of parallel religious phenomena in the ancient Mediterranean world and the Near East. This was made possible because of a major influx of new data brought to light by archeological and textual discoveries and advanced in the scientific study of ancient languages (philology), all of which had been inaccessible to earlier scholars. For the first time it was seen that early Christianity had much in common with the religions that surrounded it—in fact, that it had borrowed many conceptions in order to express its beliefs about Jesus. This meant that if one were to understand the Christian religion historically, socially, and culturally, one's net had to be cast much further than those documents which had become the church's authoritative scriptures. To that extent, the historical consciousness led to the realization that there were common elements between the myths and rituals of both Jews and "pagans" and those of early Christians.[29] Such *religionsgeschichtliche* study described Christianity with the term that had emerged to indicate its relation to the many religions of the ancient world: *syncretism.* Hermann Gunkel wrote,

Christianity is a syncretistic religion. Powerful religious motives that came from abroad were contained in it and throve mightily, both oriental and Hellenistic. For the characteristic feature—we might say, the providential

> feature—of Christianity is *that it experienced its classical era in the hour of world history when it stepped out of the Orient into Hellenism.* Therefore it has a share in both worlds. . . . These foreign religious motives must have flooded into the Church of Jesus immediately after Jesus' death.[30]

As this comment shows, the early *Religionsgeschichtler* thought of Jesus as basically unaffected by the religious movements of his own time; that is, though apocalyptic eschatology was current in Palestine, Jesus rejected it. To put it bluntly, if the Liberal portrait of Jesus was to be maintained, it was also necessary to maintain that Jesus was not influenced by the various religious movements. In contrast, Paul was finally being interpreted from the correct perspective—that of the larger Hellenistic culture or Near Eastern culture or Hellenistic Greek culture (though Paul did show some influence from his Pharisaic Jewish background). John, too, was a product of Hellenistic "pagan" religiosity. Yet it was Paul who received most attention. From the *religionsgeschichtliche* perspective, there appeared a huge gap between Jesus, the simple, ethical teacher and prophet from Nazareth, and the Hellenistic-oriental Paul, who believed in a divine Christ myth of cosmic significance. The former taught the kingdom of God within the individual; the latter formed a mystical community with rites of initiation (baptism) and a cultic meal (the Lord's Supper). To William Wrede, Paul was the "perverter" or "second founder" of Christianity, for Paul did not base his views on those of Jesus at all. Wrede wrote,

> This picture of Christ did not develop under the impress of the personality of Jesus. It has often been asserted, but never proved. . . . There remains only one explanation: *Paul already believed in such a heavenly being, in a divine Christ, before he believed in Jesus.* . . . Unless we deny both figures any historicity, it follows that to call Paul "a disciple of Jesus" is quite inappropriate if this is meant to describe his historical relationship to Jesus.[31]

Thus Wrede's assumption is that early Christians like Paul simply related Jesus to an already existing myth about a heavenly redeemer.

We conclude this chapter with the life and work of the member of the *religionsgeschichtliche Schule* who summed up much of its earlier perspective with his book *Kyrios Christos* in 1913, Wilhelm Bousset.

JESUS CHRIST IN THE THOUGHT OF WILHELM BOUSSET

Wilhelm Bousset, the oldest son of a Pietist pastor descended from French Protestant stock, was born on September 8, 1865, in Lübeck, Germany.[32] He was reared in Lübeck and received his early schooling there. After he passed his examinations, his father sent him off to the

Pietist-oriented University of Erlangen, and then to the University of Leipzig. Yet young Bousset became absorbed in the writings of the Liberals, especially Ritschl and Harnack, a turn that led to many arguments with his father. With his mother's support, Bousset finally won his father's permission to go to the University of Göttingen, where he came under the direct influence of Ritschl.

In 1889 Bousset was appointed lecturer at Göttingen. In these early years, the scholarly rediscovery of Jewish apocalyptic ideas made a strong impact on Bousset, and his first book, *Jesus' Preaching in its Opposition to Judaism* (1892), attempted to show both the continuity and discontinuity of Jesus with the apocalyptic movement. In 1894 he published critical studies on the text of the New Testament; the following year, his research on the "Antichrist" legend attempted to trace this tradition through texts over great expanses of time.

In 1896 Bousset was appointed associate professor of New Testament at the University of Göttingen. After a work on the Book of Revelation that established his reputation as a major New Testament scholar, and after launching with Wilhelm Heitmüller the *Theologische*

Wilhelm Bousset

Rundschau (*Theological Review*), Bousset published *The Religion of Judaism in the Period of the New Testament* (1903). This work successfully demonstrated that early Christianity was more indebted to Jewish and Hellenistic religions of the first century than to the Old Testament. It was revised by H. Gressmann after Bousset's death and is still considered a classic.

It was also in 1903 that Bousset wrote a book on the *general* "history of religions," *Das Wesen der Religion* (*The Essence of Religion*). Bousset's sensitivity to general religious phenomena was exceptional for a New Testament critic and historian of that period:

> . . . the whole religious life of man is a magnificent tapestry created by God who used it to entice and draw mankind up to great heights, from the imperfect to the perfect, from self-centeredness to communal life, from the sensuous to the moral, from the natural to the spiritual.[33]

Such studies did not lead Bousset to abandon his commitment to Christianity. His book *Jesus* (1903) portrayed Jesus not only as a hero of religious history but also as a powerful force that undergirded Bousset's own life.

After several other works, including an important study of Gnosticism (1907), Bousset published his masterpiece, *Kyrios Christos* (*Lord Christ*), in 1913. Still considered by some to be the foundation work for the study of beliefs about Jesus in early Christianity, this work attempted to trace the Christian movement from its inception to the second century, showing influence by Palestinian Judaism in the early stages and by Hellenistic religious piety in the later stages. This was followed by his last work, *Jewish-Christian Intellectual Activity in Alexandria and Rome* (1915).

The irony of this great scholar's life was that he was never permitted to become a full professor at the University of Göttingen, largely because of political pressure on the faculty by the German government. Thus, in 1916, during World War I, he accepted the position of full professor at the University of Giessen. There he continued to work on texts from the history of monasticism. Though he was thought by students to be remote, he was always known as a strong advocate of social justice. He died in 1920, leaving behind as his great legacy many important works, most significant of which was *Kyrios Christos*.

Wilhelm Bousset's *Kyrios Christos* was a summation of the early phase of the *religionsgeschichtliche Schule*.[34] Bousset accepted the common view of many *Religionsgeschichtler* that the New Testament was a product of syncretism. What was crucial for Bousset was the movement through four early stages from Jesus to Palestinian Jewish Christianity to Hellenistic Christianity to Paul. Then came John, more developed Gnosticism, and the early Christian writing down to Irenaeus in the late second century.

Bousset's *Kyrios Christos* had little to say about the "historical Jesus"; it perceived Jesus in the Liberal manner, as a "creative miracle" in the midst of his ancient environment, hardly affected by apocalyptic eschatology. Nevertheless, Jesus probably did accept Jewish apocalyptic eschatology near the end of his life. If he did, and spoke of himself as Son of Man, it was this conviction that gave the Palestinian community its basis for reflecting about Jesus. It did not believe that Jesus had been the *nationalistic* Messiah, the Son of David, expected to restore the glorious political kingdom of David; rather, it believed that Jesus had been "exalted" in heaven as the apocalyptic Son of Man who would return to complete his mission of judgment and defense. It was this belief, stated Bousset, that fixed the separation between the earliest church and the Jewish synagogue: Some Jews did not accept Jesus as the Son of Man; those who did became Christians. Starting from this foundation, the early church and the synoptic gospels expanded the "historical Jesus" with a number of sayings, teaching anecdotes, miracle stories, and stories of the resurrection and empty tomb—the effective and necessary symbols of the age.

Whereas the earliest Palestinian community thought of Jesus as the Son of Man, Paul thought of him as the Lord. The fact that Paul never used the apocalyptic title Son of Man suggested to Bousset that Paul's notion of Jesus Christ was built on wholly different conceptions developed in the Hellenistic churches and modeled on the mystical piety of the larger Hellenistic world. Thus the second stage of development, after the Palestinian, Aramaic-speaking church but prior to Paul, was the Hellenistic church represented by the cities of Damascus (Paul's conversion), Tarsus (Paul's birth and early childhood), and especially Antioch (Paul's home base for the mission). Here the Christ began to appear as a divine, mystical figure so familiar in the larger Hellenistic world.

The third stage of development, found in Paul himself, was the belief that the Lord was a mythical figure who had been in the form of God, had come to earth as a human, and had returned to heaven (Phil 2:6ff.). He was also the Second Adam (Rom 5). Here, Bousset saw Paul modifying the widespread oriental-Hellenistic mythical figure of a First Man, or First Adam, a supernatural, heavenly being who fell by sinking into matter, who suffered and died, but who was liberated and thereby passed on liberation to his people (the "redeemed redeemer"). For Paul, however, the First Adam was a natural man who fell and introduced sin; it was the Last Adam who was the supernatural Adam and who brought deliverance from sin. Similarly, Paul was aware of the myths of the dying and rising gods from the oriental mystery religions; but whereas those centered in the recurrent changes of the seasons, Paul

thought of a once-for-all event of the past. This event had present meaning for the Christian who died with Christ in his baptism and who
would be raised at the End as Jesus Christ was raised (Rom 6).

The second major point for Paul, according to Bousset, had to do
with the Christian's mystical identification with Jesus Christ in worship,
a conception similar to (but not exactly like) that found in the Hellenistic mystery religions. To be "in Christ Jesus" was, on the one hand, to be
in the fellowship of the body and blood of Christ (1 Cor 10:16); but it
was also to be "in the spirit," that is, under the influence of a supernatural Spirit. This Spirit seized a person and made possible such phenomena as ecstatic speaking in tongues, soothsaying and mind reading,
ecstatic prayer, healing the sick, immunity from snakebite and poison,
visions and trances, and miracle working. To be in the community also
meant that the initiate was virtually identified with Jesus Christ, whose
"body" was the church. Yet, true to his Jewish heritage, Paul was unwilling to conceive of the initiate as a god.

The third major point for Paul, according to Bousset, was that the
Lord, though a preexistent divine being who came to earth and returned, was not God but only the "Son of God." Though Jesus was, for
Paul, the object of faith (that is, a firm, unshakable conviction that
becomes the foundation for life), only God was "the Father." Jesus remained "the Son," as close as possible to the Father, yet distinguished
from him.

With Paul, the major transition to Hellenistic Christian piety was
achieved. The Johannine writings (the Gospel of John; 1, 2, 3 John),
argued Bousset, continued this basic transition, for " 'John' of course
stands on the shoulders of 'Paul.' "[35] On the one hand, the calm and
sublime Johannine piety was quite different from the ecstatic piety of
Paul, and at points John had similarities to Gnosticism. On the other
hand, John's religion was, like Paul's, not a religion of the historical
Jesus but a religion of redemption. For John, the believer who truly *sees*
the vision of the Son of God and *believes* in him *knows* God in such a
way that he is almost deified or, as John says, has "eternal life" (John
6:40). Bousset concluded:

> In spite of the fact that he wrote a fourth Gospel, John is basically
> somewhat further removed from the preaching of Jesus than is Paul. The
> gospel of the forgiveness of sins as Jesus proclaimed it has still further
> disappeared. In its place appears the message of redemption and the re-
> deemer; in place of the savior of sinners stands the one who is the friend of
> his own people, to whom the friends yield themselves in calm and radiant
> frame of mind as to the one who has for them the words of eternal life.[36]

With the Johannine writings, the history of belief had moved a long
way from the simple ethical teaching which Bousset believed was the
heart of Jesus' message. Gnosticism took up Paul's viewpoint and further mythologized his "Christ myth"—so much so that the divine re-

deemer only "seemed" to become a man in Jesus of Nazareth. Another direction was taken by postapostolic Christianity, which, Bousset believed, lost the total outlook of Paul's "Christ mysticism" by developing a highly organized and institutionalized Christianity. Yet it retained worship of the Kyrios in such a way that Christ was seen more and more as divine, the rational principle (Logos) of God, while at the same time the practical needs of the new institution made him a new lawgiver, a universal ethical teacher, in some respects not unlike the figure he had historically been. For Bousset the development concluded with Irenaeus, wherein both the deity and humanity of Jesus Christ were affirmed, leading ultimately to the Church's orthodoxy.

Wilhelm Bousset's *Kyrios Christos* sought to show the movement from the historical Jesus as an ethical teacher of the kingdom of God and the forgiveness of sins to the Christ myth of Paul and John, and beyond into the second century. That route was through the Son of Man eschatology of the earliest Palestinian Aramaic-speaking community and then through the cultic "Lord" mysticism of the Hellenistic churches. If Jesus was *expected* as the apocalyptic Son of Man at first, that future focus gradually passed into the *present* union of the believer with the "Lord" of the community in worship. It was the latter view that Paul inherited and developed, and its roots lay not in the narrower framework of apocalyptic thinking, but in the broader oriental-Hellenistic religious communities of the East, notably Tarsus, Damascus, and Antioch. For Paul, then, Jesus was the Lord whose body was the church, and the believer entered his body by baptism, through which he shared in his death and would share in his resurrection. This Lord was also present in the cult of the supper and was identical with the Spirit, which brought forth various spiritual phenomena. Yet Paul did not conclude that his Lord and Christ was God; he was still the Son of God. The Johannine literature, though quite different, took such views still further, for John's Son of Man was almost divine, and believers almost deified. It remained for Gnosticism to continue this direction and for the apostolic church to shift away from it toward a more sober, rational, and institutionalized Christ figure.

SUMMARY

By the later nineteenth century, the historical consciousness of the West had emerged in full bloom, dominated especially by materialism, positivism, and evolutionism. In New Testament study, hard-nosed historical research concentrated, first of all, on an evaluation of the sources. This research resulted in the "two-source theory" (according to which Mark and Q are the major sources for Matthew and Luke), the theory of the priority of Mark, and the Markan hypothesis (which holds that Mark is fundamentally historical and provides a relatively secure foundation for knowledge about Jesus' life). Most scholars abandoned the traditional view that Matthew was the earliest gospel, a view which had been part of the ages-old gospel harmony approach. The theory of the priority of Mark and the Markan hypothesis also went beyond historically skeptical attitudes toward the gospels (such as that of Strauss) and became the basis for the quest of the historical Jesus. The historical approach to Jesus made it possible to bypass the dominant doctrinal approach (Ch. 3).

The Jesus discovered by historical research was a human Jesus whose spiritualized, nonpolitical "Messianic (self-)consciousness" developed to include his suffering for all, and whose teaching centered in an inner, spiritual kingdom and in ethics. This Jesus became the cornerstone of Protestant Liberalism. The intellectual roots of Liberalism lay in Kant's stress on the "moral law within," in pietistic and Schleiermacherian understanding of subjective human experience, and in Hegel's conception of the activity of God within the course of human history. The Liberals stressed a God of love and a Christ who inspired Christians to live according to his higher moral values (Ritschl). Liberalism was therefore a viable alternative to orthodoxy in the minds of many modern Christian thinkers.

One of the great nineteenth-century Liberals in Germany was Adolf Harnack, who sought to replace traditional Christian dogmatics with historical understanding. Harnack's studies of the history of Christianity convinced him that the elaborate institutional Church was a distortion of the simple religion of Jesus. The heart of Jesus' teaching for Harnack was the kingdom of God and its coming, God as Father and the infinite value of the human soul, and the higher righteousness and the commandment of love. Jesus the ethical teacher was the kernel of history; the apocalyptic history was the timebound husk; and the dogmatic Christ of the creeds was to move in the wrong direction.

In the United States, Shailer Mathews found a Jesus somewhat like that of Harnack, but oriented more toward the social problems of the new industrial society. For Mathews, Jesus did not teach a fixed system of social ethics, but he did provide an attitude toward social problems that has permanent validity, notably love and good will. This, Mathews believed, was the objective result of his sociohistorical method, the distillation of the various Christian beliefs in their various social environments over the centuries.

Our final example, Wilhelm Bousset, was a *Religionsgeschichtler:* He went beyond the Liberal historians to explore the religious environment in which the myth about Jesus Christ developed in the early church's oral tradition. Jesus himself probably accepted apocalyptic views near the end of his life, and the early church stressed that Jesus as Son of Man would return shortly to complete his mission. Eventually, however, the message moved further away from Palestine into the Greco-Roman world at large. Here, thinking about Jesus was so influenced by Hellenistic religious piety that it saw him as a divine Lord, thus creating a Christ myth with its accompanying ritualistic piety. This new conception was represented in varying ways by Paul and John, the latter having been more influenced by incipient Gnosticism. Thus Christianity became a syncretistic religion.

NOTES

1. Kümmel, *The New Testament,* pp. 146–61; Paul Feine and Johannes Behm, *Introduction to the New Testament,* ed. Werner Georg Kümmel, trans. A. J. Mattill, Jr., 14th ed. (Nashville: Abingdon Press, 1966), pp. 33–59; William R. Farmer, *The Synoptic Problem* (New York: Macmillan Co., 1964).

2. William Hordern, *A Layman's Guide to Protestant Theology,* 2nd ed. (New York: Macmillan Co., 1968), pp. 73–110; Sydney E. Ahlstrom, *A Religious History of the American People,* 2 vols. (New York: Doubleday & Co., Image Books, 1975), pp. 224–49; Kenneth Cauthen, *The Impact of American Religious Liberalism* (New York: Harper & Row, 1962); Dillenberger and Welch, *Protestant Christianity,* pp. 179–231.

3. Philip Hefner, *Faith and the Vitalities of History: A Theological Study Based on the Work of Albrecht Ritschl* (New York: Harper & Row, 1966); David L. Mueller, *An Introduction to the Theology of Albrecht Ritschl* (Philadelphia: Westminster Press, 1969); Mackintosh, *Types of Modern Theology,* pp. 138–80; Durwood A. Foster, "Albrecht Ritschl," in *A Handbook of Christian Theologians,* ed. Dean G. Peerman and Martin E. Marty (Cleveland: World Publishing Co., 1965), pp. 49–67.

4. Wayne G. Glick, *The Reality of Christianity: A Study of Adolf von Harnack as Historian and Theologian* (New York: Harper & Row, 1967); Wilhelm Pauck, "Adolf von Harnack," in Peerman and Marty, *Christian Theologians,* pp. 86–111; Pauck, *Harnack and Troeltsch: Two Historical Theologians* (New York: Oxford University Press, 1968).

5. Adolf Harnack, "Über die Sicherheit und Grenzen geschichtlicher Erkenntnis," *Reden und Aufsätze* **4,** p. 7, quoted in Pauck, *Harnack and Troeltsch,* p. 19.

6. W. Bornemann in *Christliche Welt* **35** (1921), p. 315, quoted in Pauck, *Harnack and Troeltsch,* pp. 16–17.

7. The following is derived from the English translation by Thomas Bailey Saunders (New York: Harper & Row, Torchbooks, 1957).

8. Ibid., p. 238.

9. Ibid., pp. 240–41.

10. Ibid., p. 262.

11. Ibid., p. 20.

12. Ibid., p. 51.

13. Ibid., p. 62.

14. Ibid., pp. 78ff.

15. Ibid., p. 144.

16. Ibid., p. 187.

17. In addition to note 2, see Charles H. Hopkins, *The Rise of the Social Gospel in American Protestantism, 1865–1915* (New Haven: Yale University Press, 1940); Washington Gladden, *Christianity and Socialism* (Cincinnati: Jennings & Graham, 1905); *Social Salvation* (Boston: Houghton Mifflin Co., 1902); Walter Rauschenbusch, *A Theology for the Social Gospel* (New York: Macmillan Co., 1917); *Christianizing the Social Order* (New York: Macmillan Co., 1912); in addition to the works of Shailer Mathews mentioned below, see also Francis Greenwood Peabody, *Jesus Christ and the Social Question* (New York: Macmillan Co., 1900); Shirley Jackson Case, *Jesus: A New Biography* (Chicago: University of Chicago Press, 1927).

18. Kenneth L. Smith, "Shailer Mathews: Theologian of Social Process" (Ph. D. diss., Duke University, 1959); Kenneth Cauthen, "Introduction," in Shailer Mathews, *Jesus on Social Institutions*, Lives of Jesus Series (Philadelphia: Fortress Press, 1971), pp. xiii–lxxi; Charles Harvey Arnold, *Near the Edge of the Battle* (Chicago: Divinity School Association, University of Chicago, 1966).

19. The following is taken from Mathews, *Jesus on Social Institutions*, occasionally supplemented by other studies on Mathews.

20. Shailer Mathews, "Theology and the Social Mind," *Biblical World* **46** (Oct. 1915), p. 204.

21. Mathews, *Jesus on Social Institutions*, p. 11.

22. Ibid., p. 73.

23. Ibid., pp. 77ff.

24. Ibid., p. 87.

25. Ibid., p. 103.

26. Ibid., p. 113.

27. Ibid., pp. 155–56.

28. Heinz Zahrnt, *The Historical Jesus*, trans. J. S. Bowden (New York: Harper & Row, 1963), pp. 55–65; Stephen Neill, *The Interpretation of the New Testament, 1861–1961* (New York: Oxford University Press, 1966), pp. 137–90; Kümmel, *The New Testament*, pp. 206–80.

29. Kümmel, *The New Testament*, pp. 206–80.

30. Hermann Gunkel, *Zum religionsgeschichtliche Verständnis des Neuen Testaments* [On the history-of-religions understanding of the New Testament] (Göttingen, 1903), p. 95, as quoted in ibid.

31. William Wrede, *Paulus*, Religionsgeschichtliche Volksbücher I, 5/6 (Tübingen, 1904), as quoted in Kümmel, *The New Testament*, pp. 297–98.

32. Hermann Gunkel, "Gedächtnisrede auf Wilhelm Bousset," *Evangelische Freiheit* **20** (1920), pp. 141–62.

33. Wilhelm Bousset, *Das Wesen der Religion* (1903), quoted in Gunkel, "Gedächtnisrede auf Wilhelm Bousset," p. 156 (translation mine).

34. Wilhelm Bousset, *Kyrios Christos*, trans. John E. Steely (Nashville: Abingdon Press, 1970), from which the following comes.

35. Ibid., p. 240.

36. Ibid., p. 244.

VIII

Jesus Christ in Early Twentieth-Century Historical Thought

In the late nineteenth and very early twentieth centuries, thinkers in the West seemed rather sure of themselves. It seemed to them that the human race was developing its powers to a peak never reached before. Everywhere one could see progress in science, technology, and medicine; the arts flourished; social and political reform seemed to be giving more human rights to more and more people; some thought that war was an outmoded convention of the past; and some Christians, such as the American Evangelist John Mott, believed in "the evangelization of the world in this generation." Certainly, many events converged to encourage optimism about Western culture; and it seemed reasonable for the Liberal Christian to regard Jesus' ethical teachings as a great contribution to the progress and evolution of society.

Nevertheless, much thinking moved away from the historical, Liberal approach to the life of Jesus. One phase of *Religionsgeschichte* was the attempt to apply apocalyptic study to Jesus' teaching about the kingdom of heaven, as in the case of Johannes Weiss (1892), who was followed by a thoroughgoing apocalypticization of Jesus by Albert Schweitzer (1901; 1906). Almost no one accepted Schweitzer's radical view. Yet it was Schweitzer who forced the issue of the place of apocalyptic beliefs in Jesus' life and teachings, and in many respects it was Schweitzer who made the impact. Albert Schweitzer will therefore be the first major figure we discuss. We will contrast Schweitzer with William Wrede, whose view of Mark was taken up by Bousset. In many respects it was Wrede's radical criticism that pointed the way to the future. A third figure is the Roman Catholic Modernist Alfred Loisy, who accepted the apocalyptic view of Jesus and the *religionsgeschichtliche* view of the development of early Christianity, and who attacked the Liberal Protestant Harnack head-on. It is one of the great ironies of the history of the interpretation of Jesus Christ that the masterful Loisy outdid the key Protestant historian on his own ground only to be excommunicated by the Catholic Church for his historical approach. Finally, it will be interesting to compare one scholar who rejected Liberalism outright, John Gresham Machen.

JESUS CHRIST IN THE THOUGHT OF ALBERT SCHWEITZER

Albert Schweitzer (1875–1965)[1] was a professional organist, an expert on Bach, a great New Testament scholar, and a medical doctor to French Equatorial Africa (modern Gabon). He was honored by numerous universities and learned societies and was awarded the Nobel Peace Prize in 1952.

Born on January 14, 1875, in the village of Kaysersberg in Upper Alsace (then part of Germany), Schweitzer was soon taken by his family to Günsbach, where he spent his childhood. This was the home town to which he would later return on his visits to Europe. Schweitzer's father, Louis, was the pastor of the Günsbach evangelical Lutheran church, and many of his relatives were pastors, teachers, and organists. By the age of nine Albert was displaying enough talent to substitute for the organist at the Günsbach church.

In 1893, when he was eighteen, Schweitzer secured the exceptional privilege of becoming a student of the famous Parisian organist and composer Charles Marie Widor. That same year he entered the University of Strasbourg to study theology. There Schweitzer completed his doctorate in philosophy (on Immanuel Kant) and his work to qualify for the position of lecturer, published as *The Mystery of the Kingdom of God: The Secret of Jesus' Messiahship and Passion* (1901). Meanwhile, he continued his theological studies, took piano and organ, and then, after a stay in Berlin, returned to Strasbourg to become part of the pastoral staff at St. Nicholas Church, where he preached. He also made jaunts to Paris to study with Widor.

By 1903 Schweitzer had advanced to the position of principal of the Theological College at the University of Strasbourg, all the while playing and publishing Bach's music. It was in this period that he also began working on his monumental classic on late eighteenth- and nineteenth-century study of the life of Jesus, *From Reimarus to Wrede* (English title: *The Quest of the Historical Jesus*), published in 1906. Schweitzer was by now a famous musicologist and theologian; his careers seemed to be set. However, on October 13, 1905, having earlier resolved that at age thirty he would devote the rest of his life to the service of humanity, he resigned his post at the Theological College and wrote to his parents and most intimate acquaintances to tell them of his decision to enter medical school to prepare himself to become a doctor in French Equatorial Africa. Undaunted by all protestations, he stated a simple rationale: He had taught and preached; now "I wanted to be a doctor that I might be able to work without having to talk."[2] In 1911, after six hectic years of writing, playing the organ, and studying, he finished his examinations. He took a year of internship, during which he wrote his thesis (a medical defense of the sanity of his apocalyptic Jesus against the attacks of several psychiatrists), and after raising funds by begging from friends and colleagues and by performing, he and his new wife, Helen Bresslau, embarked for Lambaréné in French Equatorial Africa.

Most of Schweitzer's life from here on was dedicated to the cure of tropical diseases among black Africans. Yet he continued writing about Bach, playing a piano with pedal attachments built especially for the tropics, and developing his famous "reverence for life" philosophy (he attempted to avoid killing any living thing). Because he and his wife were German, they were confined to their quarters by the French at the outbreak of World War I. The Schweitzers were later interned at Garaison in the Pyrenees mountains and then at St. Rémy. After the war Schweitzer gave lectures on the philosophy of civilization at the University of Upsala, in Sweden. He set off again for Lambaréné, where he was to spend most of his life, returning to Europe only to raise money for his hospital.

In October 1948 Schweitzer, now seventy-three, once against visited Günsbach (and Switzerland, where his daughter lived); in 1949, partly to raise money for Lambaréné, he accepted an invitation to give a speech at Aspen, Colorado, on the two-hundredth anniversary of Goethe's birth. This visit with his wife to the United States made him even more famous, and on subsequent visits to Europe he was besieged by reporters and autograph seekers. He was awarded honorary doctorates from major universities in the United States and Europe, culminating in the Nobel Peace Prize. His wife died in 1957. Schweitzer himself passed away at the age of ninety, in 1965, at the place to which he had dedicated fifty-two years of his life, his beloved Lambaréné, where he is buried. Of his many sayings, perhaps the prayer from his early childhood at Günsbach is a fitting conclusion: "Dear God: Protect and bless everything that has breath, keep them from evil, and may they sleep in peace!"[3]

Did Jesus believe that the kingdom of God would disrupt the natural order of the world? Did he think that it was coming very soon? Did he accept the conception that "messianic woes" (tribulation and suffering) would immediately precede the End? Did he expect a Messiah from heaven, the Son of Man, to come (as the book of Daniel foretells) at the end of the world to judge the nations? Did he think that an Elijah figure would precede the Messiah? Did he actually believe that when the End came, he himself would become the Son of Man? Albert Schweitzer answered virtually all these questions with a firm yes. The view of Jesus for which he is justifiably famous is that Jesus was a thoroughgoing apocalypticist who adopted all these views from the popular Judaism of his time—with the exception of the last, his own messiahship.

Schweitzer's inspiration about the apocalyptic Jesus went back to a fateful day in the village of Guggenheim when, as a young nineteen-year-old soldier on maneuvers, he was preparing himself to impress H. J. Holtzmann (see page 203) in his upcoming examination at Strasbourg. Holtzmann, who was known for his Liberal historical view of Jesus, defended Mark as the earliest and most historical gospel and as the foundation for the view that Jesus had a developing messianic consciousness from the time of his baptism (Mark 1:9–11) to the period when he began to encounter increasing opposition and retreated to Caesarea Philippi (Mark 8:27). There, north of Galilee, he indicated that he was a *spiritual* Messiah who would suffer and die to consecrate his *earthly* kingdom, which was represented by brotherly love and ethical concern. There was no room in this Liberal portrait for either a Messiah of radical political opposition to Rome (identified with the Son of David in Schweitzer's day) or bizarre apocalyptic visions about the end of the world (identified with the Son of Man in Schweitzer's day). Jesus rejected the political and apocalyptic alternatives in Judaism for his own, more prophetic, spiritual view, said the Liberals. Schweitzer, in contrast, was forcefully struck by Matthew 10 and 11, where Jesus is reported to have sent the disciples on a mission in which he said they would experience persecution, that is, would be part of the "messianic woes" prior to the end of the world. Jesus also foretold that, before their return, the Son of Man would appear and the messianic kingdom would be revealed. All of this was Jewish apocalyptic, but it did not happen. Schweitzer reasoned that it is unlikely that the early church would have created a prediction like this and placed it in Jesus' mouth if Jesus had not really said it. It only remained to indicate *how* Jesus' apocalyptic view changed when his mission prediction did not come true.

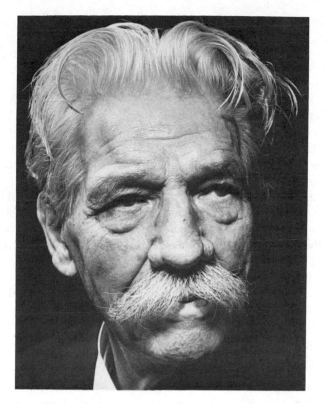

Dr. Albert Schweitzer
PHOTO BY MAX EHLERT, CAMERA PRESS LONDON

Schweitzer expressed his insight in his book *The Secret of the Messiahship and the Passion: A Sketch of the Life of Jesus* (1901) and in *The Quest of the Historical Jesus* (1906).[4] He recognized that others had verged on his view, namely, the rationalists Reimarus and Paulus; Strauss; and Wilhelm Baldensperger. Johannes Weiss, in his classic study *Jesus' Proclamation of the Kingdom of God* (1892), claimed that Jesus believed the kingdom was apocalyptic but that Jesus did not do anything to hasten its coming, for he believed that God would bring in the kingdom. What Schweitzer did was to develop the concept that everything Jesus thought, taught, and did was motivated by an apocalyptic vision. Today, his view is known as "consistent (or thoroughgoing) eschatology," a phrase borrowed from the title of the next-to-last chapter in *The Quest of the Historical Jesus*. Since there are different forms of eschatology, a somewhat more accurate description of Schweitzer's view might be "consistent apocalyptic." By custom, however, "consistent eschatology" is used and will undoubtedly remain in use.

Schweitzer's theory was that Jesus' life and teaching were dominated by an eschatological (apocalyptic) secret, first disclosed to Peter, James, and John at the Mount of Transfiguration (Mark 9 and parallels), then to the twelve disciples at Caesarea Philippi (Mark 8:27ff.; Schweitzer transposed the order of these two events), and finally to the public at Jesus' trial (Mark 14:61ff.). The heart of this secret was the combination of apocalyptic eschatology, like that found in the Old Testament (Daniel 7), and ethics, like that found in the Old Testament prophets, especially the Suffering Servant of Deutero-Isaiah (cp. Isa 52:13–53:12). Thus "ethics" was conceived within the context of the apocalyptic kingdom: It is "interim ethics," a temporary ethics for the period before the End. But it was not that Jesus simply *waited* for the kingdom (the idea Weiss developed); ethics meant that by suffering and repentance the kingdom would be brought about. For Schweitzer, the heart of Jesus' ethics in the Sermon on the Mount (Mt 5–7) was repentance. In the mission speech of Matthew 10 and 11, Jesus expected the suffering of the disciples to precede the kingdom. It would come before they returned. When that did not materialize, he shifted the suffering to his own experience, hoping himself to bring about the kingdom. Thus his secret of the *passion* was that he would take on the "messianic woes," that he would suffer like the Suffering Servant of Isaiah. With the Liberals, Schweitzer believed that Jesus' views changed. But they did not become "spiritual"; they remained apocalyptic. Jesus' Messianic Secret was that he believed he himself would become the Son of Man to judge the wicked and defend the righteous at the inauguration of the kingdom. Part of that secret was that whereas the *people* questioned whether he might not be the Elijah figure to precede the Messiah—this is Schweitzer's interpretation of the "coming one" (Mark 11:1ff.; Mt 11:1ff.)—Jesus believed that John the Baptist was the "coming one" and that he himself was the Messiah. But the kingdom did not come with Jesus' passion, and Jesus did not become the Son of Man. In the historical sense, Jesus' secret of the passion and the Messiah were still mistaken. As a result, the postresurrection church then reinterpreted Jesus' life and teaching to show that the resurrection had vindicated him, that he *had been* the Messiah, and that he would *return* as the apocalyptic Son of Man at the End, still to come.

In short, for Schweitzer apocalyptic thought did not lead Jesus to "spiritualize" the kingdom as an earthly kingdom that would be carried on by ethical activity. Schweitzer thought this Jesus was a creation of modern Liberal scholars who wanted a relevant Jesus "like ourselves." Schweitzer distressed them greatly with his comment, "This historical Jesus will be to our time a stranger and an enigma." And so he was—for Schweitzer's epoch. One may well ask whether for succeeding generations—less optimistic, torn by war and human suffering—such an image would easily die. Consider Schweitzer's concluding comment:

He comes to us as One unknown, without a name, as of old, by the lake-
side. He came to those men who knew Him not. He speaks to us the same
word: "Follow thou me!" and sets us to the tasks which He has to fulfill for
our time. He commands. And to those who obey Him whether they be wise
or simple, He will reveal Himself in the toils, the conflicts, the sufferings
which they shall pass through in His fellowship and, as an ineffable mystery, they shall learn in their own experience Who He is.[5]

JESUS CHRIST IN THE THOUGHT
OF WILLIAM WREDE

The life of William Wrede (pronounced Vrāda; 1859–1906) was short
and rather undramatic.[6] He was born on May 10, 1859, in Büchen, Germany, the son of Ernst and Justine Wrede. In 1862 his father became a
Lutheran pastor. After attending grade school in the German villages of
Fredelsloh and Gross-Freden, Wrede entered the University of Leipzig
in 1877 to study theology. Hermann Schultz, Adolf Harnack, and Albrecht Ritschl were there at the same time as professors; they had a
lasting influence on Wrede. Two years later he transferred to the University of Göttingen, and he passed his first university theology exams
in 1881. After a year as a teacher in a private school in Liebenburg,
Wrede enrolled for two and a half years in the Preachers' Seminary at
Loccum, after which he was a tutor at the theological college in Göttingen. He passed his ordination exams in 1887 and at first took a pastorate. After the death of his parents in the same year, he decided to
return to academic life, which was much more to his liking. He spent
two more years at Göttingen, preparing to qualify as a university lecturer. This he accomplished in 1889 with his study on I Clement
(1891), an early Christian writer. In 1893 Wrede was appointed to the
University of Breslau (now called Wrocław in Poland), and shortly
thereafter he married a daughter of one of his old professors, Elizabeth
Schultz. In 1895 he received a doctorate in theology from Göttingen and
was promoted at Breslau. Here he worked until 1906, when he suddenly
developed a serious lung disease, which led to a heart disorder and
eventually to his death. Whereas Schweitzer had ninety years to make
his contributions to humanity, most of them with tremendous health
and vitality, Wrede had only forty-seven.

Apart from his dissertation on I Clement and some reviews,
Wrede's career of academic publication was really launched with the appearance of his lectures on the task and method of New Testament theology. Then, in 1901, he published the work for which he became
famous, *The Messianic Secret in the Gospels,* dedicated to the person
who had so strongly influenced his thought, Albert Eichhorn. His major

studies thereafter were on the Gospel of John (1903), on the authenticity of II Thessalonians (1903), on Paul (1904), and, as he neared the end of his life, on the literary riddle of the Book of Hebrews (1906). Two volumes of his collected lectures and studies were published posthumously in 1907.

In most respects Wrede was a typical representative of the *religionsgeschichtliche Schule,* having become well known for his view that Paul was the "second founder of Christianity."[7] When Wrede turned to the Messianic Secret in the gospels, he saw that the idea was different in each gospel and that each should be interpreted independently. However, going beyond F. C. Baur, he speculated that in the preliterary oral stages, the early Christian community had *created* tradition anew. In contrast to most Liberals and *Religionsgeschichtler,* he came closer to the ideas of Strauss and Bruno Bauer in his willingness to state that Mark was further removed from the actual, historical Jesus: For Wrede, Mark elaborated much community material *about* Jesus, and indeed created a perspective on Jesus by his own portrayal of him.[8]

You will recall that the Markan hypothesis was the basis for the historical outline of the life of Jesus and that those who held it thought in terms of Jesus' progressive, or evolutionary, messianic consciousness, from his baptism to his revelation to the disciples at Caesarea Philippi. Thus the Messianic Secret was Jesus' secret interpreted psychologically by Liberal historians. For the Liberals, Jesus redefined messiahship in terms of suffering and dying in a way that had spiritual and ethical value for the individual believer; for Schweitzer, the heart of the secret was Jesus' apocalyptic view, which also underwent revision when the End did not come according to Jesus' predictions in Matthew 10. For both, it was *Jesus'* secret, and it rested on the fundamental *historicity* of Mark.

Wrede, who published his study in the same year as Schweitzer's *Secret of the Messiahship and the Passion: A Sketch of Jesus' Life* (1901), like Schweitzer opposed the prevailing Liberal view. But Wrede's view was also opposed to Schweitzer's, for it denied the historicity of Mark and the claim that the Messianic Secret was Jesus' secret, whether spiritual–ethical or eschatological–apocalyptic. For Wrede, there could not have occurred a turning point of Jesus' life at Caesarea Philippi, because certain of the disciples knew of Jesus' messianic power from the beginning. In fact, Jesus knew (according to Mark) that he was the Son of Man early in the ministry (Mark 2:10; 2:28). There were also hints of the coming passion near the beginning (Mark 2:19ff.). This meant, for Wrede, that there was no messianic development in Jesus' mind. The psychological explanation was therefore untenable.

Wrede undertook an investigation onto those passages in Mark that portrayed Jesus as concealing his messianic glory or being misinterpreted in his conception of the messiahship by those who knew him best, the disciples. Some passages in Mark indicated that Jesus expelled demons because they recognized him (Mark 1:24, 34) or that Jesus commanded the demons to remain silent about him (Mark 3:11–12). In others, Jesus commanded those whom he healed of sickness to keep silent about the miracle (Mark 1:44; 5:43; 7:36; 8:26). Still another key passage portrays Jesus as telling his parables in order to keep outsiders from understanding him (Mark 4:11–12; cp. 7:17), that is, as secret teachings for the initiated. Finally, there are a number of passages in which the disciples, to whom his identity was eventually revealed, persistently misunderstood him (Mark 6:52; 8:14–21; 9:10, 19, 32; cp. 14:37–41). Noting that Matthew toned down this emphasis (especially of the disciples' ignorance), that Luke reinterpreted their misunderstanding in terms of the traditional Jewish nationalistic concept of the messiah, and that John was partially dependent on a totally different tradition of the secret, Wrede argued that Mark, too, represented an interpretation. The key to Wrede's view was the resurrection. According to the book of Acts and Paul's writings (Acts 2:36; Rom 1:4; Wrede included Phil 2:6–11), Jesus' messiahship was linked with his resurrection. But why would this have been the case if he had already been thought of as the Messiah while he was living? For Wrede, he was not. The resurrection of Jesus was also the key to the Messianic Secret in Mark, for Mark 9:9 read: "And as they were coming down from the mountain [of transfiguration], he charged them to tell no one what they had seen, until the Son of Man should have risen from the dead. . . ." Thus the revelation of the secret Messiah awaited the ressurrection; that is, Wrede reasoned, it was dependent on the view that Jesus became the Messiah *after* the resurrection. Thus the early church had read the messiahship back into Jesus' life. For Mark this explained (said Wrede) why some of the stories he received were messianic and some were not: Jesus' glory was at points revealed, but he had commanded silence until the resurrection. Mark thus knew the *early church* tradition of Jesus' secret messiahship and made use of it to explain the non-messianic stories. Wrede concluded:

> There remains scarcely any other possibility than that the concept of the secret arose at a time when nothing was yet known of a messianic claim by Jesus while upon earth, at a time when the Resurrection was thought to be the beginning of the messiahship. . . .
> In my judgment this is the origin of the idea that we have shown to be in Mark. It is, so to speak, a transitional concept, and *it can be designated as the aftereffect of the view that the Resurrection is the beginning of the messiahship, as a concept that arose at a time when the life of Jesus is being filled positively with messianic content . . .*
> If my deduction is correct, it is of importance for critical examination of

the historical life of Jesus itself. If our view could only arise at a time when nothing was known of a public messianic claim on Jesus' part, we seem to have in it *a positive historical testimony that Jesus did not actually represent himself as the Messiah. However, this question is not finally answered here.* [9]

In short, Wrede provided a strong case for the possibility that Jesus did not claim to be a Messiah, for Mark did not write a historical account; moreover, "Mark no longer has any real conception of the historical life of Jesus"![10]

By way of summary, recall again that in 1835 David Friedrich Strauss had cast doubt on the historicity of the gospels and as a consequence had lost his job; Bruno Bauer had cast even more doubt on the historicity of Mark in 1841 and had been required to cease lecturing on the subject. In 1901 Wrede was making a strong case for Mark as a document of faith, not a simple historical document, and this time the point was not lost. Albert Schweitzer saw Wrede's views as a fundamental alternative to research on the life of Jesus in the nineteenth century, though he believed that it was the wrong one. Bousset, in the *religionsgeschichtliche* camp, eventually came to admit Wrede's logic on Mark, though he could never accept Wrede's radical conclusions with respect to the historical Jesus. Most German critics would follow in Wrede's footsteps, thereby sidestepping Schweitzer's solution, but allowing Weiss's more limited view that Jesus' *teaching* was apocalyptic. Thus arose the insight that Jesus spoke of the kingdom in eschatological (not simply ethical) terms, but that it was not possible to prove that Jesus believed himself to be the eschatological Messiah. To this day, many scholars build on Wrede's insight, taking it up and modifying it in the light of further study.

It is important to examine another scholar who was moving in a similar direction, this time a Roman Catholic. He was labeled a "Modernist," and because he had been a priest, he was excommunicated from the Catholic Church. First, then, we must describe the general issue of Roman Catholic Modernism; then it will be possible to see more clearly why Modernist views of Jesus were such a challenge to the orthodox Catholic *status quo*. The Modernist in question was Alfred Loisy.

ROMAN CATHOLIC MODERNISM

Within the context of Christianity the term "modernism" has at least two meanings. The general sense of the term refers to updating religious custom, tradition, or doctrine according to more "modern" ideas. This definition might refer to any period of history, and therefore orthodoxy itself in this broader sense was a type of "modernism." The American Protestant Liberal Shailer Mathews preferred to call himself a "modernist" in this sense.

Another sense of "Modernism"—with a capital M—includes the more general sense, but it is limited to a specific historical period and to a specific religious body. In this sense, Modernism was a movement in the Roman Catholic Church that began about 1890 under the moderate pontificate of Pope Leo XIII (1878–1903) and came to an end about 1910, having been condemned as heretical in 1907 by the conservative Pope Pius X (1903–14).[11] It is possible to study Modernism in this sense as a heresy in the history of Roman Catholic doctrine, for the encyclicals from Rome that condemned it looked upon it as an organized, programmatic, and united effort. More recently, however, scholars have become interested in studying individual Modernists, recognizing that though the Modernists were sometimes in communication, they were of many different sorts and persuasions, and the attempt to see them as a united front was a misrepresentation. Nonetheless, with this reservation in mind, we continue to refer to the phenomenon by its customary designation.

There have been many attempts to trace the roots of Modernism, but what seems to be most important was the Church's official reaction to liberal, democratic, and secular movements in the West during the late eighteenth and nineteenth centuries. As early as 1829, Pope Pius VIII (1829–30) condemned religious "indifferentism" (the belief that any religion is as good as another), individual self-reliance in matters of faith and doctrine, and individualistic, vernacular translations of the Bible (in the encyclical *Traditi humilitati*). In 1832 Pope Gregory XVI (1831–46) condemned civil, political, and religious "liberty" (in the encyclical *Mirari vos*), a condemnation that had to do in part with Italian democratic nationalist pressures on the papal states around Rome. Then Pius IX (1846–78), at first a democratic liberal, became reactionary and, with the aid of the Jesuits and others, began to develop a strategy for strengthening papal authority. First he proclaimed as an article of faith in 1854 what had previously been common belief among Roman Catholics: Mary's Immaculate Conception (that the Virgin was free from Original Sin from the moment of her conception). Pius IX's second great document, the *Syllabus of Errors*, followed in 1864. It summed up the official and unqualified condemnation of rationalism, pantheism, naturalism, indifferentism, the criticism of Scholasticism, socialism, communism, military conscription of clerics, and separation of Church and state. It culminated in the famous *denial* that "the Roman Pontiff can, and ought to, reconcile himself, and come to terms with progress, liberalism, and modern civilization."[12] The third document strengthening papal authority was the pronouncement of papal infallibility in matters of faith on July 13, 1870.

In 1878 Leo XIII came to the papal throne, facing anti-Catholic feeling in Germany, anticlericalism in France, and nationalist pressures at home. But Leo, in contrast to his predecessors, was a diplomat. Not only did he publish twelve great social encyclicals; he also encouraged historical research and opened the Vatican archives to historians. Such apparent liberalizing tendencies encouraged a new, younger generation of scholars to hope that traditional Catholic theology would come to terms with historical-critical approaches to the Bible and thus reach an evolutionary philosophy of history that would make it possible to understand, and help preserve, the institutions of Catholicism.

In 1903 the conservative Pius X replaced Leo XIII. Loisy's books were condemned; those of other scholars were put on the Papal Index (a list of books forbidden for Roman Catholics to read); and the "progressives" came under suspicion. The Irishman George Tyrrell, for example, was accused of being the "English Loisy" and was dismissed from the Jesuits in 1906. On July 3, 1907, *Lamentabili sane exitu* appeared, listing sixty-five objections to the Modernists, most of its sources being the writings of Loisy. Two months later, *Pascendi dominici gregis* denounced the "agnostic" and "imminentist" ravings of philosophers who were "thoroughly imbued with the poisonous doctrines taught by her [the Church's] enemies." What was obviously heretical was, according to the document, their duplicity: While appearing to be orthodox in matters of faith and practice, these clerics were putting scientific and historical study of the Bible outside the realm of faith, denying the divinity of Christ, and rebuking the Church. Tyrrell answered *Pascendi,* bitterly, in the Protestant-oriented London *Times.* He was excommunicated on October 22, 1907, and Loisy's excommunication followed on March 7, 1908. *Pascendi* also established guidelines for systematic repression of Modernism. This was undertaken and, in 1910, every member of the clergy was required to take the *Sacrorum antistitum,* a stringently anti-Modernist oath. Not until 1943, when Pope Pius XII eased the pressure by promoting biblical studies (*Divino afflante Spiritu*), did the situation begin to change. Today, in the period after the Second Vatican Council (1962–65), Roman Catholic biblical scholarship is in most respects indistinguishable from Protestant biblical scholarship. Among contemporary Catholics, Modernism is receiving more sympathetic treatment.

JESUS CHRIST IN THE THOUGHT
OF ALFRED LOISY

Alfred Firmin Loisy (1857–1940) was born in the village of Ambrières in the Marne, about eighty miles east of Paris.[13] His grandfathers and father were peasant farmers. Lonely, timid, and unathletic, he was also precocious and in 1868 left primary school at the top of his class. One day, after experiencing a young priest's emotional celebration of his first Mass, young Loisy, with little knowledge of other professions, decided that his vocation would be the priesthood.

After four more years of schooling, Loisy entered the Catholic theological seminary at Châlons, where his simple peasant piety was disturbed by sophisticated, Thomistic theological hairsplitting. He also had his first contact with historical and democratic thought, though it was superficial. The strain these new ideas placed on his piety and devotion grew into a tension between "science" and faith that was to be part of his continual struggle. The tension was relieved for a time by his love of studying the Hebrew language, but it was intensified when he was sent to the new Catholic Insititute at Paris to finish his studies, for there he came under the influence of the liberal historian Abbé Louis Duchesne (1843–1922). For health reasons, he returned to Châlons. He was ordained in 1889, an act he came to think of later as the tragic error of his life.

In 1881, after two enjoyable years in the parish, he was invited by Abbé Duchesne to return to the Catholic Institution as a graduate student and teacher of Hebrew. Loisy's seminary conflict between faith and science now returned and included his doubt about the accounts of the resurrection. Yet in 1882 he became a lecturer in Hebrew on the theological faculty and, on hearing the heretical Ernst Renan's lectures and studying his views, he came to believe that the gospels were not historical accounts but that they contained errors and should be studied in the same way other books are.

By 1883 Loisy was beginning to encounter opposition from the Catholic authorities. His doctoral dissertation was officially denied publication at Rome, and his teaching aroused suspicions. He was appointed professor of Holy Scripture at the Catholic Institute, but when his previously unaccepted dissertation was published in revised form in 1892, students from the seminary of Saint-Sulpice were forbidden to attend his lectures. By an ironic turn of events, in which his superior's defense of him misrepresented him, Loisy was forbidden to teach biblical subjects. Loisy's questioning of the historical veracity of Genesis and the Mosaic authorship of the Pentateuch resulted in his dismissal. Within months, the papal encyclical *Providentissimus Deus* (1893) reaffirmed the position of the Council of Trent and the Vatican Council of 1870 that Scripture was without error and written by the inspiration of the Holy Spirit. No one was specifically accused of heresy, but it was implied that Loisy was a main target of these declarations.

For the next five years Loisy found himself appointed chaplain to a girl's school in the Parisian suburb of Neuilly. Having time on his hands, he broadened the base of his thought by reading the Protestant Liberals and the views of John Henry Cardinal Newman on the devel-

Alfred Loisy

opment of doctrine. Between 1897 and 1900 Loisy published a number of articles, some under the pseudonym A. Firmin, which developed the view that the Catholic theology of absolute, unchangeable truths did not coincide with the notion of historical development. In contrast to Liberals like Harnack, Loisy argued that the institutional Church was a natural evolution from New Testament Christianity, but in accepting the Liberals' historical-critical presuppositions he encountered more opposition.

In 1900 Loisy became a lecturer at the Ecole des Hautes Etudes, a department of the Sorbonne. It was an important position and gave him a measure of independence from the authority of the Church. In 1902 he published *The Gospel and the Church*, a work which Tyrrell would call "the classical exposition of Catholic Modernism." On the surface, it was directed at Harnack's *What Is Christianity?* Like the earlier articles, however, it treated matters historically and critically. Harnack did not respond. Others did! Soon Loisy's book was a center of controversy, some claiming that Loisy was "worse than Renan" (see pages 190–96), and, though the moderate Leo XIII made no comment from Rome,

French church officials quickly condemned it. Loisy's published attempts at clarification only sharpened his views, opening them to further attack. Now the priest who said Mass daily and defended historic
Catholicism by history was convinced that he was more of a pantheist,
positivist, and humanitarian than a Christian.

Pope Leo XIII died on July 20, 1903. His successor, Pius X, had no
ambitions to fit Catholicism into the modern world. Within the year, five
of Loisy's works, including *The Gospel and the Church,* were put on the
Index as having "very grave errors" with respect to primitive revelation,
the authenticity of the gospels, the knowledge and divinity of Christ, the
resurrection, and Christ's institution of the Church and the sacraments.
Loisy offered to resign and suspend his writing, but he would not admit
his "errors," for to do so would have betrayed what had become his cardinal principle, the freedom of critical–historical scholarship. He retired
to the country to continue his writings, the most important of which
was his radical commentary on the gospels. In 1907 *Lamentabili* and
Pascendi condemned the Modernists; in 1908 Loisy was excommunicated; in 1909 he was appointed to Renan's old chair at the Collège de
France. Loisy was no longer a Catholic, and without his Catholicism he
was no longer a Christian. After a fruitful career of academic publication
he died on June 1, 1940.

Loisy's *The Gospel and the Church,* while attacking Harnack's
What Is Christianity?, was also the classic representative of a Catholic
Modernist's approach to Jesus.[14] Though he affirmed the traditional
Catholic view that there was no fundamental incompatibility between
the professions of theologian and historian, he nevertheless wished to
proceed as a historical critic, to take up Harnack on his own ground. In
so doing he was saying that in many respects Harnack himself was as
much a theologian representing a particular point of view as he was an
objective historian. Loisy believed Harnack was selecting a very few
texts from the gospels—especially "No one knows the Son but the Father; neither does anyone know the Father except the Son" (Mt
11:27)—and interpreting them to prove that Jesus' inward religion of
close relations with God was unique to the Judaism of his time, as well
as to the Old Testament. Was it not more than accidental that such
ideas coincided with modern ideas of the essence of religion? Was it not
also coincidental that they sounded very Protestant?

Loisy's classic, *The Gospel and the Church,* is appropriately titled.
He does not speak of "religion" as expressed in various institutional
churches, but of *the* Church with a capital C. As influenced by Newman
and others, Loisy has a very different view from Harnack's of the evolution of Christianity. He frequently draws upon the analogy of the seed,
which has its *natural growth:*

> Why should the essence of a tree be held to be but a particle of the seed
> from which it has sprung and why should it not be recognized as truly and
> fully in the complete tree as in the germ. Are the processes of assimilation
> by which it grows to be regarded as an alteration of the essence present po-
> tentially in the seed, or are they not rather the indispensable conditions of
> its being, its preservation, its progress in a life always the same and inces-
> santly renewed? [15]

The essence of Christianity for Loisy is not limited to a historical reconstruction of its earliest form but is to be determined by looking at the
common features of the Church from its origins to the present, despite
all the variations. The complete tree is the natural outgrowth of the
seed, and without the complete tree a distorted picture will result:

> The historian will find that the essence of Christianity has been more or
> less preserved in the different Christian communions: he will not believe it
> to be compromised by the development of institutions, of creeds, and of
> worship, so long as this development has been ruled by the principles veri-
> fied in the first commencement. He will not expect this essence to have
> been absolutely and definitely realized at any point of past centuries; he will
> believe that it has been realized more or less perfectly from the beginning,
> and that it will continue to be realized thus more and more, so long as
> Christianity shall endure. [16]

For Loisy, then, legal, ceremonial, and doctrinal structures of the
Church are not distortions, but legitimate adaptations in the world. As
he consistently says: The soul needs a body (or the soul is not alone
with its God). Whereas Harnack, as a Protestant, makes his historically
reconstructed Gospel the norm for the Church, Loisy, as a Catholic,
sees the Church and the Gospel as so intimately related that one is necessary to the other (not, however, that the Church's view of the Gospel
is normative). The "essence" is not the reconstructed historical *kernel,*
which is valid for all times and places, but the constant *principles*
present from the very beginning.

   Like Protestant Liberals, Loisy bypassed the Gospel of John and accepted the two-source theory. But unlike Harnack, he believed that the
origin of the gospels was more than a literary problem: It was really a
problem of the interaction of Scripture and tradition—already in the gospels. "The literary tradition of the gospel has followed the evolution of
primitive Christianity." [17] The contrast of approaches between Harnack
and Loisy is somewhat like the difference between a hazel nut and an
onion. With the hazel nut, removing the shell (the husk) will leave a
sizeable fruit (the kernel), and the shell may be discarded. With the
onion, the layers themselves are part of the vegetable, and Loisy saw
value in the layers themselves.

   The critical result is that Loisy is less optimistic about finding a
"modern Jesus" in the sources:

> In the Gospels there remains but an echo, necessarily weakened and a little
> confused, for the words of Jesus, the general impression He produced upon

hearers well-disposed towards Him, with some of the more striking of his sentences, as they were understood, and interpreted; and finally there remains the movement which he initiated.[18]

When Loisy looks more carefully at that echo, his Jesus does not resemble Harnack's but seems more like the Jesus of Johannes Weiss (and to a degree, of Albert Schweitzer, though Schweitzer's study of the kingdom had only appeared in 1901 and the *Quest* was not yet written). For Loisy, Jesus is a Jewish Jesus, an apocalyptic Jesus. The historical context is not husk, but kernel. The center is found in Jesus' teaching about the kingdom of God.

First, Loisy stresses that Jesus nowhere identifies the kingdom as "God's power acting on the heart of the individual," as Harnack suggests. The key text for the latter is "The Kingdom of God is within (*entos*) you" (Luke 17:21). Loisy, after noting the future orientation of Jesus' parables, the Lord's prayer, and Jesus' sayings about love, can find no such orientation in Jesus' teaching elsewhere. Moreover, in Luke the saying is inconsistent with the eschatological discourse it introduces. This leads Loisy to conclude that the difficult Greek term *entos* should be translated not "within" but "in the midst of": "The Kingdom of God is in the midst of you." The interpretation is not individual, but collective.

The key text for Loisy, on the other hand, is in Matthew 4:17: "Repent, for the kingdom of heaven is at hand." As John the Baptist taught (Harnack sees Jesus and John as contrasts), everything is to be viewed in relation to the end of the world. The Beatitudes promise the kingdom to the poor and afflicted, the needy and persecuted, but only in the future. The disciples are sent out thinking that the kingdom will come before they return. The parables of the laborers in the vineyard and the wedding feast, the one stressing judgment at the end of the day, the other the judgment of those who are invited but do not respond, are eschatological parables. In all these instances and more, Loisy indicates that the kingdom is collective, not individual; objective, not subjective (within); a future hope, not a present reality. What is already beginning is not the *fulfillment* of the kingdom, but only its inauguration. Again, the kingdom is not the Liberal's inner kingdom, but the apocalyptic kingdom of the future. Likewise, Jesus was not a teacher of ethics and inward religion so much as a Jewish apocalypticist who believed the end of the world was near.

When Loisy takes up Harnack's practical implications, each is read in terms of the kingdom. To Loisy, Harnack overemphasized the distinction between Jesus' teaching about denying self, family, and riches on the one hand and the Church's doctrine of total renunciation of self and world on the other. The latter developed naturally from the former when the End did not come. Similar arguments are made with respect to the other features of Harnack's Jesus. If Jesus did not develop a social program for the relief of the poor and oppressed, was it not because that was incompatible with his belief that the kingdom was near and that in the kingdom there would be neither rich nor poor? What difference did it make that Caesar had rights in the temporal sphere if *all* human power was nearing its end? What good was the law when the era of the Messiah was near? Of what significance was the *progress* of science and civilization if all earthly progress was soon to end? For Harnack, Jesus did not establish social, political, and economic programs because the kingdom was inner and spiritual; such programs might be appropriate, but they were not explicit to him. For Loisy, the explanation is that a simplified teaching was natural in view of the coming end of the world: Jesus was not a nineteenth-century cultural Christian; he was a first-century apocalyptic Jew.

Harnack argued that though Jesus considered himself the Messiah, the messianic conception had been transformed by his consciousness as Son. Even so, said Harnack, Jesus did not *teach* about his own sonship: The gospel he proclaimed was only that of the Father, not the Son. Loisy countered by noting that such a view was built on only one text ("No one knows the Son except the Father, nor the Father except the son . . ."). In other key passages, such as Peter's confession ("You are the Christ, the Son of the Living God" [Mt 16:16]), the titles Son of God and Messiah are equivalent. That is not surprising, since they had been so in the Old Testament and in Jewish thought. There is, however, a distinction between them, and whereas Harnack based Jesus' view of his messiahship on that of his Sonship, Loisy believed that though it was difficult to determine Jesus' own convictions from the text, the Son of God for Jesus was based on the Messiah: "Jesus named Himself the Son of God to the extent to which He avowed Himself the Messiah." [19] That extent was determined by eschatology, for Jesus was and yet was not the Messiah he would become. Again, it should be pointed out that Loisy thought Harnack was speaking in abstractions, while he, Loisy, was historically concrete. The historian will, then, relate Jesus' views to Judaism:

> The Gospel, appearing in Judea and unable to appear elsewhere, was bound to be conditioned by Judaism. Its Jewish exterior is the human body, whose Divine Soul is the spirit of Jesus. But take away the body, and the soul will vanish in the air like the lightest breath. Without the idea of the Messiah, the gospel would have been but a metaphysical possibility, an invisible, intangible essence, even unintelligible, for want of a definition appropriate to the means of knowledge, not a living and conquering reality. The gospel will always need a body to be human. [20]

For Harnack, the doctrinal question about Jesus Christ could not be answered from Jesus' teaching, for he taught not himself but God the Father. Loisy, too, does not think that Jesus taught "Christology"; however, that does not mean that his preaching and the faith it inspired were unrelated to faith in Jesus himself. Something of that was certainly *implied* in Jesus' demand on his hearers and that which was to come:

> As He did not call Himself the Messiah, and only announced the kingdom that was to come, Jesus asked no other faith in His mission than faith in His message, the promise of the kingdom; but it was nonetheless certain that, at the fulfillment of the great event, all the elect would salute the Saviour with the salutation of the Messiah. "Blessed is He that cometh in the name of the Lord" (Mt 23:39).[21]

Implicitly, then, the gospel includes also the Son, or Messiah.

In summary, the essence of Christianity seems different to the two scholars, the sources are evaluated differently, and the Church is compared to the essence in both cases, but is also different. For Harnack the spiritual essence is lost in doctrine, institutionalism, sacerdotalism, and formalistic legalism—all of which Jesus opposed in the Judaism of his day. For Loisy, however, the essence is more apocalyptic, external, and already bound up with the Church from the beginning, just as Jesus' teaching was bound up with Judaism. Jesus is therefore a man of his times and participates in the thought of his times. As in the thinking of Weiss, Jesus is a remote historical figure, a man from a different time, and must be constantly reinterpreted.

The impression should not be left that all scholars in the late nineteenth and early twentieth centuries were caught up with the historical scholarship of Liberalism, Modernism, and *Religionsgeschichte*. After all, the Roman Catholic Modernist Alfred Loisy was excommunicated for his historical views, and all priests were required to take an oath against Modernism; this mood did not begin to relax until the 1940s. It will also be recalled that church officials in Germany attempted to block the appointment of the historian Harnack to the University of Berlin but were overruled by the emperor and Bismarck. Many considered both Schweitzer's and Wrede's historical-critical views radical, despite their differences.

In the United States, the social historian Shailer Mathews and his historian-colleague at the University of Chicago, Shirley Jackson Case, found themselves locking horns with doctrinally oriented Christians from the ranks of orthodoxy. This conflict was to become one of the hottest and most divisive religious battles in U.S. religious history, the Fundamentalist–Modernist controversy of the 1920s. To maintain perspective, it will be important to consider briefly the strongest reaction to the Liberal movement, the Fundamentalist movement, and to look at a conservative Evangelical who held some of the same views, John Gresham Machen. We will consider further reactions to the Liberals in Ch. 9.

AMERICAN FUNDAMENTALISM

The roots of modern Fundamentalism in America lay in the movements of seventeenth-century Protestant orthodoxy.[22] Yet by the nineteenth century, this orthodoxy had developed new doctrines. One influence on orthodoxy was *dispensationalism,* the belief that history could be divided into a series of God's dispensations, or periods of time, the final dispensation being the period of the millennium—the thousand-year reign of the "true church," with Israel being restored to its earthly kingdom as promised by the prophets. Part of this schema was the expectation of a literal, imminent, second coming of Jesus Christ accompanied by a judgment prior to the millennium, and the resurrection of the dead and final defeat of Satan after it (Rev 20). Hence the ranks of the dispensationalists and the millennialists frequently overlapped. Other related beliefs were that the Bible is to be interpreted literally, that true Christians are "reborn," and that they make up a "righteous remnant" which cuts across denominational lines.

Another root of Fundamentalism was the "Princeton Theology." In the latter part of the nineteenth century, a prominent group of dispensationalists, largely Presbyterians and Baptists, were meeting each summer at Niagara Falls for two weeks of Bible study. In 1878 this Niagara Group wooed into its ranks another group representing the "Princeton Theology." The leader of this group was Charles Hodge, who had been inspired by Archibald Alexander, founder of Princeton Theological Seminary in 1812. Charles Hodge wrote *Systematic Theology* in 1899. He believed that he was simply defending the theology of John Calvin; yet he developed his own system by means of a highly rationalistic logic that was characteristic of seventeenth-century Protestant orthodoxy. Hodge opposed basing faith on subjective feeling or inward experience, unless it was in agreement with the experiences of people as revealed in the Bible. The central issue of the "Princeton Theology" was the authority of the Bible, and it was believed that God would not have made his will known through documents that had errors in them. For Hodge, the Word of God was identifiable with the very words of the Bible, and they were so inspired that they are free from error (verbal inspiration). Probably under the influence of new textual discoveries with many variant words in them, Hodge shifted his argument to the verbal inerrancy (infallibility) of the original autographs (plenary inspiration). Despite some differences, the Niagara Group found support from the Princeton Group on such crucial issues as rejection of "inward religion" apart from external proofs, pessimism about the possibility of social reform, logical arguments defending what they believed was Protestant orthodoxy, and, most important, the new theory of plenary inspiration of the Bible. All of this was an outright rejection of the Liberals and their historical-critical methods. In this somewhat uneasy alliance were the common weapons that would be used to do battle with the Liberals.

From 1910 to 1915, the alliance spawned a series of ninety articles called *The Fundamentals: A Testimony to Truth*. Most of its sixty-four authors were Presbyterians and Baptists. Again, it was opposed to the historical-critical methods of the Liberals, and it stressed doctrine, its central theme being the literal inspiration of the Bible as a support to certain "fundamentals" of Protestant orthodoxy. Its purpose was to check the growth of Liberalism. Though *The Fundamentals* did not ascribe to any one creed, a five-point declaration highly influential within the movement was adopted by the General Assembly of the Presbyterian Church in 1910. This declaration stated that the essential doctrines of Christianity were (1) the inerrancy of the Bible, (2) the virgin birth, (3) the atonement, (4) the resurrection, and (5) the miracles of Christ. An 1878 Niagara Creed also included such doctrinal items as the Trinity, the fall of Adam, Original Sin, justification by faith, the assurance of the "reborn" that they would receive salvation, Christ as the fulfillment of prophecy, the millennium, and the second coming of Christ. By 1920, as a result of discussions in the press, the movement became known as Fundamentalism.

As distinct from the Fundamentalist *movement*, the Fundamentalist *controversy* emerged in the 1920s. One phase of the controversy, especially in the rural South, was the attempt of a number of states to prohibit public schools and universities from teaching scientific views considered incompatible with a literal interpretation of the Bible. A famous legal case involving this controversy was that of the young high school teacher John Scopes, who was indicted and tried in Dayton, Tennessee, for teaching the theory of evolution (which, of course, conflicted with a literal view of the Genesis creation). At the trial the well-known orator, politician, and anti-evolutionist William Jennings Bryan was brought in as prosecutor; Clarence Darrow, a highly successful trial lawyer from Chicago, participated in the defense, and Shailer Mathews was one of the witnesses for the defense. The confrontation between Bryan and Darrow received tremendous publicity. When scientific evidence was consistently ruled out of court and the trial degenerated into a carnivallike atmosphere, it became something of a joke in the national press. Bryan collapsed and died a few days after the trial ended; Scopes was convicted, but the State Supreme Court overturned the conviction on a technicality. Bryan's death meant the loss of a strong representative of antievolutionary thinking, and, along with the trial itself, the debates over evolution lost momentum.

The religious side to the controversy arose within the churches in the attempt of the Fundamentalists to gain control of those denominations in which they were active, especially the Presbyterians and the Baptists in the North and the East. When Harry Emerson Fosdick, a Liberal Baptist professor at Union Theological Seminary in New York, preached a sermon (on May 22, 1922) entitled "Shall the Fundamentalists Win?" the Fundamentalists sought and won his expulsion from his guest Presbyterian pulpit. Nonetheless, he eventually went on to become minister of the prestigious interdenominational Riverside Church; thus a Liberal became the nation's most famous and influential Protestant preacher. Furthermore, though the Presbyterians reaffirmed (for the second time) the Fundamentalist five-point declaration in 1923, by 1924 the Auburn Affirmation condemned the denomination's official biblical literalism. The net effect was that in Presbyterianism the Fundamentalists failed to gain control. The same pattern occurred in other denominations. Increasingly, the Fundamentalists began to form their own denominations and to build their own colleges and seminaries.

With this general background, we can now examine an important New Testament scholar who, though he was not a strict Fundamentalist (perhaps "conservative Evangelical" or "Protestant orthodox" is more appropriate) was, like the Fundamentalists, a staunch opponent of the Liberals: John Gresham Machen.

JESUS CHRIST IN THE THOUGHT OF JOHN GRESHAM MACHEN

John Gresham Machen was born the second of three sons on July 28, 1881, in Baltimore.[23] His father, Arthur Webster Machen, was a highly successful lawyer, and his older brother, Arthur, became the same. His mother, Minnie Gresham Machen, was a remarkable woman of grace, intellect, and deep Christian faith. Machen, a lifelong bachelor, continued to be strongly influenced by these three, especially his mother, to whom he eventually dedicated one of his books, *Christianity and Liberalism* (1923).

Machen graduated from Johns Hopkins University in 1901 and, after a year of graduate study in the classics there, entered Princeton Theological Seminary, where he was deeply impressed by the "Princeton Theology." He graduated with a Bachelor of Divinity degree in 1905, having also received a Master of Arts from Princeton University the previous year. Machen then went to Germany to study for a year, and there for a time he became enamored with the theology of the great Liberal Wilhelm Herrmann. Later, however, he became convinced that Liberalism, if successful, would destroy true Christianity.

Machen returned to Princeton Seminary as an instructor in 1906. In 1914 he was ordained to the ministry by the New Brunswick, New Jersey, Presbytery, and he became professor of New Testament literature and exegesis at the Seminary, a position he held until 1929, interrupted only by overseas war service for the Y.M.C.A. from 1918 to 1919. In the 1920s Machen became one of the most articulate opponents of Liberal Christianity. At Princeton he championed the old "Princeton Theology" and, as a result, soon found himself more and more in conflict with more moderate faculty members. Machen succeeded in getting the student government to dismiss the moderate Charles R. Erdman from his position as faculty counselor. Then the students formed a League of Evangelical Students. The controversy was debated throughout the Presbyterian denomination in 1927–28. Finally, when it was decided to reorganize Princeton Seminary on the basis of a more tolerant policy in 1929, Machen and a few colleagues withdrew to form Westminster Theological Seminary in Philadelphia. When he organized a separate Board of Foreign Missions, he was suspended by the New Brunswick Presbytery in 1935, a judgment that was confirmed by higher ecclesiastical courts and supported in 1936 by the General Assembly, Presbyterianism's annual meeting. On June 11, 1936, Machen helped to form the Presbyterian Church in America, later renamed the Orthodox Presbyterian Church. He taught at Westminster until his death in January 1937.

Though Machen was a shy man, he was resolute in his belief that his interpretation of orthodox Calvinist theology was the true way to perceive Christianity—that in fact it *was* Christianity. Thus his commitment to his own views sometimes led to a certain rigidity and highhandedness in his dealing with others. Yet he has generally been considered well-intentioned and was certainly one of the best scholars of Evangelical Christianity. His *New Testament Greek for Beginners* (1923) is still used in seminaries across the country, whether Liberal, Evangelical, or Fundamentalist, and his *Virgin Birth of Christ* (1930) is considered a classic document of the Conservative wing of Protestant Christianity in America.

Machen's little classic of 1923, written at the height of the Fundamentalist-Liberal controversy, was titled *Christianity and Liberalism.*[24] He did not argue that Liberalism stood alongside orthodox Christianity as a less viable form of Christianity; he argued that Liberalism was not Christianity at all.

> The chief modern rival of Christianity is "liberalism." An examination of the teachings of liberalism in comparison with those of Christianity will show that at every point the two movements are in direct opposition.[25]

For Machen, Liberalism was grounded in a "way of life" based on feeling and will, while Christianity was based on reason. Thus Machen was critical of the postrationalist stream of nineteenth-century Protestantism, which attempted to relate human experience and emotion to Jesus' inward religion *as reconstructed by Liberal historical scholarship:* this was the approach of "feeling." Likewise, he was critical of those who stressed the "ethical" quality of Liberal Christianity and related it to *the historical Jesus* as a mere human teacher of ethics, whether individual or social; this was the approach of "will." Instead, Christianity was based on what Machen believed were the historical facts and their interpretations. These were reasoned doctrines; that is, he took the approach of "reason." The antidoctrinal, experiential, and ethical basis of Liberal historical study was, for Machen, not true Christianity.

Machen argued that the doctrinal basis for Christianity was proven by the New Testament. Paul was not interested simply in Jesus' religion or ethics; Paul was interested first in the doctrine of Christ, and then in ethics. Christ not only died; he died *for our sins*, said Machen, and that was doctrine. Moreover, Machen disagreed with Bousset that Paul was indebted to a different kind of Christianity than was current in the Jerusalem church, or that Paul was radically different from Jesus. As Paul put forth a doctrine, so did the Jerusalem church and Jesus. The Jerusalem church said not only that Jesus died but also that he was raised to redeem the world. Likewise, Jesus did not teach eternal moral principles; he included himself, his person, in his message. "It must be admitted, then, that if we are to have a nondoctrinal religion, or a doctrinal religion founded merely on a general truth, we must give up not only Paul, not only the primitive Jerusalem Church, but also Jesus Himself."[26]

In line with his denial of the Liberal stress on human experience and activity, Machen stressed three doctrinal points: (1) the doctrine of God's complete difference from man (God's transcendence) is incompatible with the Liberal historian's notion that the heart of Jesus' teaching was the universal fatherhood of God (Harnack), for the latter is characteristic of all systems that locate God within the world and man (immanence) such as natural (nonrevealed) religion and pantheism; (2) the doctrine of man's sinfulness, a correlate of God's transcendence, must be stressed against the Liberal notion of man's goodness, a notion that forgets the Christian doctrine of the separation between the creator and the creature; (3) the doctrine of the plenary inspiration of the Bible as a means of preserving the truth of the very words of God's authoritative revelation in history must be affirmed against the Liberal view of history, which holds that the Bible is full of errors and misinterpretations and that God's word is nevertheless preserved by realizing that he operates through imperfect human beings.

> It is no wonder, then, that liberalism is totally different from Christianity, for the foundation is different. Christianity is founded upon the Bible. It bases upon the Bible both its thinking and its life. Liberalism on the other hand is founded upon the shifting emotions of sinful men.[27]

It is clear that Machen believed the New Testament was interested not in Jesus' religion, but in Jesus Christ as the object of belief. Not only Paul and the early church believed in Jesus, but Jesus believed himself to be an object of faith. Machen disagreed with Weiss's view that Jesus excluded himself from the coming kingdom. He also rejected all theories that put Jesus' messianic consciousness late in life as part of his developing personality (as did Bousset) or that regarded Jesus' messianic consciousness as a product of the early church (as did Wrede). The sources taken at face value present a Jesus "who based the whole of His ministry upon His stupendous claim."[28] Not only was Jesus separate from men in his messiahship; he was also separate in his consciousness of being sinless. As such he was not an example for the disciples to rid themselves of sin; he was the means by which their sin was removed.

> There is a profound difference, then, in the attitude assumed by modern liberalism and by Christianity toward Jesus the Lord. Liberalism regards Him as an Example and Guide; Christianity, as a Saviour. Liberalism makes Him an example for faith; Christianity, the object of faith.[29]

The difference between Liberalism and Christianity was summed up by Machen in this sentence: "liberalism regards Jesus as the fairest flower of humanity; Christianity regards Him as a supernatural Person."[30]

For Machen, as all the gospels acknowledge, Jesus was a supernatural person who worked miracles.

> . . . the question concerning all miracles is simply the question of the acceptance or rejection of the Saviour that the New Testament presents. Reject the miracles and you have in Jesus the fairest flower of humanity who made such an impression upon His followers that after His death they could not believe that He had perished but experienced hallucinations in which they thought they saw Him risen from the dead; accept the miracles, and you have a Saviour who came voluntarily into this world for our salvation, suffered for our sins upon the Cross, rose again from the dead by the power of God, and ever lives to make intercessions for us. The difference between these two views is the difference between two totally diverse religions.[31]

In contrast to the Liberals' emphasis on Jesus' death as an example of human self-sacrifice, Machen stressed the Pauline teaching that a loving, yet judging, God, in the person of his divine, sinless Son, assumed human nature, sacrificed himself for sinful humanity, and was raised from the dead. Machen argued that this redeeming work was applied at the beginning of a "new life," that is, a "rebirth" by the Holy Spirit. This was an act of God which might be sudden but which could also occur momentarily and grow. In either case, salvation was linked with the faith of the believer in this act: "At the center of Christianity is the doctrine of 'justification by faith.' "[32] For Machen this was a rational decision. "For faith is essentially dogmatic. Despite all you can do, you cannot remove the element of intellectual assent from it."[33] It included not only faith, but the law of loving one's neighbor as oneself and the hope in a final victory. Machen was not a "premillennialist," but was willing to join ranks with them. The ultimate vision of Christianity focused on eternity.

This "otherworldly" approach meant that Machen was pessimistic about human institutions dealing with problems related to immigrants, industrial relations, government, and international peace, though such institutions were a necessity and would be best undertaken by what he called "Christian men." The correct Christian approach was concern with the salvation of the individual soul; then "applied Christianity" would naturally follow. The Liberal Social Gospel was again wrong-headed.

> . . . the Christian man believes that there can be no applied Christianity unless there be "a Christianity to apply." That is where the Christian man differs from the modern liberal. The liberal believes that applied Christianity is all there is of Christianity, Christianity being merely a way of life; the Christian man believes that applied Christianity is the result of an initial act of God.[34]

That was in 1923. As you will recall, Machen withdrew from Princeton in 1929, set up a separate missions board in 1933, and, when disciplined, established a new church in 1936.

Enough has been said about the Fundamentalist movement, the Fundamentalist-Liberal conflict, and conservative Evangelical Christianity to make the opposition to Liberalism, Modernism, and *Religionsgeschichte* clear. Conservatives and some Fundamentalists sought to protect what they deemed the true doctrinal faith against what they considered a "watering down" of the New Testament message by modern thought and historical criticism of the Bible. They made no quest of the historical Jesus *behind* the sources, for the sources presented the infallible truth virtually as they stood. Nonetheless, they perceived what many of those educated also in the Liberal tradition would perceive in Europe: that the Liberal quest for Jesus was a failure, a reconstruction of a particular type of historical inquiry. However, they rested their case on another type of historical inquiry, and that was informed by the dogmas of a particular religious tradition.

SUMMARY

Thinking about Jesus Christ in the early twentieth century was both an advance beyond Liberal historical scholarship and a reaction to it. The advance drew on one phase of *Religionsgeschichte,* the rediscovery of Jewish apocalyptic eschatology. Liberals and *Religionsgeschichtler* had been aware of it, of course, but they had tended to exempt Jesus' main teaching from it. In 1892 Johannes Weiss had upset his Liberal colleagues by arguing that Jesus' *teaching* about the kingdom of God was apocalyptic. Then Albert Schweitzer forced the issue by attempting to show on the basis of both Mark and Matthew that Jesus' whole *life,* as well as his teaching, was dominated by his apocalyptic eschatology. Thus Jesus expected the reign of God to arrive before the disciples returned from their mission (Mt 10), and when that did not happen, he decided to force the kingdom by taking the expected "messianic woes" on himself. When that did not happen, the early church had to revise Jesus' eschatology further by associating the End with his second coming.

Schweitzer's "consistent eschatology" approach to the life of Jesus was based on the view that Jesus had an apocalyptic messianic consciousness. But what if Jesus' messianic statements were not from Jesus, but from the early church? At the very moment when Schweitzer was taking some of the eschatology out of the early church and imputing it to Jesus, William Wrede was arguing that neither the spiritual-ethical nor the eschatological messianic consciousness could be traced to Jesus, for the whole Messianic Secret theme in Mark was a creation of the early church. This meant that at least the messiahship question was unanswerable, though the question of Jesus' apocalyptic *teaching* might still be resolved.

This direction was pursued by the Roman Catholic Modernist Alfred Loisy. In opposition to the Liberals—specifically, to Harnack—Loisy argued that the institutional Church was the natural outgrowth of the gospel, not a distortion of it. Moreover, a historical assessment of Jesus' teaching could not, as Weiss had perceived, avoid the eschatological question. Thus Harnack not only was inaccurate in his historical perception of the Church but also wrong in his historical evaluation of the message of Jesus. What Harnack considered the husk was for Loisy part of the kernel, namely, the apocalyptic elements in Jesus' view of the kingdom of God. Jesus was not a "creative miracle" in the midst of his environment, but part of it. The irony was that while Loisy was beating the Protestant Liberals at their own historical game, his developmental (evolutionary) view of history, among other things, led to his excommunication.

Reaction to the Liberals and Modernists came from orthodox quarters of the churches, both Roman Catholic and Protestant. In the United States this reaction was especially strong among the Fundamentalists, who had their roots in seventeenth-century Protestant orthodoxy. For John Gresham Machen, a conservative Evangelical Christian, pietists and Liberals alike were too oriented toward subjective human experience. What was needed was a reaffirmation of rationally conceived historical dogma, grounded in a divinely inspired Scripture. For Machen, then, Liberalism was not Christianity at all, for it too easily identified God with the world and man, seemed naively committed to the essential goodness of man, and treated Holy Scripture as it would any other ancient book. It was no wonder that Liberals discovered only a human Jesus! The liberal quest for the historical Jesus was a failure; what was needed was a return to the fundamentals of Christianity, even if that meant establishing a new church.

This orthodox-leaning reaction, though it was new in some respects, attempted to deny historical criticism. In Germany during the 1920s, there would also be an orthodox reaction to Liberalism, but one which wholly accepted and incorporated the radical methods of gospel research that had arisen. This will be the main subject of the next chapter.

NOTES

1. Albert Schweitzer, *Memoirs of Childhood and Youth* (New York: Macmillan Co., 1925; *Out of My Life and Thought: An Autobiography,* trans. C. T. Campion (New York: Henry Holt and Co., 1933); Werner Picht, *Albert Schweitzer: The Man and His Work,* trans. Edward Fitzgerald (London: George Allen & Unwin, 1964); Fritz Buri, "Albert Schweitzer," in Martin E. Marty and Dean G. Peerman, *A Handbook of Christian Theologians* (New York: New American Library, Meridian Books, 1967), pp. 112–24.
2. Schweitzer, *Life and Thought,* p. 94.
3. From his *Memoirs,* quoted in Picht, *Schweitzer,* p. 34.
4. Schweitzer, *The Mystery of the Kingdom of God,* trans. Walter Lowrie (New York: Schocken Books, 1964) (originally published in German in 1901); *The Quest of the Historical Jesus,* trans. W. Montgomery (New York: Macmillan Co., 1968) (originally published in German in 1906).
5. Schweitzer, *Quest,* p. 403.
6. A. Wrede, "Introduction," in William Wrede, *Vorträge und Studien* (Tübingen: J. C. B. Mohr [Paul Siebeck], 1907); Georg Strecker, "William Wrede: Zur hundertsten Widerkehr seines Geburtstages," *Zeitschrift für Theologie und Kirche* **57** (1960), pp. 67–91 (with bibliography).
7. Wrede, *Paulus,* Religionsgeschichtliche Volksbücher I, 5/6 (Tübingen: J. C. B. Mohr [Paul Siebeck], 1904), pp. 103–4, quoted in Kümmel, *The New Testament,* p. 299. See ch. 7, pp. 137–38, and note 31.

8. William Wrede, *The Messianic Secret,* trans. by J. C. G. Grieg (Greenwood, S.C.: Attic Press, 1971) (originally published in 1901); Schweitzer, *Quest,* pp. 330–403; Norman Perrin, *What Is Redaction Criticism?* Guides to Biblical Scholarship Series (Philadelphia: Fortress Press, 1969), pp. 7–13.

9. Wrede, *The Messianic Secret,* taken from Kümmel, *The New Testament,* p. 287.

10. Ibid., p. 286.

11. Alec R. Vidler, *The Modernist Movement in the Roman Catholic Church* (Cambridge: Cambridge University Press, 1934); John Ratté, *Three Modernists: Alfred Loisy, George Tyrrell, William L. Sullivan* (New York: Sheed and Ward, 1967); Michele Ranchetti, *The Catholic Modernists: A Study of the Religious Reform Movement, 1864–1907* (London: Oxford University Press, 1969); Bernard M. G. Reardon, *Roman Catholic Modernism,* Library of Modern Religious Thought Series (Stanford, Ca.: Stanford University Press, 1970); Manschreck, *A History of Christianity,* pp. 363–409.

12. Ann Fremantle, *The Papal Encyclicals in Their Historical Context* (New York: New American Library, Mentor Books, 1953), p. 152.

13. In addition to note 11, see Alfred Loisy, *My Duel With the Vatican,* trans. Richard Wilson Boynton (New York: Greenwood Press, 1968) (originally published in 1924).

14. Alfred Loisy, *The Gospel and the Church,* trans. Christopher Home (New York: Charles Scribner's Sons, 1912) (originally published in 1902); reprinted in the Lives of Jesus Series, ed. Bernard B. Scott (Philadelphia: Fortress Press, 1976).

15. Ibid., p. 16.

16. Ibid., p. 18.

17. Ibid., p. 35.

18. Ibid., p. 13.

19. Ibid., p. 105.

20. Ibid., p. 121.

21. Ibid., p. 114.

22. Stewart G. Cole, *The History of Fundamentalism* (Hamden, Conn.: Shoe String Press, Archon Books, 1963); Ernest R. Sandeen, *The Roots of Fundamentalism: British and American Millenarianism, 1800–1930* (Chicago: University of Chicago Press, 1970); Sandeen, *The Origins of Fundamentalism,* Facet Books Historical Series, no. 10 (Philadelphia: Fortress Press, 1968); Ahlstrom, *A Religious History of the American People,* vol. 2, pp. 274–87, 396–403.

23. Ned B. Stonehouse, *J. Gresham Machen: A Biographical Memoir* (Grand Rapids, Mich.: William B. Eerdmans Co., 1954).

24. J. Gresham Machen, *Christianity and Liberalism* (Grand Rapids, Mich.: William B. Eerdmans Co., 1923).

25. Ibid., p. 53.

26. Ibid., p. 45.

27. Ibid., p. 79.

28. Ibid., p. 87.

29. Ibid., pp. 95–96.

30. Ibid., p. 96.

31. Ibid., p. 109.

32. Ibid., p. 141.

33. Ibid., p. 142.

34. Ibid., p. 155.

Jesus Christ
and the Bultmannians

In nineteenth-century Europe and America there emerged an unusual consciousness of the march of time. It was manifest in a new awareness of "the nation," its history, and its destiny; of human progress and human achievement; and of the conquest of nature. Discoveries in geology, archaeology, and anthropology were beginning to make people think more about the past. Science, medicine, and technology were pushing toward a better future—for some at least.

Reflection *about* history paralleled this historical consciousness. For Hegel, a divine "cunning of reason" was working through the passions and activities of the individuals and peoples of the world, giving history its drive and purpose: the growth of human freedom. For Marx, class struggle was moving history toward a classless society in which the producers of goods (the laborers) would receive a just share of the benefits. For Comte, history was the progress of secular civilization; it had passed through childhood (theology) and youth (abstract metaphysics) and was now in its manhood (the "positive," or empirical, sciences). For Darwin, evolution meant the impersonal process of natural selection of mutated species over long expanses of time. For Marx, Comte, and Darwin, the notion of God directing history (providence) was replaced by either *human* progress or *natural* selection; only Hegel retained the notion of Spirit, and his thought was eclipsed by the ideas of the other three (or those like them) by the late nineteenth century.

By the turn of the century, then, science, technology, the idea of conflict among masses of people, large national states, the great and sophisticated philosophical systems—all seemed part of the common stock of Western thinking about time. It was thought, and day-to-day life seemed to prove, that historical progress was inevitable. If the divine Spirit was anywhere, it was *within* the human, historical process.

THE EXISTENTIALISTS

Not everyone, however, accepted this outlook. In the period after the First World War (1914–18), especially in the countries most devastated by the war (France and Germany), the mood became pessimistic, and strong and capable voices arose in protest against the "systems." These voices were not united or unified—that would have been considered a contradiction by existentialists. Neither were they totally new, for they had discovered kindred echoes of voices out of the past that had not been heard or, if heard, had not been accepted. The owners of these voices, past and present, came from quite different quarters; some were Christian, some were non-Christian, and some were militantly anti-Christian. For them, the great systems of thought, whether empirical or metaphysical, seemed overly academic, superficially systematic, and out of touch with the life-and-death issues. Such voices were not necessarily opposed to reason; but they opposed the type of reason that did not begin with human existence as it actually was. They were fearful that scientific progress and technological advances, while perhaps not evil in themselves, would dehumanize the individual. They warned that the uniqueness of the individual might be absorbed in a mentality of the masses. They were critical of all "schools" of thought, all bodies of accepted belief, all intellectualized doctrines. They believed that history was not necessarily going anywhere—in fact, they thought it might be regressing. They were, and are, the existentialists, and their influence has been widespread in philosophy, art, music, poetry, literature, and drama.[1]

The existentialists and existentialism are notoriously difficult to describe, because existentialism is not a unified system of thought. Certainly one characteristic of existentialism is a radical sensitivity to the disorientation of living in a confusing world, accompanied by feelings of isolation, insignificance, meaninglessness, despair, and absurdity.

> Existentialism is not simply a philosophy or a philosophical revolt. Existentialist philosophy is the explicit conceptual manifestation of an existential attitude—a spirit of "the present age." It is a philosophical realization of a self-consciousness living in a "broken world" (Marcel), an "ambiguous

world" (de Beauvoir), a "dislocated world" (Merleau-Ponty), a world into which we are "thrown" and "condemned" yet "abandoned" and "free" (Heidegger and Sartre), a world which appears to be indifferent or even "absurd" (Camus). It is an attitude that recognizes the unresolvable confusion of the human world, yet resists the all-too-human temptation to resolve the confusion by grasping toward whatever appears or can be made to appear firm or familiar—reason, God, nation, authority, history, work, tradition, or the "other-worldly," whether of Plato, Christianity, or utopian fantasy. . . . Existentialism begins with the expression of a few such isolated individuals of genius, who find themselves cut adrift in the dangerous abyss between the harmony of Hegelian reason and the romantic celebration of the individual, between the warmth and comfort of the "collective idea" and the terror of finding oneself alone. Existentialism is this self-discovery.[2]

From this perspective, philosophy is no longer a set of propositions or axioms; it is not a theoretical system or a set of valid concepts. It is poetic, without being poetry; it is deeply individual and personal, but at the same time a reflection of what is individual and personal in everyone. Existentialists know that choices are inevitable, that not making a choice is still choosing not to make a choice; that individuals know who they are in extreme crises; that when choices are difficult, there are no absolute guidelines for them, and that ultimately choices are a "leap of faith," a commitment, so that one will leap rather than fall back into the mundane, average world. Existentialists know that each person must face death, and face it with lonely anxiety.

There is no agreed-upon list of existentialists, and some thinkers included in a list might even deny being part of an existentialist movement. Yet no one would fail to have near the beginning of such a list the Danish thinker Søren Kierkegaard (1813–55). For Kierkegaard, Hegel's great speculative system of thought was comical because it did not deal with the concrete, paradoxical, "either/or" decisions of the subjective individual and his *personal* history; Kierkegaard's own tragic life was plagued by feelings of isolation, guilt, anxiety, and death. (He eventually dropped out of the university and the institutional church; he even broke off his engagement in order to write his philosophy.) Another on the list would probably be the Russian Orthodox novelist Feodor Dostoevsky (1821–81), who became convinced that the rational order of the universe was an illusion. In his *Notes From the Underground* (1864) he rebelled against that order in the name of human freedom. The suffering atheist Friedrich Nietzsche (1844–1900) believed that all the scientific, religious, and moral values taken for granted in the great philosophical and religious systems of the West could no longer be accepted. The French thinker Gabriel Marcel (1889–1973), a believer in God, found it impossible to reflect about human existence in the abstract after his terrible experiences in the First World War. In Germany, Martin Heidegger (1889–1976) stressed the analysis of concrete "Being-in-the-world" and the decisional character of human existence, without denying or affirming the existence of God. The German thinker Karl

Jaspers (1883–1969), influenced by Kant, Kierkegaard, and Nietzsche, criticized the positivist systems and stressed the contradictions in human existence. The Frenchman Jean-Paul Sartre (b. 1905), with a background in psychology and an active, Marxist-oriented political life, has written novels, plays, and philosophical works stressing the absurdity of human life. Finally, Sartre's compatriot Albert Camus (1913–60), stressed the "absurd" in the confrontation of rational minds with an indifferent universe.

How do the existentialists regard history? History is not merely what happened in the past, whether it be the "facts," the changes through time, or what one generation passes on to another. History has meaning in terms of an individual's consciousness of being in time and of having to make decisions. What the past offers are concrete possibilities of understanding one's existence so that they may be realized in the present as one decides for the future. History is therefore not simply "what happened"; it is made up of events and heroes of the past that challenge one to make a decision about the future. History must, finally, become a possibility for us; otherwise, it will become simply another system.

Such ideas had much influence among German historians and thinkers in the 1920s, among them Rudolf Bultmann. Before turning to Bultmann, however, it is necessary to backtrack and listen to another lonely voice, this one from the perspective of more traditional Christianity. He, too, challenged historical "pastness" and factuality, though he was deeply concerned about history. This was Martin Kähler, who has been highly influential in twentieth-century theological circles.

JESUS CHRIST IN THE THOUGHT OF MARTIN KÄHLER

Martin Kähler (1835–1912), the son of a German pastor, was born on January 6, 1835, in Neuhausen, Prussia, near the town Immanuel Kant made famous, Königsberg.[3] In his early school days, Kähler was a serious student who read the German romantics, especially Goethe and Schiller, as well as the philosophers Spinoza, Kant, and Hegel. Kähler entered the University of Heidelberg to study law, but became seriously ill. During this time he found that the great hymns of Paul Gerhardt gave him more solace than his beloved romantics and idealists. He gradually came to think that the latter were too "pantheistic"; that is, he thought they so identified God with everything that they reduced the creator to his creation. Though he never gave up his love for Goethe, Kähler changed his field of study to theology.

Entering the University of Heidelberg, Kähler came under the influence of Richard Rothe (1813–85), a theologian who introduced him to the historical thought of F. C. Baur and the Tübingen School. Kähler later wrote in his autobiography, "This critical cold water bath was the beginning of my own serious studies."[4] But Rothe's own lectures on the life of Jesus raised what would become for Kähler a crucial question: "How can Jesus Christ be the authentic object of the faith of all Christians if the questions what and who he really was can be established only by ingenious investigation and if it is solely the scholarship of our time which proves itself equal to this task?"[5] Did one have to be a scholar to be a good Christian?

After Heidelberg, Kähler transferred to the University of Halle, a traditional center of German pietism. There he studied with scholars who sought to find a middle ground between confessional orthodoxy in the Lutheran and pietist traditions and modern thought as represented by the sciences and biblical criticism. Eventually, Kähler would be viewed as one of these "mediating theologians," though his own historical approach was in fact closer to the "negative" critics. From Halle, Kähler transferred to the University of Tübingen, but soon he decided to return to Halle to work on his doctoral dissertation under August Tholuck.

In 1860 Kähler began teaching theology at the University of Halle. Except for three years as an instructor at the University of Bonn (1864–67), Kähler spent the rest of his active life teaching there. A prolific author (his writings included 165 titles), he was especially well known for making the Lutheran doctrine of justification by faith the center of his theology and for his views on Jesus Christ. The impact of his thought is attested by the fact that a number of major twentieth-century theologians of great fame and influence, notably Karl Barth, Rudolf Bultmann, and Paul Tillich, gave Kähler tribute for his influence on them.

In a lucid and penetrating way, Martin Kähler focused on what had become a crucial issue in late nineteenth- and early twentieth-century thought about Jesus Christ:[6] If the Bible was a fallible human document which technical historical scientists had shown to be historically "unreliable," and if such technical expertise was nonetheless necessary to go behind the documents in order to discover Jesus, how then, could the average Christian continue to believe in Jesus Christ as the one sure, historically revealed foundation for faith?

> . . . these questions, the question of the normative status of the Bible and the question of the credibility of its portrait of Christ, still retain their validity for me. These two questions, which are inseparably intertwined, basically add up to the problem of historical revelation.[7]

Like Machen in America, Kähler rejected the pietist and Liberal stress on feeling and inward religion, for it did not establish the historically objective revelation of God. Yet in contrast to orthodox Christianity—Roman Catholic, Protestant, Fundamentalist, or "mediating"—Kähler accepted modern historical criticism of the Bible. At the same time, he believed that research had come to the point of turning in upon itself. What historical research sought—the life of Jesus—it was incapable of discovering. Almost a decade prior to Wrede, Kähler had developed a highly radical view of the sources:

> I repeat: we have no sources for a biography of Jesus of Nazareth which measure up to the standards of contemporary historical science. . . . He could be taken for a product of the church's fantasy around the year A.D. 100. Furthermore, these sources cannot be traced with certainty to eyewitnesses. In addition to this, they tell us only about the shortest and last period of his life. And finally, these sources appear in two basic forms [the Gospel of John and the Synoptics] whose variations must—in view of the proximity of the alleged or probable time of origin of these forms—awaken serious doubts about the faithfulness of the recollections.[8]

For Kähler, this meant that it was impossible to go behind the sources in order to trace the developing messianic consciousness of a religious genius. The gospels were not biographies but "passion stories with extended introductions."[9] They did not permit historical reconstructions on the basis of human analogies. Filling in the gaps of Jesus' childhood, or speaking of Jesus' inner development, was more of a projection of the historian's theological position than a historical reconstruction. "The inner development of a sinless person is as inconceivable to us as a life on the Sandwich Islands is to a Laplander."[10] Any attempt to find a historically secure "minimum" or "maximum" amount of authentic material about Jesus required critical presuppositions, and those were related to one's theology. For Kähler, the entire "life-of-Jesus" movement was a blind alley, and he felt that he had to oppose it:

> I wish to summarize my cry of warning in a form intentionally audacious: *the historical Jesus of modern authors conceals from us the living Christ.* The Jesus of the "Life-of-Jesus movement" is merely a modern example of human creativity. . . . In this respect historicism is just as arbitrary, just as humanly arrogant, just as impertinent and "faithlessly gnostic" as that dogmatism which in its day was also considered modern.[11]

Who, then, was "the living Christ"? He was "the historic Christ," the "biblical Christ." At this point Kähler made a crucial distinction between "historical" (*historisch*) and "historic" (*geschichtlich*). The "historical Jesus" was the result of those who sought to arrive at the Jesus of history, but in fact this was a scholarly reconstruction varying from expert to expert; in contrast, the *historic* Christ is the figure who originated and passed on his permanent influence, the person whom history has remembered, the divine Son of God whom Christians believe redeemed them. He is God revealed, the Christ of the *whole* New Testament, including the "portrait" of Christ in the gospels and his words, for what he said of himself was in perfect harmony with who he was and what he did. He is also the Christ of the creeds and the church, and most of all he is, said Kähler, the Christ who is preached as he has been preached from the very beginning. Thus the Christ of faith is the Christ of "preaching," the "kerygmatic" Christ (Greek: *kerygma,* "proclamation").

Martin Kähler refused to choose between seventeenth-century orthodoxy and the shifting opinions of the Liberal scholarly community. In neither was there the "sure footing" he sought. Rather, he searched for the "picture" of Christ that "overpowered" him, the Christ grasped by the faith of *any* Christian, the Christ of testimonies and confessions of believers everywhere, from the beginnings to the present.

> So long as we do not substitute for faith in Christ an assent of our conscience to Jesus' religious ethic, so long as a living Christianity depends on the person of the historic Christ, and so long as the Spirit of Christ identifies himself as such by taking what belongs to the historic Jesus Christ (John 16:14), there will always remain the necessity that we encounter precisely this historic Christ, not as an ideal to be realized in the remote future by scientific investigation nor as the fluctuating result of the biographers' disputations, but, rather, within a tradition which possesses the inherent power to convince us of its divine authenticity. The datum must be "directly accessible." The Protestant Christian's independence of any form of imposed tutelage is not possible apart from the unique place occupied by the Bible. There must be for everyone a reliable means of access to the Christ of the whole Bible, who until now—in spite of all temporary obstructions and precisely in the overcoming of them—has borne the faith of Christians. It is all these considerations, then, that make it impossible for me even to differentiate the "historic" from the "biblical" Christ.[12]

Kähler accepted the fact of radical biblical criticism and recognized that the sources would not yield a biography of Jesus; he believed that nineteenth-century biographies were really products of theological imagination. He recognized the central place of the resurrection in the New Testament; he saw the "preaching" character of early Christian literature; and he believed that the biblical Christ was transmitted in Christian preaching to face new life situations. In all of this, he was a forerunner of the most influential New Testament scholar of the twentieth century, Rudolf Bultmann.

JESUS CHRIST IN THE THOUGHT OF RUDOLF BULTMANN

Rudolf Karl Bultmann (1884–1976) was born on August 20, 1884, in the town of Wiefelstede in northwestern Germany.[13] Rudolf was the oldest of three sons of an Evangelical-Lutheran pastor, Arthur Bultmann, whose father had been a Christian missionary to Sierra Leone, West Africa. His mother, Helene, was the daughter of a pastor in Baden, to the South. When Rudolf was in grade school, the family moved to Rastede. From 1895 to 1903 Bultmann attended the *Gymnasium* at Oldenburg, his father having become pastor there in 1897. Bultmann recalled in his short autobiographical sketch of 1956,

> I look back with pleasure on my school years, both in the elementary school and in the *Gymnasium*. What especially interested while at the latter, in addition to the study in religion, was the instruction in Greek and in the history of German literature. I also avidly attended the theater and the concerts.[14]

One of Bultmann's classmates at the Gymnasium was Karl Jaspers, who would one day debate the meaning of human existence with him.

In 1903 Bultmann entered the University of Tübingen to study theology, and after three semesters he transferred to the University of Berlin. In theology both universities were dominated by Protestant Liberals. At Berlin he was especially impressed with the great Harnack (see pages 205–11) and with a leading scholar of the *religionsgeschichtliche Schule,* Hermann Gunkel, who was a pioneer in the study of oral traditions in the Old Testament and in apocalyptic. In his final two semesters at the University of Marburg (eastern West Germany), Bultmann studied with the Liberal Adolf Jülicher; with Johannes Weiss, the exponent of Jesus' apocalyptic kingdom teaching; and with Wilhelm Herrmann, the great Liberal theologian who had so impressed Machen. Though Herrmann was in the tradition of Kant, Schleiermacher, and Ritschl, he also stressed divine revelation from beyond, that is, from a transcendent God who expressed himself uniquely in Jesus Christ, his divine Son. This affirmation sounded more like orthodoxy. Like Kähler, Herrmann believed that the gospel sources were insufficient to yield a "life" of Jesus, even though Jesus' ethical character was obvious in them.

Bultmann passed his first ecclesiastical exams in 1907, and after a year of teaching at the Oldenburg *Gymnasium,* he won a scholarship to Marburg. Following his dissertation on the Cynic-Stoic "diatribe" (a philosopher's manner of arguing) in Paul (1910) and his thesis on Theodore of Mopsuestia to qualify as a lecturer in New Testament (1912), he became a lecturer at Marburg. There the *Religionsgeschichtler* Wilhelm Heitmüller was one of his colleagues, and Martin Rade, the editor of the liberally oriented journal *The Christian World,* was his personal friend. He recalled enjoying the annual meeting of the journal's supporters, at which the great theological issues of the day were discussed by leading Liberals.

By now Germany was involved in the First World War. In 1917, the year he received word that his youngest brother had been killed in France, Bultmann preached a sermon that opened with comments about the pain and misery of the war, and then went on to proclaim that

God was "hidden" and "mysterious," quoting the existentialist Friedrich Nietzsche in support. Though Bultmann later claimed that the war had little effect on his thinking, this sermon no longer sounded like a typical Liberal.

Meanwhile, Bultmann had been appointed assistant professor at the University of Breslau (now Wrocław in Poland) in 1916, and soon he married and had two children. During his Breslau period, he was hard at work in his ground-breaking form-critical study, *History of the Synoptic Tradition* (1921). A year before it was published, and having written articles on the Messianic Secret (indebted to Wrede) and the contrast between Jesus and Paul (indebted to Bousset and Heitmüller), Bultmann succeeded Bousset at the University of Giessen. Though happy there, he could not resist the invitation in 1921 to return to Marburg as Heitmüller's successor, for he considered Marburg his true spiritual home. There he joined Adolf Jülicher and Herrmann's successor, Rudolf Otto, who became famous for his view that the reality of religion lay in the experience of a mysterious, fascinating, and awe-producing power outside humanity, the "Wholly Other." Such a view encouraged Bultmann's shift away from Liberalism, as it would do also to Karl Barth, an emerging leader of the new movement. In 1923 Barth (at the University of Göttingen), Eduard Thurneysen, and Friedrich Gogarten launched a new journal whose title and orientation mirrored the new eschatologically oriented mood: *Between the Times*. The new "crisis" or "dialectical" theology stressed God as "totally other," man as sinner in need of God's grace through Jesus Christ, and the "good news" *about* Jesus Christ in the New Testament—all of which were conceptions opposed to Liberalism. Bultmann's articles in this period indicated general agreement.

The existentialist philosopher Martin Heidegger, who was at Marburg from 1922 to 1928, made a strong impression on Bultmann. After 1926 Bultmann began to sound more and more like an "existentialist." Meanwhile, his critical studies continued. A 1926 article on the gospels combined his studies of the history of oral tradition in the New Testament ("form criticism") with *Religionsgeschichte*. That year he also published his little classic *Jesus* (in English: *Jesus and the Word*), in which he claimed that it was impossible to recover the life and personality of the historical Jesus. He also wrote on "dialectical theology." In 1929 he published on revelation, and in 1930 on an existentialist view of history and on Paul.

In the 1930s Bultmann became perforce a citizen of the Third Reich. Though never active in political life, he was a "charter member" of the Confessing Church, which resisted the Nazi encroachments on church and university life. Moreover, when Hitler asserted absolute power early in 1933, Bultmann prefaced the opening lecture of the summer term with a statement warning that the state is not beyond sin, that

Rudolf Bultmann

national good and evil must be judged by the standard of love, and that the Christian faith was in danger of being called into question. He then attempted to use Hitler's statements to denounce the Marburg town council for changing the Jewish names of streets and squares and to object to the distrustful atmosphere created by informers. In this context Bultmann wrote,

> As a Christian, I must deplore the injustice that is also being done precisely to German Jews by means of such defamation. . . . Keep the struggle for the German nation pure, and take care that noble intentions to serve truth and country are not marred by demonic distortions![15]

Meanwhile, Bultmann's academic output continued. He attempted to show the commonality of theme behind Jesus and Paul. In 1941 he produced his justly acclaimed commentary on the Gospel of John and the essay for which he is most famous, "New Testament and Mythology," in which he proposed an existentialist interpretation of New Testament myths. After the Second World War he published his two-volume *Theology of the New Testament* (1949, 1951), his study in *Religionsgeschichte* translated as *Primitive Christianity in Its Contemporary Setting* (1949), and his well-known discussions, mainly with his own students, on the historical Jesus.

Bultmann's impact on study of the New Testament in general and of Jesus in particular has been tremendous. He published more than fifteen books (which have gone through many revisions and editions), well over one hundred articles, some fifty more dictionary articles and word studies, about two hundred reviews, a number of short comments, and many sermons. There are also countless books that discuss his thought. His students occupied many major university professorships in Germany after the Second World War (Bornkamm, Käsemann, Conzelmann, Fuchs, Schmithals), and students of those students abound, especially in Germany and the United States. Several memorial volumes have been written for him. After a long and fruitful life that made him a profound influence on his time and one of the theological giants of the twentieth century, Bultmann died on July 30, 1976.

Rudolf Bultmann's thought is in many respects an elaboration and summation of various streams of historical, philosophical, and theological reflection derived from the preceding two hundred years; if one includes Paul, John, Augustine, and Luther, the points of contact stretch out over a much greater span of time. The following treatment does not pretend to be exhaustive of Bultmann's thinking about Jesus Christ, but it represents a selection of three important areas for which he has become especially well known: form criticism, his view of Jesus, and his proposal to "demythologize" the New Testament image of Jesus Christ.

Form Criticism

"Form criticism" is a somewhat unfortunate translation of the German term *Formgeschichte,* which literally means "history of forms."[16] One might define it as an analytical method for discovering the history of the oral tradition behind the gospels by typing the stories and theorizing about their origin and growth in their successive community "settings in life" (*Sitze im Leben*).[17] Form criticism saw biblical literature not simply as the creation of individual, creative authors recording history, but as the product of spontaneous, believing communities over long periods of time.

In the period after the First World War, there appeared three major studies that laid the foundation for form criticism of the New Testament. In 1919 K. L. Schmidt published *The Framework of the Story of Jesus,* which concluded that the vague time and place links between gospel stories (such as "In those days . . ." and "And passing along by the Sea of Galilee . . .") and a number of general summaries of Jesus' ministry scattered throughout Mark were a framework used by Mark to create a "life" of Jesus. That is, Mark had strung the stories together like pearls on a string. Martin Dibelius (in *From Tradition to Gospel* [1919]) and Bultmann were meanwhile analyzing the separate stories (the pearls), attempting to trace their separate oral histories through the various religious communities. Bultmann's comprehensive and detailed *History of the Synoptic Tradition* (1921) has become the classic work.

Bultmann accepted the existence of Palestinian Jewish Christian communities and Hellenistic Jewish Christian communities prior to Paul, as Bousset and Heitmüller had demonstrated. He then divided Palestinian Judaism and Jewish Christianity into its two major types, the one oriented to the Jewish law (preserved partly in the Midrash and the Talmud), the other oriented to apocalyptic eschatology, which Bultmann believed had been influenced by Iranian-Babylonian and oriental-Gnostic myths (see pages 43, 217–23). The Hellenistic communities were viewed much as Bousset had seen them. It was in these Palestinian and Hellenistic communities, then, that the tradition about Jesus was preserved, modified, and created.

Taking for granted such communities, Bultmann carefully observed the way Matthew and Luke had modified and interpreted Mark and, further, the way second-century noncanonical, or apocryphal, gospels continued the process of embellishment. By this means he developed a set of "laws" which he believed governed the transmission of popular oral tradition in primitive Christianity. Then Bultmann typed the stories based on forms of religious stories in the Greco-Roman world. (This approach showed the influence of the History-of-Religions School on Bultmann.) At the most general level he divided the material into two kinds: *discourses* of Jesus (including conversations with others) and *narratives* about Jesus (sometimes including his sayings). The discourses were further typed into four forms (apothegms, "words of Jesus," "I-sayings," and parables), and the narratives were further typed into two forms (miracle stories and "historical" or legendary materials). These six forms, including a few subforms, were then evaluated according to the laws of oral tradition and *religionsgeschichtliche* parallels, giving a total picture of the developing "Jesus tradition."

Extensive analysis of the tradition indicated to Bultmann that the narrative materials were the most interpretive. Though they may have represented Jesus in a vague and general way, specific historical events in the biography of Jesus were scarcely recoverable. This result, along with the parallel result derived from others that it was Mark who had strung the pearls together in the form of a "life," made Bultmann conclude:

> I do indeed think that we can now know almost nothing concerning the life and personality of Jesus, since the early Christian sources show no interest in either, are moreover fragmentary and legendary; and other sources about Jesus do not exist.[18]

What could be known about Jesus? From the *narrative* material only a little. A famous summary from a much later writing put it this way:

> Hence, with a bit of caution we can say the following concerning Jesus' activity: Characteristic for him are exorcisms, the breach of the Sabbath commandment, the abandonment of ritual purifications, polemic against Jewish legalism, fellowship with outcasts such as publicans and harlots, sympathy for women and children; it can also be seen that Jesus was not an ascetic like John the Baptist, but gladly ate, and drank a glass of wine. Perhaps we may add that he called the disciples and assembled about himself a small company of followers—men and women.[19]

Yet a critical analysis of the *discourse* material was more hopeful: "Little as we know of his life and personality, we know enough of his *message* to make for ourselves a consistent picture."[20] Bultmann was not complacent in this judgment, precisely because he knew that in many passages it was extremely difficult to distinguish between Jesus' authentic sayings and the very earliest Palestinian church creations:

> But how far that community preserved an objectively true picture of him and his message is another question. For those whose interest is in the personality of Jesus, this situation is depressing or destructive; for our purpose it has no particular significance. It is precisely this complex of ideas in the oldest layer of the synoptic tradition which is the object of our consideration. It meets us as a fragment of tradition coming to us from the past, and in the examination of it we seek the encounter with history. By the tradition Jesus is named as bearer of the message; according to overwhelming probability he probably was. Should it prove otherwise, that does not change in any way what is said in the record. I see then no objection to naming Jesus throughout as the speaker. Whoever prefers to put the name of "Jesus" always in quotation marks and let it stand as an abbreviation for the historical phenomenon with which we are concerned is free to do so.[21]

Jesus

One might think from the preceding that Bultmann would have nothing else to say on this subject. Yet some of these statements are from the introduction to a substantial book written in 1926 on Jesus, translated as *Jesus and the Word*.[22] On the basis of his form-critical studies, Bultmann located Jesus in the context of Palestinian Judaism and sought to show that as a Jew, he was both like and different from both the eschatological and rabbinic types of Judaism. Like Bousset, Bultmann thought of Jewish eschatology as having two streams, the nationalistic–political stream with its messianic hope in the Son of David, and the apocalyptic stream with its hope in the Son of Man. Jesus rejected the *nationalistic* eschatology, even though he confined his earthly ministry to the Jewish nation. Thus, for Jesus, the Jew *as Jew* had no special claim before God (Luke 13:28–29), and Jesus could even picture the Samaritan as putting the Jew to shame (Luke 10:29–37). In contrast, Jesus accepted *apocalyptic* eschatology. He expected a tremendous eschatological drama, including the coming of a heavenly messianic Son of Man, the resurrection of the dead, and the judgment of hell for some and heaven for others. Yet Jesus was unlike the apocalypticists in that he refrained from describing the details of the End and chided those who calculated when it would come or watched for signs (Luke 17:23–24). Such a "reduced apocalyptic" (Bultmann's well-known phrase) was especially obvious in the main feature of his teaching, the kingdom of God (Luke 17:20–21).

Bultmann believed that the Liberals were incorrect in seeing Jesus' idea of the kingdom as directed to individuals and their personal relations with God. In the same vein, he did not think Jesus' teaching led to mysticism, pietism, or asceticism. On the one hand, the kingdom was miraculous, coming from beyond (Rudolf Otto: "Wholly Other"); on the other hand, it was imminent, or "at hand," a future event that would have great bearing on the present. Thus the kingdom would transform the world and its communities. It was not that the world was evil as God had created it; rather, under the influence of the Devil and his demons, men had perverted it with evil wills. So Jesus appeared, proclaiming that the kingdom of God was "at hand," summoning his hearers to repent, warning them of the impending disaster, and proclaiming deliverance to those who heeded his call. He said that the kingdom was already beginning to break in, anticipated in his meals with his disciples (Luke 22:15–18), already coming upon those whom Jesus exorcized from the demons (Luke 11:20), present in the midst of the people (Luke 17:21), ultimately giving hope to the poor, hungry, and weeping (Luke 6:20–21). In short, Jesus was an eschatological prophet challenging his hearers to decide before it was too late; one had to count the cost of following him, realize that this was the last hour, and make the ultimate decision either for or against the kingdom. This decision, said Bultmann, is what Kierkegaard called "Either/Or."

As to eschatology, then, Jesus was a modified apocalypticist. Yet he was also addressed as "Rabbi" (Mark 9:5; 10:51; 11:21; 14:45), that is, as one who interpreted the law, and in this regard he was related to that other great stream of Palestinian Judaism called rabbinic Judaism. Jesus was like the rabbis in that he taught in the synagogues, gathered disciples around him, and disputed questions of the law with the rabbis' forms of argument and their style of teaching in parables. Jesus did not oppose the law, and many of his teachings are represented as being like those of the rabbis; likewise, Jesus did not openly attack temple sacrifices, prayer, alms-giving, and fasting. Yet he was different from the rabbis, at least if the later rabbinic sources were representative of the rabbis in Jesus' time. Rabbis did not associate with women, children, tax collectors, and sinners such as prostitutes; Jesus did. Moreover, Jesus could be found opposing any conventional piety that appeared to him elitist or hypocritical, and on one occasion he was accused of being a glutton and a drunkard in contrast to the ascetic John the Baptist (Mt 11:19).

Bultmann attempted to delineate the difference between the rabbis and Jesus on the basis of *how* the law was interpreted. The heart of Jewish interpretation was obedience to the commandments of the *whole* law simply because they were so commanded; if two commandments conflicted, one attempted to moderate between them in some way. Jesus, on the other hand, discriminated between what he considered essential and what he saw as nonessential. Although at this point Bultmann believed it was quite difficult to separate Jesus' teaching from that of the early church, he was willing to state that the early church probably represented Jesus' basic views here. Thus, whereas the rabbis thought of cleanness and uncleanness on the basis of externals (such as contact with a corpse or the menstruation of a woman), Jesus affirmed that cleanness was an internal matter (Mark 7:15). Whereas the law commanded assent, Jesus was willing to say, "You have heard it said [in the law] . . . , but I say to you. . . ." As Jesus himself opposed his view of the demand of God to the demand of the law, so those who followed Jesus had to do the same. For Bultmann, Jesus' notion of obedience required choice, or decision; in other words, one's will had to be in line with the intention of the command. Not simply obedience for the sake of obedience, but *radical obedience* was necessary:

> Radical obedience exists only when a man inwardly assents to what is required of him, when the thing commanded is seen as intrinsically God's command; when the whole man stands behind what he does; or better, when the whole man is *in* what he does, when he is not *doing something obediently,* but *is* essentially obedient.[23]

In contrast to a way of thinking that characterized the Greeks or, for Bultmann, many nineteenth-century ethicists, there were no unchangeable standards, no final and absolute forms for Jesus. Every new situation required a new decision, and the *now* took precedence over the past.

> This really means that *Jesus teaches no ethics at all* in the sense of an intelligible theory valid for all men concerning what should be done and left undone. . . . A man cannot control beforehand the possibilities upon which he must act; he cannot in the moment of decision fall back upon principles, upon a general ethical theory which can relieve him of responsibility for the decision; rather, every moment of decision is essentially new. For man does not meet the crisis of decision armed with a definite standard; he stands on no firm base, but rather alone in empty space. This is what shows the requirement of the good to be actually the demand of God—not the demand of something divine in man, but the demand of God who is beyond man.[24]

Bultmann then asked whether holding out a promise of reward did not contradict this demand for radical obedience. His answer was that it did, but that in Jesus' teaching the notion was paradoxical: "He promises reward to those who are obedient without thought of reward."[25]

In practice, Jesus himself stressed love of God and neighbor, but in such a way that each situation would determine the content of that love. Though one had to be prepared to surrender everything to God, that did not necessarily lead to an "ethic" of poverty, asceticism, or renunciation of property. Likewise, Jesus did not make particular pronouncements about courses of social or political action. Neither did he think that emotional love, friendship, or family love was equivalent to the radical demand for love. What he required was "perfection," that is, the Hebrew notion of "sound," "whole," "exact," or "true," which Bultmann interpreted to mean complete commitment, without divided loyalties.

For Bultmann, then, Jesus was both an eschatological prophet and a rabbi, one who had an eschatological and an "ethical" message. There was an interconnection between the imminent End and the radical demand for love, the proclamation of the kingdom and the demand for "perfection," the future and the present. Those who have thought of Jesus as an ethical teacher without real concern for eschatology (the Liberals) or as an apocalypticist with only an "interim ethic" (Schweitzer) have not found the proper balance.[26]

The interconnection between prophet and rabbi, between eschatology and "ethics," between the future kingdom and the present demand for love, had its parallel in Jesus' teaching of God as both remote and near. Bultmann wrote that in the Hellenistic world God was conceived of as part of the world or identical with the world (pantheism); for Judaism, God had been both remote and near in theory, that is, both transcendent and in contact with nature and history, while in practice, radical eschatological dualism had pushed him so far into the future that his remoteness was stressed at the expense of his nearness. When God became removed from man in Judaism, man was no longer radically conscious of standing before God in sin, but believed that his good works made his sin pardonable. By the same token, he no longer conceived grace (the gift of overcoming sin) radically enough: ". . . Judaism did not achieve a really unified idea of God, because neither the idea of sin nor the idea of God's grace is radically conceived."[27] What Jesus did was bring God's nearness back into unity with his remoteness by announcing that the future kingdom was already dawning during his own ministry. Thus Jesus naively considered God to be taking care of both nature and humanity (Luke 12:22–31; Mt 10:29–31); the remote God came near to man through Jesus' miracles (Luke 11:20); Jesus taught his disciples to pray to the remote God as though he were as close as an intimate Father (Luke 11:1–4; Mt 6:9–13); and he taught them to have faith in miracle and prayer (Mt 17:20). God's people were therefore children, or sons, and that was not a natural state, but one of God's choice. In the radicalness of man's sin, the remote God has come near to him, forgiving him:

> Thus it has finally become clear in what sense God is for Jesus God of the present and of the future. God is God of the present, because His claim confronts man in the present moment, and He is at the same time God of the future, because He gives man freedom for the present instant of decision, and sets before him as the future which is opened to him by his decision, condemnation or mercy. God is God of the present for the sinner precisely because He casts him into remoteness from Himself, and He is at the same time God of the future because He never relinquishes His claim on the sinner and opens to him by forgiveness a new future for new obedience.[28]

Bultmann's image of "Jesus" was a combination of the eschatological prophet who taught a reduced apocalyptic centering in the immediate coming of the kingdom of God and a somewhat unconventional rabbi who taught radical obedience (even to the extent of opposing the law) in the face of an ultimate decision. Similarly, God was remote, transcendent, the "Wholly Other"; yet he was near, imminent, the loving Father. On all fronts, Bultmann appeared to be keeping opposites in tension, or (to use a term from existentialism) to be presenting a "dialectic" alternating between future and present, eschatology and ethics, the distant God and the near God. Moreover, form criticism could not be absolutely certain that this was the "historical Jesus." Such a conclusion was not disturbing to Bultmann; rather, it fit his existentialized Lutheran theology: "Justification by faith" was a risk and was never built on any absolutely secure foundation, including the historical Jesus. Bultmann had wed a very radical form-critical conclusion with a very conservative theology buttressed by his Lutheranism and his existentialism: The church had never rested its faith on the ability to reconstruct the historical Jesus!

Nevertheless, Bultmann did put forth an image of "Jesus." Built within this image was a factor which both his Liberal and his *religionsgeschichtliche* teachers had, he believed, sidestepped, but which Weiss and Schweitzer had made the center: apocalyptic eschatology. Likewise, Bultmann took into consideration continuing apocalyptic influences in Paul's thinking (for example, the second coming of Jesus Christ) alongside Paul's mythic views as influenced by oriental Gnosticism. Thus, for Bultmann, Jesus and Paul were not as far apart as the *Religionsgeschichtler* had supposed: Even though Jesus' primary vision was toward the *future* kingdom of God and Paul's conception included a *past* orientation to Jesus Christ himself, both Jesus and Paul presented their messages cloaked in myth, or what Bultmann frequently called "mythology."

Demythologizing

The basic question for Bultmann as a Christian preacher and thinker was the meaning of such mythology for "the modern mind."[29] Bultmann had already addressed this question in his 1926 book *Jesus and the Word* and in several subsequent articles. However, in 1941, during the course of the Second World War, Bultmann delivered to pastors of the Confessing Church at Frankfurt a lecture that dealt specifically with the question. Titled "New Testament and Mythology,"[30] this essay and various discussions of it became the center of a controversy among pastors and theologians and provoked comment by scholars in other fields. After the war, it made Bultmann internationally famous. This essay, Bultmann's responses to criticisms of it, and his clarification of his position to English-speaking audiences in 1958 (*Jesus Christ and Mythology*)[31] provided the basis for his third major contribution to an understanding of Jesus Christ.

For Bultmann, ancient peoples lived in a "mythical" world. They thought of the universe as a three-storied structure with heaven "above," hell "below," and the flat earth in the middle. Heaven was the place of God or the gods and various celestial beings, including the angels. Hell was the place of torment, often associated with the Devil and demonic powers. The earth was the place of both ordinary, *natural* events and of interruptions of the natural course of things by either the demonic powers (resulting in natural catastrophies or human illnesses) or the divine powers (resulting in miracles of natural deliverance or healing). These outside powers, moreover, could temporarily determine the course of nature and history and were beyond the control of humans; ultimately, at the End, the divine powers would triumph, and the world would return to the paradisical state that had originally existed. In such beliefs, it was thought that the course of world history would become worse, bringing about divine intervention, resurrection of the dead, judgment of good and evil, and eternal salvation and damnation.

For Bultmann, this general way of looking at the world was "mythical." The activity of the "powers," especially of the gods, was considered on the same level as natural human activity. Apart from their exceptional powers, the gods were viewed in human terms, as acting like human beings.[32] This perception led to the following definition: "Mythology is a way of representing the otherworldly in terms of this world, the divine in terms of human life, the 'beyond' in terms of the 'near.' . . . [Myth speaks] of the other world in terms of this world and of the gods in terms derived from human life."[33] In myth, the gods and demons are conceived in terms of space (above, below), time (past, present, future), and cause and effect (interrupting the normal course of things).

Bultmann stressed that the New Testament shared this "mythical" world view. Though Jesus refrained from drawing detailed pictures, he thought that the future kingdom was already coming in his exorcisms and that it would be climaxed by a tremendous cosmic drama in which the Son of Man would come with the clouds of heaven, the dead would rise, and the judgment would follow. The early Christians also expected the kingdom to come, and Paul believed that it had already been inaugurated and that he would live to see the End. For Paul, God had already sent his Son, a preexistent divine being from heaven ("above") come to earth ("below") as a man, and that Son had died on a cross as a sinner, as a sacrifice for all others who were sinners. Through the death of this man, Adam's sin was abolished and the demonic forces were deprived of their power. This man was then raised to the right hand of God in heaven ("above"), made "Lord" and "king," and he was expected to come on the clouds to complete the work of redemption. The general resurrection and judgment would follow, and sin and death would finally be abolished. This myth was accompanied by rituals. Those who were in the church had been joined to the Lord by baptism and the Lord's supper. The Spirit was at work in them, indicating their adoption as sons of God and guaranteeing their final resurrection.

Bultmann then posed the crucial question: Cast as it is in the language of ancient apocalyptic and Gnostic redemption mythology, what possible meaning or significance can the gospel message have for modern people? Modern people do not think of space as "above" and "below," but as infinite; notions built on the three-storied universe, such as preexistence in heaven, descent to earth and from earth into hell, and ascent into heaven, have no meaning. Also, modern people understand cause and effect not as the result of uncontrollable gods and spirits who interrupt the course of nature in some miraculous fashion, but in terms of natural, physical laws which, when understood, can lead to the production of electric lights, telephones, and radios. Disease is not the product of demons to be driven out by exorcists, but of germs (sometimes) controlled by drugs prescribed by physicians. The modern person does not ascribe evil to the sin of Adam, but to human actions; neither does that person think of death as the punishment for sin, but as the inevitable natural end to life. How can a modern person believe that baptism causes an external spirit to enter into the body, or that eating food confers spiritual strength? Finally, modern people do not accept the ancient mythical view of time. Has not history refuted Jesus' belief that the kingdom would come soon and early Christian belief that Jesus himself would return soon? Why should salvation in any way be related to the death of a first-century Jew whose resurrection was perceived as a miracle? Such mythology, said Bultmann, is prescientific, the opposite of scientific thinking; it is a product of a particular historical epoch which post-Enlightenment people no longer accept; it is a false, superstitious way of thinking for the person who lives in a scientific, technological world. Bultmann concluded that to the extent that it was linked to such conceptions, the *kerygma,* or gospel message, was *"incredible to modern man, for he is convinced that the mythical view of the world is obsolete."* [34]

The task Bultmann set himself was to find a means of letting the essential proclamation of the New Testament speak to modern people without the obsolete and unbelievable mythology becoming such a barrier that no one would listen. As a Christian preacher and theologian, he was concerned that there be a way of viewing the once-for-all act of God in Jesus Christ, the incarnate, crucified, and risen one so that it might not become an affront to the intellect and might be considered seriously. In his terms, Bultmann sought to remove the false "stumbling block," the prescientific mythology, and free the true "stumbling block," the paradoxical New Testament message, the real *kerygma,* so that one could decide for or against it.

One solution was to keep the ethical teachings and abandon the eschatology. Liberals had attempted that, but Bultmann believed they had omitted the heart of the problem, the preaching message, or *kerygma,* embedded in the eschatology. *Religionsgeschichtler,* though they rightly shifted away from personal and social ethics toward the worshipping community, were inaccurate in their stress on mysticism to the exclusion of eschatology; they were also silent about the *kerygma.* Thus the problem of the Jewish and Gnostic eschatology (that is, mythology) remained.

Another solution, of course, was to accept the *kerygma* in its mythical form (as Fundamentalism did). This, however, was precisely the problem, for modern people could not do this without a sacrifice of intellectual integrity or, at best, succumbing to a form of wishful thinking that leads to a split personality—that is, accepting the scientific world view when one turns on the lights and the mythical world view when one is religious.

Bultmann's approach was to attempt an *interpretation* of the mythical statements of the *kerygma* by seeking to discover the understanding of the human condition, or human existence, that lay behind the language of New Testament myth. He called this approach "demythologizing." Here Heidegger's existentialist analysis as it was published in *Being and Time* (1927) came to his aid. [35] Heidegger was especially interested in analyzing and describing two fundamental options of human beings: true living ("authentic existence") and merely existing ("inauthentic existence"). To gain an impression of this thinking, one might consider the notion of space. It is true that humans live in the world in the sense that they have bodies which occupy space as any other object in space does. For Heidegger, however, there is a more fundamental notion of space, that is, the spheres of human activity that create concerns. Some of these are the natural concerns of survival, such as food, clothing, and shelter. But there are other concerns, such as studying and making grades, working toward success, or attempting to control the environment to make it serve humanity by science and technology. As the existentialist puts it, my existential world is not so much the world "out there," but the various spheres of meaning where I work and live. Frequently, I become too deeply concerned about these spheres of activity and become so preoccupied with "my world" that I lose sight of my possibilities for truly being. When this happens, everyday life takes over, I calculate my every move, I understand myself primarily by what "they" say about me, I live only with a trite curiosity about things, and I engage in idle chatter about mundane things. I am "lost." I am "thrown" into the round of ordinary existences, into my own little world of concerns. I experience ambiguity in my concern for "my space." I merely exist. This is "inauthentic existence."

Yet there is an alternative possibility. Some shock may cause me to develop a subtle fear that I am not on the right course. I experience an indefinable anxiety, which makes me feel as if I am not really "at home" in "my world," that my concern is not leading to my truest existence. I begin to doubt my pursuit of happiness. Without denying the reality of my ordinary concerns, I discover a deeper concern that calls into question my daily routine, and I attempt to put it into proper perspective. I perceive that I have forgotten something about the true nature of my being, and I marvel at the possibility of discovering my true self. For the moment I cease calculating, I attempt to understand myself creatively, I attempt to understand my world rather than merely being curious about it, and I replace my idle chatter with meaningful discourse. I realize that in the face of the possibility that I must decide, I really care. I decide to take my finite humanity on myself. This new freedom is my "authentic existence."

One might also consider the notion of time as Heidegger sees it. It is true that humans think of time in terms of periods and that they measure it with clocks. This is "public time." For Heidegger, however, there is a more fundamental notion of time underlying this calculated time. When the anxiety that leads to authentic existence strikes, there also occurs the threat of the end of all existence, that is, death. This is the ultimate possibility. In existentialist terms, it is the possibility that there is nothing. This future leads to an understanding of the past; the end leads to a care for the beginning. It is possible that I can forget my final end and beginning and become absorbed in my concern for what is going on now. I become complacent. I forget ultimate purpose and attempt to control the present. There is "no time to spare." My everyday concerns make me want to get control of the present, to control "my world." Then, when I awake, tomorrow will be secure. When I ignore my ultimate destiny and my past in concern for the present, I become a tool of blind fate. That is my "inauthentic existence."

Again, there is an alternative possibility. Though it is "natural" to be concerned for the present, I can also be jarred into realizing that some day I shall die; in that, I stand alone. Conscience tells me that what "they" say is not of ultimate concern. I resolve to be open to the future despite the inauthentic existence of others. I then open myself to my own future—not the future of the "world." Such a future impinges on "my present." Likewise, the past is not totally gone by, but I live out of "my past," for I was born and I am what my past decisions have made me. My present is therefore also my past and my future, all interpenetrating. In fact, the importance of any history in its several meanings is that it offers me possibilities for my own choices, my own decisions. At every point of time, I am faced with the decision either to become dominated by my world and its concerns and the time that is merely a succession of events, or to be open to the future. This openness to the future is my "authentic existence."

Bultmann found in Heidegger's analysis of human existence a contemporary language and frame of thought for understanding the meaning behind New Testament mythology. Existentialist interpretation made it possible to *internalize* the myth. Such an analysis does not project "true reality" outward into what the average person conceives to be nature (the usual notion of space) or history (the usual notion of time). What is primary is not the world as "up" or "down" or "out there," but the world as full of concerns and care, of inauthentic and authentic decisions. Likewise, it is not "time" as a progression of events in world history that is important, but the way in which one's past flows into the present and one's present into the future, the ultimate future being one's own death. Within the existentialist perspective, the eschatological and Gnostic myths of the End are transformed into one's own internalized myth.

Thus Bultmann suggested that Heidegger's "inauthentic existence" is what the New Testament calls "sin." Paul describes it as living "according to the flesh," a natural state whereby one chooses to live in the sphere of one's own interests and concerns—for example, preoccupation with sensual pleasures, pride in one's achievements, and just letting the world go by (Gal 3:3; Phil 3:4ff.). It is characterized by "boasting" (1 Cor 1:26ff.; 2 Cor 10:13ff.) and seeking the wisdom of the world (1 Cor 1–2). The Gospel of John thinks of human existence in this way when it speaks of attachment to "this world" or "this period of time." Both understand human existence as "fallen" into the world, as concern for the world, a condition characterized by a perpetual state of anxiety (1 Cor 7:32ff.). Heidegger's *theoretical* analysis of inauthentic existence, said

Bultmann, is the same as the New Testament understanding of *actual* inauthentic existence—except for one crucial difference yet to be mentioned.

In a similar fashion, Heidegger's "authentic existence" is seen in what the New Testament, specifically Paul, calls "life according to the Spirit" or "life in faith." When Paul speaks of God's free gift of grace as the forgiveness of sin, "it means faith that the unseen, intangible reality actually confronts us as love, opening up our future and signifying not death but life."[36] The orientation to the future means abandoning all security, giving up any attempt to carve out a solid "place" that one can control, surrendering self-confidence, and deciding to trust in God. This attitude of detachment from "the world" is true freedom. It is not ascetic self-denial, but living "as though" the concerns of the daily world, real as they are, did not actually exist (1 Cor 7:29–31). This is a new power, the power to become indifferent to the concerns of one's "world." It is manifested even in weakness, suffering, and death (2 Cor 4:7–11; 12:9ff.). Thus, though Paul can think of the Spirit mythically as a mysterious power entering human beings from without, his final meaning is that there is a possibility of a new life opened by faith. Such a new life is achieved by a decision, a deliberate resolve, which detaches one from "the world," delivers one finally from anxiety, and makes one capable of true fellowship (Gal 5:25). This person is a "new creature" (Gal 5:6; 6:15). A similar possibility for "new life" is found in the Gospel of John. From Paul's perspective:

> By giving up Jesus to be crucified, God has set up the cross for us. To believe in the cross of Christ does not mean to concern ourselves with a mythical process wrought outside of us and our world, with an objective event turned by God to our advantage, but rather to make the Cross of Christ our own, to undergo crucifixion with him.[37]

Furthermore, for Bultmann, Paul and John give the direction for this interpretation with their own demythologizing: The "event" is already present.

We now return to the one crucial difference between Heidegger and Bultmann, at least from Bultmann's standpoint. Heidegger thought that authentic existence is, in principle, a possibility; that is, inauthentic existence need not be inevitable, despite the fallen nature of human existence. For the New Testament, however, inauthentic existence is not only inevitable; it distorts one's perception of what authentic existence is. Simply put, the New Testament states that the fall of human existence is total and sin is inevitable. Whereas, in Heidegger's theoretical analysis, it is possible for human beings to make the transition from inauthentic existence to authentic existence in the moment of decision, Bultmann continued to assert what the New Testament proclaimed: that the transition is based on faith in an "act of God."

Is this self-confidence of the philosophers justified? Whatever the answer may be, it is at least clear that this is the point where they part company with the New Testament. For the latter affirms the total incapacity of man to release himself from his fallen state. That deliverance can come only by an act of God. The New Testament does not give as a doctrine of "nature" a doctrine of the authentic nature of man; it proclaims the event of redemption which was wrought in Christ.[38]

Here then is the crucial distinction between the New Testament and existentialism, between the Christian faith and the natural understanding of Being. The New Testament speaks and faith knows of an act of God through which man becomes capable of self-commitment, capable of faith and love, of his authentic life.[39]

But why should authentic existence take this particular form? The New Testament *kerygma,* or proclamation, is that the transition from sin to faith is rooted in the belief in an "act of God" in Christ. If sin is inauthentic existence and faith is authentic existence, does not the transition from inauthentic to authentic existence rest on a figure in time and space "out there," in world-history? Further, does it not rest on a miraculous intervention of God in that time and in that space? And is this not the very thing that Bultmann has defined as a myth? The philosopher Karl Jaspers once charged Bultmann with sliding back into the very myth that he sought to interpret; in Bultmann's view, according to Jaspers, "God localizes himself in place and time, once for all," and this is a faith that "makes God an object in the world."[40] Bultmann responded: "Does he not know that I am struggling against this very thing—fixing God as an object, and understanding revelation wrongly, as that which has been revealed?"[41]

Bultmann, of course, recognized that the New Testament related the event of redemption to an event of world history and that it gave that event a mythical framework. He also granted that many early Christians gave Jesus a mythical significance precisely because it was the real Jesus they had known as an historical person. But that did not mean that modern people could develop the same relation to Jesus. Liberal historical research had attempted to establish that relationship with Jesus, but without success.

How, then, did Bultmann attempt to show that the event of redemption is *present*? Turning to Paul, Bultmann first reduced the problem to the event of the cross. Paul not only spoke of a past event in mythical terms, that is, that the crucified one *was* the sinless, preexistent, incarnate Son of God whose sacrificial blood atoned for sin; he thought of it as an *ever-present* reality in the sacraments, in everyday life, and above all, in preaching. In the sacraments, the believer is baptized into Christ's death and is crucified with him (Rom 6:6), while the crucifixion is proclaimed at the Supper and the communicants partake of his body and blood (1 Cor 11:26; 10:16). In daily life, the believer accepts sufferings, which perfect his detachment from the world (2 Cor 4:10ff.). In preaching, the cross becomes present because it challenges hearers to be crucified with Christ.

Connected to the cross is the resurrection of Jesus, but that is also *present*. Again, the Christian believer already has a resurrected, new life in the sacraments, in daily life, and in preaching. In the sacraments, the believer has a new life through baptism (Rom 6:11); in daily life, the believer already has a new freedom from sin, however much of a struggle it is (Rom 6:11ff.; 2 Cor 13:3ff.). Most important, it is proclaimed to be new life to those who believe. The resurrection is not just a "mythical" event to prove the saving power of the cross; it is also the faith in new life in the present. For Bultmann, the meaning of God's act in Christ did not lie in a past event given mythical interpretation; it lay in the sacraments, in daily life, and most especially in the preaching that confronts human beings and challenges them to a decision.

> There is only one answer. This is the way in which the cross is proclaimed. It is always proclaimed together with the resurrection. Christ meets us in the preaching as one crucified and risen. He meets us in the word of preaching and nowhere else. The faith of Easter is just this—faith in the word of preaching . . . The word of preaching confronts us as the word of God. It is not for us to question its credentials [by historical research]. It is we who are questioned . . . In answering this question . . . , we are given an opportunity of understanding ourselves.[42]

It is therefore hardly an accident that Bultmann thought of revelation in the Gospel of John not simply as a revelation of the one "sent" by God in the past, but as the saving Word of God in the present. The "Church" then takes on special significance not as an institution of secular history to be described, but as the fellowship of believers who hear the Word proclaimed and respond to it. "In the word or preaching and there alone we meet the risen Lord."[43]

Is an "act of God" expressed in this way still a myth? Bultmann admitted that for those who choose to call any language about an "act of God" a myth, there was still myth. But he did not think that the *act of preaching* was a myth that objectifies the "facts of redemption" in the way ancient mythology did. One could not "go behind" Christian proclamation and hunt for the historical facts as a foundation for faith, however interesting that might be; neither could one prove the proclamation by belief in the resurrection. Even when the preaching of the Word contained references to a concrete historical figure from the past, it was still, paradoxically, the act of proclamation. What Bultmann wanted most of all was to remove the false "stumbling block" of the ancient mythology, which he believed interfered with communicating the true "stumbling block." It was not that there was no "stumbling block" whatever; rather, there was a "stumbling block" that modern people could see as a serious matter. This was the proclamation of the act of God in Jesus Christ, an act of preaching that challenges one to a decision.

> All these assertions are an offence (*skandalon* ["stumbling block"]), which will not be removed by philosophical discussion, but only by faith and obedience. All these are phenomena subject to historical, sociological and psychological observation, yet for faith they are all of them eschatological phenomena. It is precisely its immunity from proof which secures the Christian proclamation against the charge of being mythological. The transcendence of God is not as in myth reduced to imminence. Instead, we have the paradox of a transcendent God present and active in history: "The Word became flesh."[44]

JESUS CHRIST IN THE THOUGHT OF ERNST KÄSEMANN (THE "NEW QUEST")

For Bultmann, taking the risk of faith (his existential view of Luther's "justification by faith") in response to preaching had its intellectual parallel in taking a risk about what one could know about Jesus. One could never be *absolutely* certain: the only crucial datum for Christian faith is *the fact that* he lived in history "out there," and nothing beyond that. But how strong is the connection between the Jesus who lived and the Jesus preached by the churches? Is there a continuity between the Jesus who lived and the *kerygma* about him—both ancient and modern? Did Bultmann's approach (*the fact that* he lived) only barely make that connection? Had Bultmann not severed the Jesus who lived from the preaching?

Such questions dominated what became "the new quest of the historical Jesus."[45] The reopening of the issue in Germany is usually attributed to a gathering of "Old Marburgers" (Bultmannians) by one of Bultmann's "students," himself a professor at Tübingen, Ernst Käsemann.[46] Käsemann claimed that it is impossible to dismiss the question of the historical Jesus, since there are still Liberals who ask about it, secular historians who demand discussion of it, New Testament scholars who must face it, and most importantly, the New Testament itself, which justifies it insofar as the gospels ascribe their proclamation to a figure who lived, Jesus of Nazareth.

On the one hand, there is the history of Jesus seen as the history of the exalted Lord as well, making it impossible to understand Jesus apart from the faith of primitive Christianity ("the mythicization of history"). On the other hand, there is a narrative structure in the gospels; they do not "allow myth to take the place of history nor a heavenly being to take the place of the Man of Nazareth" (the historicization of myth).[47] Thus, for Käsemann, the gospels, especially the synoptics, rooted the eschato-logical myth in a particular history that took place in Palestine in the first century, and even the Gospel of John did not abandon it altogether. To be sure, they were interested in eschatology, not simply in the "facts"; but neither did they forget them.

> They were agreed only in one judgment: namely, that the life history of Jesus was constitutive for faith, because the earthly and the exalted Lord are identical. The Easter faith was the foundation of the Christian *kerygma* but was not the first or only source of its content. Rather, it was the Easter faith which took cognizance of the fact that God acted before we became believers, and which testified to this fact by incapsulating the earthly history of Jesus in its proclamation.[48]

For Käsemann, this meant that without the rootedness in history, the result would be a mere myth (or the ancient Christian heresy of Doce-tism, which said that Christ only seemed to become a man). To be sure, the Jesus of history was insufficient for faith and the old quest was theo-logically wrongheaded; nonetheless, as the synoptic gospels testify, faith was always tied to the Jesus of history.

Käsemann saw this dual character of the text as an embarrassment to form criticism, for (as Bultmann knew) the airtight criterion that was especially needed for distinguishing between the earliest stage of Pales-tinian primitive Christianity and the authentic Jesus material had not emerged. Yet Käsemann did produce a criterion like Bultmann's for a *minimum* amount of Jesus material where "we have more or less safe ground under our feet." This is the material that is so distinctively and uniquely different that it cannot be ascribed to the Judaism of Jesus' time, nor to the interpretation of the early church, especially where Jew-ish Christianity has clearly "re-Judaized" Jesus' bold departures from traditional Jewish teaching. From this perspective, the issue was neither what Jesus *could* have said that was like what other Jewish rabbis said, nor what Jesus *could* have said that the early church claimed he said (certainly, there were areas of overlap). The issue was, Where was his teaching *distinctive* in comparison with his environment? This criterion has become the heart of recent minimal "lives" of Jesus and today goes by the name of the "criterion of dissimilarity"; that is, it attempts to isolate material that shows Jesus as unlike both his Jewish background and his Christian followers, and then build on this material.

Käsemann, like Bultmann, wished to warn against the possibility of writing a liberal "life of Jesus." Nonetheless, he did not believe that this judgment should lead to defeatism and skepticism about the earthly Jesus, for the texts never abandoned this concern.

> The heart of our problem lies here: the exalted Lord has almost entirely swallowed up the image of the earthly Lord and yet the community main-tains the identity of the exalted Lord with the earthly. The solution of this problem cannot, however, if our findings are right, be approached with any

hope of success along the line of supposed historical *bruta facta* ["brute facts"] but only along the line of the connection and tension between the preaching of Jesus and that of his community. The question of the historical Jesus is, in its legitimate form, the question of the continuity of the Gospel within the discontinuity of the times and within the variation of the *kerygma*.[49]

Much more could be said about the "new" quest of the historical Jesus. A student of Bultmann's, Günther Bornkamm, wrote a book called *Jesus of Nazareth* to parallel Bultmann's *Jesus*. In this work Bornkamm argued that although all the stories of the gospels are molded by the faith of the church, "the gospels are a rejection of [a timeless] myth"; they justify "neither resignation nor skepticism" about the historical Jesus.[50] Another student (Hans Conzelmann) wrote a dictionary article that said much about the historical Jesus,[51] and a fourth (Ernst Fuchs) spoke of God's revelation through Jesus' conduct.[52] Still other scholars (Gerhard Ebeling and James M. Robinson) took up the discussion,[53] and some argued that the "new quest" had not advanced significantly beyond Bultmann's views (Schubert Ogden and Van Harvey).[54] At one point, Bultmann believed the discussion worthy of a response (1962).[55] As a matter of fact, more specific information about Jesus in the "new quest" looks somewhat like Ch. 1 of this book.

With the "new quest," much of the discussion within the Bultmannian camp reached a stalemate; new studies are being written, but they are either not concentrating on the historical Jesus or are taking altogether new directions. These will be mentioned in the last chapter.

SUMMARY

Bultmann was noted for many important contributions to the study of the New Testament. Three of them were form criticism, his study of Jesus, and his demythologizing program. All three were linked. Form criticism demonstrated that the Liberals in their quest for Jesus had taken a wrong path. The sources for a life of Jesus did not exist. If they did not exist, the New Testament was not interested in presenting "the historical Jesus" in the modern sense as the basis for Christian faith. Kähler had known that, and here Bultmann joined Kähler. Nonetheless, as his book on Jesus showed, something could be said about Jesus' teaching. On the one hand, Bultmann saw Jesus as an offbeat rabbi who demanded radical obedience to the will of God even when it conflicted with the law. On the other hand, Bultmann joined Weiss and, within limits, Schweitzer in seeing Jesus' kingdom teaching as eschatological. The problem was that if such teaching were taken literally, it would be unacceptable to modern man, for 2000 years of history had proven Jesus wrong. Drawing on Paul and especially John, Bultmann believed that the issue of time in the usual sense was not the crucial issue. Neither were New Testament references to space or causality. If they were to have any meaning, they must be understood existentially, that is, in reference to the individual's world of concerns and the individual's choices. For Bultmann, it was Heidegger's analysis that illuminated the understanding of existence which lay behind the New Testament myths. Thus it was possible to see that in the sacraments, daily life, and especially preaching, the believer could encounter Jesus' death and resurrection anew. Moreover, the proclamation was not tied to a mythical world view. In this proclamation context, Bultmann was willing to speak of an "act of God" that constantly happens again and again, challenging one to a decision. The true "stumbling block" was not the ancient, pre-scientific, mythical world view, but an act of God tied to Jesus. In short, the mythology was put in existentialist terms, but connection with Jesus in the *kerygma* was maintained.

After the Second World War, a number of Bultmann's students, now professors themselves, launched a "new quest" of the historical Jesus. While following Bultmann's methods closely, they believed that the synoptic gospels were more interested in history than Bultmann's focus on "the fact that he lived" would allow. Thus they were willing to say more about the "life" of Jesus, though the extent of their advance over Bultmann's conclusions has been debated. At any rate, their concern was to narrow the gap between the Jesus of history and the Christ of faith. Bultmann's response was that there is a continuity between the Jesus of history and *beliefs about* the Christ of faith; there could be no continuity between a human Jesus and a supernatural Christ—as far as the historian is concerned.

NOTES

1. For a general survey, see Alasdair MacIntyre, "Existentialism," in *The Encyclopedia of Philosophy,* 3 vols. (New York: Macmillan Co. and the Free Press, 1967), vol. 3, pp. 147–54.

2. Robert C. Solomon, ed., "Introduction," in *Existentialism* (New York: Modern Library, 1974), pp. ix–x.

3. Carl E. Braaten, "Revelation, History, and Faith in Martin Kähler," in Martin Kähler, *The So-Called Historical Jesus and the Historic Biblical Christ,* trans. Carl E. Braaten (Philadelphia: Fortress Press, 1964), pp. 1–45 (originally published in 1896).

4. *Theologe und Christ, Erinnerungen und Bekenntnisse von Martin Kähler,* ed. Anna Kähler (Berlin, 1926), p. 89, in Kähler, *Historical Jesus,* p. 5.

5. Ibid., p. 102.

6. Ibid.; for the conflict between Kähler and Herrmann, see Robert Voelkel, "Introduction," in Wilhelm Herrmann, *The Communion of the Christian with God,* trans. J. Sandys Stanton and revised from the 4th German edition by R. W. Stewart in 1906 (Philadelphia: Fortress Press, 1971), pp. xxxvii–xlii.

7. Kähler, *Historical Jesus,* p. 103.

8. Ibid., pp. 48–49.

9. Ibid., p. 80, note 11.

10. Ibid., p. 53.

11. Ibid., p. 43.

12. Ibid., pp. 121–22.

13. Rudolf Karl Bultmann, "Autobiographical Reflections," in *Existence and Faith: Shorter Writings of Rudolf Bultmann,* ed. Schubert M. Ogden (New York: Meridian Books, Living Age Books, 1960), pp. 283–88; see also Walter Schmithals, *An Introduction to the Theology of Rudolf Bultmann,* trans. John Bowden (Minneapolis: Augsburg Publishing House, 1968), pp. 1–21; Norman Perrin, *The Promise of Bultmann,* Promise of Theology Series (Philadelphia: J. B. Lippincott Co., 1969), pp. 16–21.

14. Bultmann, "Autobiography," in *Existence and Faith,* p. 283.

15. Rudolf Bultmann, "The Task of Theology in the Present Situation," in Ogden, *Existence and Faith,* p. 165.

16. "Criticism" frequently has a pejorative ring in English (even when it is constructive). "Form history" would be more accurate, but still does not fit the need. "Form criticism" as a name follows in the steps of "Literary criticism" in English, a historical method that concentrated on sources and style in their written forms.

17. The scholarly work is Rudolf Bultmann, *The History of the Synoptic Tradition,* trans. John Marsh, 2nd ed. (Oxford: Basil Blackwell, 1968) (German 2nd ed. published in 1931); for short studies, see Bultmann, "The Study of the Synoptic Gospels," in Rudolf Bultmann and Karl Kundsin, *Form Criticism,* trans. Frederick C. Grant (New York: Harper & Brothers, Torchbooks, 1963), pp. 11–76 (published in German in 1934); Edgar V. McKnight, *What Is Form Criticism?* Guides to Biblical Scholarship Series (Philadelphia: Fortress Press, 1969).

18. Rudolf Bultmann, *Jesus and the Word,* trans. Louise Pettibone Smith and Erminie Huntress Lantero (New York: Charles Scribner's Sons, 1958, p. 8 (originally published in German in 1926).

19. Rudolf Bultmann, "The Primitive Christian Kerygma and the Historical Jesus," in Carl E. Braaten and Roy A. Harrisville, eds., and trans., *The Historical Jesus and the Kerygmatic Christ* (Nashville: Abingdon Press, 1964), pp. 22–23.

20. Bultmann, *Jesus and the Word,* p. 12.

21. Ibid., pp. 13–14.

22. Bultmann, *Jesus and the Word;* see note 18.

23. Ibid., p. 77.

24. Ibid., pp. 83–84 (with one phrase slightly revised).

25. Ibid., p. 79.

26. Ibid., p. 122.

27. Ibid., p. 149.

28. Ibid., p. 211.

29. As with form criticism, the literature is vast. Bultmann's 1941 essay may now be found in Hans Werner Bartsch, *Kerygma and Myth,* revised translation by Reginald H. Fuller (New York: Harper & Row,

Torchbooks, 1961), pp. 1–44. This essay along with comments by five critics, makes up vol. 1, originally published in hardback by S.P.C.K.; vol 2 in hardback (London: S.P.C.K., 1962) has comments by more critics. The best primary source in English is Rudolf Bultmann, *Jesus Christ and Mythology* (New York: Charles Scribner's Sons, 1958), from lectures delivered in the United States. For secondary sources, see John Macquarrie, *An Existentialist Theology: A Comparison of Heidegger and Bultmann* (New York: Harper & Row, Torchbooks, 1955); *The Scope of Demythologizing: Bultmann and His Critics* (New York: Harper & Row, Torchbooks, 1960); "Rudolf Bultmann" in Marty and Peerman, *A Handbook of Christian Theologians*, pp. 445–63; Charles W. Kegley, ed., *The Theology of Rudolf Bultmann* (New York: Harper & Row, 1966); Thomas F. O'Meara, O.P., and Donald M. Weisser, O.P., *Rudolf Bultmann in Catholic Thought* (New York: Herder & Herder, 1968); James Smart, *The Divided Mind of Modern Theology* (Philadelphia: Westminster Press, 1967); Roger A. Johnson, *The Origins of Demythologizing* (Leiden: E. J. Brill, 1973); "Rudolf Bultmann: Beyond the Conflict of Science and Religion: An Existential Faith," in Roger A. Johnson et al., *Critical Issues in Modern Religion* (Englewood Cliffs, N.J.: Prentice-Hall, 1973).

30. Bultmann, "New Testament and Mythology," in *Kerygma and Myth*, pp. 1–44.

31. Bultmann, *Jesus Christ and Mythology;* see note 29.

32. Bultmann was frequently criticized for his view of myth. He responded that he was more concerned with the conception than the term. Yet he did use that term, and since his definitions were not always consistent, much discussion has centered on them.

33. Bultmann, "New Testament and Mythology," p. 10 and note 2; the translation is Bowden's in Schmithals, *Introduction*, p. 251.

34. Bultmann, "New Testament and Mythology," p. 3.

35. See Marjorie Grene, "Heidegger, Martin," in *The Encyclopedia of Philosophy*, vol. 3, pp. 459–65; the basic work is Martin Heidegger, *Being and Time*, trans. John Macquarrie & Edward Robinson (New York: Harper & Row, 1962); for an interpretation, see Thomas Langan, *The Meaning of Heidegger* (New York: Columbia University Press, 1959); for Bultmann's relationship to Heidegger, see especially Macquarrie, *An Existentialist Theology*, and secondary works in note 29.

36. Bultmann, "New Testament and Mythology," p. 19.

37. Ibid., p. 36.

38. Ibid., p. 27.

39. Ibid., p. 33.

40. Karl Jaspers, "Myth and Religion," in Karl Jaspers and Rudolf Bultmann, *Myth and Christianity*, trans. Norbert Guterman (New York: Noonday Press, 1958), p. 41; see the discussion in Schmithals, *Introduction*, p. 163, from which this translation is taken.

41. Jaspers and Bultmann, *Myth and Christianity*, p. 67.

42. Bultmann, "New Testament and Mythology," p. 41.

43. Ibid., p. 43.

44. Ibid., p. 44.

45. Chapter 1 is highly indebted to researches by Bultmann and to the "new quest."

46. Ernst Käsemann, "The Problem of the Historical Jesus," in *Essays on New Testament Themes*, Studies in Biblical Theology, no. 41, trans. W. J. Montague (Naperville, Ill.: Alec R. Allenson, 1964), pp. 15–47.

47. Ibid., p. 25.

48. Ibid., pp. 33–34.

49. Ibid., p. 46.

50. Günther Bornkamm, *Jesus of Nazareth,* trans. Irene and Fraser McLuskey with James M. Robinson (New York: Harper & Row, 1960).

51. Hans Conzelmann, *Jesus,* trans. J. Raymond Lord (Philadelphia: Fortress Press, 1973).

52. Ernst Fuchs, "The Quest of the Historical Jesus," in *Studies of the Historical Jesus,* Studies in Biblical Theology, no. 42, trans. Andrew Scobie (London: SCM Press, 1964), pp. 11–31.

53. Gerhard Ebeling, "The Question of the Historical Jesus and the Problem of Christology," in *Word and Faith,* trans. James W. Leitch (Philadelphia: Fortress Press, 1960), pp. 288–304; James M. Robinson, *A New Quest of the Historical Jesus* (London: SCM Press, 1959).

54. Van A. Harvey and Schubert M. Ogden, "How New is the 'New Quest of the Historical Jesus'?" in Carl E. Braaten and Roy A. Harrisville, *The Historical Jesus and the Kerygmatic Christ* (New York: Abingdon Press, 1964), pp. 197–242.

55. Rudolf Bultmann, "The Primitive Christian Kerygma and the Historical Jesus," in Braaten and Harrisville, *Historical Jesus,* pp. 15–42.

Some Current Approaches to Jesus Christ

The quest for the historical Jesus was inevitable. The Jesus who lived was rooted in the biblical narratives and confessions; Church doctrines affirmed that he was truly human; Protestant thinkers sought to return to the simple human Jesus of the New Testament (*sola scriptura*); the rationalists sought a human Jesus devoid of the miraculous; and Strauss's skepticism demanded a response from historians. Hence F. C. Baur, the "father of historical theology," began with Jesus' historical reality; in Baur's footsteps walked all those who desired to remove the layers of historical–doctrinal accretion and arrive at the real historical Jesus. Renan's romantic portrait, Harnack's Liberal portrait, Mathew's socially oriented portrait, and the eschatological portraits of Weiss, Schweitzer, and Loisy all sought to find that Jesus in the synoptic gospels, and especially in Mark. By the late nineteenth and early twentieth centuries, even those who defended creedal orthodoxy, such as Machen, or orthodox piety, such as Kähler, had to contend with history, the former by claiming history had been doctrinal from the very beginning, the latter by using historical skepticism as a launching pad for returning to the Christ of faith. Finally, though Bultmann spoke of the mere "fact" that Christ lived, Bultmann ranks as an excellent historian who wrote a book about "Jesus," and the post-Bultmannian "new questers" went further in their reconsideration of the historical Jesus.

Historical study of the New Testament texts about Jesus Christ continues, as can be seen in three major areas of research: redaction criticism, the method of trajectories, and social historiography.

REDACTION CRITICISM

Whereas form criticism seeks to categorize the small units or paragraphs and to trace their history through the oral tradition of the very earliest churches (*Sitze im Leben*), *redaction criticism* builds on the results of form criticism and attempts to establish the

> theological motivation of an author [German: *Redaktor*, "editor"] as this is revealed in the collection, arrangement, editing, and modification of traditional material, and in the composition of new material or the creation of new forms within the traditions of early Christianity.[1]

Form criticism isolates the material that came to the Evangelists, and redaction criticism works with the Evangelist's use and interpretation of that tradition. Whereas the former stresses the parts, the latter stresses the whole.

The redaction-critical method can be illustrated in the accounts of Jesus' baptism:

Mt 3:13–17	*Mark 1:9–11*	*Luke 3:21–22*
13) Then Jesus came from Galilee to the Jordan to John, to be baptized by him. 14) John would have prevented him, saying, "I need to be baptized by you, and do you come to me?" 15) But Jesus answered him, "Let it be so now; for thus it is fitting for us to fulfill all righteousness." Then he consented.	9) In those days Jesus came from Nazareth of Galilee	21) Now when all the people were baptized
16) And when Jesus was baptized, he went up immediately from the water, and behold, the heavens were opened and he saw the Spirit of God descending like a dove and alighting on him; 17) and lo, a voice from heaven, saying, "This is my beloved Son, with whom I am well pleased."	and was baptized by John in the Jordan. 10) And when he came up out of the water, immediately he saw the heavens opened and the Spirit descending upon him like a dove; 11) and a voice came from heaven, "Thou art my beloved Son; with thee I am well pleased."	and when Jesus also had been baptized and was praying, the heaven was opened, 22) and the Holy Spirit descended upon him in bodily form, as a dove, and a voice came from heaven, "Thou art my beloved Son; with thee I am well pleased."

The compact Markan narrative follows the statement about John's baptizing as a "baptism of repentance for the forgiveness of sins" (Mark 1:4). Presumably, Mark does not think Jesus is a sinner, but he makes no comment. We are left with the impression that Jesus is alone and that the descent of the Spirit and the voice from the split heavens, which are signs for the breaking in of the time of salvation in Jewish apocalyptic (T. Levi 18; T. Judah 24), mark Jesus' official adoption as the royal "Son of God." The redaction critic will want to see, if possible, the extent to which Mark composed this passage (out of his own imagination, so to speak) and the way it functions in the Gospel of Mark as a whole. The former is difficult, because Mark's sources are hypothetically reproduced by form-critical analysis; in this case, he is probably drawing on tradition. The latter is much clearer. In the gospel as a whole, it is said that this will be a gospel about the "Son of God" (Mark 1:1), that Jesus is acclaimed "Son of God" by a Gentile (!) at the end (Mark 15:39), that he is proclaimed "Son of God" by implication in the middle, at the Transfiguration (Mark 9:7). Another set of texts associate this designation with Jesus' miracle-working activity as a "divine man" and with the Messianic Secret (e.g., Mark 3:11; 5:7). Among the remaining "Son of God" passages is Mark 14:61ff., where the title is linked with the name "Son of Man." The point is that this is a very important title for Mark, and in the baptism, Jesus' public ministry is launched by his adoption as God's son in language from the royal psalms about the "divine" king.[2]

Though in theory it is possible to look at Matthew's and Luke's versions of the story without reference to Mark, those redaction critics who hold the two-source theory (that Matthew and Luke had access to, and used, Mark and Q) will think in terms of Matthew's and Luke's modifications of Mark as well as such matters as placement of the passage, compositional technique, and form. One must also consider the possibility that parallel texts have been cross-fertilized, that is, altered during centuries of handwritten transmission. Generally, however, redaction critics believe that the questions of textual reliability are sufficiently answered so that they can be disregarded in making judgments about similarities and differences.

Apart from variations about the Jordan River, the reassurance that the Spirit literally alighted on Jesus, and the words of the voice from Isaiah 42:1 and Psalm 2:7, the glaring difference is Matthew's preparation for the baptism by the dialogue between John and Jesus. In verse 13, Jesus *intends* to be baptized by John. Why? After all, Jesus was already a "child of the Holy Spirit" (Mt 1:18); or should it be thought that Jesus came to John confessing his sins like the others (Mt 3:5), or that Jesus was inferior to John? Why was Jesus baptized? The dialogue gives the answer: "It is fitting for us to fulfill all righteousness," says Jesus. In contrast to the other gospels, "righteousness" is one of Matthew's favorite terms (Mark does not have it; Luke has it only in 1:75; Matthew has it seven times). For Matthew, it means conduct that is in accord with God's will and therefore pleasing to God.[3] That Jesus comes after John and is baptized by him accords with God's plan: The Messiah and judge of the world humbles himself and becomes like the sinners. To be sure, the fact that Jesus is the Son of God is important for Matthew;[4] but it is also important to indicate why Jesus would be baptized at all. Thus, not only will one note the place that Matthew's view of the Son of God holds in relation to the rest of the gospel, just as in Mark, but one will determine why Matthew has such a different version of this story in particular.

A similar comparison is made with Luke. Luke makes it quite clear that the beginning of the public ministry occurs after John is imprisoned (Lk 3:19). This accords with Luke's general view of history: the period of Israel, including John the Baptist; the period of Jesus' ministry ("the middle of time"); and the period of the church in the world, which looks back to Jesus' ministry and forward to the End, when Jesus will return. So John belongs with the period of Israel; Jesus begins a new phase of history. It is also significant that Luke follows the description of Jesus' baptism with the genealogy of Jesus (Luke 3:23–28), which in turn is followed by the temptation (Luke 4:1–13). (In contrast, Matthew places the genealogy at the very beginning [Mt 1:2–16].) Luke has inserted his genealogy here because it further testifies to the fact that Jesus is the Son of God: In contrast to Matthew, who traces Jesus' lineage back to Abraham, Luke reverses the order and takes Jesus' lineage beyond Abraham to Adam, "the Son of God" (Luke 3:38). Likewise, Luke's temptation story begins and ends with the temptation of the Son of God (Luke 4:3, 9). In short, Luke's context for the baptism indicates more fully than either Mark or Matthew that Jesus is the Son of God, and again this will be compared to the place of the name "Son of God" in the gospel as a whole.

Within the baptism story, Jesus appears as one of the people who, as in the previous episodes (Luke 3:7, 10, 15), has come out to be baptized. In contrast to the impressions given in Mark and Matthew, Jesus is at least preceded by others, if he is not with them. Furthermore, Jesus then prays (Luke 3:21). This reference is characteristic of Luke's Jesus, for before every crucial turning point in the gospel, Jesus is at prayer (here; at the choice of the twelve disciples [6:12]; before Peter's confession of Jesus' messiahship [9:18]; at the Transfiguration [9:28]; before teaching the Lord's Prayer [11:1]; and in the garden of Gethsemane before the arrest [22:41]). In Luke's version, then, Jesus' individual baptism is not so important as in the other gospels, and the descent of the Spirit is highlighted. Not only does Luke point to the role of the Spirit in more than a dozen passages, but there is an analogy between the descent of the Spirit on Jesus in Luke's first book and the descent of the

Spirit on the early church in Luke's second book (Acts 1:5; 2). As a result of Luke's modifications, the baptism marks the first major event of the second major period of history (the public ministry of Jesus), and in the baptism story the one who prays receives the Spirit and becomes the Son of God.

Redaction criticism is in many respects a literary and structural method; it analyzes the parts in relation to the whole. Thus it is used not in a quest for the historical Jesus, but to establish with greater precision the images or portraits of Jesus in the gospels. To this extent, redaction critics push beyond the bounds of purely historical criticism into the territory of general literary criticism, and there is a sense in which their method might be called a "boundary discipline." Nonetheless, redaction criticism arose as a successor to form criticism and built on its results. The results of redaction criticism might be seen as the conclusion of form criticism, or as an author's contribution in a new *Sitz im Leben*. It should also be clear that the more material is ascribed to the author (the redaction), the less material is ascribed to the tradition; the method directly affects the attempt to write a history of tradition. Consequently most scholars, especially those who are exploring even less historical methods, tend to see redaction criticism as an extension of the historical-critical consciousness.

THE METHOD OF TRACING TRAJECTORIES

The term "trajectory" is usually associated with the curving path taken by a body in space, such as a planet or a rocket. In general, the critical method of trajectories is an attempt to capture the process whereby a series of interacting developments take place simultaneously, each of which might have had a different point of departure and ultimately a different destination. The charting of a number of such trajectories is the means to illuminating any one of them. Thus one might follow the course of a particular rite, or a form of literature, or a tradition, taking into account the broader cultural contexts. Furthermore, these contexts themselves are not static entities but are on the move. *Trajectories Through Early Christianity,* a series of studies by James M. Robinson and Helmut Koester, attempts in a variety of ways to trace such trajectories in Christian literature.[5] The assumption is that such categories as "Judaism" and "Hellenism" have been wrongly conceived as static entities, as cultural "background," as though an unchanging, fixed essence were involved. Robinson suggests that this is a legacy from an obsolete metaphysics:

> It is precisely the historic consciousness of modern times that has drawn attention to the inadequacy of the essentialist categorization of

science. This historic consciousness has of course also led to modern historiography, whose results have been a catalyst in accelerating the prevalence of historic thinking. Yet these results have been impeded by the burden of conceptualizations inherited from ahistoric metaphysics.

. . . As a result of the dawn of historic consciousness, New Testament studies shifted away from providing authoritative documentation for revealed eternal truth. . . . Gradually the historic in the text became of interest in its own right, and the changelessly monolithic divine eternal truth gave way to a history of dogma, a process in the history of ideas.[6]

What *Trajectories Through Early Christianity* attempts to do is to carry through the radical historical consciousness and overcome the crisis in scholarship that has been caused by the obsolete metaphysics.

Koester gives an example of an attempt to trace trajectories in "One Jesus and Four Primitive Gospels,"[7] in which he attempts to show how various "gospel" forms not made canonical in the Church (and now collected in the New Testament Apocrypha) had prototypes in the period before the writing of the gospels that did become canonical. This study is important for the problem of the historical Jesus because it raises the question whether such "pregospel gospels" reflect Christian beliefs more consonant with Jesus of Nazareth or his teachings. This question is especially important because these "pregospel gospels" do not reflect the emphasis on the passion and resurrection so characteristic of the gospels that were eventually accepted as canonical. Moreover, the historical Jesus is not their major concern.

Koester first draws on Robinson's attempt to trace a trajectory of the form of literature that collects "sayings of wise men."[8] Robinson noted that such collections were found in Egypt and Mesopotamia, then in both canonical and noncanonical Jewish writings (Proverbs, Ecclesiastes; Sayings of the Fathers; apocalypses such as the Similitudes of Enoch, the Apocalypse of Adam, and the Testaments of the Twelve Patriarchs), then in early Christian collections of Jesus' sayings (Q; the parables in Mark 4; the exhortations in the *Didache;* Jesus' teachings ordered in speeches by the Gospel of Matthew), and finally in Gnostic collections of Jesus' teachings, especially the Coptic Gospel of Thomas from Nag Hammadi in Egypt. What struck Koester was that the Gospel of Thomas has many Q sayings of Jesus of the type that form criticism called "prophetic and apocalyptic sayings," but that it contains no future apocalyptic Son of Man sayings or elaborate apocalyptic predictions characteristic of Mark 13. Since Thomas does have kingdom sayings, and since these focus on the presentness of the kingdom for the believer, it may be that this "sayings gospel" continues Jesus' original emphasis on the kingdom, namely, its *presence already* for the believer. A similar conclusion is made about many parables in Thomas which Koester judges are earlier *in form* than those in the synoptic gospels and which "are never understood as eschatological parables but rather as admonitions to find the mysterious treasure in Jesus' words and in one's own self."[9] Koester also analyzes "I-sayings," "wisdom sayings and proverbs," and "rules for the community" in Thomas with less speculation about whether the material might go back to Jesus. However, this is not Koester's main point. What is most significant is that the material represents a "gospel" of *sayings,* not a passion–resurrection gospel, and that its roots are primitive:

> The basis of the *Gospel of Thomas* is a sayings collection which is more primitive than the canonical gospels, even though its basic principle is not related to the creed of the passion and resurrection. Its principle is nonetheless theological. *Faith is understood as belief in Jesus' words, a belief which makes what Jesus proclaimed present and real for the believer.* The catalyst which has caused the crystallization of these sayings into a "gospel" is the view that the kingdom is uniquely present in Jesus' eschatological preaching and that eternal wisdom about man's true self is disclosed in his words. The gnostic proclivity of this concept needs no further elaboration.
>
> The relation of this "sayings gospel," from which the *Gospel of Thomas* is derived, to the synoptic sayings source Q, is an open question. . . .[10]

In addition to a pregospel "sayings gospel," Koester is interested in a pregospel "miracle gospel" and its particular rationale. This is the question of the aretalogy mentioned in Ch. 2.[11] Koester generally accepts that behind the Gospels of John and Mark lie collections of stories of Jesus' miracles and that in them Jesus is characterized as a "divine man" who works miracles as a sign of his divine power, a conclusion indicated by the original ending of John's miracle source: "Now Jesus did many other signs in the presence of his disciples, which are not written in this book; but these are written down that you may believe that Jesus is the Christ, the Son of God . . ." (John 20:30–31). And as those followers who put forth this view believe that Jesus has divine power, so they believe that they are recipients of this divine power (2 Cor, esp. chs. 10–13). Except for the "infancy gospels," which attempt to demonstrate Jesus' miraculous power as a child, the miracle gospels did not survive but were taken up into the type of gospel that became canonical.

Koester develops still a third "pregospel gospel," the "revelation gospel," characterized by a secret revelation of Jesus to his disciples on a mountain. Such a literary genre can be traced behind the apocalyptic speeches of Jesus, especially in the Book of Revelation, the "little apocalypse" of Mark 13, and the "farewell discourse" of John 13–17. At the other end of the trajectory there are Gnostic revelation discourses such as the *Apocryphon of John.*

All three types of gospels were taken up into what became the canonical gospel form, a unique creation of Mark, stressing Jesus' death and resurrection. As it developed further, it included Jesus' birth and infancy as well (Matthew, Luke). Indeed, the gospel and the creeds of orthodoxy grew together, so that these elements in Jesus' story were further combined with the myths of preexistence, virgin conception by Mary, resurrection, descent into hell, and ascension into heaven. Consequently the trajectories of the "sayings gospel," the "miracle gospel," and the "revelation gospel" continued, but not within what became orthodoxy, for orthodoxy had absorbed them *within* the canonical gospels.

The study of trajectories is inherently historical and continues to shed light on development of forms of literature about Jesus, as well as possible connections with Jesus himself.

SOCIAL HISTORIOGRAPHY

A third example of continuing interest in history and historical methods in approaching the sources about Jesus Christ is found in *social historiography*. But it should be pointed out that, like redaction criticism, this is a "boundary discipline" that moves away from traditional historical approaches. A good example of this approach is found in John Gager's study *Kingdom and Community*.[12] Gager acknowledges that earlier scholars such as Shailer Mathews, Shirley Jackson Case, and certain of the *Religionsgeschichtler* had a social orientation to Jesus and early Christianity. However, at that time sociology and social theory were in their infancy, and (what is in retrospect more obvious) most Christian historians sacrificed historical rigor to their theological defense of the uniqueness of Jesus and/or early Christianity in their social environments. Even the form critics, who appeared so radical and, to some, destructively critical, did not make use of social-anthropological studies of the transmission of oral tradition in nonliterate societies or the psychology of rumor formation and transmission.[13] Today, suggests Gager, it is easier and most likely for historians of early Christianity and social scientists to exchange ideas.

At the most general level, Gager focuses not on the traditional historian's interest, the uniqueness of nonrepeatable events through time, but on the recurrent patterns of social phenomena that can be compared cross-culturally. One selects data, classifies it, compares it with other data, abstracts a theory, and tests it with more data. Gager identifies Peter Berger as an important sociologist who thinks that all societies are products of human attempts to establish meaning, truth, values, goals, duties, social roles, and so on, and to adapt, maintain, and legitimize these things. The process of establishing them is *world-construction*," and their perpetuation is *world-maintenance*. Without such activities there is no society. Moreover, one of the activities that supports world-construction and world-maintenance is religion, "the human enterprise by which a sacred cosmos [world] is established."[14] Religion grounds the society in the realm of the sacred, the eternal nature of things. A new religion will necessarily participate more in world-construction; an established religion will necessarily participate more in world-maintenance. Given this general premise, Gager proposes as a method

> to examine specific problems in terms of theoretical models from recent work in the social sciences. In each case the model has been formulated independently of Christian evidence. My procedure will be to test them against information based on early Christian documents.[15]

Gager's proposal can be illustrated with his comparison of early Christianity with "millenarian movements" around the world, especially the "cargo cults" of the Pacific islands, which attempt by strange and exotic rites to gain possession of European manufactured goods. Such movements, according to I. C. Jarvie,[16] have four common traits: (1) the promise that heaven will soon come to earth; (2) the reversal or overthrow of the current social order; (3) the release of strong emotional energies; and (4) the limited duration of the movement. To these traits Gager adds one that is frequently discussed by students of the millenarian cults: (5) the appearance of a prophetic, charismatic, or messianic leader. Gager assumes that early Christianity fits this general picture, with the exception that Jarvie's fourth trait in the case of Christianity did not apply—but only because Christianity ceased to be a millenarian cult in the strictest sense. Gager also gives a word of caution about the fifth trait:

> For the early Christians, the figure of Jesus stood at the center of their world. In speaking of that world, it is impossible to avoid speaking about him. But our present concern is not with the historical Jesus, i.e., with what he "really" said and did. Thus when we refer to Jesus' words and actions in what follows, we do not mean to imply that they are to be taken as authentic. Instead we will be focusing on *images* of Jesus in the literature of early Christianity. Often these images will correspond to real moments in the life of Jesus, but for present purposes this correspondence is not germane. Our chief concern will be to emphasize the extent to which the role of Jesus as portrayed in the Gospels conforms to the role of the millenarian prophet as one who articulates aspirations in such a way that a visible movement will erupt from a bed of amorphous discontent.[17]

Thus, like redaction criticism and the method of trajectories, social historiography does not make the quest of the historical Jesus its major consideration. Rather, it raises the question how the biblical images of Jesus compare to the theoretical model of the millenarian prophet. Here a word should be said about that particular aspect of Gager's study.

Students of millenarian cults have noted especially two traits that characterize the millenarian prophet.[18] First, such a figure either is able to articulate a system of rewards or benefits limited to a special "in-group," which shares traditional assumptions with the "out-group" (for example, the notion of a chosen people), or is able to express a new set of values that challenges traditional assumptions altogether. To put it bluntly, the millenarian prophet challenges "the system." To the followers the prophet is believed to have charisma; he is believed by them to exert a powerful influence among them, teaching them that they will receive the benefits of traditional values or that a new set of values must occur. The second trait of the millenarian prophet is that he himself becomes the symbol of the "new man," or the new state of existence. By means of the "life" of the prophet, whose authority is sometimes increased by death, imprisonment, or some mysterious disappearance, the followers are able to interpret their own struggles and aspirations.

Gager's proposal is that the gospel images of Jesus fit the model of the millenarian prophet.[19] In his interpretation of Scripture, Jesus reverses the traditional Pharisaic notion that the pious are the chosen ones while "tax collectors and sinners" are outsiders (new values; a new "in-group"); as a result, he is claimed to have prophetic charisma (e.g., Mark 1:22: "he taught them as one who had authority, and not as the scribes"; cp. 1:27). Likewise, in his purification of the temple and prophecy of its destruction he challenges the Sadducees' priestly authority; as a result there emerges a new community (one could say, a "temple not made with hands") with its own rites and moral standards, and Jesus is seen as the "new man," the one whose life is the measure of the redemption to come in the millennium. As examples, Gager suggests two texts that were important in the "new quest" discussion: "For whoever is ashamed of me and of my words in this adulterous and sinful generation, of him will the Son of man also be ashamed, when he comes in the glory of his Father with the holy angels" (Mark 8:38; cp. Luke 9:26); and "And I tell you, every one who acknowledges me before men, the Son of man will acknowledge before the angels of God; but he who denies me before men will be denied before the angels of God" (Luke 12:8–9). The way one responds to Jesus will be the measure of the way the Son of Man will respond in the millennium.

Jesus' death further enhanced his authority. When the kingdom did not come as he promised, the new community did not collapse but, like many millenarian groups, undertook zealous missionary activity as a response to its disappointed hopes and as a way of reinforcing its convictions. Nonetheless Jesus' followers felt uneasy because of their unfulfilled expectations. This tension, suggests Gager, was resolved by a myth that alternated between the symbols of oppression and despair on the one hand and the symbols of victory and hope on the other: the myth of the Book of Revelation, which alternates between beasts, plagues, Satan, etc., on the one hand, and the Lamb, the elders, the New Jerusalem, etc., on the other. The myth culminates in the vision of the new heaven and the new earth (Rev 21:1–22:5).

A CRISIS IN THE HISTORICAL CONSCIOUSNESS OF THE WEST?

Gager's suggestion that the early Christian community developed a myth as a response to its despair about the realities of history has a touch of irony about it, for one of his authorities for this function of myth is Mircea Eliade, who has raised serious questions about the "historical consciousness" that has come to dominate much of Western thinking.[20] Whereas Gager applies Eliade's analysis to a period of history that he studies as a historian, Eliade himself applies his analysis to the period of history in which he lives. Another of Gager's analysts of myth, Claude Lévi-Strauss, has made his strongest impact on various fields by his nonhistorically oriented "structuralist" methods. The importance of Lévi-Strauss for new approaches to Jesus Christ will be considered later; for the moment, as a transition, a further word should be said about Eliade.

Mircea Eliade is a major exponent of the field called *the history of religions*.[21] Scholars in this field attempt as a preliminary step to study the history of particular religions, but they are ultimately more interested in comparing the phenomena of religions cross-culturally, including religions of nonliterate societies whose histories are difficult or impossible to trace. Thus the historical and comparative data are gathered, empirically investigated, and generalized, frequently with the aid of other fields such as archeology, anthropology, psychology, sociology, philosophy, and literary criticism. Though it is descriptive in intention, it is also sympathetic to religion, and historians of religion believe that religion has the right to be studied on its own terms. In these interests, the study of the history of religions has not limited itself to historical methods.

Eliade, highly influenced by the religions of nonliterate societies, believes that modern Western civilization is in many respects on the wrong track, for it is in danger of losing its spiritual moorings.[22] Thus there is an increasing sense among Westerners of the "terror of history": Tiny countries are caught in the power struggles of great nations; nuclear energy is potentially destructive of all; human control of the environment may result in its ultimate destruction, and so on. Since many people increasingly see no reason or purpose to these events, skepticism is rampant. Many people feel that "nothing really matters." The pressure of historical events causes a despair that is not overcome by the intensification of the "historical consciousness" itself. Eliade suggests that such despair might be overcome with an ultimate reference beyond history in "archetypal patterns," that is, universal patterns of meaning which can be repeated and which give meaning and coherence to life, just as myth is enacted in ritual. With this background, Eliade wishes

> to confront "historical man" (modern man), who consciously and voluntarily creates history, with the man of the traditional civilizations, who . . . had a negative attitude toward history.[23]

Such a confrontation with Western "historical consciousness" is not new. Eliade notes in passing those philosophers and philosophers of history who have opposed the progressive "linearism" of the "historical consciousness," such as Friedrich Nietzsche (1844–1900), Oswald Spengler (1880–1936), and Arnold Toynbee (1889–1975). In one way or another, these thinkers have proposed the theory that there are great patterns of history which repeat themselves. Toynbee, for example, suggested that such patterns of rise, growth, and decline were "mythical" and that such patterned myths portray the drama of the individual's inner life. Eliade comments on these authors:

> Basically, it may be said that it is only in the cyclical theories of modern times that the meaning of the archaic myth of eternal repetition realizes its full implications.[24]

From this perspective, historical explanation itself may be mythical!

Whether or not one accepts Eliade's judgment, it is clear that there are those who are examining Jesus Christ in a nonhistorical manner. Three examples of the nonhistorical approach follow: structuralism, analytical psychology, and an attack on historical criticism by one interested in the sociology of knowledge and in analytical psychology.

STRUCTURALISM

Structuralism is a method of interpretation that emerged from the study of the structures of language-systems.[25] There is a widespread philosophical point of view that human beings can be distinguished from the animals by language and that language makes more complex social relationships possible. Human beings have the capacity to abstract the ideas of emotions, things, and events they experience and to name them with word-symbols. For example, the idea of something upon which one sits can be designated by the word "chair." In a language there is developed a *system* of signs that makes it possible to speak in more complicated ways (sentences, paragraphs, etc.), and such a system is the prerequisite for thinking. When the linguist tries to understand how the parts of the language go together to make up the whole "structure," the major concern is not the history of the language—how it grew and developed over a period of time—but the way the structure looks at one particular moment. When a student learns a language, he or she does not normally treat it as a changing, developing organism, but as a fixed structure of dictionary definitions, noun declensions, verb paradigms, and grammatical relations. Similarly, the structuralist is not concerned with the historian's history, with "through-time" (*diachronic*) realities, but with structures, with a whole reality seen "all together at once in a slice of time" (a *synchronic* reality).

There are several levels to structure; that is, there are several structures that relate to language and human thinking. The structuralist acknowledges that speaking involves an *intent* to communicate something in a specific situation. There are also the limitations of the specific language, which are conditioned by the culture and its thought patterns, both of which normally lie beneath the level of consciousness in the act of communication. However, the structuralist thinks that these are rooted in a more fundamental structure of the unconscious mind, which characterizes the thinking, communicating human being. One linguist, Roman Jakobson, believes that all language, learning, and development in human beings arises from the contrast between consonant and vowel, loudness and softness, high pitch and low pitch.[26] These are *opposites* in speech patterns. As a result of this analysis of language, one of the most famous structuralists, the French anthropologist Claude Lévi-Strauss, proposed that the basic structures of human minds operate in the form of opposites, or what he called "binary opposition."[27] For Lévi-Strauss, the mind is in a constant process of seeking a compromise between these poles. Edmund Leach proposes as an example the street light: Between "stop" (red) and "go" (green) is placed "caution" (yellow).[28] The theory is that all minds operate by mediating these oppositions, which are buried in the unconscious. "Deep structures" like these are what give rise to underlying oppositions in literature, and structuralists have attempted to reduce these oppositions to their minimum number. Though structuralists may study various "surface structures" in a work of literature, their ultimate concern is with the "deep structures" in the human mind; thus it is the operation of the human mind, not history, that dominates structuralism.

How does this relate to the study of Jesus Christ?[29] In contrast to the historians, structuralists do not study how biblical texts came to be what they are "through time" (the chief concern, for example, of the form critics). Rather, they look at a portion of the text somewhat in the manner of a crossword puzzle, trying to arrange the words, phrases, sentences, and groups of sentences into a structure that will ultimately reflect the "deep structure." In many cases, they do not begin without any patterns; rather, after isolating some of the smallest units of expression ("Jesus wept"; or "when he saw him") and determining various sequences, they categorize the units into options for "doing" something or "being" someone. They attempt to determine what the functions of persons, objects, animals, etc. are, until finally there is a general picture of the structure of the narrative.

This analysis of the narrative structure is a prelude to another analysis, of the *mythical structure*. The mythical structure of a text is an underlying, subconscious "deep structure" that appears most clearly in specifically mythical narratives but is not limited to them. Nonetheless, the study of a number of explicitly mythical narratives will in theory yield a common mythical "structure." Such a "structure" can be expressed in a number of variations, just as a musical theme can occur in a number of variations. If Lévi-Strauss is correct that human minds operate with "binary opposition," the function of myth will be to resolve the basic contradictions of human existence.

A study by Dan O. Via illustrates the possibilities further. He builds on the observation of *Religionsgeschichtler* that the idea of dying and rising gods was widespread in Mediterranean literature in Jesus' time.[30] However, whereas *Religionsgeschichtler* attempted to show historical connections between such beliefs, Via suggests that in this cultural arena the binary opposition of death and life in the human mind was coming to expression. The various myths about Jesus Christ, and even nonmythical narratives, will reflect this binary opposition. Interestingly, one of his conclusions is that the rejected prophet represents a mediation between the poles of the ideal religious people ("life") and the religious outcasts ("death").

Whatever one thinks of structuralism, it is clear that here is a *method which is distinctly ahistorical,* at least in its initial stages.

ANALYTICAL PSYCHOLOGY

The notion of "deep structures" common to all minds leads to a consideration of one of the broadest approaches to Jesus Christ. This approach is found in the thought of the eminent Swiss analytical psychologist Carl Gustav Jung (1875–1961).[31] Jung was a collaborator with Sigmund Freud (1856–1939) from 1906 until 1913, when their differences in theory resulted in a split. Freud had led Jung to use the interpretation of dreams as one means for understanding the unconscious bases for mental illness. However, whereas Freud stressed that dreams were largely the result of childhood repression of sexual instincts combined with images of recent events, Jung became more and more interested in explaining certain "cosmic" dreams which he did not think could be due solely to personal experiences. Reared among superstitious farm folk, but widely read in myth, and absorbed since his student days with the attempt to explain occult phenomena, Jung became fascinated with the fact that dream images, symbols, and narratives had close parallels in the images, symbols, and myths of nonliterate societies. To an extent that Freud could not accept, Jung theorized that a deeper level of the unconscious had evolved and was shared by human beings from all times and places; it was not biologically inherited but was an "instinctive trend." On one level of the psyche there was the tendency, Jung believed, to form images, symbols, and mythlike narratives. These universal, cross-cultural patterns, or motifs, he called *archetypes*. Jung believed that Western technical civilization had caused moderns to strip away the spontaneous, instinctive, and emotional sides of the whole personality but that total psychological equilibrium was restored in the images and symbols of the dreams, which communicated messages to the rational parts of the mind. Indeed, Jung believed that dreams could sometimes reveal the unconscious trends that would indicate future occurrences; if they were ignored, they would lead to psychological disorders. In the collective unconscious, Jung thought, were all the archetypes: the accumulation of human experience from its remote origins, expressed in dream images, symbols, and narratives, and illuminated by cross-cultural study of myths.[32]

It is perhaps not surprising that Jung believed that Jesus Christ was a Western expression of an archetypal image and that Christ was an archetype of the self. For Jung, the Christian Trinity was a variation of the primordial image of the parent-god, the child-god, and the life-creating power common to, and uniting, both.[33] In the patriarchal monarchies of the ancient Near East (Babylon and Egypt), for example, there was normally a world-creating father who transferred his power and rights to the mediator between him and his world, the heroic son (sometimes a third god or goddess appeared as well). In Greece, Pythagoras speculated that "one" was the source and unity of all numbers, "two" appeared as the first even number, and "three" as an uneven yet perfect number containing the beginning, the middle, and the end. The Trinity of Christian orthodoxy, stated Jung, did not arise from the *direct* influence of oriental and Greek ideas; it arose as the reemergence of the archetypal "three-in-oneness," the "one," the "other," and the life-giving power from both: Father, Son, and Holy Spirit.

> The archetype *an sich* [in itself], as I have explained elsewhere, is an "irrepresentable" factor, a "disposition" which starts functioning at a given moment in the development of the human mind and arranges the material of consciousness into definite patterns. That is to say, man's conceptions of God are organized into triads and trinities, and a whole host of ritualistic and magical practices take on a triple or trichotomous character, as in the case of thrice-repeated apotropaic spells, formulae for blessing, cursing, praising, giving thanks, etc. Wherever we find it, the archetype has a compelling force which it derives from the unconscious, and whenever its effect becomes conscious it has a distinctly numinous quality. There is never any

conscious invention or cogitation, though speculations about the Trinity have often been accused of this.[34]

> Thus, the history of the Trinity presents itself as the gradual crystallization of an archetype that moulds the anthropomorphic conceptions of father and son, of life, and of different persons into an archetypal and numinous figure, the "Most Holy Three-in-One." The contemporary witnesses of these events apprehended it as something that modern psychology would call a psychic presence outside consciousness. If there is a consensus of opinion in respect of an idea, as there is here and always has been, then we are entitled to speak of a collective presence.[35]

Jung believed that from a psychological perspective, the development of the doctrine of the Trinity was a natural but incomplete evolution in human consciousness and in history. The one, dependable, disciplinarian father was characteristic of a dependent, passive childhood; the separate "person" of the Son was characteristic of a growing self-consciousness and a moral discrimination of free choice, that is, a conflict of decision that faces youth in its transition to adulthood; the "person" of the Holy Spirit was an achievement of adulthood when the Son tempered rationality with a voluntary return to the child's recognition of authority—an acceptance of humility, self-criticism, and irrationality. From his analytical-psychological perspective, Jung believed that the Trinity archetype needed to be rounded out to include a fourth element (recognition of the evil side of the personality), for the four-in-one was an even more widespread archetype (the *mandala,* or mystic circle).

In Jung's analytical view, then, the Christian doctrine of the Trinity was a manifestation of the "three-in-one" archetype of the collective unconscious, and each person of the Trinity was a manifestation of a developmental stage of the self: childhood, youth, maturity. Jung also suggested that the interpretation of Jesus Christ in Christianity was the expression of a primordial archetype and that Christ was an archetype of the self. This primordial archetype, said Jung, recurs in dreams and hero fantasies, and is expressed symbolically.

> The content of all such symbolic products is the idea of an overpowering, all-embracing, complete or perfect being, represented either by a man of heroic proportions, or by an animal with magical attributes, or by a magical vessel or some other "treasure hard to attain," such as a jewel, ring, crown, or, geometrically, by a mandala. This archetypal idea is a reflection of the individual's wholeness, i.e., of the self, which is present in him as an unconscious image. The conscious mind can form absolutely no conception of this totality, because it includes not only the conscious but also the unconscious psyche, which is, as such, inconceivable and irrepresentable.[36]

For Jung, the Greco-Roman "divine man" (discussed in Ch. 2) was an expression of the archetypal "man of heroic proportions" in the collective unconscious.

> The general idea of Christ the Redeemer belongs to the worldwide and pre-Christ theme of the hero and rescuer who, although he has been devoured by a monster, appears again in a miraculous way, having overcome whatever monster it was that swallowed him. . . . The hero figure is an archetype, which has existed since time immemorial.[37]

Thus

> The most important of the symbolical statements about Christ are those which reveal the attributes of the [archetypal] hero's life: improbable origin, divine father, hazardous birth, rescue in the nick of time, precocious development, conquest of the mother and of death, miraculous deeds, a tragic, early end, symbolically significant manner of death, post-mortem effects (reappearances, signs and marvels, etc.).[38]

Jesus Christ, said Jung, is "our culture hero," a symbol of the self. Christ is the *perfect* self, an ideal self. To reduce him to a "mere man," as the historicists have done, produces a distorted image. To strive for Christ's sinless perfection is legitimate from a psychological perspective. Yet there is a difference between perfection and wholeness or completeness. The complete or whole self must take account of the "shadow" side of the personality, the evil self, represented in Christian tradition as the demonic Antichrist. This does not mean that Jung considered the archetypal symbol false, but only that the natural human condition must admit the presence of evil. Thus Jung believed that Christ as the archetypal symbol of the self retains its valid meaning.

Jung's voice may be added to those who seek the truth elsewhere than in simple historical reconstruction. For Jung, the meaning of Jesus Christ lies in timeless archetypal symbols. The "three-in-one" archetype is manifested historically in the Father, Son, and Holy Spirit of Christian orthodoxy, while at the same time it is suggested that an individual self passes through stages representing the three persons. Similarly, the "hero archetype" is manifested historically in the "divine man" who becomes a model for interpreting Jesus Christ, while at the same time Jesus Christ becomes the ideal archetype of the self.

AN ATTACK ON HISTORICAL-CRITICAL SCHOLARSHIP FROM "WITHIN"

"Historical biblical criticism is bankrupt." So begins a little book by Walter Wink entitled *The Bible in Human Transformation: Toward a New Paradigm for Biblical Study*.[39] What Wink opposes is not history itself, but the dominant method of studying history in the Bible. Moreover, he does not claim that the method has accomplished nothing or is without value, just as a bankrupt business is not without assets. Rather, it is simply incapable of accomplishing what it set out to accomplish: an interpretation of the Scriptures which makes them so alive that present meaningful possibilities for personal and social transformation can occur. This judgment, unlike those of Lévi-Strauss or Jung, is made by a Christian whose profession is primarily interpreting the New Testament.

Wink develops a set of interrelated reasons why he thinks "the historical-critical method has reduced the Bible to a dead letter."[40] Whereas the biblical writers sought to bring forth, encourage, or foster faith (the books were written "from faith to faith"), biblical criticism was a historical method that sought to emulate the "objective neutrality" of the natural sciences, that is, to examine the phenomena by suspending emotional involvement, personal bias, value judgment, and social commitment. For Wink, the error of this supposed objectivity was that it did not admit its own commitments:

> Objectivism is a false consciousness because evidence of its error is systematically repressed. It pretends detachment when in fact the scholar is attached to an institution with a high stake in the socialization of students and the preservation of society, and when he himself has a high stake in advancement in that institution by publication of his researches. It pretends to be unbiased when in fact the methodology carries with it a heavy rationalistic weight which by inner necessity tends toward the reduction of irrational, subjective, or emotional data to insignificance or invisibility. It pretends to search for "assured results," "objective knowledge," when in fact the method presumes radical epistemological doubt [doubting is the means to knowing], which by definition devours each new spawn of "assured results" as a guppy swallows her children. It pretends to suspend evaluations, which is simply impossible, since research proceeds on the basis of questions asked and a ranked priority in their asking.[41]

Thus biblical study became subject to a "technique" that asked questions the texts never intended to answer. Moreover, biblical critics were accountable to the professional guild of scholars and became increasingly separated from the vital community of faith for which the biblical texts were intended. The scholars' quest for freedom to search for the truth without censorship or interference was noble, but it also brought isolation from the communities that had originally given such a quest its significance. Finally, it arose in part as a weapon against a naive orthodoxy that accepted a more direct and literal view of biblical origins and inspiration.

> Bluntly stated, biblical criticism was a certain type of evangelism seeking a certain type of conversion. No depreciation is intended by those terms, loaded as they are. Only those still under the illusion that biblical criticism was ideologically neutral should be offended by their use. Far more fundamentally than revivalism, biblical criticism shook, shattered, and reconstituted generation after generation of students, and became their point of entree into the "modern world."[42]

In short,

> To say that biblical criticism has now, like revivalism, become
> bankrupt, is simply to summarize the entire discussion to this point. It was
> based on an inadequate method, married to a false objectivism, subjected to
> uncontrolled technologism, separated from a vital community, and has out-
> lived its usefulness as presently practiced. Whether or not it has any future
> at all depends on its adaptability to a radically altered situation.[43]

Wink does not propose the abandonment of biblical criticism, but
he believes that it should come under new management. What is occurring is a *paradigm shift.* A *paradigm* is a set of presuppositions, values,
beliefs, and methods that gives one a total picture and a way of operating with information. T. S. Kuhn has advanced the discussion of paradigms by showing how a particular perspective operates in the scientific
community until it no longer explains adequately the new influx of
data.[44] At that point a new paradigm begins to emerge, though against
the resistance of those who accept the prevailing paradigm. A characteristic example from the history of science was the stress caused by a shift
from the geocentric (earth-centered) view of the world to the heliocentric (sun-centered) view in the sixteenth and seventeenth centuries. For
Wink, the old paradigm is the historical-critical method of biblical study.
What is the "paradigm shift" that is now occurring?

Wink begins by noting a progression of thought about the history of
interpretation of the Bible, which helps in understanding the nature of
the process of interpretation itself. First, there is what he calls *fusion:*
the paradigm in which the interpreter is so fused with the tradition that
it is immediately meaningful. There is a naive and direct relation to the
past, and it forms the channels through which one thinks. To interpret
Wink, the Bible is a holy text read directly for inspiration. Then,
suggests Wink, the past begins to be questioned; a certain doubt arises
about the tradition. This brings about a negation of the fusion between
the bible and direct, immediate belief. The Bible is a writing to be examined like other writings. Criticism arises. For Wink, the positive value of
this new paradigm, *critical distance,* is that it gathers much new information unimpeded by the constrictions of the tradition. Yet it should be
clear that this perspective commits the biblical scholar to secularism.
Even if the interpreter is a believer, from the point of view of method he
or she is a functional atheist. Moreover, criticism tends to become
mired in its concern for correct methods and in its inability to do what it
must finally do: criticize itself. To be consistent, criticism must turn to
itself, "negate the negation," and develop what the philosopher Paul
Ricoeur called a "second naivete." The new paradigm into which it is
now possible for the biblical interpreter to move does not stop at a critical distance but goes on to engage in self-criticism and allows the texts
to interpret the reader once again.[45]

For Wink, the movement toward a new paradigm is aided especially
by two approaches: the sociology of knowledge and analytical psychol-

ogy. The former is especially helpful in understanding the interpreter's approach to the text from the viewpoint of his or her social position; the latter is especially important for suggesting how the interpreter may pass beyond a superior attitude in examining the text (critical distance) to encountering the text. Two examples relate to Jesus Christ.

Jesus' parable of the Pharisee and the tax collector (Luke 18:9–14) reads:

> He also told this parable to some who trusted in themselves that they were righteous and despised others: "Two men went up into the temple to pray, one a Pharisee and the other a tax collector. The Pharisee stood and prayed thus with himself, 'God, I thank thee that I am not like other men, extortioners, unjust, adulterers, or even like this tax collector. I fast twice a week, I give tithes of all that I get.' But the tax collector, standing far off, would not even lift up his eyes to heaven, but beat his breast, saying, 'God, be merciful to me a sinner.' I tell you, this man went down to his house justified rather than the other; for everyone who exalts himself will be humbled, but he who humbles himself will be exalted.

Wink states that the biblical critic confines himself to interpreting the social roles of the Pharisee as one who has religious and social position and the tax collector as one who is a "sinner," thus leaving untouched the tendency of the modern reader to identify with the tax collector. As a result, this interpretation fails to bring out the paradox of the story: that it is precisely the outcast who is justified. To identify immediately with the supposed "good guy" misses the social implications of the story, namely, that it is Jesus who justifies the sinner and that "he who exalts himself will be humbled, but he who humbles himself will be exalted."

> To enter the space in which the parable speaks requires that we hold Pharisee and publican together as dual aspects of a single alienating structure, represented here by the temple; to locate both kinds of responses [the Pharisee's and the tax collector's] within our own experience; and to transcend both by their reconciliation under the justifying love of God. But to *begin* by identifying with the *publican* as if he were the "good guy" is simply to flip the righteous/unrighteous tag. The story is then deformed into teaching cheap grace for rapacious toll collectors. All this because the exegete hid behind his descriptive task without examining the recoil of the parable upon contemporary self-understanding.[46]

Wink's second aid is derived from Dr. Elizabeth Howes (who is indebted to Jung's analytical psychology) and the Guild for Psychological Studies in San Francisco. What he intends is a study of the texts with reference to the interpreter's *personal* history. The story of the paralytic is found in Matthew 9:1–8, Mark 2:1–12, and Luke 5:17–26. Though it should be studied in all three versions, it will be enough to quote one (Mark):

> 1) And when he returned to Capernaum after some days, it was reported that he was at home. 2) And many were gathered together, so that there was no longer room for them not even about the door; and he was preach-

ing the word to them.   3) And they came bringing to him a paralytic carried by four men.   4) And when they could not get near him because of the crowd, they removed the roof above him; and when they had made an opening, they let down the pallet on which the paralytic lay.   5) And when Jesus saw their faith, he said to the paralytic, "My son, your sins are forgiven."   6) Now some of the scribes were sitting there, questioning in their hearts,   7) "Why does this man speak thus? It is blasphemy! Who can forgive sins but God alone?"   8) And immediately Jesus, perceiving in his spirit that they thus questioned within themselves, said to them, "Why do you question thus in your hearts?   9) Which is easier, to say to the paralytic, 'Your sins are forgiven,' or to say, 'Rise, take up your pallet and walk'?   10) But that you may know that the Son of man has authority on earth to forgive sins"—he said to the paralytic—   11) "I say to you, rise, take up your pallet and go home."   12) And he rose, and immediately took up the pallet and went out before them all; so that they were all amazed and glorified God, saying, "We never saw anything like this!'"

Wink proposes that a group in a circle examine the text in all its versions with the supervision of a leader. The first object is to get the group to see the critical problems themselves, thus achieving critical distance. The second object is to get the group to work through the account again and recreate the story by historical imagination, using the critical results as a check on random speculation. The third object is to get members of the group to see how they respond inwardly to the text. Questions are asked such as, "Who is the 'paralytic' in you?" and after discussion, "Who is the 'scribe' in you?" followed by more discussion and more questions and answers. Afterward, the members of the group are encouraged to portray their ideas of the "paralytic" or the "scribe" in clay, paints, written dialogue, silence, music, movement, or role-playing, that is, to allow the "feeling" side to emerge. The purpose is to discover insights and integrate them into one's self-understanding. *"For an insight never strikes us as really true or truly real until it can be related to those symbols which most profoundly inform our lives."* [47]

Wink leads his group *through critical distance* as a process of their own discovery. Then they move on to a "second naivete" that once again understands the personal and social dimensions of the text in the present. Such a process, he suggests, will perhaps aid in restoring dialogue and interpersonal relations.

SUMMARY

The purpose of this final chapter has been to indicate some contemporary approaches to Jesus Christ. A number of scholars are still very much involved in historical questions and the methods of historical criticism. Redaction criticism, building on form criticism, attempts to understand a whole gospel, and thus a particular gospel writer's view of Jesus Christ for his own time. The method of trajectories attempts to trace the path of themes and forms of literature through time and thereby illuminate the growth of materials about Jesus. And social historiography attempts to understand Jesus and the early church in terms of models such as the millenarian prophet and millenarian cults. In such studies, it is clear that there is less emphasis on the historical Jesus as such.

Structuralism attempts to understand the various structures of literature and move to the "deep structures" of the human mind, including perhaps the binary opposition life/death as it emerges in the Jesus story. Jungian analysis seeks to discover the archetypes of the collective unconsciousness, including the "three-in-one" archetype as expressed in the Trinity and the "hero archetype" as expressed in the stories about Jesus. Jung concluded that for Western culture Jesus Christ is an archetype of the ideal self. There is another method of biblical study that attempts to overcome the critical distance of biblical scholarship, thus fostering a "second naivete" through the sociology of knowledge and group interaction.

This chapter began with the statement that the quest of the historical Jesus was inevitable. But the Scriptures do not present simply a historical Jesus; neither do the creeds or Christian piety. Orthodoxy had its point to make, in both its uncritical and its critical forms, and perhaps the emergence of Bultmann's existentialism in the context of neo-orthodoxy in the Germany of the 1920s was also inevitable, for it made the most of the radical historical work of Strauss, Bruno Bauer, Wrede, and *Religionsgeschichte*—but, following Kähler, it returned to the "Christ of faith." This was the state of affairs for the historical movement between the two World Wars, and though modified in the "new quest," it was clear, as Käsemann put it, that the historian was in an embarrassing position. In a sense, history had doubled back on itself: The most critical research had shown that the sources were truly historical but not extremely valuable for the history of *Jesus*. Thus, however ironic, it is nevertheless appropriate that a study whose theme is Jesus Christ through history should end with a consideration of contemporary thinkers who are challenging the very historical presuppositions on which our study has been built.

NOTES

1. Norman Perrin, *What is Redaction Criticism?* Guides to Biblical Scholarship, ed. Dan O. Via (Philadelphia: Fortress Press, 1969), p. 1. The example that follows is in part an extension of Perrin, *The New Testament: An Introduction* (New York: Harcourt Brace Jovanovich, 1974), pp. 13–14.

2. Philipp Vielhauer, "Erwägungen zur Christologie des Markusevangeliums," in *Zeit und Geschichte,* ed. Erich Dinkler (Tübingen: J. C. B. Mohr, 1964), pp. 155–69.

3. Gerhard Barth, "Matthew's Understanding of the Law," in G. Bornkamm, G. Barth, and H. J. Held, *Tradition and Interpretation in Matthew,* trans. Percy Scott (Philadelphia: Westminster Press, 1963), pp. 137–41.

4. Jack Dean Kingsbury, *Matthew: Structure, Christology, Kingdom* (Philadelphia: Fortress Press, 1975), ch. 2.

5. James M. Robinson and Helmut Koester, *Trajectories Through Early Christianity* (Philadelphia: Fortress Press, 1971).

6. Robinson, "Introduction: The Dismantling and Reassembling of the Categories of New Testament Scholarship," in Robinson and Koester, *Trajectories,* pp. 9–10.

7. Koester, "One Jesus and Four Primitive Gospels," *Harvard Theological Review* **61** (1968), pp. 203–47, reprinted in Robinson and Koester, *Trajectories,* pp. 158–204.

8. Robinson, *"LOGOI SOPHŌN* ['Sayings of the Wise']: On the *Gattung* of 'Q,' '" in Robinson and Koester, *Trajectories,* pp. 71–113, an enlargement of an article that appeared as a contribution to *Zeit und Geschichte,* pp. 77–96 (originally in German).

9. Koester, "One Jesus," p. 177.

10. Ibid., p. 186.

11. See Ch. 2, page 58, and below on Jung's "hero archetype," pages 303–4.

12. John Gager, *Kingdom and Community: The Social World of Early Christianity* (Englewood Cliffs, N.J.: Prentice-Hall, 1975). See also Wayne A. Meeks, "The Man from Heaven in Johannine Sectarianism," *Journal of Biblical Literature* **91** (1972), pp. 44–72; L. E. Keck, "On the Ethos of Early Christians," *Journal of the American Academy of Religion* **42** (1974), pp. 435–52; Jonathan Z. Smith, "The Social Description of Early Christianity," *Religious Studies Review* **1** (1975), pp. 19–25; H. C. Kee, *Community of the New Age: Studies in Mark's Gospel* (Philadelphia: Westminster Press, 1977).

13. Gager refers to J. Vansina, *Oral Tradition: A Study in Historical Methodology* (Chicago: Aldine Publishing Co., 1965); G. Allport and L. Postman, *The Psychology of Rumor* (New York: Henry Holt, 1947); and T. Shibutani, *Improvised News: A Sociological Study of Rumor* (New York: Bobbs-Merrill, 1966).

14. Peter Berger, *The Sacred Canopy: Elements of a Sociological Theory of Religion* (New York: Doubleday & Co., 1969), p. 25. Note also Berger and T. Luckmann, *The Social Construction of Reality: A Treatise in the Sociology of Knowledge* (New York: Doubleday & Co., Anchor Books, 1967); Robert Bellah, "Religious Evolution," in *Beyond Belief: Essays on Religion in a Post-Traditional World* (New York: Harper & Row, 1970), pp. 20–45; C. Geertz, "Religion as a Cultural System," in *Anthropological Approaches to the Study of Religion,* ed. M. Banton (London: Tavistock Publications, 1966), both of which are found (the latter in abridged form) in W. Lessa and E. Vogt, eds., *Reader in Comparative Religion: An Anthropological Approach,* 3rd ed. (New York: Harper & Row, 1972), pp. 36–50, 167–78.

15. Gager, *Kingdom and Community,* p. 12.

16. I. C. Jarvie, *The Revolution in Anthropology* (Chicago: Henry Regnery, 1967), p. 51.

17. Gager, *Kingdom and Community,* p. 22. In general see Sylvia

Thrupp, ed., *Millennial Dreams in Action: Studies in Revolutionary Religious Movements* (New York: Schocken Books, 1970); Norman Cohn, *The Pursuit of the Millennium: Revolutionary Messianism in Medieval and Reformation Europe and Its Bearing on Modern Totalitarian Movements* (New York: Oxford University Press, Oxford Paperbacks, 1970); in particular, S. R. Isenberg, "Millenarism in Greco-Roman Palestine," *Religion* 4 (1974), pp. 26–46.

18. Yonina Talmon, "Pursuit of the Millennium: The Relation between Religious and Social Change," *Archives Européennes de Sociologie* 3 (1962), reprinted in Lessa and Vogt, *Reader,* 2nd ed. (1965), pp. 522–37; Kenelm Burridge, *New Heaven, New Earth* (New York: Schocken Books, 1969).

19. Gager, *Kingdom and Community,* pp. 29ff.

20. Mircea Eliade, *Cosmos and History: The Myth of the Eternal Return,* trans. Willard R. Trask (New York: Harper & Row, Torchbooks, n.d.), pp. 141–62; *Myth and Reality,* trans. Willard R. Trask (New York: Harper & Row, Torchbooks, n.d.), pp. 75–91; extensive discussion of the problem in general and Eliade's views in particular appears in Lee W. Gibbs and W. Taylor Stevenson, eds., *Myth and the Crisis of Historical Consciousness* (Missoula, Mont.: Scholars Press, 1975).

21. Mircea Eliade and Joseph M. Kitagawa, *The History of Religions: Essays in Methodology* (Chicago: University of Chicago Press, 1959).

22. Eliade, *Cosmos and History,* pp. 141ff.

23. Ibid., p. 141.

24. Ibid., p. 146.

25. Michael Lane, *Introduction to Structuralism* (New York: Basic Books, 1970), pp. 11–39; Robert Scholes, *Structuralism in Literature: An Introduction* (New Haven: Yale University Press, 1974).

26. Roman Jakobson, *Fundamentals of Language* (New York: Mouton & Co., 1956). The acknowledged father of this linguistic development is Ferdinand de Saussure, *Course in General Linguistics* (New York: McGraw-Hill, 1966) (originally published in 1915).

27. Claude Lévi-Strauss, *Structural Anthropology,* trans. Claire Jacobson and Brooke Schoepf (New York: Doubleday & Co., 1967); Lévi-Strauss, "The Structural Study of Myth," in *Myth: A Symposium,* ed. Thomas A. Sebeok (Bloomington: Indiana University Press, 1955), pp. 81–106. Helpful studies are Edmund Leach, *Claude Lévi-Strauss* (New York: Viking Press, 1970) and O. Paz, *Claude Lévi-Strauss: An Introduction* (London: Jonathan Cape, 1971).

28. Edmund Leach, *Genesis as Myth and Other Essays* (London: Jonathan Cape, 1969), p. 13.

29. Edmund Leach, *Genesis; Interpretation: A Journal of Bible and Theology* 28 (April 1974); R. Barthes et al., *Structural Analysis and Biblical Exegesis,* Pittsburgh Theological Monograph Series, trans. Alfred M. Johnson, Jr. (Pittsburgh: Pickwick Press, 1974); Jean Calloud, *Structural Analysis of Narrative,* trans. Daniel Patte (Philadelphia: Fortress Press, 1976); Daniel Patte, *What Is Structural Exegesis?* (Philadelphia: Fortress Press, 1976); Vernon K. Robbins, "Structuralism in Biblical Interpretation and Theology," *The Thomist* 42 (1978), pp. 349–72; *Semeia, An Experimental Journal for Biblical Interpretation,* vols. 1 and 2 (Missoula, Mont.: Scholars Press, 1974).

30. Dan O. Via, *Kerygma and Comedy in the New Testament* (Philadelphia: Fortress Press, 1975), ch. 2.

31. Helpful introductions to Jung's thought are Robert A. Clark, *Six Talks on Jung's Psychology* (Pittsburgh: Boxwood Press, 1953); E. A. Ben-

net, *What Jung Really Said* (New York: Schocken Books, 1967); Anthony Storr, *C. G. Jung* (New York: Viking Press, 1973); C. G. Jung et al., *Man and His Symbols* (New York: Dell Publishing Co., Laurel Editions, 1968).

32. Eliade has written positively about Jung's theories; see his *Images and Symbols,* trans. Philip Mairet (New York: Sheed and Ward, 1969), pp. 14n., 20, 52n., 89.

33. C. G. Jung, "A Psychological Approach to the Dogma of the Trinity," in *Psychology and Religion: West and East,* The Collected Works, vol. 11, trans. R. F. C. Hull (London: Routledge & Kegan Paul, 1958), pp. 109–200. A development of the symbolism of the number three is found in Philip Wheelwright, *The Burning Fountain* (Bloomington and London: Indiana University Press, 1968), ch. 7.

34. Jung, "Trinity," pp. 148–49.

35. Ibid., pp. 151–2.

36. Ibid., pp. 155–6; see also Jung, "Christ, A Symbol of the Self," in *Aion: Contributions to the Symbolism of the Self,* Collected Works of C. G. Jung, Bollingen Series, vol. 20, trans. R. F. C. Hull, reprinted in *Psyche and Symbol: A Selection from the Writings of C. G. Jung,* ed. Violet S. de Laszlo (New York: Doubleday & Co., Anchor Books), pp. 35–60.

37. Jung, "Approaching the Unconscious," in Jung et al., *Man and His Symbols,* p. 61; see also Joseph L. Henderson, "Ancient Myths and Modern Man, in Jung et al., *Man and His Symbols,* pp. 95–156; Joseph Campbell, *The Hero With A Thousand Faces,* Bollingen Series, vol. 17 (Princeton: Princeton University Press, 1949).

38. Jung, "Trinity," pp. 154–55.

39. Walter Wink, *The Bible in Human Transformation: Toward a New Paradigm for Biblical Study* (Philadelphia: Fortress Press, 1973).

40. Ibid., p. 4.

41. Ibid., pp. 6–7.

42. Ibid., pp. 14–15.

43. Ibid., p. 15.

44. Thomas S. Kuhn, *The Structure of Scientific Revolutions* (Chicago: University of Chicago Press, 1970).

45. Wink, *Bible in Human Transformation,* ch. 3.

46. Ibid., p. 43.

47. Ibid., p. 64.

Subject Index

The Author Index begins on page 318, and the Biblical Index begins on page 321.

Abraham, 291
Absolute Idea, 170
Absolute Mind, 170–71, 196–97
Acts of the Apostles, 173, 292
Adam, 12, 56–57, 69, 81, 91, 111, 117, 123, 135, 143, 221, 274, 291
Adoptionism, 68, 74, 94
Agrapha, 7
Albertus Magnus, 90
Alexandria, School of, 72–76, 79, 83, 95, 106
Ambrose, 80
Anabaptists, 112–13, 118, 129
Anselm of Canterbury, 88, 91, 95, 98n, 108, 154
Antichrist, 304
  legend of, 219
Antioch, School of, 73–75, 78–79, 83, 94, 106
Apocalypse of Adam, 293
Apocalyptic, 183, 189, 194–95, 197, 214–16, 218–19, 221, 224, 227, 229–32, 234, 236, 243–45, 253, 263, 267–69, 272, 274, 290, 293
Apocrypha, 7–10, 28
Apollinaris, Apollinarianism, 78–79, 80, 83, 95
Aquinas, Thomas, 85, 89–96, 102–3, 106–7, 124
Aramaic church, 15, 221
Aramaic gospel, 187, 202
Archetype, 161–63, 169, 302–4, 309
  hero, 309
  patterns, 299
  primordial, 303
Aretalogy, 58, 294
Arianism, 75–80, 83, 95
Aristotle, 88–90, 96, 163, 170
Arius, 75, 78, 97n
Ascension, 180, 294
Athanasius of Alexandria, 74–78, 81, 83, 95
  Festal Letter of, 2
Atheism, 136–37
Atonement, 247, 279
  in Anselm, 89

in Calvin, 113–18
in Luther, 108
in Ritschl, 204
in Schleiermacher, 162
in Wesley, 154-55
Auburn Affirmation, 248
Augustine of Hippo, 2, 80–82, 84, 89, 91, 95, 97n, 106, 120, 140, 154, 201–2, 266

Bach, Johann Sebastian, 228–29
Bacon, Francis, 136
Baptism, 17, 118, 163, 182, 218, 222–23, 230, 274, 279–80, 289–92
Baptists, 110
Bar Cochba, revolt of, 187
Baur, F. C., 184–90
Beatitudes, 155, 187, 194, 209, 243
Benedict of Nursia, 85
Berkeley, George, 136
Bismarck, Otto von, 205, 245
Bousset, Wilhelm, 218–23
Bryan, William Jennings, 247
Bultmann, Rudolf, 262–81

Caesarea Philippi, 210, 230, 232, 234
Calvin, John, 113–18
Calvinists, 152–53, 159, 165, 249
Capitalism, 172, 212
Caraffa, Gian Pietro, 119
Cargo cults, 296
Carmelites, 125, 129
Carthusians, 85
Catherine of Siena, 128
Catholic Reformation, 118–22
Cenobitism, 84
Chalcedon, Council of, 83–84, 95
Chalcedonian Creed, 82
Christological hymns, 43–52, 54, 57, 59
  Titles, 13, 165, 183, 189, 194–95
  Lord, 221, 223, 225
  Son of David, 13, 21, 195, 221, 230, 268

Son of God, 13, 35–38, 60, 66, 71, 73, 77, 117, 143, 154, 165, 183, 194–95, 222–23, 244, 261, 290–94
Son of Man, 20–21, 33, 38–43, 165, 183, 189, 195, 197, 210, 221, 223, 225, 230, 232, 234–35, 268–69, 274, 290, 293, 297
Christology, 159, 209–10, 244
Church, 161, 195, 197, 204, 207–8, 210, 216, 218, 221–24, 230, 235, 238, 240–42, 245–46, 250–51, 253–54, 270, 274, 280–82, 289, 291–93
Church of the Brethren, 110
Cistercians, 85
Clement of Alexandria, 72
Cluny, 85
Communism, 171–72, 237
Constantinople, Council of, 77–78, 83, 95
Cop, Nicholas, 114
Copernicus, Nicholas, 135
Creationism, 175
Critical distance, 306–9
Criticism
  Biblical, 139, 141–43, 164, 260, 262, 305–6
  form, 4, 264, 266–68, 272, 282–83, 289, 290–93, 295, 308
  historical, 101–2, 106, 129, 179, 184, 190, 201–3, 205, 208, 241, 245, 247, 252–54, 261, 292, 304–8
  literary, 201
  redaction, 289–92, 295–96, 308
  tendency, 186
Cyril of Alexandria, 79, 82–84, 95

David, 11–13, 21, 35–39, 42–43, 53
Dead Sea Scrolls, 17, 21, 23, 44, 50
Deists, 137–40, 143, 148, 164, 194

313

Author Index

Biblical Index

Old Testament Apocrypha
(Canonical in the Roman Catholic Bible)

Old Testament Pseudepigrapha

B
C
D
E
F   4
G   5
H   6
I   7
J   8